Brenda Barker

The Human Group

Other books by the author

MASSACHUSETTS ON THE SEA (*with* S. E. Morison)

AN INTRODUCTION TO PARETO (*with* Charles P. Curtis)

ENGLISH VILLAGERS OF THE 13TH CENTURY

FATIGUE OF WORKERS (*Report of the Committee on Work in Industry, National Research Council*)

THE SOCIETY OF FELLOWS (*with* O. T. Bailey)

THE HUMAN GROUP

George C. Homans

HARVARD UNIVERSITY

HARCOURT, BRACE & WORLD, INC.

NEW YORK, CHICAGO, SAN FRANCISCO, AND ATLANTA

To the memory of

Robert Shaw Barlow

Social Philosopher

Contents

Foreword

EARLY in his book Mr. Homans asks a question of his fellow sociologists: "What single general proposition about human behavior have we *established?*" In other words, has sociology succeeded in making even one statement about the way men act that can be relied on in all circumstances where it should apply? Has it made one theoretical formulation that is uniformly descriptive?

Considering that sociology is the study of men living in society, the question is a startling one, and so is Mr. Homans' admission that it must be answered "no." Since the question and the answer lie at the center of his effort in the book, it will be well to try to say precisely what he means by them. What he has in mind—ultimately, much thinking, many researches, perhaps many generations beyond his book—is a general theory which will be as applicable to society as any *general* scientific theory is to the data of its field. The importance of such a theory is obvious: it is the general statements of science that phrase the uniformities science sets out to find, that make the results of inquiry and experiment applicable, that make prediction possible, and that serve to suggest, direct, and test further research. There is also the importance outside the field of sociology itself, that such a general theory would be incalculably useful in what may be called the applied sciences of government, politics, legislation, industrial management, and whatever other practical skills take social data or social functions into account. No one needs to be told that there have been a good many general theories of sociology, or that none of them, as a series of generalized statements about society, holds good throughout.

Perhaps a parallel is called for. There *are* general theories in, say, thermodynamics, which fascinates Mr. Homans and from which he draws a good many examples and analogies herein, or again in chemistry, but there are none in medicine. Either a research chemist beginning a new kind of investigation or a chemical engineer setting out to develop a new kind of product works within a generalized theoretical system to which he can appeal with confidence and to which at every step he turns for guidance, critical testing, prediction, or proof. Neither a medical researcher nor a practising physician has any such set of basic theoretical statements at his disposal. Medicine has many adequate *limited* theories, and it has complexly interwoven series of them, but there is no General System of Medicine. There have been such theoretical general systems in the more or less remote past, but since they were *a priori* and deductive they were always overthrown by the advance of factual knowledge. Whether or not a general medicine consisting of a single theoretical system will ever be worked out, it would be idle to speculate: perhaps the nature of the data medicine deals with forbids, perhaps it does not. But there is none now. Sociology has not reached the advanced stage of scientific generalization that medicine has, still less the stage that thermodynamics and chemistry have. Again, perhaps it never will, perhaps the nature of its data forbids. But to work in that direction is certainly desirable, and any advance it can make toward wider generalizations than it now has will be extremely useful. To try to achieve them is one of the efforts sociologists must continually make.

What Mr. Homans' statement means, then, is this: so far as that particular effort is concerned, sociology has so far established no general proposition about human behavior *of a kind sufficiently valid throughout for a general theory of sociology to be erected on it.* This is not to say that sociology has not established uniformities or that it lacks limited theories which can be applied satisfactorily within their fields.

In *The Human Group* Mr. Homans calls attention to a different way of looking at familiar sociological data and analyzing them to the end of discovering a different kind of uniformity. His deliberate purpose is to establish, if it can be established, the *kind* of general statement about human behavior that can be used to form increasingly more general sociological theories. That and that only. His is necessarily a humble effort, since in the present state of knowledge it must necessarily focus on only a few aspects of behavior. But, though it is only what is called a first approximation—that is, a first step—it is also ambitious, since it attempts to point out the way and the direction in which further steps may most rewardingly be taken.

That is not to say that the kind of sociology Mr. Homans is practising here desires or is destined to overthrow any other kind, or that Mr. Homans invented it. He is trying merely to devise more effective intruments for dealing with the specific problem I have just defined, one which has so far resisted solution. Actually, herein he is following clues that have been proving fruitful in a variety of sociological investigations for a full generation, and to some extent his methods of following them have likewise developed in response to those clues, wherever they have appeared. In studies of the peoples it pleases us to call primitive, in studies of industrial operations, in studies that apply a multiple approach to single communities, and even in the application of mathematics to abstract sociological data—in all these fields an increasing literature has been pointing in the same direction. It would be improper to call this literature a school, though eventually it may create one; rather, a good many very different minds have found a common ground. Mr. Homans' originality, and it is impressive, consists of having stated what the common ground is and having formulated a theory about it. That is, in this book, besides describing the methods, pointing out the significance of results, and codifying a procedure, he derives a theory which makes them systematic. There is as yet no name for the kind of sociology which these studies foreshadow or for the theory Mr. Homans works out here. We may describe the latter, however, by pointing to its principal emphasis and calling it a theory of the dynamic interrelationships in social behavior.

With that phrase may I for a moment relinquish the vocabulary so necessary to working sociologists, who must give exact value to words? What Mr. Homans describes can be expressed simply enough in the layman's idiom. Sociology has repeatedly tried to make usable generalizations about large organizations of people— Comte and Spencer, say, about nations, or Marx about societies, or Toynbee about civilizations. Such generalizations frequently yield valuable insights and may roughly describe parts, perhaps even large parts, of what actually happens. But they do not hold good throughout. Though they are complete systems, they do not correspond to all the facts, nor can they be used throughout to serve the basic scientific functions of criticism, verification, and prediction. They cannot be used as what they were intended to be, reliable descriptions of men in society; they are always leading to dead ends, and experience is always proving them wrong. Mr.

Homans' remarks about the limited and rigorous system of Durkheim, for instance, point out that as a general theory it leads to disappointing results. With such an elaborate system as Toynbee's there can be no empirical test. The theory is neither "true" nor "untrue," and though it may be beautiful or moving, though it may contain many important observations, it cannot be used as a guiding principle for further inquiry.

The trouble with generalizations about such large units of people is that we do not know enough to generalize well. The units are too complex, too many forces are operating for us to take account of, and we have as yet not developed adequate or reliable means of analyzing them. What Mr. Homans does is to reverse the classic procedure. He deals not with the largest organized aggregations of people but with the smallest ones, groups that are deliberately formed for specific purposes and, more basically, those that arise and cohere naturally. He studies five such small groups here. Each is organized and functional, each has specific characteristics, but all are so small that it is possible to subject them to accurate analysis. If they can be satisfactorily analyzed, then perhaps the findings can be extended step by step to larger groups. If uniformities of the kind I have defined are found among them, then the same uniformities can be intelligently searched for in the larger ones. To find any uniformities of that kind which can be generalized as theory will be important in itself and will create the hope that they may lead to reliable general theories. Moreover, Mr. Homans points out, the only historical continuity of men in society is that of small groups. Trades, guilds, religions, classes, nations, empires, cultures, civilizations have all been disrupted, broken, and extinguished, but through every social disintegration small groups have survived. We know of no society that does not contain them. Small groups have survived the destructive forces. The fact is so striking as to suggest that the small group is the basic social unit. The structure of society may be built of just these bricks. Anything that may be learned with certainty about them will be invaluable. And it may be by studying them we can arrive at theoretical statements which describe society no matter where, from whatever angle, or in whatever interest we approach it.

The study of even the smallest group, however, is exceedingly complex. The simplest associations of men involve so many actions, relationships, emotions, motives, ideas, and beliefs, and there is so much interpenetration and interdependence, that it is impossible to take account of them all. We need a way of investigating groups and a way of thinking about them that will disclose which of these are significant for hypotheses that can lead to further studies which will in turn lead to wider hypotheses. There have been innumerable studies of small groups. But what Mr. Homans does is to concentrate on certain activities and processes he observes in them, and apply a new kind of systematic analysis. He studies three of them as static societies, though in doing so he must for the most part ignore their dynamic components (this is, of course, the kind of selective, arbitrary procedure that science must adopt), and two of them as dynamic societies. The first three groups are: a team of workmen engaged in manufacturing an industrial product, a metropolitan street-corner gang, and a tribe of Pacific islanders. One of the groups treated as dynamic is a small New England town, and it is studied here as a society that is disintegrating. The other is a company that manufactures electrical equipment, and it is studied as a society in conflict. In all five Mr. Homans selects the same phenomena for analysis, though with a somewhat different emphasis and elaboration each time. And the import of his book is that, different as these groups are, their behavior shows fundamental similarities: they reveal social uniformities.

His procedure is semantically controlled. The limitations of language require him occasionally to use words which carry a high if accidental emotional charge, and there is nothing to do but to keep pointing at the things for which the words stand till the charge is dissipated. Sociology cannot use the purely denotive vocabulary of the natural sciences or the symbols of mathematics. Thus to many laymen, and even to some social scientists, Pareto's expression "the free circulation of the élite" seems to carry an opprobrious suggestion of conservative bias, if not indeed fascism, whereas they find no such taint in *"la carière ouverte aux talents,"* which expresses precisely the same idea, and accept uncritically such a phrase as "full opportunity for self-development." That particular reef does not lie in Mr. Homans' course, but several similar ones do. For instance, it is curiously possible for an analyst to observe the fact that classes exist in society and at the same time to feel that the word "class" is deplorable or repugnant. Mr.

Homans has no alternative but to keep on designating the fact, the thing for which the word stands, till he can be sure it has become a datum. Again the words "leadership" and "leader" have an overtone of "exploitation" or "subverter," or even "Il Duce" and "Der Führer," and are likely to inject a subjective element into a study that will fail if it is not kept objective. There is nothing to do but to keep on pointing to the wholly neutral fact that whenever men form groups there are always those who initiate or direct or supervise and those who accept or act on the initiative or direction of others—that squads have corporals and armies generals, clubs have presidents, and orchestras conductors, shops have foremen, and parliaments presiding officers. It is necessary, even, to point out repeatedly that forces other than marital infidelity and drunkenness may have united to produce an increase in the divorce rate, or that the desire for higher pay may not fully explain unrest or inefficiency in a factory's labor force or the same factory's board of experts. Mr. Homans is required to define his terms with great rigor, and the reader must keep in mind that the definitions always apply.

My job here is not to describe his method or summarize his book, but I may serve the reader by pointing out the pivotal, recurring terms. He scrutinizes three elements of behavior: activity, what members of a group do as members of it; interaction, the relationship which the activity of one member of the group has to that of another; and sentiment, the sum of interior feeling, whether physical or mental, that a group-member has in relation to what the group does. To these he adds another carefully defined concept which he calls "the norms": the code of behavior which, implicitly or explicitly, consciously or unconsciously, the group adopts as just, proper, or ideal. He joins to these the concept of "the external system," such relations between a group and its environment as may affect its behavior, and the "internal system," such sentiments of the group toward one another as may affect its behavior. These elements and processes of behavior are what he studies in each of his five groups. He finds that in all five they act in the same way to perform the same functions, and have the same relationships to one another. In the course of studying them he uncovers two related, facilitating processes which he calls "the build-up" and "the feed-back" and which are to be thought of as mechanisms of social adaptation and elaboration.

The core of his findings is that in all five groups the forces which
affect behavior are in a constant state of mutual dependence.
"Interaction" and "sentiment" depend on each other; the oftener A
and B do things together, the more they will tend to like each
other; the more they like each other, the oftener they will tend to do
things together; both tendencies affect their behavior and that of the
group. But each is also dependent on all the other elements, processes, and relationships that have been considered. If either the
liking of A for B or the way they do things together produces any
considerable departure from what the group considers proper behavior, a reaction will be set up to bring them into line, and this too
will affect other relationships and group behavior as a whole. That is
the external system in operation; but the nature, degree, and extent
of the group action thus required, and of the individual actions subsidiary to it, will be affected by feelings inside the group which have
no direct bearing on the group's relation to the environment, by subgroups and cliques, by jealousies and rivalries and admirations.
Moreover, this system of dependent relationships, which reacts on
the environment and may to some extent change it, is itself in some
degree modified by the environment, and is constantly adjusting and
readjusting within itself. If numerical values could be assigned to
these forces, the coefficients would always be changing in relation
to one another. All affect one another, each is a resultant of the
others, the operation of all conditions the working of all.

These are ideas of marked (but deceptive) simplicity and of
extreme importance. What the small group reveals when thus studied
is a social system reacting with its environment as a self-adjusting
organization of response whose parts are mutually interdependent.
What acts, and what reacts, is not any single part or function of
the social system, nor any combination of parts or functions, but the
system as a whole, a totality whose mutual interdependence *is* the
system. Cause and effect disappear; what must be looked for is the
resultants of complexes of interacting forces. The group is a dynamic
social equilibrium. It sets up its own responses organically, determines its own measures of control, derives its own possibilities of
adaptation, elaboration, and change. To state just one of Mr.
Homans' conclusions—I have no space for more—direction or leadership can be imposed on it only so far as the group as such

is willing to accept either. It will accept them only as they fit its own pattern of group necessity and only to the degree that fulfills its own conception of what is proper *in its own terms*. This is a startling illumination of a thesis familiar to us as "government rests on the consent of the governed." Given the theoretical statement it receives here, it is an important idea for sociology. All the principles which Mr. Homans finds related to it, and to which his book is devoted, are equally important.

His first point, then, is that the elements he isolates are true uniformities: they appear in all small groups. His second is that the dynamic equilibrium probably characterizes the larger units of society with which sociology is ultimately concerned, that his generalizations probably apply there. If so, then this book is a first approximation of—a first step toward—a general theory of society. But what is more important is that these are also prime forces of adhesion and coherence in society, since they are, so to speak, the physiology of the smallest units. The inference is that since the primary groups that people form have these characteristics, they are basic in all human association.

But it is when he turns in his last chapter to applications that Mr. Homans makes the points which will seem most significant to readers outside his profession. The vigor and durability of small groups seem to him to be the stability of society. The almost universal fear is that ours is an age of disintegration. If it is, or if 'it is not to become one, then the problem of so controlling society that the forces of disintegration will be overcome is paramount. Metropolitan society has seriously restricted and enfeebled the natural processes that enable people to form small coherent groups which live together and share the whole sum of experience. Industrial society has provided no functional substitutes. It may be that the restriction and enfeeblement of the forces that make such organizations possible are in themselves disintegrative. It may be that the preservation of our society depends on our finding ways to strengthen what has been weakened, to make the natural formation of basic small groups easier and more inevitable, or on our finding ways to transmit their vital essence to the larger groups that so tragically lack it.

BERNARD DE VOTO

Cambridge, Massachusetts

Introduction

LIKE OTHER fields of intellectual inquiry, sociology has experienced periodic shifts in the problems that are of central interest to theorists and research workers. Not too long ago, sociology was devoted largely—never wholly, as it sometimes seemed—to such worrisome and interesting difficulties of social life as crime, delinquency, and divorce. At another, when its horizon was broader and its analysis perhaps deeper, concern centered on the search for regular sequences of change in cultures and civilizations. These shifts in interest were more than eddies in the current of sociological thought. Each left a more or less permanent precipitate that was caught up in new and, we like to think, accumulating knowledge.

One such recent shift in sociology, and in the affiliated field of social psychology, is evidenced by the rapidly mounting interest in the study of the small group. This interest cannot fairly or accurately be called new; it is, rather, a renascence. An earlier generation of sociologists—Cooley and Simmel are only the best remembered among numerous others—had been much interested in the small group, within limits dictated by the primitive research methods and the scantily developed theory of the time. But though their writings were much quoted, their ideas were little advanced by those who came after. And since the beginnings they provided were not systematically followed up, sociological knowledge about the small group remained stagnant.

Within the past decade or so, this condition has greatly changed. From the most varied sources there has developed a revival of sociological interest in the small group, an interest that bids fair to grow with the accumulation of new empirical findings, interrelated in systematic theory. Diverse strands of thought have converged in this development. As the sociological implications of

Freudian theory were progressively drawn out, for example, they were seen to involve numerous hypotheses about interpersonal relations in small groups, notably but not exclusively, the family. Social psychologists, among whom Kurt Lewin must be accorded preeminence, began to study the interaction of men in experimentally contrived little groups. Moreno tenaciously followed out the implications of researches on reciprocal and unilateral attractions and repulsions among the members of a group and, by his achievements in what he called sociometry, encouraged further sociological interest in the study of the small group. Utilitarian as well as academic considerations have promoted this interest. Practical concern with the development of effective techniques for conference and discussion groups has lately led to controlled observation of patterns of interaction in such periodically assembled groupings. And empirical studies of industrial, political, and military bureaucracies—often conducted for reasons extraneous to the advancement of sociological theory—have unexpectedly rediscovered the importance of the small groups which typically form, often not according to plan, at many places in these large social organizations.

This notable convergence of varied lines of theory and varied methods of research on the small group strongly suggests that this subject will for some time to come remain one of the chief growing points in the systematic study of the behavior of men in society. And the appearance of *The Human Group* lends weight to that supposition.

Mr. Homans' major purpose is to work toward a sociological theory which will state, in convenient and compact form, the interconnected uniformities detected in the behavior of men in groups. The book is largely based on intensive and systematic scrutiny of five small groups, and proceeds on the assumption that close study of these particular groups will enable us the better to understand the workings of groups in general. What starts as analysis of particulars tentatively ends as synthesis of generalizations.

It will be evident to the reader that Mr. Homans has effected a mutually advantageous partnership between his theory and his data. Just as the theory lends significance to the data, the data lend cogency to the theory. The partnership is strengthened by Mr. Homans' method of presentation. He first sketches the bare outlines of his conceptual scheme, so that one may have a preliminary way of looking at the facts. This is followed by a detailed recording of facts about a particular group. With these facts in hand, he begins their analysis, utilizing the conceptual tools which have been laid out. Consequently, his conceptions (or abstractions) do not depart very far or for very long from the facts of observation. And thereafter, whenever the data require it, new concepts are introduced to enlarge our understanding of the observed behavior. Thus the reader sees sociological theory at work, organizing, clarifying, and benefiting from otherwise inert data.

Because Mr. Homans lets the reader in on his method of analysis, rather than confronting him with readymade findings, his book becomes an effective instrument for training students. It is a document which the student of group behavior can *use*, not merely cite. For the student who, under Mr. Homans' guidance, conscientiously works through these five intensive studies of groups should be able to utilize this same method of analysis and this same general theory in the study of other groups. Thus the student, with this work, gains an active skill in sociological analysis rather than a passive knowledge about the contents of a textbook.

Mr. Homans' book facilitates this kind of active learning in many ways, of which I can here mention only a few. Underlying the whole is the sustained practice of *systematically* analyzing small groups in terms of specific variables and their mutual relations, rather than presenting an assortment of splendid but disconnected insights. Comparison between the analysis of a sociological problem set forth in this book and in earlier, more discursive, writings should help the student to appreciate the importance of thinking in terms of relations between specified variables. The analysis of social control in Chapter 11 of this book and in the writings of Edward Ross, for example, provides one such instructive comparison.

In its analysis of small groups in terms of variables, this book profits from not attempting to do too much too soon. L. J. Henderson, the distinguished biochemist to whom Mr. Homans avowedly owes so much of his conception of scientific method, liked to advise the use of "as few variables as you dare, as many as you must," and the wisdom of this advice is here abundantly illustrated. No

more than other men are sociologists prepared to juggle a score
or so of variables simultaneously and come out with any determinate result. An initial quartet of variables—what he calls interaction, sentiment, activities and norms—enables Mr. Homans to go
a long way, though of course not all the way, toward analyzing
basic processes in the small group. And as occasion demands, he
introduces additional variables, so that his first approximation becomes successively closer to the concrete facts of group behavior.
The student who is so often tempted to deal at once with "all the
facts of the case" only to discover that his understanding is diminished by an excess of facts will gain an instructive lesson in the
virtues of the more modest and more productive procedure of successive approximations.

Threaded through Mr. Homans' limited array of analytical variables is an unflagging emphasis on their mutual dependence. Much,
of course, remains to be done by way of working out sharper tools
for the study of such mutual dependence, but the reader who follows Mr. Homans' account with care is not likely again to overlook the salient fact that parts and elements are interdependent,
not only in small groups but in social organization generally. For
by taking account of interdependence in his studies of group behavior, Mr. Homans succeeds in converting what has often been an
empty figure of speech into a tool of analysis.

Interdependence not only characterizes the relations of variables
within a group, but also the relations of that group to its social environment. By recognizing this fact, Mr. Homans has escaped the
tendency, already marked in many sociological researches, to consider small groups as though they were in fact wholly isolated.
To be sure, the sociologists and social psychologists who adopt
this latter assumption would, upon second thought, acknowledge
it to be entirely provisional. They know, of course, that no Chinese
wall shuts off the group from the world about it. Nevertheless,
research, particularly research on experimentally contrived groups,
is still largely carried forward on this assumption, with the result
that there has been little systematic analysis of the interconnections between the internal organization of groups and their social
surroundings. In Mr. Homans' scheme of analysis, however, these
interconnections take a central place, and he has made good prog-

ress in mapping out their character. And in addressing himself to the question of how groups maintain themselves in their environment, he relates his analysis to one of the major problems of that important emerging trend of social theory called functional sociology.

Just as the book advances the theory of small groups by taking into account the often neglected environment of groups, so it advances that theory by systematic examination of the processes of change in group structure. This is not merely a study in social statics. Furthermore, and particularly important, social change is not considered in descriptive terms only. The processes of change are bound up theoretically with the internal organization and the environment of the group. Structure, process, and function, statics and dynamics, find their integral place in this analytical scheme.

In so tight-knit a book as this, it is difficult to single out passages or sections of special worth. Excursus though it is, the handful of pages dealing with the modern urban family will be judged by some as having more than its share of seminal ideas rigorously and methodically stated. Others will regard as most rewarding those numerous passages in the several case studies that analyze in detail the mutual dependence of activity, sentiment, interaction, and norms. They will note that much said here about social norms emerging from ongoing activities is a refreshing reminder of what has often been forgotten in current anthropological discussions of culture as a thing virtually set apart from society. Here, and elsewhere, Mr. Homans does not believe in letting abstract nouns—for example, "culture," "society," and "civilization"—get the better of him.

But though choice is difficult, the student interested in the development of functional sociology will want to give topmost place to that part of Chapter 10 which reconciles the theories of Malinowski and Radcliffe-Brown regarding ritual and anxiety. Here Mr. Homans succeeds, not adventitiously, but through methodical application of the theory developed earlier in his book, in establishing a linkage between the functions of social patterns for the individual members of a group and for the group considered as a whole. Sociologists have lately come to recognize that *both* kinds of function—or dysfunction, if the consequences of the behavior are disruptive rather than adaptive—must be taken into account in a functional analysis, and in this book they have a series of object lessons in how this can be done. Pursuing the same tradition of social theory, Mr. Homans points repeatedly to the unforeseen and unintended consequences of human action—another common and familiar fact setting important theoretical problems for functional sociology—and seeks to show that often these are unforeseen precisely because significant relations within the group and between the group and its environment have not been taken in account. Throughout, special problems of this nature are analyzed, not with the aid of improvised hypotheses, but through use of the general scheme of analysis, a practice as sound as it is rare in sociological theorizing.

But it would be a mistake to suppose that readers will uniformly agree with Mr. Homans' concepts, methods, and results. Indeed, I myself happen to differ here and there with certain passages; for instance, the brief and, in my opinion, tendentious discussion of "manipulation" of men by leaders, and the references in one study to questionnaire results in which the author attaches significance to the sheer percentages of people answering a question in one way rather than another. (In regarding this as a highly defective procedure, the research sociologists who work systematically with numerical data on expressions of attitudes are likely to be more critical than their critics who, like Mr. Homans, make occasional use of such data. For, as is well known, the absolute percentages of people responding in a given fashion to a questionnaire are very largely affected by the mere wording of the questions, and therefore change appreciably as the wording is slightly modified.)

Moot points there certainly are in this book, as Mr. Homans periodically reminds us, but since he is careful to say that his is only one, and not necessarily the sole, mode of interpretation, and since he gives us the grounds for his interpretation, his book will be of value even to those who may occasionally differ with it. For it forces them—as I believe it did me—to work out and clarify the bases for their disagreement. In short, the reader who has a bone to pick with the author will typically find that it is a bone worth picking and will profit from the lucid exposition of a theory with which he does not always agree. And because salient theoretical issues are thus brought out into the open, the book has great didactic value for training students in the application of a sociological theory of group life.

But it is not necessary to report further uses of Mr. Homans' analytical scheme; the book itself does that in sturdy and lucid prose. With proper words in proper places, the book never fights shy of technical terms when these are really needed, but is careful to make each such term genuinely denotive. In this respect, as with respect to the scientific temper which pervades the whole, it is reminiscent of that little gem of a book by L. J. Henderson, *Pareto's General Sociology* (recognized as a classic both by those who find little of merit in Pareto's immense bulk of sociological writing and by the dwindling few who still abide by him). And like Henderson, Mr. Homans is not averse to aphorisms: "To the classic peril of being impaled on the horns of a dilemma, we moderns should add a new one, being split by a false dichotomy." Or another, aptly self-illustrative in its own unconditional phrasing: "a new statement must be an overstatement, and sometimes it is more important that the statement be interesting than that it be true." But it would be a pity if the reader were so taken with Mr. Homans' frequent aphorisms as to miss the essentially systematic character of his sociological analysis. The style may be the man, but the systematic analysis is the science. And this unpretentious book is first and last a work of social science, not a collection of epigrams or random insights.

In closing these remarks, and despite my occasional disagreement with certain details in the book, concerning which the author rather than the editor has rightly enough had the last word, I should like to express this considered judgment: not since Simmel's pioneering analyses of almost half a century ago has any single work contributed so much to a sociological theory of the structure, processes, and functions of small groups as George Homans' *The Human Group.*

ROBERT K. MERTON

Columbia University
August 1950

Preface

IN THIS BOOK as elsewhere, my chief intellectual debt is to three great men, Lawrence Joseph Henderson, Elton Mayo, and Alfred North Whitehead, under whose influence I was lucky enough to come rather early in life. Other intellectual debts will be readily apparent in the pages that follow. This book also relies heavily on the field research of certain sociologists and anthropologists, in the sense that it tries to state, in a single conceptual language, some of the generalizations implicit in their work. Thanks are therefore due to Fritz Roethlisberger and William Dickson, the authors, and to the Harvard University Press, the publisher, for permission to reproduce quotations and charts from *Management and the Worker;* to Conrad Arensberg, Solon Kimball, and the Harvard University Press for permission to reproduce quotations from *Family and Community in Ireland;* to William F. Whyte and the University of Chicago Press for permission to reproduce quotations and one chart from *Street Corner Society;* to Raymond Firth and George Allen and Unwin, Ltd., for permission to reproduce quotations and charts from *We, the Tikopia;* to Raymond Firth and Routledge and Kegan Paul, Ltd., for permission to reproduce quotations and one chart from *Primitive Polynesian Economy;* to David L. Hatch for permission to reproduce quotations from his unpublished Harvard Ph.D. thesis, "Changes in the Structure and Functions of a Rural New England Community since 1900;" and to Conrad Arensberg, Douglas Macgregor, and the editors of *Applied Anthropology* (now *Human Organization*) for permission to reproduce quotations and charts from an article entitled, "Determination of Morale in an Industrial Company." The concrete field data cited in this book come largely from these sources. Permission to use other quotations and figures is acknowledged in the text. In my thinking, and in some societies, a debt does not divide debtor and creditor but links them closer together. I am therefore particularly happy to acknowledge my heavy indebtedness to my friends Florence Kluckhohn and Robert Merton for reading and criticizing in detail the manuscript of this book, to my friend Bernard DeVoto for much good advice, not always taken, on publishing problems, and to my wife, Nancy Parshall Homans, for redrawing all the charts.

GEORGE CASPAR HOMANS

Cambridge, Massachusetts
August 1950

THE ANCIENT EMBLEM *that represents life by the circle formed by a snake biting its tail gives a sufficiently just picture of the state of affairs. In effect, the organization of life in complex organisms does form a closed circle, but one that has a head and a tail, in the sense that all the phenomena of life are not equally important although all take part in the completion of the* circulus *of life. Thus the muscular and nervous organs maintain the activity of the organs that make blood, but the blood in turn nourishes the organs that produce it. There is in this an organic or social solidarity that keeps up a kind of perpetual motion, until a disturbance or cessation of the action of a necessary vital element shall have broken the equilibrium or brought about a trouble or stoppage in the play of the bodily machine.*

CLAUDE BERNARD
Introduction a la medicine experimentale:
Paris, 1865.

CHAPTER 1

Plans and Purposes

Why Study the Group? ... A New Synthesis ... Socio-logical Theory ... What Kind of Theory? ... How Shall the Theory Be Built? ... The Problem of Abstraction ... Clinical and Analytical Science ... Rules of Theory-Building ... Social Science and Literature ... Method of Presentation ... Separation of Fact from Theory ... The Human Qualities Needed

IN THIS book we shall study the most familiar features of the most familiar thing in the world—the human group. We mean by a group a number of persons who communicate with one another often over a span of time, and who are few enough so that each person is able to communicate with all the others, not at secondhand, through other people, but face-to-face. Sociologists call this the primary group.[1] A chance meeting of casual acquaint-ances does not count as a group for us.

The study of the human group is a part of sociology, but a neg-lected part. As the science of society, sociology has examined the characteristics and problems of communities, cities, regions, big organizations like factories, and even whole nations, but it has only begun to study the smaller social units that make up these giants. In doing so, it has not followed the order of human experience, for the first and most immediate social experience of mankind is small group experience. From infancy onward we are members of fami-lies, childhood gangs, school and college cliques, clubs and teams— all small groups. When, as grownups, we get jobs, we still find our-selves working with a few persons and not with the whole firm, association, or government department. We are members of these

[1] C. H. Cooley, *Social Organization*, 23-31.

larger social organizations, but the people we deal with regularly are always few. They mediate between us and the leviathans. The group is the commonest, as it is the most familiar, of social units, and on both counts it is at least as well worth study as any of the others. Sociology might have begun here.

WHY STUDY THE GROUP?

We here—and this is the collaborative, not the editorial *we:* author and reader are learning together—will have two reasons for studying the group: the sheer interest of the subject and the desire to reach a new sociological synthesis. In a utilitarian age, the first reason must get special emphasis. If we want to study social behavior at all, we shall want to study the commonest of social units, and in this book we shall study the group primarily because the study is interesting and not because it is useful. The story goes that an English politician came to visit Faraday in his laboratory just after he had built the first electric motor.[2] The politician is supposed to have asked him—the business of politicians is to ask these questions—what the gadget was good for. At this point the story splits into two versions. One has it that Faraday replied, "Someday you can tax it." Another, that he asked the counterquestion, "What good is a baby?" Either way the moral is clear. For the great men of science, knowledge was good because it might have a future, but in the meantime it was, like a baby, good in itself. Knowledge is power, but it is also, for some men, happiness. *Felix qui potuit rerum cognoscere causas.* We must no longer quake at the question: "Knowledge for What?"[3] It need not put us in the wrong. There is only one paramount reason for studying anything but the multiplication table. Either you are so interested in a subject that you cannot let it alone, or you are not. In the end, it is a matter of intellectual passion. Willard Gibbs, the greatest of American theoretical physicists, said of his own work, "Anyone with the same desires could have made the same researches."[4] The stress is on desire. Accordingly the chief motive for writing or reading this book

---

[2] The same story with variations has been told of other scientists, including Franklin.

[3] The title of a book by R. S. Lynd.

[4] M. Rukeyser, *Willard Gibbs*, 381.

is the interest of the subject, and the aim of the book is sheer intellectual enlightenment.

A NEW SYNTHESIS

The second reason for studying the group is that through this study a new sociological synthesis may be reached. The first generation of sociologists, the generation of Comte and Spencer, and the second, the generation of Pareto, Durkheim, and Max Weber, made great, if inadequate, syntheses. The third generation, which flourished between World War I and World War II, shunned the example of its predecessors, but it followed up their many suggestions and made a number of excellent, detailed studies of particular social groups. In the course of the work of this generation, many hypotheses were hammered out, but they remained bound to the material from which they came. They were so stated as to apply to the particular groups being studied, but not beyond. They were not generalized to apply to all, or at least many, groups. Although this provincialism was wise in its time, the present, or fourth, generation of sociologists feels once more the need for synthesis, for putting together, making explicit and general, the ideas that special studies have brought out. Sociology has been gorged with facts; it needs to digest them. And yet, if there is a need for synthesis, the last generation has taught us to be modest in our aims. We now know something of the endless complexities in the study of society. Perhaps we cannot manage a sociological synthesis that will apply to whole communities and nations, but it is just possible we can manage one that will apply to the small group. Synthesis of the microcosm—that may be an attainable end. The group may be small enough to let us get all the way around it.

SOCIOLOGICAL THEORY

To say that a study is synthetic and general is to say that it is theoretical. "It is the office of theoretical investigation," said Willard Gibbs, "to give the form in which the results of experiment may be expressed." [5] If he had put "observation" for "experiment," Gibbs would have stated the purpose of this book. It is to provide

[5] *Ibid.,* 232.

one form—not the only possible form—in which may be expressed the results of observation in sociology. We now have, besides the treasury of human history and literature, many good studies of social groups of various kinds, from primitive societies to modern factories and communities. Granting that these studies are not everything they may sometime become, for what we see grows with what we are taught to see and in turn helps the latter to grow, many of us still feel that they sum up close observation in clear exposition. In what form, then, can the results of this work be expressed so that we can see whether or not they apply, not merely to single groups, but to many or all groups?

If we have a great deal of fact to work with, we also have a great deal of theory. The elements of a synthesis are on hand. We shall only put together ideas that have been lying around for some time in the literature of the social sciences, so that our novelty—if we are new at all—will consist not in what we combine but how we do so. Some theoretical work has illuminated the descriptions of particular groups: it needs to be expressed with full generality. Some of it has been hinted at in asides and suggestions, cryptically: it needs to be spelled out. Some of it has been beautifully general and explicit, but partial: many elements need to be added to make a satisfactory whole. Yet whatever the weakness of this statement or that, there have been signs of convergence in the body of theory as a whole. This book tries to make the most of the convergence and state one way in which the meeting of minds, the agreement on a synthesis, might take place.

The behavior of men, usually in small numbers, has inspired the largest part of human literature and eloquence. If we investigated no further than we have today, we should have plenty of material to study. But until recently this great mass of observation has led to nothing. Some leaders, perhaps those of the past more than those of the present, have shown great capacity for handling men in groups, but their know-how could not easily be communicated in words from one man to another. There have been a few maxims of practical wisdom, always at odds with one another because the limits of any single maxim were never stated. Whatever a man did, he could always find a rule to back him up. But until recently there has been little growth. Our knowledge is Babylonian.

Our proverbs are carved on the pyramids. A new fact in physics or biology fits into an old theory, or by not fitting starts a new theory. Either way one can build on it. Think of the mass of old work summarized and new work suggested by the periodic table of the elements. But every adventurer in the science of human behavior from Aristotle to Freud has had to make a fresh start, or something like it.

If the outlook has changed since the opening of this century, the reason is that we have begun to sketch out systematic theories of human behavior and to use them. Einstein taught the world, what it ought to have known long ago, that no theory is permanent. If an old theory survives new conquests of science, it survives as a slave. But even the most fragile theory has its uses. In its lowest form, as a classification, it provides a set of pigeonholes, a filing cabinet, in which fact can accumulate. For nothing is more lost than a loose fact. The empty folders of the file demand filling. In time the accumulation makes necessary a more economical filing system, with more cross references, and a new theory is born.

But in sociology we have not made as much progress as we might have, and the reason is clear. We have pursued the higher branches of our science before the trunk was strong. We have not grown because we have had nothing to grow from. We have given ink-blot tests to Navahos; we have computed differential fertility rates among ethnic groups in Kansas—all worthy subjects if we had also studied ordinary, everyday social behavior. Make no mistake about it, *that* we have not done. Perhaps we were afraid that, if we studied the commonplace, we should lay ourselves open to the familiar charge that a sociologist is a man who discovers at infinite pains what everybody knows. Or, as one novelist put it, a sociologist is a man who spends forty thousand dollars to find a whorehouse. We should have had enough self-confidence and enough sense to forget such fears. The fact is that the popular diagnosis of our shortcomings is wholly mistaken. Far from discovering facts that are too familiar, we have not discovered facts that are familiar enough. Prostitution is not one-millionth as common as some of the behavior we shall study in this book. The basic characteristics of social behavior are well known in the sense that everyone, so far as he leads a social life, has some intuitive familiarity with them, but they are not well known in another, and more important sense. They have not been stated in such a way that a body of scientific knowledge can be built on them. Above all, the links between the different aspects of social behavior have not been made clear. A fact is commonplace or not according to its connection with other facts. The fact that an apple would fall was the dreariest fact in the world until Newton showed that an apple and a planet obeyed the same laws of motion. The theoretical synthesis developed in this book will attempt to state some perfectly familiar ideas about social behavior—the more familiar the better—in such a way that their relation to other equally familiar ideas will become clear. We shall try to make the commonplace strange by showing it in new connections.

This book has, then, a twofold purpose: to study the small group as an interesting subject in itself, but also, in so doing, to reach a new sociological synthesis. Since this book will try to state one general form in which the results of particular observations may be expressed, it will be, in Gibbs' sense, a book of theory. These observations include some excellent modern studies of groups of various kinds. The book aims to be true to them, to make explicit what is implicit in them and to make general what is partial. And the book will deliberately concentrate on the most familiar aspects of group behavior.

WHAT KIND OF THEORY?

We have spoken of the need for sociological theory. The next question is: What kind of a theory shall we try to develop in this book? The rest of the book is the answer to this question; we can now anticipate our results only briefly. First, group behavior will be analyzed into a number of mutually dependent elements. Second, the group will be studied as an organic whole, or social system, surviving in an environment. Third, the relations of the elements to one another in the system will be found to bring about the evolution of the system with the passage of time.

Perhaps we can illustrate our meaning by a cursory analysis of one of the simplest groups: two friends. The two men like one another. If we ask why they do so, we are told that they have interests in common or that the personality of the one is compatible with that of the other. That is, their emotional feeling for one another is not something in itself; it does not exist in a vacuum, but is determined in part by other factors. What we perceive next is that the relation between their friendship and these other factors is a two-way one. They are friends, for instance, because they have interests in common, but if we are good observers of human behavior, we know that the reverse is also true: if they are friends they will develop interests in common. Which comes first, the friendship or the common interests? The answer is that neither comes first, but that they wax or wane together. In this book we say that the two factors, or elements, are mutually dependent. But personality, interests, and the sentiment of friendship are not the only factors that need to be considered. We must also take into account the number of times the two men meet. If they meet and have interests in common, they are apt to become friends; on the other hand, if they are friends, they will find occasions for getting together. And if they do not meet, their friendship is apt to ebb away. Absence makes the heart grow fonder for only a short time. As before, the two factors: the feeling the two men have for one another and their association with one another, are mutually dependent. But "getting together" is not something in itself, any more than friendship and common interests are. People do not just get together; they get together to do something. Let us suppose that the two friends are interested in camping, and go off on a camping trip together to the north woods. We now perceive that the emotional tie between them will be affected by the success of the trip. If everything goes well, or if difficulties are met and overcome, their friendship is, we say, cemented. If everything goes badly, they may get disgusted with one another. Their friendship and the success of the joint enterprise are mutually dependent. For if the success of the enterprise affects their friendship, so their friendship— their *morale* we might call it now—affects the success of the enterprise, enabling the friends to carry on through difficulties, to *make* a success of their trip. Moreover, the success of the enterprise is determined in part by the environment in which the pair find themselves. Does a bear eat the food? Are the rivers low, so that the canoe is holed on a rock? And finally, the nature of this little group will change or develop with time. If the two men associate with one another, undertake activities in which both are interested, and are successful in carrying them through, their friendship will grow.

We have not carried the analysis as far, or made it as rigorous, as we might. After all, we do not want to tip our hand as early in the book as this. But we have said enough to make our points clear. What have we done? We have separated the concrete behavior of the two men into factors or elements: emotion, personality, interests, association, activities, and the success of those activities. We have seen how these elements are mutually related to one another, and how their mutual relations make a recognizable, ongoing entity: not just two men, but two men linked together; not just two individuals, but a new kind of unit, a group. We have seen that this unit exists in an environment, and that some of its characteristics are determined by the nature of the environment. And we have seen how the relations between the various factors in the group life tend to make the group develop or evolve with the passage of time. The problems we encounter in analyzing this pair are the problems we shall encounter in analyzing any group.

By way of further illustration, we turn from our statement, which was tied to a particular group, to a much more general statement of the nature of a complex whole. Mary Parker Follett, social worker and one of the most sensitive writers on problems of human organization, struggled, far more eloquently than we, to say what we have tried to say. In her study of administrative control, she argued, as others had done, that in studying any organized social activity we must study the "total situation." But we must not merely "be sure to get all the factors into our problem." We must examine "not merely the totalness of the situation, but the nature of the totalness. . . . What you have to consider in a situation is not all the factors one by one, but also their relation to one another." The relation is such that the parts make a whole, the elements make an organism. And Mary Follett affirmed "that the whole determines the parts as well as that the parts determine the whole." She recognized that the unity is not a static, finished thing, but an ongoing process: "The same activity determines both parts and whole. . . . We are speaking of a unity which is not the result of an interweaving, but *is* the interweaving. Unity is always a process, not a product. . . . I have been saying that the whole is determined not only by its constituents, but by their relation to one another. I now say that the whole is determined also by the relation of whole and parts. . . . It is the same activity which is making the whole and parts simultaneously." Finally, the activity, the process, she spoke of always leads to something new. Something emerges. She summarized her ideas as follows: "My first point concerned the total situation; my second, the nature of the interacting which determines the total situation; my third, the evolving situation. We have come to see that reciprocal adjustment is more than mere adjustment; that it is there we get what the psychologist has called the 'something new,' 'the critical moment in evolution.'" Here perhaps we had better leave Mary Follett, but in the pages to come we shall be concerned with all three processes she called the interacting, the unifying, and the emerging.[6]

Writers of great sensitivity, like Mary Follett, may give us a vision of our subject: the unity that is at the same time a process, the unity whose parts taken separately slip out between our fingers like sand but in integration are as strong as steel. And yet the vision is not enough. It is one thing to see where we are going and quite another to get there: to build up, piece by piece, a picture of the dynamic unity of a group when, in taking the pieces out of the whole, we may falsify them and it. In his discussion of "internal relations," that is, the relations between the parts in a whole, Alfred Whitehead, perhaps the greatest of modern philosophers, stated the difficulty clearly: "The difficulty which arises in respect to internal relations is to explain how any particular truth is possible. Insofar as there are internal relations, everything must depend upon everything else. Apparently, therefore, we are under the necessity of saying everything at once." [7] We shall indeed, in the rest of this book, know the despair that comes when one cannot follow up immediately all the connections in an interconnected whole, when one cannot ride off in all directions. But we may take comfort in Whitehead, who went on to say: "This supposed necessity is palpably untrue. . . . [The

---

[6] All quotations from "The Psychology of Control," in H. C. Metcalf and L. Urwick, eds., *Dynamic Administration: The Collected Papers of Mary Parker Follett*, 183-209.

[7] A. N. Whitehead, *Science and the Modern World*, 235.

general scheme of relationships] discloses itself as being analysable into a multiplicity of limited relationships which have their own individuality and yet at the same time presuppose the total relationship within possibility." [8] That is, a statement of the relation between any two parts of a whole is not incorrect just because it says nothing about the relation of each of the two to all the other parts. Remember these words of Whitehead's. We are glad to have his reassurance, as we shall be forced in any event to work with limited relationships. Whether or not it is a philosophical necessity, it is certainly a literary impossibility to say everything at once.

HOW SHALL THE THEORY BE BUILT?

The group will be described as an organic whole, surviving and evolving in an environment. We do not want just to get the feel of this whole. We want to be men and *understand*. We want to build up in detail the articulation of the whole, and in these mazes we shall certainly go astray unless we have a method of attacking our problem, a method that we can apply patiently, repeatedly, and systematically, at whatever risk of dullness. The question then is: How shall we go about constructing our theory of the group?

We shall begin with semantics, the science of tracing words back to their references in observed fact. In sociology we are devoted to "big" words: status, culture, function, heuristic, particularistic, methodology, integration, solidarity, authority. Too often we work with these words and not with observations. Or rather, we do not wed the two. No one will make progress with this book who does not train himself to extensionalize,[9] who does not habitually catch himself as he mouths one of the big abstractions and ask: What does this mouthful mean in terms of actual human behavior that someone has seen and reported? Just what, in human behavior, do we *see?* The question is devastating, and we do not ask it half often enough. Carefully working out the referents of existing concepts will help us to reach a simple method of classifying what we see, and in the classification itself we shall gain a new set of concepts more adequate than some of the old ones for the purposes we have in mind.

[8] A. N. Whitehead, *Science and the Modern World*, 239.
[9] See S. I. Hayakawa, *Language in Thought and Action*, 58-60.

Let us take an example. Let us take the concepts *status* and *role*, which are commonly used in social science. What do they mean? Ralph Linton, the anthropologist, who gave these concepts an important place in his social theory, has this to say: "A *status*, in the abstract, is a position in a particular pattern [of social behavior] . . . A status, as distinct from the individual who may occupy it, is simply a collection of rights and duties . . . A *role* represents the dynamic aspects of a status. The individual is socially assigned to a status and occupies it with relation to other statuses. When he puts the rights and duties which constitute the status into effect, he is performing a role. Role and status are quite inseparable, and the distinction between them is of only academic interest. There are no roles without statuses or statuses without roles." [10]

Now let us try, if we can, to translate these words into observations, and, leaving out of consideration the fact that a person may hold several statuses—he may be a *father*, an *officer* of a lodge, a *deacon* of a church—let us consider only a single status, that of *foreman*. Foreman is a status in that the position may be occupied by a number of individuals in succession; the position does not disappear when an individual leaves it. Let us suppose that a man is foreman in a factory, and that we are watching him at work. What do we see and hear? We watch him, perhaps, overseeing a battery of punch presses, going from one man to another as they tend the machines, answering their questions and showing them, if they have made mistakes, where they have gone wrong. We see him also at his desk making out records. That is, we see that he has a certain kind of job, that he carries on certain activities. We see also that he deals with certain men in the plant and not with others. He goes to certain men and talks to them; others come to his desk and talk to him. He gets his orders from a boss and passes on the orders to members of his own department. That is, he communicates or, as we shall say in this book, interacts with certain persons and not with others, and this communication from person to person often takes place in a certain order—for instance, from the boss to the foreman and then from the foreman to the workers—, so that we can say, in Linton's words, that the foreman occupies a posi-

[10] R. Linton, *The Study of Man*, 113-4.

tion in a chain of communications. If, moreover, we stay in the factory and listen sharply, we shall hear remarks to the effect that a foreman's job is lower or worse than the president's but higher or better than the ordinary workingman's. That is, the foreman's job is given an emotional evaluation. We shall also hear statements of one kind or another about the way the foreman ought to behave, statements that may come both from the boss he works for and from the men who work for him. That is, we hear norms of behavior being expressed. These make up "the collection of rights and duties" that Linton speaks of: notions of what the foreman's behavior ought to be, not necessarily what it really is. And finally, if the foreman's behavior departs outrageously from the norms, we shall see his boss and even his own men take action to bring him back into line. That is, we see men acting so as to control the behavior of others.

No doubt we could make other observations, but we have cited enough to illustrate our point. We do not directly observe *status* and *role*. What we do observe are activities, interactions, evaluations, norms, and controls. Status and role are names we give to a complex of many different kinds of observations. Or, as an expert in semantics would say, a word like *interaction* is a first-order abstraction: it is a name given to a single class of observations; whereas a word like *status* is a second-order abstraction: it is a name given to several classes of observation combined. Second-order abstractions are useful for some purposes but for others have serious drawbacks. They spare us the pain of analysis when we should not be spared. To speak of a man's status as if it were an indivisible unit is a convenient kind of shorthand, but to think of status in this way may prevent our seeing the relations between its components. It may prevent us, for instance, from seeing that as a man's position in a chain of communications changes, so the way he is evaluated by his fellows will change. Since it is just this kind of relation that we shall be examining in this book, the concepts that enter our theories will be, so far as possible, first-order abstractions. At least we shall not use the higher abstractions until we have established the lower ones.[11]

[11] See G. C. Homans, "The Strategy of Industrial Sociology," *American Journal of Sociology*, LIV (1949), 336.

What we have been saying, though it may sound complicated, is in fact too simple. If we follow out its implications, we shall find it naïve. We have implied that we can gaze passively on human behavior and then, all of a sudden, find it has fallen into several classes of observations. But no one just "sees" human behavior. The eye is never quite innocent, but comes to its task sensitized. We see what our experience and ideas teach us to see—and this is never the whole story. The world and its meaning are always negotiating with one another, with experience as the go-between. Even common-sense language implies a theory of behavior and tells us, for instance, to look for actions and motives. We have some notion how to cut the cake. But for the time being we need not worry about the subtlety of the mutual relation between thinking and observation. The great point is to climb down from the big words of social science, at least as far as common-sense observation. Then, if we wish, we can start climbing up again, but this time with a ladder we can depend on.

When we divide our observations of social behavior into classes and give names—our concepts—to the classes, we take the first step in the analysis of the group. We shall take this step in the next chapter. When we examine systematically the relations between the facts to which the concepts refer, we take the first step in synthesis. We shall take this step in the later chapters of the book. By "examining systematically" we mean only that we shall consider in regular order the relation of each set of facts to each of the others. In so doing, we shall be patient, methodical, and slow. We must be so if we are to keep control over the whole of our material while giving special attention to each part of it in turn. Unless we hold our material down in this way, it may get away from us. It has a lot of spring.

THE PROBLEM OF ABSTRACTION

Let no one be deceived by our systematic attack. It means that we shall study methodically the aspects of social life we choose to take up; it does not mean that we shall study every aspect of social life. There are always more observations than can possibly be summed up in any one theory; or rather, if the theory is to be formulated at all, it must leave many observations out of account. Galileo took a fateful step for science when he left friction out of the study of motion. He framed, for instance, his law describing the motion of a ball rolling down an inclined plane on the assumption that there was no friction between the ball and the plane. He was justified in doing so because he could set up his experiments in such a way that they approximated this ideal state more and more closely, although they never quite got there. And he could not have framed a simple, general law if he had not used this method. It is, in fact, the necessary method, but its victories are abstract. As every one of us knows, friction always does exist in any piece of machinery and for practical purposes must be taken into account, often by methods far from elegant. Abstraction is the price paid for generalization.

The method of abstraction seems to create no such mental conflict in physics as it does in sociology. Electrons are members of a group—the atom—, and if we were electrons and knew man's theory of the atom, we might be amused by it, as an educated Hindu might be amused by a missionary's picture of Hindu culture. The theory would seem so gross, so statistical, so simplified, even if it was adequate enough to show man how to split electrons out of the group. But we are not electrons; we study the atom from the outside; we have no way of comparing the theory with the reality, and therefore our shortcomings create no mental conflict in us. This is not true of our social theory. We have inside knowledge of our own society, and this immediate familiarity with group behavior is at once an asset and a liability. It is an asset because we always have our experience to check our theories against. They must be in some degree true to experience. It is a liability because people are too easily able to say of any social theory, "You have left such and such out." They are quite right: we always leave something out. We must if we are to make theories at all. But such people make no attempt to see what we have got in. For them, the social equivalent of friction is a ghost at the table. They do not understand that a theory may be true, and yet not the whole truth.

CLINICAL AND ANALYTICAL SCIENCE

It is high time we knew the difference between clinical and analitical science. Clinical science is what a doctor uses at his patient's bedside. There, the doctor cannot afford to leave out of account anything in the patient's condition that he can see or test. He cannot leave it out either in itself or in its relation to the whole picture of a sick human being. It may be the clue to the complex. Of course the doctor has some general theories at the back of his mind, theories of the connections between a limited number of physiological factors: what the others will do when one is changed. These doctrines may turn out to be useful, but he cannot, at the outset, let them master his thinking. They may not take into consideration, and so may prevent his noticing, the crucial fact in the case before him.

In action we must always be clinical. An analytical science is for understanding but not for action, at least not directly. It picks out a few of the factors at work in particular situations and describes systematically the relations between these factors. Only by cutting down the number of factors considered can it achieve this systematic description. It is general, but it is abstract. As soon as he left friction out of account, Galileo's science became analytical. To return to our medical illustration, a description of particular cases of anemia is clinical science, whereas a theory of blood chemistry is analytical. When progress is rapid, clinical and analytical science help one another. The clinicians tell the analysts what the latter have left out. The analysts need the most brutal reminders because they are always so charmed with their pictures they mistake them for the real thing. On the other hand, the analysts' generalizations often suggest where the clinicians should look more closely. Both the clinician and the analyst are needed. We ought to be sick and tired of boasts that one is better than the other. This is a book of analysis, but it relies heavily on work that is clinical, as the word is used here, and this work was stimulated by earlier analyses.

Elton Mayo, a pioneer in the field of industrial psychology and sociology, used to say that it was better to have a complex body of fact and a simple theory—a working hypothesis—than a simple body of fact and a complex theory. Of course it is better, and many a social scientist has damned himself by taking the second course. Yet you can be just as damned by the first. You may become a man who is sensitive and intuitive about people, and yet incapable of communicating any but your most obvious intuitions; or one who theorizes in spite of his theories but always at the highest level, never among those middle-level generalizations that Francis Bacon felt were the most fruitful.[12] But we need not, unless we insist, be impaled on a nonexistent dilemma. There are always more choices than two. What we need is a theory neither more nor less complex than the facts it subsumes, but adequate to them. If we hesitate to generalize, we lose both our generalization and the observation it might have suggested. If there is a body of fact crying for theoretical synthesis, no doctrinaire stand need stop us from making it. Let us follow Rabelais' advice and do what we like. Above all, let us not be merely sensitive souls; let us be men and understand.

RULES OF THEORY-BUILDING

All these ideas can be summed up in a set of rules that, as experience seems to show, are wisely followed in setting up a theory of the kind we propose. A theory, we will remember, is a form in which the results of observation may be expressed. The rules are:

1. Look first at the obvious, the familiar, the common. In a science that has not established its foundations, these are the things that best repay study.

2. State the obvious in its full generality. Science is an economy of thought only if its hypotheses sum up in a simple form a large number of facts.

3. Talk about one thing at a time. That is, in choosing your words (or, more pedantically, concepts) see that they refer not to several classes of fact at the same time but to one and one only. Corollary: Once you have chosen your words, always use the same words when referring to the same things.

4. Cut down as far as you dare the number of things you are talking about. "As few as you may; as many as you must," is the

[12] *Novum Organum*, Bk. I, aphorisms lxvi, civ.

rule governing the number of classes of fact you take into account.

5. Once you have started to talk, do not stop until you have finished. That is, describe systematically the relationships between the facts designated by your words.

6. Recognize that your analysis must be abstract, because it deals with only a few elements of the concrete situation. Admit the dangers of abstraction, especially when action is required, but do not be afraid of abstraction.[13]

SOCIAL SCIENCE AND LITERATURE

The men of letters, novelists and poets, may be, as some tokens suggest, resentful of the social scientists. They see the latter moving into their territory. But they have no reason to be afraid. If the social scientists are to do their job, they must follow a rigorous code, and it could not be better calculated to make their books and articles hard reading. The rules of theory-building contradict the rules of art at every point. Thus the obvious, or what looks like it, is the thing that a writer is most careful to avoid. Since most efforts at serious conversation shows that it hurts people to think about one thing at a time, a writer uses words that refer to several things at once. He also uses different words for the same thing, or he will be told he lacks variety. For the same reason, he must not repeat himself, whereas systematic discussion is notoriously repetitious, because the same things must be considered in several different connections. Finally, a writer, in a novel or poem, is always concerned with evoking a vivid and integrated sense of concrete reality, either physical or psychological, and his success in doing so is the measure of his charm. A theory begins by breaking up concrete reality and ends by leaving out most of it. The social scientists are not competing, and cannot compete, with the literary artists. They are doing a different job.

METHOD OF PRESENTATION

This is a book on social theory; the theory will show the group to be an organic whole; and the theory will be built up through

---

[13] See G. C. Homans, "A Conceptual Scheme for the Study of Social Organization," *American Sociological Review,* XII (1947), 13. Many of the ideas developed in this book were stated briefly in this paper.

careful examination of the link between social concept and social observation. These facts determine the method of exposition we shall use in this book. We shall use a case method.

A case method means, in the first place, that general theories are shown to arise out of, and to be supported by, specific, detailed matters of observation. For this reason, the method is particularly useful in sociology, where many of the concepts are of so high a level of abstraction that they have lost their connection with observation. But we still have not described the method fully. Any theoretical work has something to do with facts, cites facts. It is not the mere use of facts but the way they are used that makes a case method. A theory is usually supported by fact in the following way. Suppose a sociologist believes that sexual desire can be used to reinforce other motives for action. He needs data to clinch his theory, and he writes: "Thus the natives of North America are accustomed to seeing pictures of the lightly-clothed female figure used to induce the purchase of commodities, whereas the natives of Greece in the fourth century B.C. were accustomed to seeing the female figure used as a symbol of victory rewarding patriotism. In both cases, the logical connection does not appear." Two independent facts, one from America and one from Greece, are used to support the theory. Facts back up theory, it is true, but they are isolated facts. Many theories, many good theories, have been established in this way.

A case method does not deal with isolated, but with connected, facts. Each case gives a connected body of information about a particular situation. But we still have not succeeded in describing the method as we shall use it, and for this purpose let us compare two ways in which the method is now being used. When they use case discussion as a method of teaching, many law schools have a special end in view. The welter of information about a particular lawsuit is brought into the discussion only in order that the student may learn to weed most of it out, narrow the issues down to the crucial one, and pick out the small number of facts that will settle it. Some schools of business administration also teach by cases, but with almost the opposite purpose. Instead of narrowing the focus of the student, these schools want to widen it, to show the student the large number of factors that must be taken into consideration if a wise decision is to be reached in the situation described. These schools want to make the student aware of the "total situation."

The case method used in this book will be nearer to the business-school practice than to the law-school one. It will be concerned with the total situation, and more. We must remember Mary Follett's warning that we should be interested not merely in the totalness of the situation but in the nature of the totalness. If we want to develop a theory of group behavior that will show every element of group life related to every other element in a system, then the material we use must be as connected as the theory. If we are to show connections, there must *be* connections. We must not, in the classical manner, use isolated facts to back up our theory, but related facts.

What we shall do is examine in detail five studies of social behavior. Each is a description of a particular group and deals with more than one side of the life of the group. Our theory will arise out of these cases and not out of a set of isolated facts. It will provide one form in which the results of this body of observation may be expressed. By taking only five cases, we shall sacrifice wide coverage but we shall gain in intensity of analysis, and in important places. For the studies we shall use are among the best of modern sociology and anthropology. We shall try to be true to the best.

SEPARATION OF FACT FROM THEORY

These cases will be presented in a special way. Each group will first be described in ordinary common-sense language, or language as close to that as an academic person can get. This does not mean that the investigators who originally made these studies were guided in their work by common sense alone. On the contrary, each investigator was stimulated and controlled by thoroughly sophisticated ideas. It does mean that in this book the results of each investigation will be presented so far as possible with no more interpretation than is built into our everyday manner of speaking. They will be merely reported.

The descriptions of the various groups will be briefer here than in the original reports, some of which were very long. This is not a collection of sources, a set of reprints. There is no room to include every bit of information about every group, and no need to do so. Enough will be included to support our theories, but nothing left out that is contrary to them. To be sure, if the original reports were in any way inadequate, ours must needs be inadequate in their turn, but we shall try to avoid any other slanting of the data. Should a reader feel that a crucial fact has been suppressed, he is perfectly at liberty to consult the original reports. All are in libraries; all but one are in print. Yet in practice a reader will be less apt to think that important data have been left out than that trivial ones have been kept in. Let him remember that the triviality or importance of a fact in sociology depends on the meaning it has for the members of the group in question and not on the meaning it has for him. In the light of eternity, the question whether a girl should wear a short or a long dress is trivial. It is not trivial if you are the girl and you are going to a party.

After each group has been described in ordinary common-sense language, the description will be analyzed in terms of the theory we shall develop. This separation of the data from their interpretation is designed to have several advantages. Since he has been presented with a body of fact to which he can give his own interpretation if he is unwilling to accept ours, the skeptic need not feel that anything has been put over on him. As we have said so often, one of the purposes of this book is semantic: to re-establish the connection between what we see and hear in social behavior and the concepts with which we analyze our observations. If we begin by separating the two, we may in the end be able to link them together more firmly. We sociologists are not trained in making a report containing nothing more than things actually seen and heard and then, after the report is in, making an abstract analysis of it. Too often our fact and our interpretation are confused with one another, and our thinking is confused as a result. The final advantage of our method is drill. By watching our method being applied systematically in case after case, the reader may learn to use it himself, if he finds it useful, for the analysis of any new group he may later encounter.

If our method has some advantages, it has also obvious disadvantages. It means that each group will be described twice, first in an observational report and second in an abstract analysis. Let us face the fact: although the subject of this book is inherently interesting, its method is triply dull. Its plan of presentation is inevitably repetitious. Its emphasis is on the familiar, the obvious, the trivial. And its abstract analysis may take away what little vividness the obvious once had. This is not an apology, but a warning of what lies ahead. No one need apologize for necessity. We can gain our ends only by adopting these means.

To sum up, this book is a study of the human group—the primary group as sociologists call it. All grander sociologies must be true to the sociology of the group. This book is also a theoretical study in that it tries to give one general form in which the results of observations of many particular groups may be expressed. Like any theoretical study, it begins with analysis, separating concrete observation into classes of fact. But the analysis is only a step toward an organic synthesis. The final picture of a group will be one in which all aspects of group life are mutually dependent, the mutual dependence forms a system, a total configuration, and the mutual dependence carries the seeds of emergent evolution. The book will first report detailed investigations of particular groups and then make an analysis of each group in terms of the developing theory.

THE HUMAN QUALITIES NEEDED

Finally, something must be said about the human qualities we shall need in this undertaking. We shall need, first, the innocence of the child, not the good little boy or girl but the *enfant terrible* who stops the conversation by asking the wrong questions. For we shall have to ask, "What do I actually see?" And, as we have said, no question is more devastating.

We shall also need the sophistication of the man of the world in order to make use of the past experience of the intellectual disciplines in dealing with problems of complicated fact. As Mary Follett said, "I do wish that when a principle has been worked out, say in ethics, it didn't have to be discovered all over again in psychology, in economics, in government, in business, in biology, and in sociology. It's such a waste of time." [14] The critical attitude is the heart of sophistication. We must recognize that many of the methods we should like to follow were late products of old sciences such as physics, sciences, moreover, whose problems can be made to look as if they brought in only a few variables. The study of the group is not an advanced science and can seldom pretend to manage with a small number of variables. Let us get what help we can, without feeling that we must imitate everything.

Sophistication includes knowing when not to be sophisticated. No one is more a creature of fashion than the average intellectual. He is quite ready to believe, at any moment, that certain kinds of work are the only respectable ones to go into. We are told, for instance, that our data in sociology should be quantitative, that is, should be cast in numerical form, and of course they should. But good observation ought not to be discarded just because it is not numerical. Sociology may miss a great deal if it tries to be too quantitative too soon. Data are not nobler because they are quantitative, nor thinking more logical because mathematical. The old-fashioned naturalist, who used only his eyes, was also a scientist, and his counterpart in sociology is very useful in the stage the science has reached. Let us make the important quantitative, and not the quantitative important. The final emphasis must always be on the group before us. Lord Nelson, greatest of all admirals, after explaining to his ship captains the plan of attack he intended to use at the battle of Trafalgar, went on to say, "No captain can do very wrong who places his ship alongside that of an enemy." In the same way, no one who studies a group will go far wrong if he gets close to it and, by whatever methods are available, observes all that he can. Nothing that can illuminate the group should be ruled out for doctrinaire reasons. We shall be blind enough without willfully narrowing our vision. At the same time we do not have to learn the hard way. The older sciences have already struggled with many of the problems that now face sociology. If the solutions have been stated mathematically, they are not to be disregarded just for that reason. No matter where it comes from, we shall need all the help we can get. The man of the world remembers this and is above fashion.

[14] *Dynamic Administration,* 16.

Above all, we need humility. Always, in the end, we must remember Francis Bacon's counsel: "The subtlety of nature is greater many times over than the subtlety of the senses and understanding." [15] The stupendous discoveries that have been made only teach us how much remains unknown. "If I were more sensitive, or more comprehensive, or even more energetic, what strange truth, with the strangeness of the new embracing the old, might I not discern?" The thought is appalling, but it does not appall us often enough. Nothing we have said already, or will say hereafter, can be taken to imply that this book tells the whole story about the group, or anything like the whole story. It will be incomplete partly by reason of human frailty and partly by design. In any event it will be incomplete, but incompleteness may be creative, if one man's lack becomes another's incentive.

[15] *Novum Organum,* Bk. I, aphorism x.

CHAPTER 2

The Elements of Behavior

*Events in the Single Group . . . Custom . . . Definition
of Concepts . . . Activity . . . Interaction . . . Sentiment
. . . Sociometry . . . Summary . . . Usefulness of the
Concepts*

THIS chapter is a tough one, perhaps the toughest
in the book, but we had better know the worst at once. It tries to
do two things at the same time. First, it tries to show how the
kinds of generalization we shall be interested in are reached: how
we go from simple descriptions of social events to uniformities in
the behavior of a limited number of persons and groups and finally
to generalizations that may apply to all groups. Second, it tries to
define the words, or concepts, that will come into these highest
generalizations. As we shall see, the two jobs mesh with one another and must be carried on together.

One of the big problems of sociology, as of all social science, is
semantic: the problem of the relation between the words used and
the observations made. The meanings of words are usually given
by definitions, but the trouble with definitions, as one of the first
great semanticists, Lord Bacon, pointed out, is that "the definitions
themselves consist of words, and those words beget others: so that
it is necessary to recur to individual instances, and those in due
series and order." [1] Bacon meant that the end of the chain of words
must be anchored in an act something like the one by which a
mother teaches her child the meaning of the word *cow:* she points
at the beast and says the word. Acts of this kind are not available
to us. We are not in the open air watching a group in action, and
we cannot learn the meaning of sociological concepts by having

[1] F. Bacon, *Novum Organum*, Bk. I, aphorism lix.

someone point to various items in the behavior of the group and, as he does so, name the concepts. But we can do the next best thing. We can take the descriptions of group behavior made by good observers, persons who, unlike ourselves, have been watching groups in the open air; we can point to certain things they saw and give these things names. The names are the concepts.

Our work presupposes the direct observation of human behavior. It does not for the most part deal with what men write in answer to a questionnaire or what they say when a research assistant has his foot in the door. It deals with what men say and do on the ordinary occasions of ordinary life. This kind of fact is surprisingly hard to collect; it demands an observer who is not himself so much a part of the situation that he cannot view it with a fresh eye, and one who does not, by the mere fact of his presence, change what would otherwise be said and done. Anthropologists who live with the tribes they study and who back up their lengthy questionings of native informants with firsthand observations of daily life collect this kind of material, and so do a few sociologists who study groups and communities in our own society. Our work relies on theirs. Some social scientists find this kind of material hard and unsatisfying to work with: it can seldom be converted into statistics and always leaves unanswered many interesting questions—and they shy away from it. Nevertheless it is the stuff of everyday existence, and we start with it here.

EVENTS IN THE SINGLE GROUP

We are going to begin with a description of everyday social events in a society not our own. The world is a stage, and one of its many scenes opens:

The room is low and rectangular. The left wall is filled by a door, closed, and a big stone fireplace, fitted for cooking. Chairs and benches are set around the fireplace. Against the back wall a table stands, and to the right of the table a colored picture hangs over a cabinet containing a small figure. The right wall is taken up by a dresser, full of kitchen gear and crockery, on one side of which is a door and on the other a staircase leading upstairs. Through a window over the table a yard, with a cart in it, is seen in dim light.

A woman opens the door, right, and comes into the room. She goes to the fireplace, rakes together the ashes on the hearth, some of them still alive, puts on new fuel, and rekindles the blaze. Then she fills a kettle with water and hangs it on a hook over the fire. When it boils, she makes tea; meanwhile she lays out dishes, cutlery, bread, and milk on the table, and gets ready to cook eggs.

A middle-aged man and two younger ones enter, exchange a few words with the woman, pull up chairs, sit down at the table, and begin to eat. The woman herself does not sit, but stands by, ready to bring up more food and drink if the men ask for them. When the men have eaten, the older one says to the younger ones, "Well, we'd better be off." They go out.

By this time a girl has joined the woman in the room, but not until the men have left do the two sit down for their meal. Before they have finished, crying is heard outside, right. The woman leaves and later returns carrying a young child in her arms. She fondles and comforts it, then feeds it in its turn.

She turns to the girl, who is already washing the dishes, with a remark about making butter. . . .[2]

We need not go on. This scene, or something much like it, has been enacted millions of times in the history of mankind, and it shows, of course, a farm family beginning a working day. It is not an American farm family, though families of this sort were common not so long ago in America and survive in some places still. It is a countryman's family in the southwest of Ireland. Farm families, differing from this one in some outward appearances, but perhaps not very different in essentials, have for centuries formed the foundations of society in Europe, the Near East, India, China, and much of the Americas. This social unit is characteristic of many of the countries that have the largest populations. Only in recent years and in a few places have we begun to see the appearance of a new kind of family. The old-fashioned farm family—if we may call it that—is still the commonest of human groups.

The scene is familiar. We begin and end with the familiar and are lucky to be able to do so, but the important point at the moment is not the familiarity of the scene. It is rather that a scene like this is part of the raw material of sociology: a description of a series of *events*, in each of which at one particular place and time

[2] Adapted from C. M. Arensberg and S. T. Kimball, *Family and Community in Ireland,* 35.

a person did certain things, in certain physical surroundings, perhaps with certain implements and together with certain other persons. All science begins with process, the flux of things, the passing scene. Generalization must be true to events. We forget their vividness at our peril. And how refreshing they are! "Here," we can say, "is one kind of certainty. No matter how we interpret them, and no matter how far they fall short of telling the whole story, these things, at least these things, *happened.*"

There can be little interpretation of, generalization from, single events. We can learn much—and it is good discipline, too—from trying merely to report, that is, from trying to describe human behavior in words altogether flat, simply descriptive, devoid of interpretation. In any strict sense, it cannot be done. Any noun implies some context; even a word like *table* implies something about the use of a physical object. But in the effort to leave out at least the higher levels of meaning, we can discover how much meaning we regularly put into our descriptions. Perhaps we shall see how easy it is to commit ourselves to an interpretation before we know what we are doing.

Our description of the farm family beginning the day is just such a flat description as a playwright might write in setting the opening scene of his play. The meaning unfolds only as the action of the play develops. Thus the older woman is not called the mother of the family, nor the man the father. "Mother" and "father" assume a certain scheme of social relationships, and from the single scene we cannot be sure that we are dealing with that kind of scheme. It is better to begin with distinctions like those between man and woman, youth and age. In the same way, the cabinet is not called a shrine. If we had called it that, we should have been assuming something that the single scene cannot tell us. Nevertheless, there are items in the description that might be remembered, should he run across them again, by anyone anxious to build up a picture of the relationships between the members of the family. For instance, the older man gives orders to the two younger ones or at least gives the signal to go out and begin the day's work. The woman likewise points out to the girl the job—making butter—that the two of them will do in the course of the day. Both women wait for the men to finish eating before they sit down themselves. The older woman comforts and plays with the baby. And so on. An observer builds up his picture of social relationships from repeated events like these.

CUSTOM

The next stage in the analysis of human behavior—and it always implies the first—is reached when we recognize simple recurrences in events, recurrences at different intervals. To go back to our farm family, we note that almost every day the men go out to work in the fields; that every year, at about the same season, they dig potatoes; that in this work the father directs the activities of the sons. The women do the chores around the house but do not work in the fields; so long as there is a youngster in the house, the mother feeds it, goes to it when it cries, comforts and protects it. And so on. The behavior of the members of a group is a symphony, a symphony that may have discords. There are different voices—as the wood winds are a voice in a symphony—each with its themes, which come in at different intervals, sometimes quietly, sometimes loudly, sometimes in the foreground, sometimes in the background. Often there is a conductor who is himself a voice, and there are recurrences in the group of voices, in the movement as a whole. Like lazy listeners, we who are at the symphony never hear all the voices and all their harmonies. We hear only the ones we are interested in hearing.

These recurrences in social behavior, when recognized as recurrences, are called customs. For the moment we are simply going to accept custom as a fact, giving notice at the same time that the fact raises an important question, which will be considered in a later chapter. We mention the question now only to show we are aware of it. Some students of society are inclined to take the recurrences in the behavior of a group for granted. They are interested in the details of particular customs, but not in custom itself as an aspect of group life. Other students go further, as Edmund Burke did years ago, and see custom as useful, even necessary. Men cannot plan for the future without relying on the massive regularities of expected behavior. Yet when everything intelligent has been said about the usefulness of custom, one more profound question remains: What makes custom customary? For the brute fact is that customs do change. In view of the constantly varied forces playing on society, it is amazing that anything can be recognized as persistent. The recurrences are miracles, not commonplaces; and miracles, if they happen often, are just the things we should study most closely. As soon as we do, we find that nothing is more defenseless than a custom, alone. Not single customs, but systems of custom, survive. Anthropologists used to talk about the "tyranny of custom" as if custom were a mold pressing social organization into a shape. This view is misleading. Custom is not something outside of, and apart from, social organization but is implicit in organization. These are large generalizations. We state them now, but only in a much later chapter shall we try to back them up. By that time we hope to have the tools to do the job.

The usual descriptions of groups consist of statements of custom, that is, recurrences in human behavior at different places or at different intervals. 'The Irish countrymen live on isolated farms." . . . "The men of a Tikopia village commonly put out to sea together when they go fishing." The books and articles that are our sources, that we must work with, are full of such remarks. But we must never forget, having a lively sense of the shifting sands on which we build, that statements of custom, if they are worth anything, are founded on repeated observations of individual events in single scenes. With this in mind, let us return to the Irish farm family, and now study a description of the relationships between its members, particularly father, mother, and son. The description is a statement of custom: a summary of the recurrences in many single scenes like the one with which this chapter opened.

The growing child ordinarily sees his father as owner and principal worker of the farm. When the whole family group of father, mother, children, and whatever other relatives may be living with them, works in concert, as at the potato planting, the turf cutting, and the haymaking, it is the father who directs the group's activities, himself doing the heavy tasks. . . .

In his earliest childhood, of course, the mother looms larger in the child's consciousness than the father. The child's first duties, as soon as he can speak and walk, are to run on petty errands to neighbors and near-by "friends." Soon he is taking his father's meals to him in the fields or going on errands to the nearest shop. Until he is seven and has gone through First Communion, his place is in the house with the women, and his labor is of very little importance. After First Communion, at six or seven, he begins to be thrown more with his elder brothers, and comes to do small chores which bring him more and more into contact with his father and with the other men of the neighborhood . . . But not till he passes Confirmation and leaves school (generally at the same time) does he take on full men's work. Even then, as he becomes adult and takes on more and more of the heavy tasks of the farm work, he never escapes his father's direction, until his father dies or makes over the farm to him at his marriage . . .

It goes without saying that the father exercises his control over the whole activity of the "boy." It is by no means confined to their work together. Indeed, the father is the court of last resort, which dispenses punishment for deviations from the norm of conduct in all spheres. Within the bounds of custom and law he has full power to exercise discipline. Corporal punishment is not a thing of the past in Ireland, and, especially in the intermediate stages of the child's development, from seven to puberty, it gets full play.

It is during those years that the characteristic relationship between father and son is developed in rural communities. The son has suffered a remove from the previous almost exclusive control of its mother, in which an affective content of sympathy and indulgence was predominant, and is brought into contact for the first time with the father and older men. But the transfer is not completed. There is a hiatus in his development through the years of school when his participation in men's work and his relationship with his father has little chance of developing into an effective partnership. A real union of interests does not take place until after Confirmation and school-leaving, when for the first time his exclusive contacts and his entire day-to-day activity, particularly in farm work, will be with his father and the older men.

This fact colors greatly the relationship of father and son, as far as affective content goes. There is none of the close companionship and intimate sympathy which characterizes, at least ideally, the relationship in other groups. Where such exists, it is a matter for surprised comment to the small farmers. In its place there is developed, necessarily perhaps, a marked respect, expressing itself in the tabooing of many actions, such as smoking, drinking, and physical contact of any sort, which can be readily observed in any small farm family. Coupled with this is the life-long subordination . . . which is never relaxed even in the one sphere in which farmer father and son can develop an intense community of interest—farm work. Nothing prevents the development of great mutual pride, the boy in his experienced and skillful mentor, tutor, and captain in work, and the man in a worthy and skillful successor and fellow workman, but on the other hand everything within the behavior developed in the relationship militates against the growth of close mutual sympathy. As a result, the antagonisms inherent in such a situation often break through very strongly when conflicts arise . . .

On the other hand, the relationship of mother and son has a very different content. Like that between father and son, it is the product of years of development. It is marked, too, by a similar retention of subordinate status on the part of the son. In farm work the boy is subject to the commands of his mother even when, fully adult, he has passed over exclusively to men's work. . . . But within the scope of such a subordination there is a quite different affective history. The relationship is the first and earliest into which a child enters. It is very close, intimate, and all-embracing for the first years of life; only gradually does the experience of the child expand to include brothers, sisters, and last, the older male members of the household.

Until seven, the child of either sex is the constant companion of its mother. If the family is numerous an elder child, usually a sister, may take over much of the mother's role, but the mother is always near-by. As the woman works in the house or fields, the child is kept by her side. In the house it usually sits in a crib by the fire or plays about on the floor, but always within sight and sound. It learns its speech from its mother, amid a flood of constant endearments, admonitions, and encouragements. The woman's work never separates her from the child. Custom imposes no restraints or interruptions in her solicitude. She looks after its comforts, gives it food, dresses it, etc. She constantly exercises restraints and controls over it, teaching it day by day in a thousand situations the elements of prudery, modesty and good conduct.

The controls she exercises are of a different kind from those of the father. She is both guide and companion. Her authority most often makes itself felt through praise, persuasion, and endearment. Only when a grave breach of discipline demands a restraining power greater than hers, or when an appeal to ultimate authority is needed, does the father begin to play his role. Especially in the years before puberty, the farm father enters the child's cognizance as a disciplinary force. The barriers of authority, respect, extra-household interests, and the imperatives of duty rather than of encouragement make it difficult for any intimacy to develop.

Even after Confirmation the child's relationship to his mother is not materially weakened. He becomes confirmed, it is true, in a masculine scorn for feminine interests and pursuits, but he can and must still look for protection to his mother against a too-arbitrary exercise of his father's power. In family disputes the mother takes a diplomatic, conciliatory role. From her intermediary position she can call upon the strongest ties between herself and her sons to restore rifts in parental authority and filial submission.

Throughout the years of the son's full activity in the farm economy under the father's headship, the mother still remains the source of comfort and the preparer of food and is still infinitely solicitous of his welfare. It is only at marriage that the bond is broken . . . If the child must leave the farm for other walks of life, the closest possible relationship is still maintained. When one goes home, it is to see one's mother. There is always an attempt to carry on a correspondence. In exile, the bond lingers as a profound sentimental nostalgia.[3]

Before we go on to our main purpose, we must get some preliminaries out of the way. This passage describes a relationship between three persons, not the conventional triangle of a love story but the triangle that has father, mother, and son at its corners. The pattern of the relationship is clearly marked—which is a reason why we chose a description of an Irish family and not one of an American family. The latter is more familiar to us but its pattern is not so easily characterized. In the Irish family the relationship between mother and son is one of warm affection, the relationship between father and son is one of admiration mixed with respect. Moreover, these relationships are not peculiar to Ireland: it is interesting how often the pattern repeats itself in farm families, and indeed in other families, all over the world. Nor are these relationships inevitable. It is not simply "natural" that a son should love his mother, though we all like to think it is. He loves his mother because the repeated, thousand-times-repeated, events in which the two are brought together are of a certain kind. From earliest childhood she cares for him; but change her behavior and the emotion would change too. In like manner, the son's feeling for the father is colored by the father's control over him in the many-times-repeated events of farm work. Nor, to go a step further, are the two series of events—the events determining these mother-son and father-son relationships—isolated from the rest of the world. Instead they are related to the division of labor and assignment of authority in a going farm enterprise, surviving in an environment.

[3] Reprinted by permission of the publishers from Conrad Maynadier Arensberg and Solon Toothaker Kimball, *Family and Community in Ireland,* Cambridge, Mass.: Harvard University Press, 1940, pp. 51-60.

We shall not be misled by the use of the words "the child," "his mother," and "his father" in the singular. These are shorthand for "children," "mothers," and "fathers." An anthropologist would say that the passages quoted above tell us some of the customs of Irish countrymen, a statistician that they may perhaps express some kind of average in the behavior of a certain number of groups—Irish farm families—over a certain span of time. The statistician might find fault with the passages for not letting him know the relation between the "sample" and the "universe," that is, the relation between the number of groups directly observed and the larger number for whose behavior the average is supposed to hold good. He might also find fault with the passages for giving us no idea of the number of groups—there must be a few—whose behavior deviates in some degree from the average. He might say that the statements are by implication quantitative but that they do not let an outsider make any judgment of their quantitative reliability. His criticisms are good, and they can be answered only by raising new questions: How much more effort, in men, time, and money, would be needed to get the kind of data he wants? Given a limited supply of all three, how far would getting his kind of data interfere with getting a wider, though admittedly less reliable, coverage of group behavior? These are questions not of scientific morality but of strategy and, in the broad sense, economics: getting the most for one's money. They themselves beg for quantitative answers. And we might finally ask the different and more searching question: How far does the craving to get the kind of data a statistician considers reliable lead social scientists to take up questions for which this kind of data can easily be secured instead of questions that are interesting for other reasons? To which the statistician might reply: If we are not getting what I want, are we getting anything on which we can found a science? We should keep these questions in mind, for much of the material we shall be working with is not of the kind the statistician wants.

DEFINITION OF CONCEPTS

Let us go back over our work so far. We began with a flat description of events within a single group; then we went on to a statement of the customs of an unspecified but limited number of groups: the families of Irish countrymen. The next step is a long one; in fact it will take up the rest of this book. We shall set up some hypotheses—and they will remain hypotheses because we shall only set them up, not prove them—that may sum up a few aspects of social behavior in an unlimited number of groups all over the world. There is no use saying now what these hypotheses are; we shall find out soon enough, and one move in particular we must make before we can formulate any hypotheses of high generalization, such as ours will be. We must define a few of the concepts that come into them. Though we cannot do so by pointing at objects and saying the concept, we can take the next best step. We can examine a passage like the one above, point out certain words in it, ask ourselves whether the aspects of social behavior to which the words refer have anything in common, and then, if they do, give a name to this common element. The name is the concept. We might have written a passage of our own for this purpose, but anyone can solve a problem if he sets it up himself. It is much more convincing to use someone else's passage, as we have done.

ACTIVITY

Let us look, then, at certain words and phrases in this passage, and first, perhaps, at words like these: *potato planting, turf cutting, haymaking, corporal punishment, smoking, drinking, gives food, dresses, looks after, plays, sits, walks, speaks, talks, First Communion, Confirmation.* In the passage we can pick out many more such words, and also some of greater generality, like *work* and *activity.* Let us agree that they have something in common, without committing ourselves on the question whether this something is important. They all refer to things that people do: work on the physical environment, with implements, and with other persons. If we want to be precise, we can say that all these words and phrases refer in the end to movements of the muscles of men, even though the importance of some of the movements, like talk and ceremonies, depends on their symbolic meaning. We shall speak of the characteristic they have in common as an *element* of social behavior, and we shall give it a name, as a mere ticket. It might be

called *action,* if *action* had not been given a more general meaning, or *work,* if *work* did not have a special meaning in the physical
sciences and may yet have an analogous one in sociology. Instead of
either of these, we shall call it *activity,* and use it, in much the same
way that it is used in everyday speech, as an analytical concept
for the study of social groups.

We call activity an element, not implying that it is some ultimate,
indivisible atom of behavior. It is no more than one of the classes
into which we choose to divide something that might be divided
in other, and less crude, ways. In fact we call it an element just
because the vagueness of that word gives us room to move around
in. Above all we must realize that activity is not a variable like temperature in physics: it cannot be given a single series of numerical
values. Instead, a number of aspects of activity might be measured.
We are sometimes able to measure the *output* or rate of production
of certain kinds of activity, for instance, factory work, and sometimes the *efficiency* of activity, the relation of input to output. We
might even be able to assign an index to the degree of *similarity* of
one activity to another. And so on. These are true variables, at least
in possibility, though we could not give them numerical values in
every piece of research. In later chapters we shall have to make
sure, when we speak of activity, which particular variable we have
in mind.

INTERACTION

Going back now to the passage we are working with, let us look
at expressions like these: the boy is *thrown with* his elder brothers;
he comes more and more *into contact with* his father; he never
escapes from his father's direction; he *participates* in the men's
work; he is a *companion* of his mother; he goes to *see* his mother,
and so on. The element that these phrases have in common is more
or less mixed with other things, for in our language one word seldom states one clear idea. For instance, what does the word *see*
mean in the phrase "going to see someone"? Yet there is a common
element, and it seems to be some notion of sheer interaction between persons, apart from the particular activities in which they

interact. When we refer to the fact that some unit of activity of one man follows, or, if we like the word better, is stimulated by some unit of activity of another, aside from any question of what these units may be, then we are referring to *interaction*. We shall speak of interaction as an element of social behavior and use it as an analytical concept in the chapters that follow.

We may find it hard to think consistently of interaction as separate from the other elements of behavior, but we shall have to do so in this book, and the fact is that in our everyday thinking we often keep it separate without realizing as much. When we say "Tom got in touch with Harry," or "Tom contacted Harry," or "Tom was an associate of Harry's," we are not talking about the particular words they said to one another or the particular activities they both took part in. Instead we are talking about the sheer fact of contact, of association. Perhaps the simplest example of interaction, though we should find it complex enough if we studied it carefully, is two men at opposite ends of a saw, sawing a log. When we say that the two are interacting, we are not referring to the fact that both are sawing: in our language, sawing is an *activity*, but to the fact that the push of one man on the saw is followed by the push of the other. In this example, the interaction does not involve words. More often interaction takes place through verbal or other symbolic communication. But when in the armed forces men talk about the chain of command, or in a business ask what officers report to what other ones, they are still talking about channels of communication—the chains of interaction—rather than the communications themselves or the activities that demand communications.

Just as several variables are included under the concept of activity, so several are included under interaction. We can study the *frequency* of interaction: the number of times a day or a year one man interacts with another or the members of a group interact with one another. We can measure the ratio between the amount of time one man is active, for instance, talking, and the *duration* of his interlocutor's activity. Or we can study the *order* of interaction: Who originates action? Where does a chain of interactions start and where does it go? If Tom makes a suggestion to Dick, does

Dick pass it on to Harry? [4] Once again, we shall have to make sure from time to time that we are talking about one variable under interaction and not another. Our observations of this element can often be rather precise and definite, which gives them infinite charm for persons of a certain temperament.

When we called the first of our elements *activity,* we may have been using the obvious and appropriate word. But in calling the second element *interaction,* are we not needlessly using a strange word when a familiar one is on hand? Why not speak of *communication* rather than *interaction?* Our answer is: The word *communication* is neither general enough in one sense nor specific enough in another. When people think of communication, they think of communication in words, but here we are including under interaction both verbal and nonverbal communication. What is more, the word *communication* is used in several different ways in everyday speech. It may mean the content of the message, signal, or "communication" being transmitted, or the process of transmission itself, as when people speak of "methods of communication," or to the sheer fact, aside from content or process of transmission, that one person has communicated with another. Only to the last of these three do we give the name of interaction, and the unfamiliarity of the word may underline the fact that its meaning is specific. Nevertheless we shall, from time to time, when there is no risk of confusion, use the word *communication* in place of *interaction,* so that our language will not sound hopelessly foreign.

SENTIMENT

Now let us go back to our passage again and consider another set of words and phrases: *sentiments of affection, affective content of sympathy and indulgence, intimate sympathy, respect, pride, antagonism, affective history, scorn, sentimental nostalgia.* To these we shall arbitrarily add others, such as *hunger* and *thirst,* that might easily have come into the passage. What can we say these words have in common? Perhaps the most we can say, and it may not be very much, is that they all refer to internal states of the human

---

[4] For a systematic discussion of interaction as an element of social behavior, see E. D. Chapple, with the collaboration of C. M. Arensberg, *Measuring Human Relations* (Genetic Psychology Monographs, Vol. 22 (1940)).

body. Laymen and professional psychologists call these states by various names: drives, emotions, feelings, affective states, sentiments, attitudes. Here we shall call them all *sentiments*, largely because that word has been used in a less specialized sense than some of the others, and we shall speak of *sentiment* as an element of social behavior.

Notice the full range of things we propose to call sentiments. They run all the way from fear, hunger, and thirst, to such probably far more complicated psychological states as liking or disliking for individuals, approval or disapproval of their actions. We are lumping together under this word some psychological states that psychologists would certainly keep separate. Our employment of the concept *sentiment* can only be justified by what we do with it, so that at the moment all we can ask is indulgence for our failure in orthodoxy.

We must now consider a question that may not seem important but that has come up again and again, in one form or another, ever since the behaviorists first raised it. We can *see* activities and interactions. But if sentiments are internal states of the body, can we see them in the same way? It is true that a person may say he feels hungry or likes someone, and that in everyday life, if we are dealing with him, we take account of what he has to say about his own feelings. But scientists may be forgiven for believing that subjective judgments are treacherous things to work with. They are not reliable; we cannot tell whether two persons would reach the same judgment under the same circumstances, and reliability is the rock on which science is built. Some scientists even believe that they can reach important generalizations, in psychology and sociology, without paying any attention whatever to subjective judgments; and they would ask us whether there is anything we can point to as sentiment that has not already been included under activity and interaction. Can it be independently observed? Perhaps in some animals the more violent sentiments can be so observed. In a dog or cat, pain, hunger, fear, and rage are marked by measurable changes in the body, particularly in the glands of internal secretion.[5] We assume that this is also true of human be-

---

[5] See W. B. Cannon, *Bodily Changes in Pain, Hunger, Fear, and Rage.*

ings, but few of the necessary measurements can easily be made. For mild sentiments such as friendliness, and these are the ones we shall be working with most often here, we are not sure how far the bodily changes occur at all. The James-Lange theory that a sentiment and a set of visceral changes are one and the same thing cannot be driven too far. On an occasion that might conceivably have called for emotion, the undamaged human being reacts so as to cut down the amount of visceral change taking place. The body mobilizes for action, if that is appropriate, and reduces the merely emotional changes.

Science is perfectly ready to take leave of common sense, but only for a clear and present gain. Lacking more precise methods for observing sentiments, since the biological methods can only be used in special circumstances, have we anything to gain by giving up everyday practice? Have we not rather a good deal to lose? And what is everyday practice? In deciding what sentiments a person is feeling, we take notice of slight, evanescent tones of his voice, expressions of his face, movements of his hands, ways of carrying his body, and we take notice of these things as parts of a whole in which the context of any one sign is furnished by all the others. The signs may be slight in that the physical change from one whole to another is not great, but they are not slight so long as we have learned to discriminate between wholes and assign them different meanings. And that is what we do. From these wholes we infer the existence of internal states of the human body and call them anger, irritation, sympathy, respect, pride, and so forth. Above all, we infer the existence of sentiments from what men say about what they feel and from the echo that their words find in our own feelings. We can recognize in ourselves what they are talking about. All those who have probed the secrets of the human heart have known how misleading and ambiguous these indications can sometimes be, how a man can talk love and mean hate, or mean both together, without being aware of what he is doing. Yet we act on our inferences, on our diagnoses of the sentiments of other people, and we do not always act ineffectively. In this book we are trying to learn how the elements of our everyday social experience are related to one another. Leaving out a part of that experience—and sentiment is a part—would be reasonable only if we had a better kind of observation to take its place. Some sciences have something better; ours does not yet.

We may end with a practical argument. This book is, in one of its intentions, an effort to bring out the generalizations implicit in modern field studies of human groups. If the men who made the studies felt that they could infer and give names to such things as sentiments of affection, respect, pride, and antagonism, we shall see what we can do with their inferences, remembering always that a more advanced theory than ours may have to wait for more precise and reliable observations. No theory can be more sophisticated than the facts with which it deals.

Under the element of *sentiment,* several different kinds of studies can and have been made. Perhaps the best-known ones are carried on by the public opinion pollsters and attitude scalers using questionnaires they get people to answer. Especially when they try to find out the *number* of persons that approve or disapprove of, like or dislike, a proposal for action or a candidate for public office, they are studying at least one variable under this element. Often they go further and try to discover not only how many persons approve or disapprove but the *conviction* with which they do so: whether they are sure they are right, feel somewhat less sure, or remain undecided. The pollsters may also try to find out the *intensity* of the sentiments concerned: a man may disapprove of something intellectually and yet not feel strongly about it. His emotions may not have been deeply aroused.

SOCIOMETRY

Especially interesting from our point of view are the methods of studying the likes and dislikes of persons for one another developed by J. L. Moreno and given by him the name of *sociometry.*[6] In the course of his work in the New York State Training School for Girls at Hudson, New York, a fairly large community but one in which the girls lived in several small houses rather than under one single institutional roof, Moreno found himself asking this question: How can we choose the membership of a house in such a way that the

[6] See especially J. L. Moreno, *Who Shall Survive?*, and the journal *Sociometry.*

girls will be congenial and that the work of the house, its house-keeping, will be carried on pleasantly and effectively? And he decided to take a very obvious step. He decided to ask the girls whom they would like to live and work with. In particular, he called all the girls in the community together, supplied each one with a pencil and paper, and then gave what he later came to call the *sociometric test*. That is, he asked the girls to answer the following question:

You live now in a certain house with certain other persons according to the directions the administration has given you. The persons who live with you in the same house are not ones chosen by you and you are not one chosen by them. You are now given the opportunity to choose the persons whom you would like to live with in the same house. You can choose without restraint any individuals of this community whether they happen to live in the same house with you or not. Write down whom you would like first best, second best, third best, fourth best, and fifth best. Look around and make up your mind. Remember that the ones you choose will probably be assigned to live with you in the same house.[7]

Moreno asked a question of the same kind about dislikes. In his discussion of the test he argues that its results are apt to be meaningless unless the persons taking the test believe their choices make a difference, and that two conditions must be realized before they can hold this belief. In the first place, one person does not like another in a vacuum but in a definite setting, and if the setting changes the liking may change too. Therefore, the choice of likes and dislikes must be made according to some definite criterion. At Hudson the girls were asked whom they would, or would not, like to live with. In the second place, the person who administers the test must have the power to put its results into effect; he must be able to do something about it. At Hudson, Moreno had to have the power to assign girls who liked one another to the same house.

The two conditions are seldom realized, so that the sociometric test is not a universal weapon of research and action in sociology. When it can be used, it may be very helpful. The results of the sociometric test were used at Hudson in assigning girls that were fond of one another to the same house, and the administration believed that morale improved. The test, suitably reworded, was also

[7] *Who Shall Survive?*, 13-4.

used during the depression in planning resettlement communities. Since then it has been put to work in many different situations.

But we are not immediately interested in the use that can be made of the sociometric test in social action. We are interested in it as a method, available under some circumstances, for mapping out interpersonal sentiments. From one point of view its results are crude, yet they could not otherwise be achieved without direct observation of a group and interviews with its members, carried out over a long period. The test, in short, is economical. It can bring out several main types of relationship between two persons: mutual liking or, as Moreno calls it, mutual attraction; mutual disliking or repulsion; attraction on one side but repulsion on the other; attraction or repulsion on one side but indifference, that is, no choice, on the other; and finally mutual indifference. Using suitable symbols for these relationships, Moreno can diagram various simple types of group structure: the isolated individual, chosen by no one and repelled by many; the isolated pair; the triangle in many forms; the star, or popular girl, liked by many others; and the influential or powerful girl with her followers: she likes and is liked by rather few persons, but they are strategically placed not only in her own house but in others, and they themselves are chosen by many persons, so that the original girl is at the center of a complex web of attraction. We shall want to ask why such a person is in fact influential. From these simple structures Moreno goes on to plot out larger emotional networks.[8] Later we shall look at some of the other results of his work. At the moment we must recognize the sociometric test as one simple method of mapping out some of the sentiments that relate members of a group to one another.

Before we take leave of sentiment for the time being, one more point needs to be made. Many studies of sentiments and attitudes are made without any great effort to relate their results to studies of activities and interactions. Some psychologists study attitudes alone. In the future, fruitful results will come increasingly from using several methods in conjunction with one another. If social fact must be analyzed as a mutual dependence of many elements in a whole, then we shall have to investigate social fact with mutually dependent methods.

[8] See especially, *Ibid.*, 53, 89, 90, 115.

And now let us go back to our passage for the last time. Of course it includes many words besides the ones we have taken up for scrutiny. In particular there are words like *status, role, direction, control, subordination,* and *authority.* We all use some of these words; we all think we know what they mean, and they all do mean important things. But carefully examined, they seem to refer to complicated combinations of our simpler elements: activity, interaction, sentiment. In Chapter 1 we have already seen that this is true of *status.* In the same way, a word like *direction* refers not just to the giving of orders by one man to another but to the giving of orders that are obeyed, which is, if we think about it for a minute, a much more complex idea. We shall come back to these things, because they are important in the study of social groups, but we shall avoid real pitfalls if we do not begin with them.

SUMMARY

To use the language of the sciences, our *conceptual scheme* consists, so far, of *persons* and three elements of their behavior: *activity, interaction,* and *sentiment.* We shall add other concepts as we go along; these we begin with. Using these concepts, we shall try to reach analytical hypotheses describing the behavior of persons in groups. These hypotheses are a third level in the process of generalization. At the risk of repetition, let us take an example from the material we have just been studying. The first level consists of descriptions of individual events. Thus, on a certain day in a certain farm in County Clare, Mary Shaughnessy took up her little son, fed him, and fondled him. The second level consists of descriptions of the average behavior of a limited number of persons in a limited area over a limited span of time. Thus, among the Irish countrymen the women's work never separates them from their children, and custom imposes no restraints or interruptions on their solicitude. The third level consists of descriptions of behavior that may, we hope, apply to many groups, and to persons in many kinds of relationship to one another, not necessarily mothers and sons. Thus, the greater the interaction between two persons, the greater, in general, the sentiments of affection they feel for one another. This last kind of description is an analytical hypothesis. We must not worry yet about whether it is true. That question comes up later; at the moment we are only illustrating what we mean. If, moreover, it does turn out to be true, it will be true only as one of a series, or system, of such expressions, each of which qualifies the others, but again this is not a question that need disturb us now.

When all is said and done, let us not delude ourselves. This classification of the elements of behavior is old and crude, both. The concepts, sentiment, activity, and interaction, are close to common-sense ideas. They have all been used by social scientists before, though not all together. And there are many other ways of breaking group life down into its elements, other classifications and cross classifications far more subtle than this. We may have to elaborate on this one as the work progresses. It is not the last word but the first.

USEFULNESS OF THE CONCEPTS

The real question is not whether the classification is old and crude but whether it is useful, and this can hardly be settled now. It can hardly be found either useful or useless before it is used. Here, as at a play, we must practice what Coleridge called "the willing suspension of disbelief." However skeptical we may be as to its worth, we can still take the scheme on trial and give it a chance to show what it can do.

Even if this particular breakdown or classification does not turn out to be useful, experience seems to show that some classification is immeasurably better than no classification at all. It can at least serve as a check-off list. In making a study of a group, or in reading a description of one, a classification will help us decide whether a minimum of important facts has been gathered. It serves as a filing cabinet or set of pigeonholes where data can collect until they are needed. It may also help us stick to the subject. In sociology we tend to wander all over our material; we never quite know what we are talking about at any particular moment. The reason is not that we are incompetent, but that we have no device for fixing our attention. Any classification, no matter how crude, provided only it is used regularly, forces us to take up one thing at a time and consider systematically the relations of that thing to others. This is one of the roads that leads to generalization.

So much for classification in general. A classification of this particular kind may help us to extensionalize, that is, to go behind the big words and phrases so common in this field to the actual observations to which they refer. We do not want to get rid of the big words but to give them underpinnings, to show their relation, through concepts of a lower degree of abstraction, to the things we see and hear in human behavior. Interaction, sentiment, and activity are such low-order concepts.

There seem to be two kinds of sociologist, both contributing much, both running into difficulties. We may call them the pedestrians and the intuitives. Take first the pedestrian. Sociology, with the other social sciences, has completed a large number of researches, scrupulous in method, thorough in execution, and illuminating in results. Yet it is often true that something is lacking. It is curious how often one reaches the end of a good, stubborn, down-to-earth research report, crammed with common sense, and finds the author floundering when, not a moment before, he was sure of his ground. If you will examine what has happened, you will discover that, when he tried to state his conclusions in the most general terms, these terms suddenly could not bear the weight put upon them.

Take now the intuitive. He has judgments on the evils of the present social order that we feel sure are great with meaning, yet the meaning never quite comes to light—once more because the medium used, the language, breaks down under the strain. Here is an example; a sociologist writes: "No society can function as a society unless it gives the individual member social status and function, and unless the decisive social power is legitimate power. The former establishes the basic frame of social life: the purpose and meaning of society. The latter shapes the space within the frame: it makes society concrete and creates its institutions. If the individual is not given social status and function, there can be no society but only a mass of social atoms flying through space without aim or purpose." [9] We feel that this man is saying something important

[9] P. F. Drucker. *The Future of Industrial Man,* 25.

and something forgotten by most students of our fearful ills. Yet the truth is that he uses a lot of big words like "social status and function," "the purpose and meaning of social life," "power," and "the basic frame of social life" which are left wholly unrelated to observed fact.

The "pedestrian" does not get through from fact to adequate generalization; the "intuitive" does not get through from generalization to adequate fact. For the former, the conclusions, as he states them, tend to hold good only within the imposed limits of his research. For the latter, his intuitions, however suggestive, tend to remain just intuitions, of which there have been millions in human history. You cannot *do* anything with them. Neither man contributes to a growing body of social theory, summing up much work. Yet without such a theory neither individual research nor individual intuition can issue in wise social action. A science, like an army, cannot advance unless it keeps its lines of communication clear—the lines of communication between its words and its facts. To this problem our present method is addressed.

Finally, a classification of this kind may help us out of a dilemma that seems to threaten a science like anthropology. On the one hand, some of the students of culture—the "design for living" of a society —emphasize "cultural relativity" so far that each culture, tribal or national, becomes a unique entity, inherently different from all others. In one sense each culture is indeed unique, and certainly this emphasis has been necessary and useful, but carried far enough it almost implies that the differences between cultures are matters of kind, not of degree, and that there are no common elements in which cultures differ by amounts that might be measured, however crudely. On the other hand, some students have been trying to discover what specific institutions appear in every society, and they have found very few. Something that can be recognized as marriage—a man and at least one woman living together—is almost the only one, and even this is somewhat ambiguous, as some of the circumstances surrounding marriage itself, for instance, the rules governing the choice of marriage partner, vary greatly from society to society. Not that marriage is a small smatter—far from it. But to say that marriage is the only institution all societies have in common is a little like saying that the only things we can be sure of are death and taxes. It does not take us very far. In comparing groups, do we have to choose between radical difference and commonplace similarity?

Some of the natural sciences have been able to avoid this dilemma, largely because their problems have been simpler than those of the social sciences. For instance, a mixture of fruit juice, liquor, and ice in a cocktail shaker is a very different thing, looked at in one way, from a mixture of hot air and gasoline in an automobile engine cylinder. Superficially they seem to have only two traits in common: both are mixtures and both exist in enclosed spaces. In the study of cultures, anthropology has hardly gone beyond this kind of comparison. But in the science of thermodynamics, the liquid and the hot gas find a new and different kind of similarity and difference. On the one hand, some aspects of the behavior of both can be described in terms of the same three variables: pressure, temperature, and volume. On the other hand, the two differ in the values, and in the rates of change of the values, of these three variables, as also in some constants characteristic of water, fruit juice, air, and gasoline. The liquid and the hot gas are alike in that the same kinds of measurement can be applied to both; they differ in the values that these measurements take. Similarity is no longer superficial, nor difference radical. Anthropology and sociology have not reached this stage of sophistication, and perhaps they never will, but they certainly never will if they fail to recognize the kind of logical problem they face. Pressure, temperature, and volume are true analytical concepts. Activity, interaction, and sentiment, though we may call them analytical concepts, are not quite the same kind of thing. Let us be clear about that. But they may be steps in the direction of such things.

Now we are ready to go to work. We have laid out the job and our conceptual tools. Remember what our procedure is to be. We are going to study cases: descriptions of the behavior of particular groups. First, each case will be stated in ordinary literary language; it will simply be reported. Then an analysis will be made of the case, using the concepts defined so far. With each new case, moreover, the analysis will develop in complexity, and new concepts will be added as the need for them arises. In this way, the relationship between fact and theory should be clear at every step.

CHAPTER 3

The Bank Wiring Observation Room

The Plan of the Study . . . The Plan Put into Effect . . .
The Organization of Work . . . Method of Payment . . .
The Output Situation . . . Social Organization . . . Some
Individual Personalities . . . Norms of the Group . . . End
of the Study

OUR FIRST case describes a group of workingmen in a modern American factory, a group that was studied in the course of the Western Electric researches. These researches have become well known to sociologists and businessmen, but we do not need to explain what they were in detail, even to persons who have no professional knowledge of them: only a few facts must be remembered.[1] They were carried out from 1927 through 1932 at the Western Electric Company's Hawthorne Works in Chicago. This company is a subsidiary of the American Telephone and Telegraph Company, and it manufactures, among other things, telephone equipment for the Bell System. In the direction of the investigations, the research organization of the company worked with the Department of Industrial Research of the Harvard Graduate School of Business Administration. The chief aim of the researches was to inform industrial management about the sources of employee satisfaction or dissatisfaction at work, but that aim is in no sense our concern here. We are interested in the researches only so far as they tell us how workingmen behave. But perhaps we had better be more careful: we are interested in the researches so far

[1] The chief books in which the researches are described are: E. Mayo, *Human Problems of Industrial Civilization* (1933); T. N. Whitehead, *The Industrial Worker* (1938); F. J. Roethlisberger and W. J. Dickson, *Management and the Worker* (1939); G. C. Homans, *Fatigue of Workers* (Report of the Committee on Work in Industry, National Research Council, 1941).

as they tell us a part of the behavior of a particular group of workingmen over a particular span of time. We are not interested in the question whether this is all that might have been said about their behavior, whether this is the way they ought to have behaved, or whether management should have tried to get them to behave differently. For our present purposes these questions raise false issues. So long as we can say, "A group of people behaved in these ways, among others, for a certain period of time," we are satisfied.

We should also bear a couple of other points in mind. The researches were carried out in the last years of the boom and the first years of the great depression. How far was the behavior of the men in the group we shall study affected by their knowledge that in their company, as in others, layoffs were impending? The original descriptions of the research say nothing on this point, but it is one that we should be thinking about. Then, too, the reader will find nothing to show that a labor union was affecting the behavior of the group, and this may seem odd in view of the importance of unions in factories today. The fact is that the Western Electric researches were completed before the great C.I.O. organizing drives of the mid-thirties. The only union in the Hawthorne Plant was a so-called company union. Union membership was simply not a factor in the behavior of the men.

THE PLAN OF THE STUDY

The particular group we shall study is the so-called Bank Wiring Observation Room group, which is described at much greater length than here in *Management and the Worker*, by F. J. Roethlisberger and W. J. Dickson.[2] This was the last in the series of researches, and the fact that it was an end product and not a trial run is important. The research workers at Hawthorne had been made to feel perfectly free to follow up the leads given by the facts. Their scheme for interpreting the behavior of factory workers became steadily more adequate as it became more complicated. By the

[2] Fritz Jules Roethlisberger and William John Dickson, *Management and the Worker*, Cambridge, Mass.: Harvard University Press, 1939. All quotations and figures from this book are reprinted by permission of the publishers.

year 1931 they had decided that they must make a study of a group of workingmen under as nearly as possible normal industrial conditions. This may seem a strange decision. After all, what is industrial research trying to do but study normal conditions? Yet the fact was that the earlier investigations at Hawthorne had been of men and women under unusual conditions, and the conditions were unusual because, unintentionally, the very process of setting up the studies had made them so. The story is told in any of the accounts of the researches. What we must realize is that the Bank Wiring Observation Room was designed to avoid this particular pitfall.

To study workers under normal industrial conditions is not easy. The researchers decided that they could not study a whole shop department. Too much change of personnel would be going on; too many research workers would be needed if a thorough job was to be done; it would be impossible to overcome, in so large a body of men, the suspicion that the presence of outsiders would arouse. Therefore only one section of a shop department was chosen for study. Like most decisions, this made new difficulties while meeting old ones. It was clear, for instance, that the chosen section could not be studied while still a part, geographically, of the whole department. The influence of men who knew they were not being investigated upon those who knew they were might be disturbing. Therefore the section would have to be taken from the department and put in a room of its own. The research staff knew from much experience that the move itself might change those normal industrial conditions they were so anxious to maintain, but they felt they had to take the risk. There was no other way out. The section would be put in a room of its own, but in every other respect an attempt would be made to keep the conditions of work what they had been in the main department.

The group chosen for study should, the investigators felt, meet several lesser specifications if possible. It should be a group that could be removed from the department without undue inconvenience and, in particular, without moving bulky and costly equipment to the new room. The members of the group should be experienced workers, all doing the same job. An operator's work pace should be set by his own effort and not by a machine or conveyor, and it should be possible to measure individual output exactly. Finally, it should be reasonably certain that the members of the group would remain in the room and in the employ of the company. From these specifications it is clear that the research staff was particularly interested in factors affecting output and in the use of output as an index of other characteristics of group behavior.

These specifications were not altogether easy to meet. It was finally decided to study a section from a department that assembled switches for step-by-step central office telephone equipment. This section was responsible for wiring banks of terminals: hence the name Bank Wiring Observation Room. Fourteen men were taken from the department and placed in a room by themselves: nine so-called wiremen, three soldermen, and two inspectors. The group was a unit that needed to have no contact with the main department except through supervisors and a trucker who brought in materials and removed completed work.

The research staff wanted to be sure that the behavior of the men while they were in the room was not greatly different from what it had been in the main department. As a check, and without the knowledge of the men, records of their output were kept for eighteen weeks before the beginning of the study. If output in the room showed any significant change from output in the department, the assumption would be that conditions in the room had made the difference. As it turned out, there was no great change. All of the thirty-two men in the department were interviewed to give them a chance to express their attitudes toward jobs, supervisors, and working conditions. This was no new departure. An Interviewing Program had been in progress in the plant for some time, and 20,000 interviews had been conducted by methods which came closer and closer to what is now called the nondirective interview. Finally, for ten days before the men were asked to take part in the study, an investigator was placed in the department and given a desk near the foreman's in order that he might get an over-all impression of the men's work habits and behavior. His judgment was that behavior in the room was not greatly different from what it had been in the department.

The plan was to divide the work of studying the group between an observer and an interviewer. The observer was put in the room as a disinterested spectator. Twice a day he took records of output and the quality of work. The operators were used to having such records kept: this would create no disturbance. The observer was to keep no other records except a log of events and conversations that he considered significant. The research staff had a great deal of experience and reading behind it by the time the Bank Wiring Observation Room study began, and much more than common sense guided the observer's choice of significant events. But this chapter is a mere report of what was done and not a critique of the theory behind it. We shall see later what kinds of events the observer recorded.

The investigation was conceived as a study of the men as they would have worked in the main department. If they were to work as they worked there, they would have to feel at ease in the presence of the observer. He would have to be on friendly terms with everyone in the room. To this end, it was decided that he should abide by the following rules: (1) He should not give orders or answer questions if answering implied that he had power to take official action. So that he could keep his records, he was given a desk in the room, but it was put at the back, facing towards a side wall. Putting him at the front of the room and at a desk facing the operators would have given him by implication the kind of authority a schoolteacher has. (2) He should not willingly enter into any argument. If forced to do so, he should be as noncommittal as possible. (3) He should not thrust himself into a conversation; he should not seem anxious to overhear what the men said or over-interested in what they did. (4) He should not violate any confidence or give any information to supervisors whatever their rank. (5) He should not by his behavior or manner of speech set himself off from the group. The evidence is that the observer lived up to the letter and spirit of these rules.

Unlike the observer, the interviewer was to keep out of the room unless absolutely required to be in it. His relation to the men raised no such problem as did the observer's, since, as we have noted, the Interviewing Program was a familiar feature of the Hawthorne scene. The interviewer merely got in touch with, and interviewed, the men in the room rather more often than he would have done had they still been working in the main department. Apparently the operators accepted the interviewer as doing his normal job, and they even became rivals in an attempt to hold the interviewing record, that is, to keep an interview going longest.

THE PLAN PUT INTO EFFECT

The plans were laid; next they had to be set in motion. First the department foreman told the operators that they had been chosen for the study and asked their co-operation. He explained that in every way their life would be the same except that they would be placed in the special study room. Their work would be the same, their rates, their method of payment, and their supervision. The research staff would have no responsibility over them. All they were asked to do was work as they had been working in the department. Then the foreman took them to the observation room and introduced them to the research director and the proposed observer. The director explained the purpose of the study: that describing an ordinary department under ordinary conditions seemed a sensible step to take in industrial research. He said that the observer would be in the room to record output and any other facts he considered important. He promised, finally, that no record of what the men did in front of the observer would be used to their disadvantage.

The research staff believed that it would be hard to get the men's co-operation in continuing to work just as they had been working. It did not turn out to be. Habit may be too strong for people even when they know they are being watched. In the background, moreover, were the earlier researches, in which the staff had made pretty intimate studies of workers' lives without once violating a confidence. No promises had been broken; no persons hurt. After all, the observer did not in the least resemble a spy. The operators had been told just what he was in the room to do, and he did just that. After a period of constraint and misunderstanding, they first became used to the observer, then friendly with him, and they drew him into their conversations. The clearest sign that they had lost all suspicion of him was their willingness to do and say things in front of him that broke or implied breaking various rules of the company. There is little evidence, either in output and earnings, or in general activities and conversations, that the workers' behavior was unlike what it had been in the main department. Perhaps they were a little more noisy and boisterous. They were in a room by themselves, and their regular supervisor, who had never incommoded them very much, could not remain in the room all the time. Just as the researchers had hoped, the transfer to the room had not greatly changed "normal' industrial conditions.

THE ORGANIZATION OF WORK

Of the fourteen men, or operators, as they were called in the Western Electric Company, who were regularly in the Observation Room, nine were wiremen, who will be called Winkowski, Mueller, Taylor, Donovan, Capek, Krupa, Hasulak, Oberleitner, and Green, and who will also be numbered, to make the diagrams compact, W1 through W9; three were soldermen, who will be called Steinhardt, Matchek, and Cermak and numbered S1, S2, and S4; and two were inspectors, who will be called Allen and Mazmanian and numbered I1 and I3. In the original report of the research by Roethlisberger and Dickson, the men were only given numbers. The names have been assigned for the first time here to add vividness and ease in identification. They are, of course, not the real names, though they are appropriate to the national backgrounds of the operators. With the exceptions of Matchek (Yugoslavia) and Mazmanian (Armenia), all the men were born in this country, mostly the sons of German and Bohemian immigrants, but with some sprinkling of so-called older Americans. With the exception of Mazmanian, who was 40, all the men were between 20 and 26 years old, and, again with the exception of Mazmanian, who had completed three years of college, none had any college education. Their average service with the company was four years. Matchek had been longest with the company—nine years. Mazmanian came next with seven. Only four were married; but each of the others, except one, had someone in his family dependent in whole or in part upon him. Two other persons, a solderman (S3) and an inspector (I2) were in the room for a time, but they did not stay there long and will not be mentioned further.

Besides these men, two others were in the room a good part of the time: a trucker, who kept the group supplied with materials and removed completed equipments, and a group chief, that being the title of the lowest grade of supervisor in the Western Electric Company. Above the group chief in the chain of command came, in this order, a section chief and a foreman, the latter being in charge of the whole department. Both the section chief and the foreman visited the room from time to time.

As we have stated, the men were engaged in making parts of switches for central office telephone equipment. Specifically, they were connecting wires to banks of terminals. A bank was a piece of plastic about one and one half inches high and four inches long, convex in shape, with 100 or 200 terminals or points—the number varied with the type of bank—sticking out from it fanwise. A finished equipment was ten or eleven of these banks long and two or three banks high. A wireman took the necessary number of banks for an equipment and placed them in a holder or fixture on a workbench. Then he connected the terminals of the banks together in a certain order with wire. He made each connection by looping the wire, from which the insulation had been stripped at the proper intervals, over a point and pulling it tight. When all the points of all the banks had been connected according to plan, he was said to have wired one level. A wireman worked on two equipments at a time. Having finished a level on one equipment, he moved to the second equipment.

In the meantime, a solderman fixed in place the finished connections of the first equipment, and an inspector tested and scrutinized the work of both men. He had an electrical test set which he connected to two terminals of the equipment. If the set buzzed, the circuit was complete. If it was not complete, he had to determine by close examination what the trouble was. And even if the circuit was in good order, he still had to inspect the equipment visually for other defects. As for the wireman, after he finished a level on his second equipment, he came back to the first and started a new level on top of the old one, first slipping fiber insulators over the connections already made, while the solderman and inspector went on to the second equipment. When ten levels had been completed, a second row of banks was placed on top of the first, and the wiring was continued on them.

Wiring, soldering, and inspecting took different lengths of time. Thus one solderman could solder the connections made by about three wiremen. Therefore the company had divided the men into

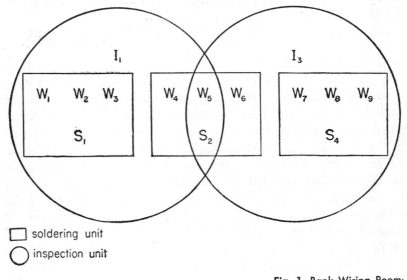

soldering unit

inspection unit

Fig. 1. Bank Wiring Room:
Division of the group into inspection and soldering units

soldering units. Steinhardt (S1) was supposed to solder for Winkowski (W1), Mueller (W2), and Taylor (W3), and these four men made up soldering unit 1. In the same way, Donovan (W4), Capek (W5), Krupa (W6), and Matchek (S2) made up unit 2, and Hasulak (W7), Oberleitner (W8), Green (W9), and Cermak (S4), unit 3. Two inspectors could handle the work of all the men. Inspection unit A consisted of Allen (I1), the first four wiremen, and S1; inspection unit B, of Mazmanian (I3), the last four wiremen, and S4. The work of Capek (W5) and Matchek (S2) was divided between the two inspectors (Fig. 1). Because the inspectors and soldermen could work on the equipments only when the wiremen were not busy with them, the wiremen as a rule set the pace for the other operators, but it was quite possible for either

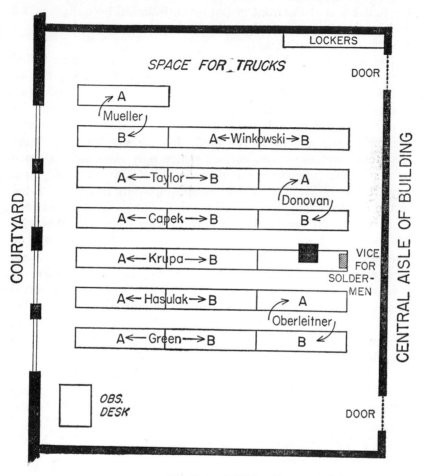

Fig. 2. Bank Wiring Room: Spatial arrangement

the soldermen or the inspectors to limit output by refusing to keep up with the wiremen.

The Observation Room was separated from the main department by high partitions. Fig. 2 shows its layout. The men faced toward the end of the room occupied by a row of lockers, and this end was considered the front. Since he went back and forth between two equipments, each wireman had two working positions. Soldering unit 1 was at the front of the room, followed by units 2 and 3 and by the observer's desk at the back. On one side of the room windows opened on a courtyard.

The wiremen worked on equipments of two kinds, one called connectors and the other selectors, these being the names of two different kinds of central office telephone switches. The method of wiring was the same for both equipments, and aside from the names, the differences between the two were slight. A connector equipment was usually eleven banks long, a selector never more than ten; a connector equipment weighed only about half as much as a selector, but neither weighed enough to give a young man any trouble lifting it, and only two equipments had to be lifted in the course of an average working day. The differences between equipments were important only because they were associated with differences between people. In the department, the men who worked on connectors, the connector wiremen as they were called, were all placed at the front of the room, with the selector wiremen behind them, and this arrangement was maintained in the Observation Room. The men in front worked on connectors, while Hasulak (W7), Oberleitner (W8), and Green (W9) worked on selectors. Beginners in the department were soldermen. Later they became wiremen, with a raise in wage rate. The newer and slower wiremen usually started "in back" and as they became more skillful moved forward to connectors. At the same time their efficiency ratings and earnings were apt to increase. The wiremen in the department expressed a preference for connector wiring and looked upon "going on connectors" as a promotion even if their hourly rates were not changed.

METHOD OF PAYMENT

The men in the Observation Room were paid according to a system called group piecework; that is, the department as a whole counted as a unit. For each equipment completed and shipped, the department was credited with a fixed sum, and from the total amount thus earned in a week the individual employees in the department were paid. Thus the more units turned out by the whole group, the more pay each employee received.

How was the individual's share of this sum determined? In the language of industry, a man is on daywork when he is paid by the time he spends at work; the number of hours or days, and he is on piecework when he is paid by his output: the number of "pieces" of work he turns out. In the Bank Wiring Department, each employee was assigned an hourly wage rate—a certain number of cents an hour—based largely on his efficiency as shown by his output record, and this rate, multiplied by the number of hours he worked during the week, made the daywork value of the work he accomplished. By adding together the daywork value of the work of all the employees in the department, and subtracting the figure thus obtained from the total earnings of the department, the excess of piecework earnings over daywork earnings was determined. This surplus, divided by the total daywork earnings, was called the "percentage." The weekly daywork earnings of each man were then increased by this percentage, and the resulting figure constituted his weekly take-home wage. The company guaranteed that actual wages should never be less than the daywork value of the work done.

Clearly there was a logical reason for each feature of this wage incentive system. His hourly wage rate remaining constant, a man could increase his earnings only if the output of the department as a whole increased. A rise in his own output, unless that of others rose in the same measure, would hardly show at all in his pay envelope. A fall in his output, if that of others did not fall, would also hardly affect him. On the other hand, his wages would rise if he could raise his wage rate, and this did depend, through his efficiency record, on his output. The assumption of the men who designed this scheme was that an employee would work up to the limit set by fatigue to increase not only his own output but that of the group as a whole. Only thus could he maximize his earnings, and this, it was taken for granted, was what he wanted to do. Furthermore, he would do what he could to cut down waste time, since time that did not go into output did not help the earnings of the department.

THE OUTPUT SITUATION

Whether or not the men were expected to behave as described, the fact was that they did not. They had a clear idea of a proper day's work: about two completed equipments, or 6,600 connections, for a man working on connectors, 6,000 for a man working on selectors. The wiremen in the room felt, as they had felt in the department, that no more work than this should be turned out, and this much was well within the capacity of most of them. They tended to work hard in the morning, until the completion of a day's work was in sight, and then to take it easy in the afternoon as quitting time approached. As the pressure lessened, conversation, games, and the preparation of tools and equipment for the next day's work took more and more time. It appears impossible to determine how the figure of two equipments per day was reached. Perhaps a good round number was wanted, with no connections left over. Moreover, the figure was not objectively low. The output of the department was considered wholly satisfactory by the company. The foreman was proud of his "boys" and thought that if they produced any more output they would work their fingers to the bone. Yet output was clearly not as great as it would have been if it had been limited only by fatigue. Only in this sense could the investigators refer to the men's adoption of an output limit as "restriction of output." Many workingmen would have called it "doing a fair day's work for a fair day's wage."

If a man did turn out more than was thought proper, or if he worked too fast, he was exposed to merciless ridicule. He was called a "rate-buster" or a "speed king," but at the same time a man who turned out too little was a "chiseler." He was cutting down the earnings of the group. The fact that the men had set an upper limit on output did not mean they believed in doing no work at all. And ridicule was not the only penalty a nonconformist had to suffer. A game called "binging" was played in the Observation Room, especially by Hasulak (W7), Oberleitner (W8), Green (W9), and Cermak (S4). If, according to the rules of this game, a man walked up to another man and hit him as hard as he could on the upper arm—"binged" him—, the other then had the right to retaliate with another such blow, the object being to see who could hit the harder. But binging was also used as a penalty. A man who was thought to be working either too fast or too slow might be binged.

Together with the belief that a man's output ought not to go above a limit of two completed equipments a day went the belief that a man's output record, that is, his average hourly output, ought to show little change from week to week. When workingmen put a plan like this into practice, industrialists speak of it as "straight-line" output, because output records plotted on a graph will then approximate a straight line. In the Observation Room, output records were to be held constant and not earnings. A man's earnings depended on the output of the whole group, not just on his own, and so were only partly within his control. Nevertheless, since a man's output record helped determine his efficiency rating and this in turn his hourly rate, his record was, in the long run, not unrelated to his earnings. In keeping his record constant, he was again acting contrary to the assumption of the wage incentive scheme, that he would do everything in his power to increase his hourly rate.

Since average hourly output is calculated by dividing total output by hours of work, the men wishing to keep their output records constant had, as they could easily see, two methods of doing so open to them. They could manipulate either the dividend or the divisor—they could claim more or less output than they really produced, or they could claim that they had taken more or less time. In practice they used both methods.

As for output, the group chief kept the output records and was supposed to take an actual count every day of the number of connections made by each wireman. It was a big job, and he did not have time for it. Instead he let the wiremen themselves report their output to him. He was aware that their reports were not always accurate. As he said, "They like to have a few saved up in case things don't go so good." If a man was a little ahead one day, he would not report all his connections but save up a few to be applied in a slump. Unlike the group chief, the observer kept an accurate record of output by making a count every day at noon and evening. He discovered that the wiremen always knew just where they stood and that most of them, in the long run, kept a remarkably close balance between actual and reported output. Most reported more connections than they had in fact completed but except for Hasulak (W7) and Green (W9) the differences were not large. Taylor (W3) and Krupa (W6) reported a little less than they had done. Note that this manipulation of the output records had no immediate effect on the men's earnings. These depended on the earnings of the whole department, which were determined by an accurate and independent count of the number of equipments shipped out.

The men could also keep average hourly output constant by controlling the amount of time admitted as available for work. In the department and in the Observation Room, the employees were permitted to claim "daywork allowance" for time lost through reasons beyond their control. In making up the output records, this allowance was subtracted from total time on the job. The reasons given for lost time were shortage of materials, defective materials, waiting for another workman, making repairs, and power turned off. The group chief was responsible for admitting daywork allowance claims, as he was for keeping track of output. Few of the reasons for lost time were in fact wholly beyond the men's control, but as it was impossible to draw any hard and fast line between those that were and those that were not, the group chief tended to let most of the daywork allowance claims go through. Once again, the men varied in the amount of daywork allowance they asked and got. Taylor (W3) claimed least: 18 seconds per hour on the average. Hasulak (W7) and Green (W9) claimed most, with 3 minutes 42 seconds, and 3 minutes 48 seconds, respectively. Note the similarity of this pattern to that of differences between reported and actual output. Men like Hasulak and Green not only reported a good deal more output than they really completed but also claimed a good deal of time out. These two facts meant of course that their hourly output was considerably less in fact than the group chief's records showed it to be.

The group chief was in a difficult position. He was a representative of management, and his duty was to enforce the rules laid down by management. He was supposed to keep an accurate count of connections completed and to admit daywork allowance claims only for stoppages that were beyond the men's control. In fact he took the men's word on both points. As we shall see, there were a good many other things going on in the Observation Room, as in the department as a whole, of which higher management would not have approved. The group chief knew this, but there was little he could do about it. To enforce the rules would have required his standing over the men all day, and by so doing he would have sacrificed all hope of establishing good relations with them. He would have lost even that minimum of influence that he needed if he was to do any kind of a job at all. Under these circumstances he chose to side with the group and wink at much that was going on, especially as he was in a position to protect himself. Output was considered good. There was no easy way of showing that his output figures were wrong, and he did not have to show them to anyone. They were not checked against the output of the department as a whole, but used only for establishing efficiency ratings. So indefinite were the reasons for work stoppages that he could throw the blame where he pleased if someone protested that too much daywork allowance was being given. The workers liked the way he treated them and they respected him, but they did not stand in awe of him.

The men's idea of a proper day's work—two equipments a day, or 6,600 connections on connector equipments, 6,000 on selectors, or about 825 connections an hour—was exactly maintained by few persons in the room. Taylor (W3) came closest: his output record as kept by the observer showed an almost straight line at 825. Capek (W5) and Krupa (W6) fluctuated around 825. Mueller (W2) was consistently higher, around 900, and the rest were consistently lower. Hasulak (W7), Oberleitner (W8), and Green (W9) were lowest in actual hourly output, Green never getting above 600, though he reported more.

It occurred to the research staff that these individual differences in output might be connected with differences in intelligence or dexterity. Wiring seemed to require both. Therefore the men were given a standard intelligence test (Otis) and a dexterity rating combining the results of two pegboard tests and a soldering test in which the subject was asked to solder as many terminals in a bank as possible, without error, in a given length of time. The results of neither the intelligence nor the dexterity test correlated with average hourly output. Green, (W9), for instance, the lowest man in output, ranked first in intelligence. And Mueller (W2), the highest man in output, ranked lowest in intelligence. But Mueller was a difficult person, and there is reason to doubt that he cooperated in the test. In any event, whatever was determining the output figures, it was not native intelligence or native dexterity—if indeed there are such things.

If the men were asked why they tried to keep their output at, or below, a standard and their output records close to horizontal straight lines, their replies were rather vague. "Something" might happen if they did not. The slower men would get bawled out; someone would be laid off; hours would be reduced; above all, a rate—it was never specified what rate—would be cut so that the men would be in the position of doing more work for the same amount of money. In point of fact, none of the men in the Observation Room, and some had been with the company for as long as nine years, had any experience of the things they said they were guarding against. For instance, the policy of the company was that piecework rates, once established, would not be changed unless there were a change in manufacturing process, and restriction of output, by keeping labor costs up, may actually hasten instead of delaying the introduction of a new manufacturing process. What the experience of the men, young men though they were, had been outside of the Western Electric Company is another question, and certainly the explanations they gave have been common talk among American workingmen for years. In order to understand the attitude of the workers in the room, we certainly need the answer to one question: About how much money did the group or an individual lose through every equipment that might have been turned out but was not? The original report does not answer this question.[3]

SOCIAL ORGANIZATION

So far we have been looking at the organization of work and the behavior of the group in the matter of output. But these were not the only sides of group life studied. The observer kept a log in which he recorded all events that he thought would be of interest —interest not being defined by common sense but by the investigators' previous experience in research and by the questions they

---

[3] For indirect evidence, see *Management and the Worker*, 479.

wanted to answer next. We now turn to this other material and some further aspects of group behavior that it revealed, but first we had better cite the very words of Roethlisberger and Dickson, saying how the material was analyzed:

First, each person entering into the study, whether operator, inspector, or supervisor, was considered separately. The observation material and interview material were examined carefully, and every entry in which a particular person was mentioned or referred to was lifted out and listed under his name. Through this method of classification, the degree and kind of social participation of each individual in the Bank Wiring Observation Room became apparent.

Secondly, the material thus listed for each person was examined for evidence of the extent of his participation. Two questions were asked: (1) To whom do this person's relations extend? Does he associate with everyone in the group, or are his social activities restricted to a few? (2) Does he enter a great deal or relatively little into social relations with the people with whom he associates? In other words, if S1 converses and associates with the men in his soldering unit to the exclusion of everybody else, does he do so frequently or infrequently?

Thirdly, an attempt was made to determine the kind of participation manifested by each person. Such questions as the following were considered: Does he assume a superordinate or subordinate role? Does he strive for leadership? If so, is he permitted to do so, or are his attempts in that direction opposed by others? Are most of his social contacts related to his job, or are they in the nature of arguments, conversations, or games which have no immediate relation to his work?

Fourthly, each occurrence in which a person entered into association with another person was examined to see whether the relation thus manifested expressed an antagonism, a friendship, or was merely neutral. Each incident, of course, had to be related to its social context before its significance could be determined.[4]

This statement provokes a comment on the side. We can hardly help noticing that the material was broken down by (*a*) persons, (*b*) the extent of their participation, (*c*) the kind of participation, and (*d*) whether the relations between persons were antagonistic, friendly, or neutral. These four correspond at least roughly to the concepts that we set up at the end of the last chapter and that we shall use, to start with, in our analysis of group behavior; that is, persons, and the three elements of their behavior: interaction, ac-

[4] *Ibid.*, 493-4.

tivity, and sentiment. In this book we are hardly doing more than bringing out the unstated implications of some good modern field studies, and so this chance to show the similarity between our concepts and the way the Bank Wiring Observation Room data were analyzed has been too tempting to pass up, but we must now go back to sheer reporting.

Let us now turn to some of the activities, over and above each man's special job, that were observed in the room. One of the

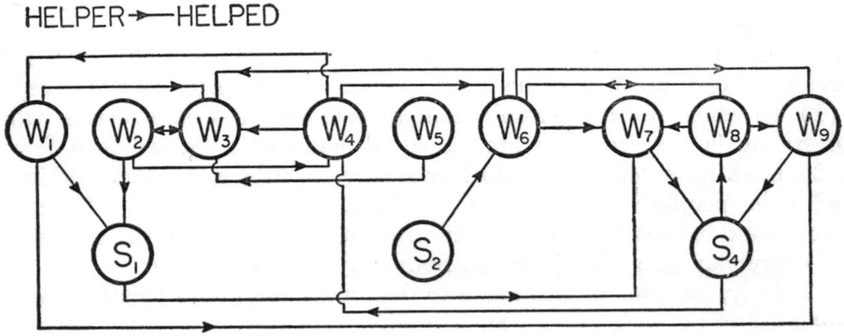

HELPER→—HELPED

Fig. 3. Bank Wiring Room: Men who helped one another

commonest was helping another man out by doing some of his wiring for him when he had fallen behind. Although no formal rule of the company said that one man should not help another, helping was in practice forbidden, on the theory that the jobs were one-man jobs and that each man could do his own best. Nevertheless a good deal of help was given. The wiremen said it made them feel good to be helped. Donovan (W4) said in one of his interviews: "It seems like if a fellow is loafing and gets behind, nobody will help him out, but if he is making an honest effort he will be helped. . . . Some people are friendlier than others, you know, and where that's the case you will find them helping each other out." [5] The observer kept track of instances of helping, and they are summarized in Fig. 3. In this figure, certain points should be noticed especially. Everyone took part in helping. Unlike some other activities, it was not confined to one social group. As for in-

[5] *Management and the Worker,* 505.

dividuals, Taylor (W3), although he was a good worker and did not need help, was helped more than anyone else in the room. Krupa (W6), on the other hand, gave more help than anyone else but rarely received it. Capek (W5) and Matchek (S2) gave help a few times but never received it.

Job trading between wiremen and soldermen was, like helping, forbidden in theory but tolerated in practice. Until recently, industrial thinking has held that the more specialized a man is, the more efficient he is. Efficient or not, an occasional change of job was enjoyed by the men in the room. But there was more at stake

INITIATOR→—ACCEPTOR

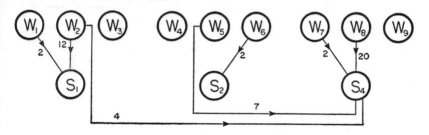

Fig. 4. Bank Wiring Room: Men who traded jobs

in job trading than a bit of variety in the work. In practically every case, the request for a trade came from the wireman, and the solderman concerned traded without protest. Records were kept of job trading, and Fig. 4 summarizes them, the figures indicating the number of times trading took place between each pair of operators. Note that most of the trading was requested of Cermak (S4), the solderman for the three selector wiremen. In 33 out of the 49 times job trading was recorded, it was with him. Furthermore, wiremen from soldering units 1 and 2 traded with Cermak, but no man from soldering unit 3 ever traded outside his own unit. "In other words, the connector wiremen apparently felt free to change jobs either with their own soldermen or with the solderman for the selector wiremen, but the latter did not feel free to trade outside of their own unit." [6]

[6] *Ibid.*, 504.

Something of the same sort came out in the choice of the "lunch boy," as he was called, who went out of the room every noon to order and pick up, from the plant restaurant, the lunches for all the men. When they first came into the room, Steinhardt (S1) had reluctantly agreed to do the job. Cermak (S4) came into the room after the study was under way, and when he did, he took over the duties of lunch boy as a regular part of his job. Cermak was the solderman for the selector wireman.

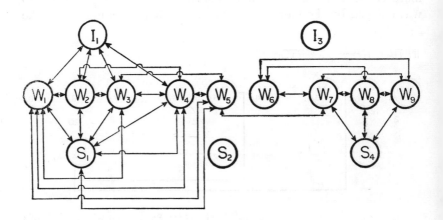

Fig. 5. Bank Wiring Room: Men who played games together

In the lunch hour and from time to time during the work, the men in the room took part in all sorts of games. Almost anything was an excuse for a bet: matching coins, lagging coins, shooting craps, cards, combinations of digits in the serial numbers of weekly pay checks. Pools were organized on horse racing, baseball, and quality records. In the games, the money at stake was not the important thing. Bets were small—one to ten cents—except in horse racing, which was a serious matter. The group picked out a "Test Room Horse" and bet on him fairly consistently. The observer also included under the heading of games the practices the men adopted of "binging" one another and chipping in together to buy candy.

The pattern of participation in games is shown in Fig. 5. The arrows connecting the circles indicate that the persons thus joined took part in one or more games, either as pairs or as members of a larger group. The figure demonstrates that participation in games occurred for the most part within two groups. Allen (I1), Winkowski (W1), Mueller (W2), Taylor (W3), Donovan (W4), and Steinhardt (S1) made up one group, a group at the front of the room. Krupa (W6), Hasulak (W7), Oberleitner (W8), Green (W9), and Cermak (S4) made up another, a group at the back. Capek (W5) is shown participating in both groups, but since the

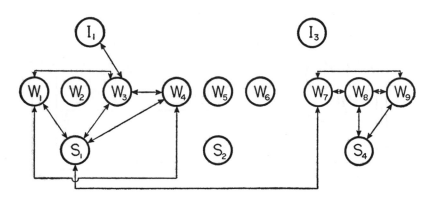

Fig. 6. Bank Wiring Room: Men who were friends

frequency of participation is not recorded, the figure misrepresents his position. He took part in only one game with the group in front, and on one other occasion played a game with Hasulak (W7). Matchek (S2) and Mazmanian (I3) never took part in games.

The material collected by the observer could also be interpreted to show that friendships or antagonisms existed between certain men in the room. These emotional relationships are plotted in Figs. 6 and 7. In Fig. 6 we must note that, except for a friendship between Steinhardt (S1) and Hasulak (W7), all friendships occurred within one or the other of the two groups already mapped out on the basis of participation in games. Several of the men, and it is worth while to notice which ones, were not particularly friendly with any of the others. As for antagonisms, a large number of them centered around Mazmanian (I3) and Capek (W5), while neither

Winkowski (W1) nor Taylor (W3), was the object of any antagonism at all. The antagonisms of soldering unit 3, the selector
wiremen, were more marked than those of any other unit. Their
antagonism for Mueller (W2) is noteworthy.

Roethlisberger and Dickson sum up all this evidence by saying
that, although the members of the Bank Wiring Observation Room
were pulled together in some ways, for instance, in mutual help

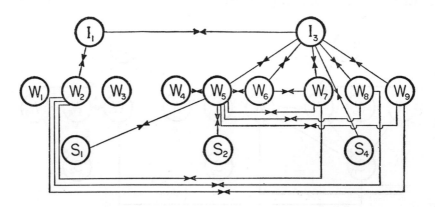

Fig. 7. Bank Wiring Room:
Men who were antagonistic to one another

and in restriction of output, in others they were divided. In particular, there were two cliques in the room, whose membership
was approximately that revealed by participation in games (Fig.
8). "The group in front" as it was called in the room, clique A as
it will be called here, had as its nucleus the connector wiremen of
soldering unit 1 but was not identical with that unit, since Donovan (W4), a wireman of unit 2, was also a member. Winkowski
(W1), Taylor (W3), and Donovan (W4) were members of this
clique, as was Steinhardt (S1), the solderman of unit 1, and Allen
(I1), the inspector who looked over its work. Mueller (W2) took
part in the games of clique A, but otherwise had little to do with
it; he entered little into conversation. "The group in back," or
clique B, had as its nucleus the selector wiremen of soldering unit

3. Hasulak (W7), Oberleitner (W8), and Green (W9) were members, as was Cermak (S4), the solderman of the unit. Krupa (W6) associated a good deal with clique B. He was always "horsing around" with the selector wiremen and had little to do with clique A. Yet he sought leadership, and the selector wiremen resisted and disliked his attempts to dominate them. In many ways he was an outsider even in their group. Mazmanian (I3), Capek (W5), and

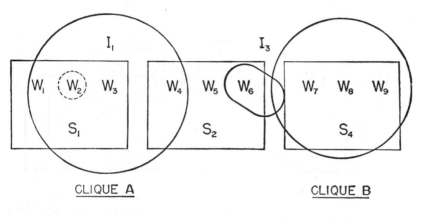

CLIQUE A   CLIQUE B

Fig. 8. Bank Wiring Room:
Division of the group into cliques

Matchek (S2) were in no sense members of either clique, Mazmanian and Capek attracting much antagonism.

Each clique had its own games and activities, noticeably different from those of the other group, and clique A felt that its activities were superior to those of clique B. The members of clique A did not trade jobs nearly so much as clique B, and hardly entered at all into controversies with one another as to whether, in the winter, the windows should be open or shut. Nine-tenths of these controversies took place between members of clique B or between them and other members of the room (Fig. 9). Most of the gambling games occurred in clique A, most of the binging in clique B.

Both groups purchased candy [from the store of the Hawthorne Club], but purchases were made separately and neither clique shared with the other. Clique A bought chocolate candy in small quantities, whereas clique B bought a less expensive kind in such large quantities that W9 at one time became ill from eating too much. Clique A argued more and indulged in less noise and horseplay than clique B. The members of clique A felt that their conversations were on a higher plane than those which went on in clique B; as W4 said: "We talk about things of some importance." [7]

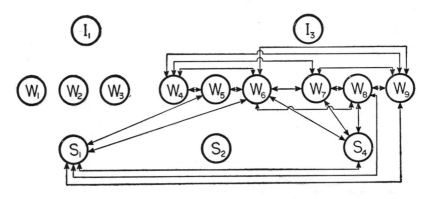

Fig. 9. Bank Wiring Room:
Men who got into arguments about windows

We are still recording facts and not analyzing them, but this does not forbid our noticing some correlations that were more than mere coincidence. If, as we have seen, the output rates of the wiremen could not be correlated with their intelligence or dexterity, they could clearly be correlated with clique membership. Look at Fig. 10. The selector wiremen not only had the lowest output; they also put in for much more daywork allowance than the others and reported that their output was much greater than it really was. If their reported output was low, their real output was even lower. The members of clique A came much closer to attaining the norms of the group in the matter of output. It was true that Mueller (W2) was first in output and the only man in the room who consistently went above the agreed standard for a fair day's work, but then he was only in a small degree a mem-

[7] *Management and the Worker*, 510.

ber of clique A. Krupa (W6) and Taylor (W3) came nearest to
having output records that were neither too low nor too high but

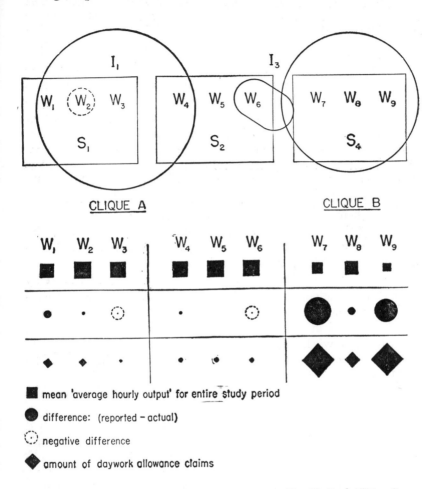

Fig. 10. Bank Wiring Room:
The relation between output and clique membership

took the form of straight lines at an average output of 825 connections an hour. They were also the only two men that reported
less work than they really turned out. Krupa was striving after

leadership, and Taylor, as we shall see, was probably the most popular man in the room.

SOME INDIVIDUAL PERSONALITIES

The present account of the Bank Wiring Observation Room has been faithful to the original in saying a good deal about interpersonal and intergroup relationships, little about the personalities of the individual workers. This has meant a certain lack of vividness, for we are used to thinking of group behavior as a matter of the clash or harmony of individual personalities. We miss them when we are told nothing about them. For this gap in the original report there were good reasons. Besides the observer, an interviewer was assigned to the room, and he had several long talks with each of the workers. They told him much about their past histories, their present situations and problems outside the plant, and all of this material would have added to our picture of the individual personalities. Nevertheless, in writing their book, Roethlisberger and Dickson decided to leave most of it out. The men who had worked in the room could be rather easily identified by other Hawthorne employees. Information about their personal lives and characters might easily have been embarrassing to them if it had appeared in print. The result is that for the understanding of individuals we have to fall back on the much less complete material collected by the observer in the room, though what he could add is better than nothing.

Mazmanian (I3), as the chart of antagonisms shows, was the most disliked person in the room. He was also by far the oldest, and the only one who had any college education. Though he had been an inspector for more than seven years, he was a newcomer to the department. He had trouble at first catching on to the use of his test set and thus slowed up the men whose work he inspected. They were irritated and did nothing to help him out. Instead they made fun of him, arranged their work so that he could not possibly keep up, and when he was not looking adjusted his test set so that it would not work. They also made many claims for daywork allowance on the ground that he delayed them. He returned the favor **by** finding their work unsatisfactory. Mazmanian did better in his job as time went on, but the antagonism between him and the men increased. Finally he could stand it no longer. He went to the Inspection Branch Personnel Division and charged that the men were slowing down and interfering with his work. The Personnel Division took the matter to the foreman of the Bank Wiring Department, who denied the charges. The news got back to the men that Mazmanian had "squealed." They were furious; co-operation broke down completely, and Mazmanian had to be transferred out of the room. He had never taken part in the group's activities, except for arguments, and in them he tended to pose as a man of superior knowledge, who knew big words.

As this incident shows, the inspectors were outsiders in the room. They were responsible to their own supervisors in the Inspection Branch of the plant, and not to the supervisors of the Bank Wiring Department. Since they had to pass on the work of the men, they were themselves much in the position of supervisors and faced the same dilemmas: their work became easier at the price of abandoning any hint of superiority over the men. Allen (I1), unlike Mazmanian, who identified himself with the management, decided on this course. He took part freely in all the activities of clique A. He was also the man who told the group that Mazmanian had squealed and let them know of other news affecting their welfare, and, while the rest of the men were submissive toward the foreman, Allen was not so in the least and spoke to him as they would never have dared to speak.

Mueller (W2) was the fastest workman in the room, earning for himself the nicknames "Cyclone" and "Phar Lap," the latter the name of a famous racehorse of the day. As we have seen, he took part in games of chance with clique A, but otherwise was rather unsociable. He worked with great concentration; he was not talkative; he had nothing to do with arguments. The other men left him alone. He was especially contemptuous of "the group in back," the men with low output, and won their antagonism in return. He seldom helped others, but it may be significant that he often traded jobs with Steinhardt (S1). Wiremen, we will remember, originated proposals to trade.

Capek (W5) was next in unpopularity to Mazmanian and unquestionably the least popular of the wiremen. Like Mueller he was a fast and efficient worker, contemptuous of those who could not do as well. Several times he took it upon himself to bawl out Green (W9) because he was not doing enough work. He thought Steinhardt (S1) "horsed around" too much and should work harder. He often referred to Hasulak (W7) as a "fairy" and petulantly commanded Krupa (W6) to shut up. To show his disdain for the selector wiremen he soldered one day for all three positions while also trying to do as much wiring as Oberleitner (W8) ordinarily did. But he went much further than this: he did not hesitate to squeal if he saw fit. "Thus, one day he purposely made a number of derogatory remarks about Mazmanian (I3), so that Mazmanian's supervisor, who was in the room, could hear him."[8] The only persons with whom he approached friendliness were Winkowski (W1) and Taylor (W3). He helped Taylor a few times, but was never helped himself. "The observer noted that Capek rarely smiled. He seemed unhappy and very discontented with his job. He was constantly asking his supervisors for a transfer, and once when he thought he was going to get one he was more cheerful than he ever was before or afterwards."[9]

Krupa (W6) was so short that he had a hard time wiring the top levels of his equipment. The foreman suggested that the group chief hang him up by his heels to stretch him out a little. To his fellow workmen, he was "Shorty," "The Shrimp," "The Runt." In spite of his low stature, he was an extraordinarily fast workman, a fact which won him his other title of "Speed King." Yet he reported less work than he turned out and stayed close to the approved output limit. At work or off, it was impossible to keep him still. He talked to everyone, jeering at one moment, friendly at the next. He helped more persons than anyone else but was seldom helped himself. Above all, he liked to draw attention to himself with wisecracks and dirty stories. His imitation of Popeye the Sailor was celebrated. This tendency of his also showed itself in a drive for leadership: he could not help telling people what to do. He thrust himself in on other men's arguments with the group chief and pleaded their cause. But the group would not accept his pretensions. It constantly belittled him with nicknames and made

[8] *Management and the Worker*, 468.
[9] *Ibid.*, 470.

fun of his national origin—he was of Polish descent—although there was another Pole in the room, Winkowski (W1), who was never called a "Polak." Krupa helped the men at the rear of the room, Hasulak, Oberleitner, and Green, and associated with them, but neither clique fully accepted him. In one incident, Hasulak and Oberleitner made fun of Krupa while he was arguing with the section chief over the rate of pay. Again, "on one occasion Hasulak, Oberleitner, and Green ordered some candy from the Hawthorne Club store and asked Krupa to contribute to the purchase price, but when the candy came they would not give him his share." [10]

Like Mazmanian (I3) and Capek (W5), Matchek (S2) was a member of neither clique, but for a different reason from theirs. He had a speech difficulty, which made him seem backward and prevented his taking part easily in the activities of the group, although he appeared to enjoy watching and listening to the others. He was a good solderman and towards the end of the study was beginning to take a more active part in the life of the room. If the study had gone on longer, his social position might have changed.

We have looked briefly at the behavior of the men that did not become, or did not easily become, members of a clique. Perhaps a word or two about some of the others is needed. Green (W9) was lowest in output and in the quality of his work and claimed more daywork allowance than anyone except Oberleitner (W8). Yet he received the highest score in the intelligence test. He was more easily distracted from his work than any of the others and was always going out of the room to get a drink of water. He often complained of feeling tired and lacking interest in his job, though physical examination showed he was in good health and he was always eager to take part in sports after hours. Because he was so slow at wiring, Green was often razzed by others in the room, but he took the jeers in good part and was well liked. He was the room's intellectual, liking to impress the rest with his use of big words like "voluptuous." Once when the group chief asked him what kind of job he would like best, he said: "I'd like a job reading. Some job where I could sit and read all day." [11]

[10] *Ibid.*, 475.
[11] *Ibid.*, 480.

Still another kind of man was Taylor (W3), whose output was consistently good, ranking second only to that of Mueller (W2). He came closer than anyone else to realizing the group's ideal of a straight-line output record at 825 connections per hour. Like Krupa (W6) he reported less work than he completed. His quality was high. He was on good terms with everyone in the room and always willing to take part in a game or conversation. "All the men in the observation room had a standing invitation to play poker at his house." The men showed the way they felt about him by helping him more than any other operator in the room, although he did not always return the favor.

The other important facts about him are well stated by Roethlisberger and Dickson:

Taylor was an indefatigable talker. Whether working or not, he kept up a continual stream of chatter which he directed chiefly toward Winkowski (W1), Steinhardt (S1), and Allen (I1). He seldom lost an argument whether it was about baseball, horse racing, movie stars' salaries, the interest rate on postal savings, or the cost of shipping a dozen eggs a hundred miles by express. His superiority was demonstrated not only by the fact that he usually won out in arguments but also by the way in which he advised and cautioned the men. Thus when Steinhardt said he was thinking of getting a transfer to a subsidiary of the Western Electric Company, Taylor told him that he should consider his chances of getting back on his present job in case he didn't get along well on his new job. He told Capek (W5) which horses to bet on in the races. When Krupa (W6) and some of the others got too boisterous, it was Taylor who warned them to "pipe down." If he thought an argument was going too far, as in an argument about religion between Winkowski and Steinhardt, he tried to put a stop to it.

The following incident serves well to show Taylor's position in the group. The men were complaining about poor wire, but the group chief told them they had to use it up. Contrary to his orders, Winkowski and Oberleitner went out to the department and got some wire for themselves. They were rather proud of themselves and thought they had "got away with something." Taylor then went out to the department and in a short time came back accompanied by the trucker, who had a whole truckload of wire.[12]

NORMS OF THE GROUP

We have been looking at differences between cliques and differences between individuals. At the end we must come back to the group as a whole, and especially to its norms. Roethlisberger and Dickson conclude that the men in the Bank Wiring Observation Room had adopted a definite code of good behavior, revealed by what the men said and, in different degrees, by what they did. Even the men who did not live up to the code knew what it was. It had, like most codes, many articles, of which the following were the most important:

1. You should not turn out too much work. If you do, you are a "rate-buster."

2. You should not turn out too little work. If you do, you are a "chiseler."

3. You should not tell a supervisor anything that will react to the detriment of an associate. If you do, you are a "squealer."

4. You should not attempt to maintain social distance or act officious. If you are an inspector, for example, you should not act like one.[13]

To these we should, perhaps, on the evidence of the group's reaction to Krupa's (W7) behavior, add one more: You should not be noisy, self-assertive, and anxious for leadership.

END OF THE STUDY

The Bank Wiring Observation Room study lasted for six and a half months, from November 1931 to May 1932, when the deepening depression and lack of work put an end to it. In this time the research staff had made no changes in the conditions in the room; it had simply watched and recorded the behavior of the men. The short time spent on the study meant that the pattern of social life did not have much chance to change. Given more time, Matchek (S2) might have participated more often, and Taylor (W3) might have achieved acknowledged leadership. We do not know. But what change did take place seems to have been in these directions. One other point: the amount of space devoted in the report to

13 *Ibid.*, 522.

descriptions of games, arguments, and breaches of rules may leave the impression that this was an undisciplined group. It was not. All these activities were significant in revealing social relationships, but they tend to make us forget the long hours the men spent turning out wired equipments. The men worked hard and produced much.

When the Observation Room study was stopped, the men went back to the department where they had been in the beginning. There they were again interviewed, so that the research staff might find out whether their attitudes had changed during their life in the room. Some claimed that working in the room was the same as working in the department, others, that the illumination was worse but that they felt freer to do as they pleased. Some who had said in earlier interviews that the room was small and made them feel shut in, now asked to be taken back into it, saying that they liked it much better than the department. The chief change seemed to have been in the relation of the wiremen to the other workers. As the study went on, they felt further and further removed from the department, more and more a group by themselves. This attitude showed itself in claims that the men in the main room discriminated against them, sending them all the poor wire and taking all the *Microphones* (a weekly plant newspaper). In short, the isolation of the group created some antagonism between the group and the rest of the department.

We have now carried out for one group the first part of our procedure for studying group behavior. We have looked at the productive and social life of fourteen factory workers. The description has been made, by design, as flat as possible: a statement in ordinary language of what was said and done, avoiding inference or explanation. Of course the attempt has not been perfectly successful. Inferences always creep in, and the reader who is worth his salt will make his own as he goes along. But perhaps it has been successful enough to provide a person who dissents from our interpretation with the material to defend his own position. To this interpretation we now turn. We analyze what happened in the Bank Wiring Observation Room no longer in ordinary language but in terms that may perhaps be applicable to more groups than one.

CHAPTER 4

The External System

*Definition of the Group . . . System and Environment . . .
The Nature of the Environment . . . The External System
. . . Sentiment . . . Activity . . . Interaction . . . Pair Rela-
tionships . . . Mutual Dependence of Sentiment and Ac-
tivity . . . Mutual Dependence of Activity and Interaction
. . . The Pyramid of Interaction . . . Conclusion*

IN THE NEXT three chapters we shall make an
analysis of the Bank Wiring group, using the concepts defined in
Chapter 2, and at least one new concept which we shall introduce
when necessary. In the first two of these chapters, we shall try to
establish only a few general ideas, taking the Bank Wiring group
as little more than a point of departure, but in the third chapter
the analysis will get very detailed indeed.

There would be no reason for doing this work, which takes us,
in analysis, over ground we have already covered in common-sense
description, if it did not help us accomplish our main purpose.
Human groups differ greatly in externals: one group is connecting
wires to banks of terminals, while another is hanging out on a
street corner, and a third is gathering coconuts on a South Sea
island. Only if we apply the same scheme of analysis to all groups
can we bring out the similarities in human relationships that underlie these differences in externals. Or perhaps, instead of speaking of similarities, we had better say that a general scheme of
analysis helps us to see that the underlying human relationships
differ from group to group in degree rather than in kind. The Bank
Wiring Observation Room would be nothing to us if it did not let
us show how such a scheme can be set up and used.

DEFINITION OF THE GROUP

The subject of this book is the human group. We all think we know what we mean by this word, but if one of our purposes is to make explicit what we already understand intuitively, perhaps we should be more rigorous in defining it than we have been so far. Here, if anywhere, is the place for clarity. How do we determine that a certain number of persons form a group? Let us study one method of determination that is not far different from our intuitive attack on the problem. Suppose we are in a position to observe, or get records of, the social participation, within a given community, of a certain number of persons, let us say eighteen women.[1] We follow their participation over a period of time, and we notice that each woman is present on occasions or at events when some others of the eighteen are also present. The events are various: a day's work behind the counter of a store, a meeting of a women's club, a church supper, a card party, a supper party, a meeting of the Parent-Teacher Association, etc., but we make a note of the women present at each one. Then, since we are methodical social scientists, we begin to make a chart, divided into squares by lines and columns. Each column stands for a single social occasion or event, identified by date; each line, for a single woman. (See Fig. 11; but this is the chart in its final, not its original form.) Then we begin to fill in the squares. If Evelyn, Theresa, Brenda, and Charlotte were present at a bridge party at Brenda's house on September 26, we put a cross opposite each of their names in the column that stands for this social event, and so on for the other events, until we end with a chart showing for a period of time which women were present at social events at which at least one of the others was also present.

The chart in its rough form will not reveal very much. (If you do not believe this, try making such a chart for yourself.) For one thing, the columns are probably arranged in the chronological order of events, and the women are probably in no particular order

[1] This is an example from actual field research: see A. Davis, B. Gardner, and M. R. Gardner, *Deep South*, 147-51. Fig. 11 is reproduced, with modifications, from this book, by permission of The University of Chicago Press, the publishers.

at all. But then we begin to reshuffle lines and columns. As far as columns are concerned, we put in the center the columns representing events, such as a meeting of the Parent-Teacher Association, at which a large number of the women were present, and we put toward the edges the columns representing the events, such

NAMES OF PARTICIPANTS	DATES OF EVENTS (MONTH AND DAY)													
	6/27	3/2	4/12	9/26	2/25	5/19	3/15	9/16	4/8	6/10	2/23	4/7	11/21	8/3
1. Evelyn	x	x	x	x	x	x		x	x					
2. Laura	x	x	x		x	x	x	x						
3. Theresa		x	x	x	x	x	x	x	x					
4. Brenda	x		x	x	x	x	x	x						
5. Charlotte			x	x	x		x							
6. Frances			x		x	x		x						
7. Eleanor					x	x	x	x						
8. Pearl						x		x	x					
9. Ruth						x		x	x	x				
10. Verne								x	x	x		x		
11. Myra									x	x	x	x		
12. Katherine									x	x	x	x	x	x
13. Sylvia							x	x	x	x	x	x	x	x
14. Nora						x	x		x	x	x	x	x	x
15. Helen							x	x		x	x	x		
16. Dorothy								x	x					
17. Olivia									x		x			
18. Flora									x		x			

Fig. 11. Social participation plotted
so as to reveal group membership

as supper parties, at which only a few of the women were present. As far as lines are concerned, we put together toward the top or bottom the lines representing those women that participated most often together in social events. A great deal of reshuffling may have to be done before any pattern appears.[2]

The final form of the chart is shown in Fig. 11. It reveals that there were some events, such as those of March 15, April 8, and

[2] For the logic of this method, see E. Forsyth and L. Katz, "A Matrix Approach to the Analysis of Sociometry Data," *Sociometry*, IX (Nov., 1946). 340-7.

September 16, at which most of the women were present. It also reveals that Laura, to take one example, participated more often in events at which Evelyn, Theresa, Brenda, Charlotte, and Frances were present than in events at which Nora was present, and that Nora participated more with Myra, Katherine, Sylvia, and Helen than with Laura. Count the participations and see. We can make the same kind of analysis for the other women, and we generalize these observations by saying that the eighteen women were divided into two groups. The pattern is frayed at the edges, but there is a pattern. The first seven women, Evelyn through Eleanor, were clearly members of one group; numbers 11 through 15, Myra through Helen, were just as clearly members of another. Some women participated about equally with both groups but not very much with either; Pearl is an example. And some participated, though not very often, only with the second group. Pearl, Olivia, Flora, and their like are marginal group members. There may be a sense in which all eighteen women formed a group, distinct from the other groups in the community, but that would take further research to find out.

It should be clear that a modification of this method could have been used—in fact, was used—to map out the two cliques in the Bank Wiring Observation Room and to divide the Bank Wiring group as a whole from the other groups in the department. It could probably be applied to any group whatever. So let us generalize the method to give us a definition of the word *group*. We have been looking at the persons that participated together in social events. Our word for "participating together" is *interaction:* a group is defined by the interactions of its members. If we say that individuals A, B, C, D, E . . . form a group, this will mean that at least the following circumstances hold. Within a given period of time, A interacts more often with B, C, D, E, . . . than he does with M, N, L, O, P, . . . whom we choose to consider outsiders or members of other groups. B also interacts more often with A, C, D, E, . . . than he does with outsiders, and so on for the other members of the group.[3] It is possible just by counting interactions to map out a group quantitatively distinct from others. This is

[3] See E. D. Chapple and C. S. Coon, *Principles of Anthropology*, 287.

what we do crudely in everyday life when we say that certain persons "see a lot of one another," "go around together," "work together," or "associate with one another," and that they make up a clique, a gang, a crowd, a group. We are saying that they interact frequently with one another, irrespective of the particular activities in which they interact.

A couple of further points about this definition need to be brought out. The definition certainly does not imply that a person belongs to only one group. That would run counter to common sense, and we are here to sharpen common sense, not to outrage it. In our stalking horse, the Hawthorne Plant, a wireman like Taylor (W3) was, in his working hours, a member of the Bank Wiring Observation Room and of clique A within it, but after working hours he was a member of other groups: his family, his church, his lodge, interacting in each of these groups only within limited spans of time.

Note also that our definition of the word *group* is relative: the meaning depends on what persons and groups one chooses to consider outsiders to the group in question. For some purposes we choose to consider cliques A and B in the Bank Wiring Room as groups in their own right, but they were at the same time subgroups of the Bank Wiring Room, which was itself a group. In like manner, the room itself was a subgroup of the department, and the department a subgroup of the Hawthorne Plant. But we have now pushed our definition too far. We are especially concerned with those groups—an older generation of sociologists called them primary groups—each member of which is able to interact with every other member.

The decision, then, as to what will be called a group and what a subgroup depends on the level at which we wish to make the analysis. This does not mean that the division between groups is merely conventional, that we can draw the line where we please. Given the reported facts, a sociologist could hardly cut the Bank Wiring Observation Room into cliques in any other way than Roethlisberger and Dickson did. The cliques were matters of observation, not convention. At whatever level we look at the web of interaction, it always shows certain thin places, and the lines between groups fall there. Any group with a population larger than two can be divided into subgroups, but even in a group of three persons, the question as to which pair makes the "company" and which individual the "crowd" cannot be settled by a flip of a coin.

Perhaps we have gone far enough in spelling out our definition of the word *group*. How much of any theory needs to be set down for the record beyond the possibility of misunderstanding—though anyone can misunderstand if he is bound he is going to—and how much left to the intelligence of the reader is always a hard question, but certainly the reader will be insulted if he is not allowed to do any independent thinking of his own. One point does need to be made clear. Saying that a group is defined by interaction is not the same thing as saying that interaction is the whole of group life. Every page of this book will tell about other elements that need to be taken into account. Unfortunately one has to begin, and begin somewhere. The charm of interaction for some sociologists is that it can be observed rather unambiguously, that it can in fact be counted. It may be a good place to start.

SYSTEM AND ENVIRONMENT

This definition of the group implies, and is meant to imply, that the group has a boundary and that outside the boundary lies the group's environment. A scheme of analysis that breaks down the phenomena being studied into organized wholes, or systems, and environments in which the systems exist has turned up again and again, and has again and again been found useful, in sciences as far apart as physics and biology. Sometimes the organized wholes can easily be identified; their boundaries are clear; they have skins. But even when the wholes are not so definitely marked off from the environment, much intellectual illumination is gained by stating what shall be taken as the boundary of the system—by drawing an imaginary line around it—and then studying the mutual relations between the system and its milieu. In thermodynamics—the study of phenomena such as hot, compressed gas in a cylinder—you may be able to say something about the energy generated by the system or the work done on the environment: energy and work are functions of the system as a whole. In biology and physiology

—the study of animal bodies—you may be able to show how the system, this time the living organism, reacts as a unit to changes in the environment. Whitehead says that the idea of an organized whole, or system, existing in an environment is "a fundamental concept which is essential to scientific theory." [4]

Our definition of the group draws a line between the systems we shall study and their different environments. The activities, interactions, and sentiments of the group members, together with the mutual relations of these elements with one another during the time the group is active, constitute what we shall call the *social system.* The rest of the book will be made up of detailed analyses of social systems. Everything that is not part of the social system is part of the environment in which the system exists. Note that, as the definition of the group is relative, so must be that of the group's environment. If the group we are interested in is the Bank Wiring Observation Room, then the rest of the Hawthorne Plant is part of its environment, but if the Hawthorne Plant itself should be the group in question, then the environment would become everything outside this new system.

Whenever we use the words *organized whole* or, still worse, *organism* in connection with groups and societies, we are laying ourselves open to misinterpretation. People will at once think we mean that a group is an organism like that most familiar one, the living body, and of course it is not. Organized wholes have some things in common with one another but also differ greatly among themselves, especially in the capacity to maintain a steady state in the face of changes in the environment. A thermodynamic system like hot coffee, cream, and sugar in a thermos bottle does pretty well in solving this problem, but only for a short time and for small changes in outside temperature. The healthy human body does very much better. Indeed the steady state kept by its internal organs sets it free to take aggressive action on the environment. Somewhere in between, if we were arranging systems in the scale of their *organicity,* would come social systems. The group is never quite passive. The various attempts to show that it is the mere creature of its surroundings have never been clinching, though

[4] A. N. Whitehead, *Science and the Modern World,* 68.

they have helped social scientists to be tough-minded. The demands of the environment cannot be disregarded, but they by no means wholly determine the constitution of the group. In fact, in the favorable instance, the group spontaneously evolves the behavior necessary to improve its standard of living in the environment. In the curious coincidence between the needs for survival and the organism's capacity to meet those needs, the group and the animal body are the same in kind if not in degree. The ability of the group to survive gross changes in its milieu seems less than that of the animal body, but both are struggling toward the free life.

THE NATURE OF THE ENVIRONMENT

We are getting too philosophical, though it is a man's philosophy that makes what he sees. In our standard procedure for analyzing social behavior, we ask first: What is the nature of the group's environment? and next: Given that the group is surviving in the environment, what are the limits that this condition places on the interactions, sentiments, and activities of the group? If you prefer the latter question in the form: What is the response of the group to the demands of the environment? you are welcome to it, but it is probably less rigorous. Answering these questions, in whatever form they are put, is the first step in the study of a social system.

The environment may be broken down into three main aspects: physical, technical, and social, all of which are interrelated, and any one of which may be more important than the others for any particular group. But let us get back to the Bank Wiring Observation Room, and first take the physical and technical aspects together. The men were working in a room of a certain shape, with fixtures such as benches, oriented in a certain way. They were working on certain materials with certain tools. These things formed the physical and technical environment in which the human relationships within the room developed, and they made these relationships more likely to develop in some ways than in others. For instance, the sheer geographical position of the men within the room had something to do with the organization of work and even with the appearance of cliques. In just the same way, we should begin with the physical and technical environment if we were studying some other kind of group, say a primitive tribe or a medieval village. Thus we might observe that the villagers worked in a cool, wet climate, on clay soils, using a wooden plow drawn by eight oxen to till the land for planting winter wheat. Then we should ask ourselves how these physical and technical factors helped determine the relationships between villagers. Note that we say "helped determine." Seldom does the environment wholly determine social relationships in the sense that, if the group is to survive, only *one* scheme of organization is possible.

As for the social environment, the Hawthorne Plant and the Western Electric Company in general was, through its supervisory force, an important influence on the wiremen. The management had chosen the men; it wanted them to accomplish results of a certain kind; it had an organization plan for reaching these results; it had a method of wage payment by group piecework, and so on. We do not need to repeat what we have said already. The management tried to put these plans into effect, and in a large measure succeeded, though not altogether. In output, in helping, in exchanging jobs much was going on in the room of which the higher-ups in the company would not have approved. In this respect, again, the environment set limits on the behavior of the group, which would certainly have been broken up if it had not conformed to the company's plans to some degree.

Another important influence—we cannot say which is the most important—came from the other workers that the wiremen met in the plant and department. Many of the ideas about the restriction of output must have been picked up from them. Important also was the Chicago of the early years of the depression, and so were the groups in which the men participated outside of their work. Their membership in families certainly had a direct effect on their behavior, particularly on their motives for work, and so did their looser membership in neighborhoods, social classes, and churches. We mention these aspects of the environment, not because we know enough about their effect on the wiremen, but because they ought to be looked at in the study of a group. We are not just analyzing

the environment of the Bank Wiring Observation Room but setting up a check list for future use.

Another and pervasive environmental influence on the Bank
Wiremen was *culture,* to use a word some anthropologists have
taken as their central concept. The wiremen were Americans, and
they were soaked in American culture: the values and norms of
American society. We shall have something to say about culture
later; it can be taken up most conveniently at another point in
the study of the social system, so let us say no more about it now,
except to underline its importance.

THE EXTERNAL SYSTEM

We have studied the nature of the environment and the kinds
of influence the environment may exert on the behavior of a group.
The environment and its influences will be different for each group
considered, but we are now focusing on the Bank Wiring Observation Room. We turn next from the environment to the behavior
of the group itself; we note that the group is, at the moment we
study it, persisting or surviving in its environment; and we infer,
not unnaturally, that the behavior of the group must be such as
to allow it to survive in the environment. Then we turn to the elements of group behavior: sentiment, activity, and interaction, and
we say that the *external system* is the state of these elements and of
their interrelations, so far as it constitutes a solution—not necessarily the only possible solution—of the problem: How shall the
group survive in its environment? We call it external because it
is conditioned by the environment; we call it a system because in
it the elements of behavior are mutually dependent. The external
system, plus another set of relations which we shall call the *internal system,* make up the total social system.

At the risk of anticipating some later steps in our argument, let
us take everyone into our confidence on what we are trying to do.
When we study a group, one of the first observations we can make
is that the group is surviving in an environment, and therefore we
say of the group, as of other organisms, that it is, for the moment
at least, adapted to its environment. But this word *adaptation* is
ambiguous. Does it mean that the characteristics of the group are

determined by the environment? No, it does not, for the second observation we can make is that the characteristics of the group are determined by two classes of factors and not one only. These characteristics are determined by the environment, in greater or lesser degree according to the nature of the environment and of the group in question, and also by what we shall call for the time being the internal development of the group. But we are not yet at the end of our difficulties, for the third observation we can make is that the two classes of factors are not independent of one another. Full explanation of our meaning will take the rest of this book, but we can outline our argument now. Assuming that there is established between the members of a group any set of relations satisfying the condition that the group survives for a time in its particular environment, physical and social, we can show that on the foundation of these relations the group will develop new ones, that the latter will modify or even create the relations we assumed at the beginning, and that, finally, the behavior of the group, besides being determined by the environment, will itself change the environment.

In short, the relationship between group and environment is essentially a relationship of action and reaction; it is circular. But perhaps it is safer to say that it sounds circular when described in words and sentences. When we describe a phenomenon in ordinary language, we are bound to start with a particular statement, going on from there to a sequence of further statements, and if the phenomenon is complex and organic, the sequence has a way of coming back sooner or later to the statement with which we started. No doubt a series of simultaneous equations could describe the characteristics of the group more elegantly than words and sentences can, but we do not yet have the equations, and it may be that the equations cannot be set up before the verbal description has been made. If, then, we are limited to ordinary language, and if the tendency of ordinary language is to make the analysis of complex organic wholes sound circular, we propose in this book to relax, to fall in with this tendency of language rather than fight against it, and to analyze the relationship between group and environment as if it were a process having a beginning and an end, even though the point at which the process ends may be the point from which it started. Let us be candid and admit the method is clumsy, though it may be the best we have.

Our method has many analogies in the verbal description of physical processes. In describing a group, our problem is, for instance, a little like the problem of analyzing without the help of mathematics what happens to a set of interlinked springs when one of them is compressed. How shall a man describe in words what happens to a set of springs in a cushion or mattress when he sits on them? If he begins by sitting on any one spring and tries to trace from there the changes that take place in the rest of the springs, he will always find that the last spring in the series is linked back to the first and prevents the first from giving way under his weight as much as he thought it would. This, in fact, is the virtue of the set of springs.

Now let us use a more complicated analogy. We are all more or less familiar with the operation of the gasoline, or internal-combustion, engine. Let us ask ourselves how the operation of this engine was originally explained to us, or, better, how we should go about explaining it to someone else. We should, perhaps, begin by considering only one cylinder, instead of all the cylinders a real engine would have, and we should, just to get our exposition going, assume the cylinder and its contents to be in a certain state. We might, for instance, assume that the piston has reached the top of its stroke, and that the mixture of air and gasoline above the piston is hot and compressed. From then on, we should describe the operations of the engine as proceeding in sequence. A spark explodes the hot mixture; the explosion drives the piston downwards, and the moving piston transmits turning energy to the shaft. As the shaft turns, a system of cams opens valves in the cylinder head that admit a fresh mixture and allow the burnt gas to escape. The turning shaft also causes the piston to rise once more in the cylinder, compressing and heating the fresh mixture; and we are back where we started from, except that we have yet to account for the spark that set the whole process going. A generator is turned by the shaft, and this generator produces the electric current that explodes the mixture in the cylinder. And so the process goes on as long as the gasoline holds out.

The point we want to make is that although these operations in fact take place in a continuing cycle, we must nevertheless, language being what it is, describe them as if they took place in a sequence having a beginning and an end. Therefore we must assume a certain state of affairs at the beginning of our exposition, the existence of which we can account for only at the end. Thus we assume at the beginning the hot, compressed gas and the spark that ignites it, but we cannot account for the gas being in the cylinder, and being heated, compressed, and ignited, until we have reached the end of our explanation. At our convenience, we can choose any point in the cycle as the point from which our exposition starts, but, whatever point we choose, the problem of describing a cycle as a sequence of events still remains.

Now a group is obviously not an internal-combustion engine—our analogy is *only* an analogy—but we shall analyze the characteristics of the group as if we were dealing with some kind of ongoing circular process. No doubt this is not the only way in which the group could be analyzed, and no doubt, once we have finished making our analysis in this way, we shall be able to adopt a better way and throw away the old, just as one discards the scaffolding that has surrounded a house during construction. But having adopted this method of exposition, we encounter the same kind of difficulty we encountered with the gasoline engine. In describing the circular process in ordinary language, we are at liberty to begin at whatever point in the process we choose, but no matter what point that is, we must still assume at the beginning of our description the existence of certain conditions that we can account for only at the end. We choose to begin the analysis of the group with the external system, which we have defined as a set of relations among the members of the group that solves the problem: How shall the group survive in its environment? We do not say that the external system is the only possible solution to the problem. We do not say either that the group could do no worse or that it could do no better and still survive. We merely say that the external system is *one* solution of the survival problem. For us it is the equivalent of the assumption we made in describing the gasoline engine that the mixture was originally hot and compressed and that a spark was ready to explode it. Then, having assumed that some set of relations such as the external system must exist, we shall go on, as we did with the gasoline engine, and try to show why they do in fact exist or why the assumed relations are modified. The emphasis had better be on modification, for there is one great difference between describing the gasoline engine and describing the group. With the gasoline engine we show how the later events in the cycle create the very conditions we assumed in the beginning, whereas with the group we shall show that the later events in the cycle may modify the conditions we assumed in the beginning. We shall have to allow scope for emergent evolution.

Thus the external system first gives us a set of initial conditions from which our exposition can take its departure and then takes account of the fact that the adaptation of the group to its environment is partly determined by the nature of the environment, while leaving us free later to show how this adaptation is also in part determined by the internal development of the group.

To return from the general problem to the particular group we are studying at the moment, the first question we ask of the Bank Wiring group is this: What does this group need to have in order to keep going in its particular environment? It needs motives (sentiments) on the part of its members, jobs (activities) for them to do, and some communication (interaction) between them. In other words, the members of the group must meet in some degree the plans of the Western Electric Company, and they must be adequately motivated to do so. We shall first take up each element of the external system separately and then in its mutual relations with the others. Until we have done this job we had better not try to define the external system any more rigorously. We must show, and not just say, what we mean.

SENTIMENT

The Bank Wiremen came to the Hawthorne Plant in the first instance with certain motives. The motives were generated by the circumstances of their lives outside the plant, but they were also part of their behavior within it. Some of the motives the men would have recognized: they were working for money, money to get food, to support a family, to buy and keep a car, to take a girl to the movies. These motives were the only ones the planners in the company took into account in devising the wage incentive scheme. Perhaps these were the only motives they thought they could successfully appeal to. At any rate, the men must have had many other reasons for working at Hawthorne that they might not have admitted so easily: a feeling that a man was not a fully self-respecting citizen unless he had a job, a desire for the prestige outside the factory that comes from working up to a good job within it, the wish to belong to a company that was said to be a good place to work, and so on. These are all, by our definition, sentiments, and these were the motives for work that the men brought to the Bank Wiring Observation Room. Whatever other sentiments their association with their fellow workers might release in the men, these would still have had to be satisfied in some degree. Man does not live by bread alone, but he lives by bread at least. These sentiments were assets to the company in that they led to hard work; they were liabilities in that the company had to satisfy them. Sentiment as an element of co-operation always has this double aspect.

The sentiments we have been talking about are part of what is often called individual self-interest. Let us be clear as to what we mean by this famous phrase. In the first place, it may be that all motives are motives of self-interest in the sense that, given the situation in which he is placed, a man always tries to do as well as he can for himself. What he does may look to outsiders as if it were hurting rather than helping him; it may look impossibly altruistic rather than selfish, and yet modern psychology teaches us that, if we knew the full situation, both the social relationships and the psychological dynamics of the person concerned, we should find all his actions to be self-enhancing. But this is an aside; let us take up the question from another point of view. If we examine the motives we usually call individual self-interest, we shall find that they are, for the most part, neither individual nor selfish but that they are the product of group life and serve the ends of a whole group not just an individual. What we really mean by the celebrated phrase is that these motives are generated in a different group from the one we are concerned with at the moment. Thus from the point of view of the Bank Wiring Observation Room, the desire of a man to earn wages was individual self-interest, but from the point of view of his family it was altruism. Motives of self-interest in this sense are the ones that come into the external system. Sentiments, on the other hand, that are generated within the group we are concerned with at the moment include some of the ones we call disinterested. Friendship between wiremen is an example. While sentiments of self-interest affected or influenced the behavior of the men in the room, they did not solely determine that behavior. If these sentiments had been alone decisive, output would perhaps have been higher. That both self-interest *and* something else are satisfied by group life is the truth that is hardest for the hard-boiled—and half-baked—person to see. As Mayo says, "If a number of individuals work together to achieve a common purpose, a harmony of interests will develop among them to which individual self-interest will be subordinated. This is a very different doctrine from the claim that individual self-interest is the solitary human motive." [5]

ACTIVITY

The activities of the group were in the first instance planned by the Western Electric Company engineers. Some of the men, with tools and fixtures, wired one kind of equipment; some of the men wired another. Some of the men soldered the connected wires into place on the terminals. Two men inspected the completed switches, both visually and with testing sets. A group chief supervised the whole. A trucker brought supplies into the room and took completed equipments out. Here were a number of different kinds of activity, ranging from manual work with tools through visual observation to activity that was largely verbal: supervision and direction. The activities were in theory different for different persons, and they were organized: each had a part in the production of a completed whole. Furthermore, the men were paid for their work in different amounts, according to a complicated system of group piecework. Note that the Western Electric organization tried to control more of the activities of the group than it was actually able to control. Nevertheless, it did to a very large extent settle what the men should do.

[5] E. Mayo, *The Political Problem of Industrial Civilization*, 21.

INTERACTION

In the same way, observing the behavior of the men, one could have mapped out a scheme of interaction among them, in abstraction from their sentiments and their activities, and one could have recognized that a part of the scheme was set by the company. There were the necessary interactions between a solderman and the three wiremen he worked for, between an inspector and the wiremen and soldermen whose work he passed judgment on, between the group chief and all the men in the room. Then there were the almost inevitable interactions between the men who were thrown together by the physical geography of the room, especially between the wiremen and soldermen who worked together, some at the front, some in the middle, and some at the back of the room. Finally, the mere fact that all the men were together in a single room tended to increase interaction between each member of the group and every other.

PAIR RELATIONSHIPS

So far we have been doing with the description of the Bank Wiring Observation Room no more than we did, two chapters back, with the description of the Irish countryman's family. We have, to be sure, limited ourselves to that part of group behavior that is under the direct influence of the environment, but within this field what we have been doing is the same. We have been making a crude analysis, breaking the behavior of the men down into its elements of sentiment, activity, and interaction. We shall now take a new step in the application of our method, the first step in synthesis. What has been separated must be put together again. We shall study the relationships of mutual dependence among sentiment, activity, and interaction in the external system. More particularly, we shall study the relationships between pairs of elements, of which there are, logically, three: sentiment-activity, activity-interaction, and interaction-sentiment.

There is nothing complicated about the idea of mutual dependence. Just the same, we had better say what we mean by it, as it will come into our thinking over and over again. In physics, Boyle's law states that the volume of a gas in an enclosed space varies inversely with the pressure upon it. The greater the pressure, the smaller the volume of the gas. This statement, which is usually put in the form of an equation, expresses a relationship of mutual dependence, mutual because if either pressure or volume changes, the other variable will change too. If pressure is increased, volume will decrease. But if we choose to begin with volume instead of pressure, we say that if volume increases, pressure must decrease. This kind of relationship is most elegantly expressed in an equation, but in the field of sociology we should not pretend to use equations until we have data that are thoroughly quantitive. Instead we shall have to describe this kind of relationship in ordinary language, and here we are at once in trouble, because this is just the kind of relationship that ordinary language—at least any of the Western languages—is least well equipped to describe. Ordinary language, with its subjects and predicates, is geared to handling only one independent factor and one dependent factor at a time: someone is always doing something to somebody. Cause-and-effect thinking, rather than mutual-dependence thinking, is built into speech. Yet a situation that can accurately be described in cause-and-effect terms is just the kind that is encountered least often in sociology. Here the cause produces an effect, but the effect reacts upon the cause. In these circumstances, the very first effort to use ordinary language shows how crude a tool it is. Yet we shall do what we can with it, as we have nothing else. We may, for instance, say that an increase in the complexity of the scheme of activity in the external system will bring about an increase in the complexity of the scheme of interaction, but that the reverse is also true. The two are mutually dependent.

One other point should be made but not elaborated at this time. According to Boyle's law, the volume of a gas in an enclosed space varies inversely as the pressure put upon it only if the temperature is held constant during the process. If the temperature does vary, the relationship between volume and pressure will not have the simple form stated by the law. When we study the mutual dependence of two variables, we must somehow take account of the effect on these two of the other variables that enter the system. In the same way, when we make a statement about the mutual dependence of, for instance, interaction and activity, we must never forget that sentiment also comes into the system and may effect the relationships described. It is never enough to say that the relationship holds good "other things being equal." We must try to say what these other things are, and where they are "equal." This raises immense problems, which we shall not try to cope with at this time, if indeed we can ever cope with them adequately in social science.

MUTUAL DEPENDENCE OF SENTIMENT AND ACTIVITY

When we are thinking of the relationship of mutual dependence between sentiment and activity, we speak of sentiments as motives or drives. In the simplest form of the relationship, a motive gives rise to activity, and once the activity is successfully completed, the motive disappears. A man feels hungry; he gets something to eat and his hunger disappears. If his activity does not result in his getting something to eat, new sentiments, which we call frustration, will be added to his original hunger, and we say that the activity was unrewarding or even positively punishing. He may then try a new one; if it ends in his getting something to eat, his hunger is allayed, and he will tend to repeat the activity the next time he feels hungry. We now say that the activity is rewarding, but do we mean anything more by this word than that we saw the man eat the food and repeat the activity leading to it?

This is the relationship at its simplest. It is much more complicated when the motive is not something like hunger but something like a man's fear that he will be hungry in the future. Suppose that a man is afraid he will be hungry in the future if he does not now start plowing his field and doing other tasks in co-operation with other men that will lead in the end to loaves of bread on his table. The man's hunger is allayed when he gets food, but the fear does not necessarily disappear when the appropriate activities are carried out. Future hunger is still a threat. In these circumstances, *both motives and associated activities persist, both continuously recreated, but if either side of the relationship is changed, the other will be affected.* Returning to our example, we can say that, if for any reason the man is less afraid he will be hungry, he may not

work so hard. And if, on the other hand, he finds some new set of
activities that will yield more food than the old, he may become
less fearful. The relationship between motive and activity is mutual.

This relationship seems to hold good whether the activity in
question is obviously and directly useful or, like magic, takes the
place of a useful activity that is unknown or impossible. In the
absence of anything better to do, men must find even magic rewarding. The relationship also seems to hold good both for the
sentiments we share with all men, such as fear, hunger, thirst,
cold, and the like, and for the sentiments generated in a particular
social situation, such as the need to be paid wages. Note how in
the Bank Wiring Observation Room the company's wage incentive
plan tried to establish a particularly close link between one sentiment (the desire for money) and one set of activities (production).
That the plan did not altogether achieve its intended results does
not mean that this link was unimportant. It means that other sentiments besides the need for money affected output. It is clear, for
instance, that the sentiments of Green (W9)—"I'd like a job reading"—, sentiments that presumably were generated by his whole past
history and experience in groups outside the plant, were among
the forces making his output the lowest in the room. If the interviews with the workers had been reported more fully, we should
know much more about the outside influences on the motives of
the men.

We need not go further into the mutual dependence of sentiment and activity. After all, most of the science of psychology, and
particularly that part called "learning theory," is devoted to studying it, and if we tried to compete with psychology our hopeless
inadequacy in that field would be revealed even more clearly than
it is already. All we can do is show how some of the problems
studied by psychology fit into a general scheme for analyzing group
behavior. Remember also that we are now considering only the
sentiments that come into the external system. The sentiments of
the internal system are rather different in kind, though their mutual dependence with activities is the same as that we have just
described.

MUTUAL DEPENDENCE OF ACTIVITY AND INTERACTION

In the external system, the relationship of mutual dependence between activity and interaction links the division of labor with the scheme of communication in the group. In the Bank Wiring Observation Room, the total job of turning out completed equipments was divided into a series of separate activities: wiring, soldering, inspection, trucking, and, not least in importance, supervision. Each separate activity was assigned to a different individual or subgroup, and in many of the activities each unit of work—for instance, completing a single level of connections—took a certain length of time. But what has been broken up must be put together again. If finished equipments were to be turned out, interaction had to take place in a certain scheme between the men doing the different jobs.

Thus when a wireman had completed a level on one equipment he moved over to a second one, and that act was the signal for the solderman to begin soldering in place the connections of the first terminal. The wireman had interacted with the solderman: remember that by our definition interaction takes place when the action of one man sets off the action of another. And note that, in this instance, the wireman originated interaction with the solderman: he gave the signal to which the other responded. We can without danger call interaction communication provided we remember that communication is not necessarily verbal. There was no need for words to pass between wireman and solderman in order that communication between them should be effective. In the same way, the solderman's completion of his part of the task was the signal for the inspector to go to work, and if he discovered any defect, he would initiate interaction, almost necessarily verbal this time, with the workman responsible. Thus a continuous process of interaction brought together the separate activities that went into the completion of the product. Finally, if one of the company's regulations was too flagrantly violated, or the process of co-ordination failed at any point, the problem would come to the group chief's attention. Someone would bring the matter up to him, or he himself would initiate interaction to restore the established order.

Generalizing from the Bank Wiring Observation Room, we can say, then, that any division, among the members of a group, of the partial activities that go into the completion of some total activity implies a scheme of interaction among the persons concerned, and that *if the scheme of activities is changed, the scheme of interaction will, in general, change also, and vice versa.* The two are mutually dependent. Sometimes, and this is perhaps the more common situation, a man who is organizing a piece of work begins by dividing it up into separate activities, and then makes the scheme of interaction conform to his division. That is, he treats the scheme of activity as the independent or governing factor. Thus the management of a plant may decide how an operation shall be divided among the workers and then devise an appropriate method of co-ordination. But this presupposes that an appropriate method of co-ordination can be put into effect, and the presupposition may be wrong. That is, the scheme of interaction may sometimes be the governing factor. Surely certain forms of the division of labor among the members of an industrial group were prohibitively expensive in the days before the conveyor belt was invented and made new schemes of interaction possible. In most circumstances, *both* factors are important.[6]

The division of labor makes the cost of work less in human effort or money. For this reason all societies have gone some distance in making their members specialists. From Adam Smith to Henry Taylor the uncriticized assumption was apt to be that the further the division was carried, the greater were the savings effected, that the further a job like shoemaking was broken down into its component specialties, and each assigned to a workman who did nothing else, the less would be the cost of making the shoe. Now we have begun to understand that the division of labor, like any other process, has its point of diminishing returns. Peter Drucker has shown how, in World War II and in some kinds of industrial work where conventional assembly lines could not be set up, the assigning of all the component specialties of any one job to one person or a group of persons, rather than to a number of separate individuals, turned out to be a cheaper way of manu-

[6] In this and the following discussion, much reliance is placed on C. I. Barnard, *The Functions of the Executive*, ch. VIII.

facturing than any other.[7] Why the division of labor may reach a point of diminishing returns should be clear from our analysis. The division of labor is not something in itself; it always implies a scheme of interaction by which the different divided activities are co-ordinated. The indirect costs of setting up this scheme, including the costs that arise if supervision is inadequate, may offset the direct savings from specialization.

THE PYRAMID OF INTERACTION

What we said two paragraphs ago we must now take back in part. It is not universally true that as the scheme of activity changes, the scheme of interaction will change too. It is not true when the activity in question is supervision or leadership: the process by which departures from a given plan of co-operation are avoided or new plans introduced. In groups that differ greatly in the activities they carry on, the schemes of interaction between leaders of different levels and their followers tend nevertheless to be strikingly similar. Let us see what this means by taking up the problem of the *span of control,* as organization experts call it: How many men can be supervised by a single leader? When the activities of a group are of such a kind that they can be co-ordinated largely through one-way interaction from the leader to the followers, then the leader can supervise a rather large number of persons. An example is the conductor of a symphony orchestra, who may direct as many as a hundred men. But in general the interaction must be two-way: the leader gives orders, information, and exhortation to his followers, but they must also supply him with information about themselves and the situation they face. In these circumstances the span of control becomes much smaller. It is significant how often a group of between eight and a dozen persons crops up under the supervision of a single leader in organizations of many different kinds. The old-fashioned squad in the army is an example. And since the same kind of considerations govern the relations between the leaders of the first level and their own leaders, and so on for higher and higher leaders in groups of larger and

[7] P. F. Drucker, "The Way to Industrial Peace," *Harper's Magazine,* Vol. 193 (Nov., 1946), 390.

larger size, it is easy to see how the scheme of interaction, especially in big organizations, piles up into its characteristic pyramidical, or hierarchical, form. The leader-in-chief appears at the apex of the pyramid, working with a small group of lesser leaders; each lesser leader, level by level, works with his own small group of leaders of still lower rank, until finally at the broad base the rank and file are reached.

No matter what activities an organization carries on, this characteristic form of the interaction scheme tends to appear; it appears in the Catholic Church as surely as it does in an industrial firm or an army. Therefore we must modify our earlier rule and say that *whatever changes occur in the scheme of activities of a group, the scheme of interaction between the leaders of various levels and their followers tends to keep the same general pyramidical form.* Yet the modification is more apparent than real. If the conflict between the two rules distresses us, we can readily reconcile them. The pyramid scheme of interaction seems to make possible the supervision of the activities of a large number of persons, through two-way interaction between them and leaders of different levels. Whenever, therefore, this particular activity, supervision, remains largely the same from organization to organization, then the scheme of interaction—the pyramid—through which supervision is exercised remains largely the same too. Our rule stated that if the scheme of activity changed, the scheme of interaction changed too. But the rule also implies that if the activity does not change—and the job of supervision is much the same from group to group—the interaction does not change either. The first rule holds after all, the second rule being merely one of its special cases.

The relation between the scheme of activities and the scheme of interaction in an organization is usually represented by the familiar organization chart, which shows the organization divided into departments and subdepartments, the various officers and subofficers occupying boxes, connected by lines to show which persons are subordinate to what other ones. Every such chart is too neat; it tells what the channels of interaction ought to be but not always what they are. The pyramid-type chart is particularly misleading because it shows only the interaction between superiors and subordinates, the kind of interaction that we shall call, following Barnard, *scalar*.[8] It does not show the interaction that goes on between two or more persons at about the same level of the organization, for instance, between two department heads or, in the Bank Wiring Room, between a wireman and an inspector. This kind of interaction we shall call *lateral* interaction, though we must remember there are borderline cases where the distinction between scalar and lateral interaction disappears. The conventional organization chart represents the scalar but not the lateral interaction. If it were not for the unhappy association with predatory spiders, the facts would be much better represented by a web, the top leader at the center, spokes radiating from him, and concentric circles linking the spokes. Interaction takes place along the concentric circles as well as along the spokes. But even the web is too neat a picture.

It is a mistake to think of the pyramid—or the web—scheme of interaction as always created by conscious planning. It is so created in only a few instances, for example, the large formal organizations of modern Western society, and these, in their origins, modeled themselves on previously existing patterns. The pyramid occurs not only where it is planned, as in the Western Electric Company, but also where it is not planned, as in a street gang or primitive tribe. Sometimes the pyramid is imposed on a group, as supervision was imposed on the Bank Wiremen; sometimes, as we shall see, a group spontaneously creates its own pyramid. Sometimes a group, if it is to operate successfully on the environment, needs the pyramid; sometimes a group does not need the pyramid but creates it anyhow. In any event, the fact that a pyramid of interaction may be a practical necessity of effective operations on the environment is no guarantee that the pyramid will appear. As we mentioned earlier, the possibility of coincidence between the practically necessary and the spontaneously produced is one of the fascinating discoveries that comes from the study of groups as of other organisms, but we shall never explain the existence of the pyramid of interaction or any other such item of group behavior by pointing out that it helps the group to survive in an environment. Even

[8] C. I. Barnard, *Organization and Management*, 150.

if we assume for the moment that it does help the group to survive, we shall sooner or later go on to examine in detail the mechanisms by which the item in question is produced. We shall study what the philosophers call efficient, rather than final, causes. But we are again running ahead of our argument. The immediate point is that the principles of organization are universal; they are not an invention of the Prussian general staff or of American big business.

The relationship between the scheme of activities and the scheme of interaction is the problem of *organization,* in the narrow sense of that word. When the leaders of military, industrial, and other concerns speak of organization, this is what they mean. For us the word has a much broader meaning, but the narrow one will do no harm so long as we know what it is. Since our concern is with the small group, we had better not try to attain the higher reaches of organization theory, which apply only to large concerns. But one last point should be made. The complexity of organization does not end with the appearance of the hierarchy of leadership. In big concerns, several different hierarchies arise and intersect one another. The pyramid, from being two-dimensional, becomes three- and multi-dimensional, with several different chains of interaction between the followers and the upper leaders. In the jargon of the experts, a line-and-staff form of organization develops, and we shall have something to say about it in a later chapter, where the subject comes in naturally. For the moment we can summarize in the words of Eliot Chapple and Carleton Coon: "The coordination needed in any complex technique is impossible without interaction. As we have seen, most complex techniques involve the activities of more than one person, and, in fact, where people practice a number of complex techniques, extensive interactions must take place to coordinate the work of manufacturing, to secure raw materials, and to exchange the goods produced. In other words, the growth of complexity in technical processes goes hand in hand with an increase in the amount of interaction and in the complexity of the interaction pattern." [9]

[9] E. D. Chapple and C. S. Coon, *Principles of Anthropolgy,* 250.

CONCLUSION

Logically, of course, a third relationship of mutual dependence exists: the mutual dependence of interaction and sentiment, but we shall choose to consider this a part of the internal system, to which we turn in the next chapter. The two aspects of group life that we call the external and the internal systems are continuous with one another. The line between them can be drawn where we choose, arbitrarily, and we choose to draw it here. The only reason for drawing a line at all is to save words: we now can talk about the external system without repeating everything we have said in this chapter.

What goes into the external system is what we have shown goes in: the best definition is a process of pointing. If we must have a definition in words, we can say that the mutual dependence between the work done in a group and the motives for work, between the division of labor and the scheme of interaction, so far as these relationships meet the condition that the group survives in an environment—this we shall regularly speak of as the external system. But remember that when we talk of a group's survival in an environment we always deceive ourselves to some degree. The group is not passive before the environment; it reacts. It even defines what its environment shall be. Its purposes make different aspects of the environment important. The relationship between group and environment is never a one-way matter. But we are weak creatures, and our tools of language and analysis are soft. We ought to say everything at once, yet in our desperation we find we have to start somewhere. We have chosen to begin with the environment and its influence on the group. We shall then show how the group, on the foundation of the relationships thus established, elaborates further tendencies of its own, which react so as to modify the adaptation to the environment. This again is not the truth, but a manner of speaking. Yet it is forced on us. What we need now is a willing and provisional suspension of disbelief. Until we have said everything, we shall have said nothing. We shall have to keep many balls in the air at the same time. Regard all our statements as partial truths until the last word and the last modification are in.

CHAPTER 5

The Internal System: The Group as a Whole

The Elaboration of Group Behavior . . . Mutual Dependence of Interaction and Sentiment . . . The Nature of the Hypotheses . . . Mutual Dependence of Sentiment and Activity . . . Mutual Dependence of Activity and Interaction . . . Elaboration and Standardization . . . Norms . . . Culture . . . The Relation of Norms to Behavior . . . Assumptions or Values . . . Technical, Social, and Religious Systems

LONG AGO Aristotle wrote: "The city comes into existence in order that men may live; it persists that they may live well." [1] For Aristotle the city meant the small Greek city-state, such as Athens, which was much closer to the small group we are studying in this book than to the mass cities of modern times. At least the members of the governing class could have some direct contact with one another. For Aristotle the city was also the most familiar and important of organized human groups, and much that he says about it, including the remark just quoted, applies to all human groups. Elton Mayo used to make Aristotle's point in different language. He said that there is a tendency for any group of men to complicate the conditions of their life, to make the conditions more interesting, and that any circumstances interfering with the complication were felt emotionally as frustration. Chester Barnard's statement is still more elaborate.

When the individual has become associated with a cooperative enterprise he has accepted a position of contact with others similarly associated. From this contact there must arise interactions between these persons individually, and these interactions are social. It may be, and

[1] *Politics,* I, 1, 1252b12.

often is, true that these interactions are not a purpose or object either of the cooperative systems or of the individuals participating in them. They nevertheless *cannot be avoided*. Hence, though not sought, such interactions are consequences of cooperation, and constitute one set of social factors involved in cooperation. These factors operate on the individuals affected; and, in conjunction with other factors, become incorporated in their mental and emotional characters. This is an effect which makes them significant. Hence, cooperation compels changes in the motives of individuals which otherwise would not take place. So far as these changes are in a direction favorable to the cooperative system they are resources to it. So far as they are in a direction unfavorable to cooperation, they are detriments to it or limitations of it.[2]

THE ELABORATION OF GROUP BEHAVIOR

Each of these men—Aristotle, Mayo, Barnard—is talking about the same phenomenon. When a number of persons have come together to form a group, their behavior never holds to its first pattern. Social life is never wholly utilitarian: it elaborates itself, complicates itself, beyond the demands of the original situation. The elaboration brings changes in the motives of individuals. This is the point that Barnard stressed especially; and the change in the attitudes of persons, brought about by their membership in groups, is perhaps the central topic of social psychology. But the elaboration also means changes in their activities and interactions—changes, in fact, in the organization of the group as a whole.

This elaboration is the subject of the present chapter and the one following. In the last chapter we studied the *external system* —the behavior of a group so far as that behavior represents one possible answer to the question: How does the group survive in its particular environment? In the present chapter we shall begin the study of the *internal system*—the elaboration of group behavior that simultaneously arises out of the external system and reacts upon it. We call the system "internal" because it is not directly conditioned by the environment, and we speak of it as an "elaboration" because it includes forms of behavior not included under the heading of the external system. We shall not go far wrong if,

[2] Reprinted by permission of the publishers from Chester Irving Barnard, *The Functions of the Executive*, Cambridge, Mass.: Harvard University Press, 1938, p. 40. See also pp. 45, 52, 120, 286.

for the moment, we think of the external system as group behavior that enables the group to survive in its environment and think of the internal system as group behavior that is an expression of the sentiments towards one another developed by the members of the group in the course of their life together.

In analyzing the internal system, we shall, as before, use the Bank Wiring Observation Room to illustrate our points, and we shall do so according to a definite plan. In the present chapter we shall take up the internal system as exemplified in the behavior of the group as a whole; in the next chapter we shall take it up as exemplified in the division of the group into cliques. In Chapter 3 we saw that the group was in some sense a unit and in some sense also a grouping of sub-units.

We shall again work with the three main elements of group behavior: activity, sentiment, and interaction, but in describing the internal system we shall find that these elements do not take quite the same form they do in the external system. Instead of the motives for getting a job, we shall have to deal with sentiments developed on the job, such as liking or disliking for other persons, approval or disapproval of the things other persons do. Instead of activities demanded by the job, we shall have to deal with activities spontaneously evolved that serve to express the attitudes of persons toward one another. And instead of interactions required for the co-ordination of practical activities, we shall have to deal with interaction elaborated socially—for fun, so to speak. We call the internal system a system, just as we called the external system one, because in it all three of the elements of social behavior are mutually dependent, and we shall, as before, take account of the mutual dependence by considering three pair relations: interaction-sentiment, sentiment-activity, and activity-interaction.

MUTUAL DEPENDENCE OF INTERACTION AND SENTIMENT

By the very circumstances in which they were placed, working together in the same room, the Bank Wiremen almost inevitably interacted with one another. They were, as we often say, thrown together. In our description of the external system, we did not go beyond statements like this, but the internal system takes up where the other leaves off. Interaction in the external system gives rise to sentiments that we treat as part of the internal system because they are not brought into the group by its members but released in the members by their life in the group. Specifically the Bank Wiremen, interacting with one another frequently, also became friendly. No doubt there were social isolates in the group, like Capek (W5) and Mazmanian (I3), and no doubt the specially close friends were also members of the same clique, but it is all too easy in emphasizing the cliques and the anti-social individuals to lose sight of the wide-spread friendliness within the group as a whole. The relationship between association and friendliness is one of those commonly observed facts that we use all the time as a guide for action in practical affairs but seldom make an explicit hypothesis of sociology. We assume that if only we can "get people together," they will like one another and work together better. We also assume that the relationship between interaction and sentiment works in the other direction. If it is true that we often come to like the persons with whom we interact, it is also true that we are prepared to interact with persons we already like. That is, interaction and this particular kind of sentiment are mutually dependent.

Now let us try to make the hypothesis a little more explicit. We can begin by saying that *persons who interact frequently with one another tend to like one another.* But this does not do justice to the quantitative and relative aspects of the relationship. Our words "like" and "dislike," "friendship" and "antagonism," are misleading. They make us think that there are only two values on the scale. We should think instead of a continuous gradation from hatred to love, with our usual words for the sentiments representing many different values on the scale. And even if we think in these terms, we are still in difficulties. When we say that Hasulak (W7) liked Steinhardt (S1) and disliked Mueller (W2), we may only mean that he liked Steinhardt more than he liked Mueller. If forced to choose between Mueller and some outsider as a companion, he might have found that he liked Mueller well enough. All our words for liking and disliking have relative and not absolute values. We cannot say how much Hasulak liked the men he knew, unless we have determined a zero point on the scale, a point, perhaps, where one man is indifferent, neither friendly nor hostile, to another. Setting up such a point and measuring the strength of sentiment with reference to it is not an easy task, as the social psychologists who study attitudes know, and we shall not undertake it here. Instead we shall allow for the quantitative aspect of sentiment and the other elements of social behavior by stating some of our hypotheses in differential form; for instance, by stating what small change will take place in the strength of sentiment if there is a small change in the frequency of interaction. Thus we can restate our original hypothesis as follows: *If the frequency of interaction between two or more persons increases, the degree of their liking for one another will increase, and vice versa.* This kind of hypothesis takes account of the fact that some sentiments form a scale without raising the question where the zero point on the scale lies. We should probably state all our later hypotheses in differential form, but we shall not in fact be tediously careful to do so.

But our hypothesis still does not take adequate account of the facts of group behavior. It does not take account of group elaboration or development. For instance, it is not hard to think of the original relationships among the Bank Wiremen being those of the external system. The members of the group began by being thrown together in a certain room and working on certain jobs. But obviously the observed behavior of the Bank Wiremen went far beyond the original plan of work set up by the company. How shall we describe the process of growth and development? We can at least reformulate our hypothesis as follows: *If the interactions between the members of a group are frequent in the external system, sentiments of liking will grow up between them, and these sentiments will lead in turn to further interactions, over and above the interactions of the external system.* The interactions between Bank Wiremen were in fact more frequent than the setup of work required. It is not just that favorable sentiments increase as interaction increases, but that these sentiments then boost interaction still further. Our theory is that through processes like these a social system builds up or elaborates itself. But how far can the elaboration go? Clearly it cannot go on indefinitely; there must be forces bringing it to a halt; for one thing, the limitations of time will prevent the frequency of interaction from going beyond a certain level.

But what is the level and what determines it? We raise these questions without being able to answer them.

A further complication can now be brought in. It was observed that the Bank Wiremen, after a time in the Observation Room, found themselves to some degree antagonistic toward the men remaining behind in the department, and that they expressed their antagonism in claims that the men in the department were in various small matters discriminating against them. In this instance, then, as in so many others, the liking of friends within a group carries with it some dislike of outsiders. The greater the inward solidarity, the greater the outward hostility. As before, this hypothesis is familiar. It is almost the principle of organization in some primitive tribes. A dictator may try to use it, believing that if he can cut down his subjects' interaction with, and inflame their distrust of, foreigners, he can maintain his own power and a primitive unity in his nation. Stated more precisely, the hypothesis is that *a decrease in the frequency of interaction between the members of a group and outsiders, accompanied by an increase in the strength of their negative sentiments toward outsiders, will increase the frequency of interaction and the strength of positive sentiments among the members of the group, and vice versa.* This hypothesis is in turn a special case of a more general one, which we shall consider later and which may be stated as follows: *the nature of the relationships between the individuals A, B, C, . . . is always determined in part by the relationships between each one of them and other individuals M, N, O, . . .* In the present case, A, B, C, etc., are members of a particular group; M, N, O, etc., are outsiders, and we are considering, in the relationships between these persons, only the elements of interaction and sentiment.

THE NATURE OF THE HYPOTHESES

The hypothesis that an increase of interaction between persons is accompanied by an increase of sentiments of liking among them is one of those analytical statements about the behavior of human groups that it is an aim of this book to make. Underneath their obvious differences, human groups are alike—this is our belief—in that some parts of their behavior will sooner or later be summed up in a series of such hypotheses, though it may be a very long series. Perhaps, then, we need to take a little time to explain the nature and limitations of a hypothesis of this kind.

In the first place, let us be clear that it is only a hypothesis, not a theorem. We have offered no proof, except what is provided by the behavior of the Bank Wiremen, and a statistician would say that a single instance is not nearly enough. Plenty of confirmatory evidence could be found in anthropological and sociological studies of small groups. What is more important, the hypothesis could conceivably be tested by an experiment using modern methods of measuring interaction and attitude. In fact one of our aims is to state hypotheses in such a way that they can be tested by experiment. To quote Willard Gibbs once more: "It is the office of theoretical investigation to give the form in which the results of experiment may be expressed."

In the second place, we do not pretend that the hypothesis is original with us. Why should it be? Men have not been studying atoms for thousands of years, but they have been studying their own behavior, and passionately too. We have no doubt that they have intuitively known and acted upon all the hypotheses we shall present. Many of the hypotheses have also been explicitly stated in the literature of social science. The relationship expressed in our present hypothesis is, for instance, a part of the phenomenon that sociologists call "in-group solidarity." Make no mistake about it—we are not trying to be original here. Our aim is of another kind. We are trying to develop a general sociology, and therefore, on the assumption that the most familiar phenomena are apt to be the most general, the banal and obvious hypotheses are just the ones we want to state. We are also trying to state the hypotheses in such a way that the observations to which the words in the hypotheses refer are unmistakable—something which, we submit, is not true of "in-group solidarity." And we are, finally, trying to state the hypotheses in a language or conceptual scheme common to them all, so that their relationship to one another is explicit and they form a coherent series, each one illuminating the others instead of wasting its light in isolation. Unless we do all of these things we shall never have the foundations on which a developing science of sociology can be built. Too easily have sociologists assumed that the foundations were already laid, for there are still good reasons for asking the question: What single general proposition about human behavior have we *established?* And we shall find ourselves waiting for an answer.

In the third place, in stating that an increase of interaction between persons is accompanied by an increase of sentiments of friendliness between them, we have offered no explanation why this should be so. Perhaps we could begin to make an explanation. "Friendliness" unquestionably conceals a complicated process. For one reason or another, you associate with someone for a period of time; you get used to him; your behavior becomes adjusted to his, and his to yours; you feel at home with him and say he is a good fellow. The friendliness may be no more than the emotional reflection of adjustment, and it is perhaps for this reason that your liking for someone is so often independent of his personality. You can get to like some pretty queer customers if you go around with them long enough. Their queerness becomes irrelevant. Along such lines as these we might begin to make an explanation, but even if we make none our hypothesis is not invalidated. A hypothesis sums up certain facts; so long as it does so it stands, whatever the explanation of the facts may be. For instance, the force of gravitation was long used to "explain" such things as the path of a planet around the sun. Then the physicists saw that they could, by Newton's laws, simply *describe* the paths of the planets and the motions of many other bodies, without invoking any gratuitous explanation such as "gravitation." The science of mechanics "dropped the question as to the 'why' and inquired into the 'how' of the many motions that can be observed." [3] In a much less exact manner than mechanics we ask how the elements of interaction and sentiment are related, and drop the question why they are related in a particular way. No doubt a more general hypothesis than ours will provide the explanation, but it will do so by including or subsuming ours as a special case and not by invalidating it. Only fact can invalidate.

Finally, this hypothesis, like all our hypotheses, holds good only so long as "other things are equal." Nothing is vaguer than this

[3] E. Mach, *The Science of Mechanics*, T. J. McCormack, trans., 155.

commonplace phrase. In order to make sense of it, we need to know
what the "other things" are and what we mean by their being
"equal." We have conceptually isolated interaction and sentiment
in order to investigate the relationship between the two, but in
real social behavior interaction and sentiment cannot be isolated
from the third element, activity, and from other factors we have
not yet considered. Activity is one of the "other things." Two persons that interact with one another tend to like one another only
if the activities each carries on do not irritate the other too much.
If either of them behaves in an irritating way, the mere fact of
bringing them together, increasing their interaction, may increase
negative rather than positive sentiments. Interaction and friendliness are positively associated, not on the assumption that the element of activity is out of the concrete phenomenon, for we know
it comes in, but rather that this element is at least emotionally
neutral.

Again, interaction and friendliness are positively associated only
if authority is not one of the "other things" and does not enter the
situation being considered. When two men are working together
and one is the boss of the other, as, for instance, when a son is
working for his father on an Irish farm, the interaction between
them, required by the job they are doing together, may be frequent, and yet the superior and the subordinate will scarcely become friends. Instead their sentiments toward one another are apt
to be ambivalent, and ambivalent for a perfectly good reason: two
influences are at work and not just one. There may be an element
of friendliness in the feelings of the subordinate or perhaps, if
the boss is capable and wise, one of admiration, but there is also
an element of constraint, respect, or even awe, which seems to
derive from the authority the boss exercises over the subordinate.
Moreover, the interaction between the two, instead of tending to
increase, is held close to the amount strictly required for "business"
—that is, to the amount required by the external system. This kind
of behavior we can observe in the Irish farm family; we can observe it also in different degrees wherever authority is strong, as
in armies and on ships. We shall have much to say about it later,
but one point cannot be made too strongly at the outset. To have
authority it is by no means enough that a man should give orders

to others. He must give orders that they will obey, and the process by which obedience to orders is secured is not a simple one. In studying it we shall be led into the whole problem of social control.

Interaction is accompanied by friendliness among the members of a group only if the group as a whole is maintaining itself in its environment. If the group fails in its purposes and starts to break up, its disintegration will be hastened by the increasing antagonisms and mutual incriminations of the members. On the other hand, the warmth of feeling between companions may be vastly heightened by their joint and successful confrontation of a dangerous environment.[4] Hence the particularly intimate fellowship of shipmates, of fliers who are squadronmates or crewmates, of partners working underground in a coal mine. In short, certain characteristics of the group as a whole may modify in one way or another each one of the relationships within the group.

We have brought forward a number of factors—and there must be others—that may modify the relationship between interaction and sentiment expressed in our hypothesis. Some of these factors, such as authority, tend to nullify the relationship: frequent interaction is not accompanied by friendliness. Others, such as the successful confronting of danger, tend to make interaction especially frequent and sentiment especially intense. The fact that these "other things" cannot be disregarded in the behavior of many groups does not invalidate our hypothesis, but does require that the influence of these factors be stated in further hypotheses. These become, with the original one, a series or system of hypotheses in which the degree of applicability of any one hypothesis to any particular group is limited by the applicability of all the others. In this book we are trying to set up such a series of hypotheses, or make a start at doing so. What we have had to say about one of them applies to all the others and need not be repeated. The logical problem we are wrestling with is, in the end, the mathematical problem of setting up and solving a system of differential equations. Our system cannot be as elegant as that, but it can at least take the mathematical system as a model of what it would like to be.

[4] R. R. Grinker and J. P. Spiegel, *Men under Stress*, 21-5.

MUTUAL DEPENDENCE OF SENTIMENT AND ACTIVITY

In the Bank Wiring Observation Room group as a whole, we can see the mutual dependence of sentiment and activity most easily in the wide web of helping. There were few occasions when helping another man was required by the necessities of the work —indeed it was forbidden by the company; yet it took place just the same, and many of the men testified that helping and being helped made them feel better. Everyone took part in helping; it was not confined, as were some other activities, to soldering units. In fact it was one of the activities that united the whole group instead of dividing it into cliques, though there were some men, like Taylor (W3), who were helped more than others. On the basis of the Bank Wiring Room, we can, therefore, state the hypothesis that *persons who feel sentiments of liking for one another will express those sentiments in activities over and above the activities of the external system, and these activities may further strengthen the sentiments of liking.* In the same way persons who dislike one another will express their disliking in activity, and the activity will increase the disliking. The circle may be vicious as well as beneficent. Stating the relationship quantitatively, we can expect that any change in the sentiments of persons for one another will be followed by a change in the activities in which they express those sentiments. And the reverse will also be true: any change in the expressive activities—for instance, in the amount of help given— will be followed by a change in the sentiments of liking.

All sentiment seeks expression in action, and if the action is rewarding it will be repeated. The mechanism we are describing here is universal; it applies to the external system as much as it does to the internal. But in the external system the sentiments being expressed are those a person brings to the group from his life outside the group, whereas in the internal system the sentiments—favorable or unfavorable attitudes toward other members of the group —are generated or released in a person by his experience within the group. The activities in which the latter sentiments find expression may be of many kinds. In the Bank Wiring Room they took the form of mutual help. In other groups we shall see other ways of exchanging gifts and favors, and we shall see the appearance of new co-operative activities undertaken by the group as a whole.

MUTUAL DEPENDENCE OF ACTIVITY AND INTERACTION

The intimate relation between activity and interaction is obvious, here as in the external system. In fact it takes an uncomfortable effort of mind to separate them only to put them together again. In the Bank Wiring Room an activity like helping clearly implied interaction between the persons who helped one another and, moreover, an increase of interaction beyond what the wiring job demanded. The process is general. A great deal of social activity —dances, parties—is enjoyed less for the sake of the activity itself, which may be trivial, than for the possibilities of social interaction it affords.

ELABORATION AND STANDARDIZATION

In describing the mutual dependence of sentiment, interaction, and activity in the internal system, we have so far been exclusively concerned with what we may call the *mode of elaboration.* Interaction between persons leads to sentiments of liking, which express themselves in new activities, and these in turn mean further interaction. The circle is closed, and by the very nature of the pair relations the whole system builds itself up. How far it can build itself up we do not know, and of course it can build itself down. If for any reason interaction in the internal system decreased, then activity would decay and sentiments of friendliness weaken. In describing the process we could begin with any other one of the elements instead of interaction, but the important point is that the circle, or better the spiral, can be vicious as well as beneficent. The same relationships that cement the group may dissolve it, provided the process once gets going in the wrong direction. In most groups there is a precarious balance between the two tendencies.

We have been emphasizing the appearance of new sentiments, activities, and interactions. In the internal system there is another kind of development, which we may call the *mode of standardization,* and which we mention here, not because we have evidence from the Bank Wiring group as a whole to illustrate it, but because of its general importance. *The more frequently persons interact with one another, the more alike in some respects both their activities and their sentiments tend to become.* Moreover, the more a person's activities and sentiments resemble those of others, the more likely it is that interaction between him and these others will increase. The process as usual works both ways. Whatever may be the explanation of this relationship—and it may not be necessary to assume a general tendency to imitate—the relationship exists. The social climber knows all about it and, consciously or unconsciously, uses it for all it is worth. He wishes intimate and frequent interaction with members of a certain social class. When he has that, he will by definition be a member himself. To gain this end, he models his behavior and attitudes on those of the members of the class. So far as he is successful in doing so, social interaction will follow. On the other hand, the more extensive his interaction, the more extensive will be his awareness of the "right" activities and sentiments, and therefore his ability to imitate. These connections hold good even if the class members pride themselves on their unconventionality. The unconventional can be as conventional as anything else.

A spectacular example of the mode of standardization is given by another one of the Western Electric researches, the so-called Relay Assembly Test Room. In this room, five young women sat in a row at a bench doing identical work: assembling small electrical relays. Each relay took only about a minute to complete, and the output and output rate of each girl was measured precisely over a period of years. Many interesting understandings came out of the Relay Assembly Test Room; we need only speak of one of them. The work required such concentration that social interaction —conversation—was easily possible only for those girls who sat next to one another. For certain spans of time, and for certain pairs of girls who were both neighbors and close friends, not only was the output of each girl practically identical with that of the other, but also the fluctuations of their output rates correlated to an astonishing degree. Each relay was turned out in so short a time that deliberate correlation was impossible: the correlation was unconscious. Moreover, when the seating order was changed, the former pair correlations almost disappeared, and though later, while close friends were still sitting apart, the correlations showed a tendency to build up again, they never reached their former extent.[5] Here we can see clearly the relation between interaction, sentiment, and the standardization of activity. In fact this group can be analyzed in exactly the same way as the Bank Wiremen. The only reason we do not do so here is that the group looks far more artificial, far less like real life, though its behavior has the advantage of being describable in more nearly precise quantitative terms.

Just as friendliness within a group tends to be accompanied by some degree of hostility toward outsiders, so the similarity in the sentiments and activities of the members of a group tends to be accompanied by some dissimilarity between their sentiments and activities and those of outsiders. A mode of standardization is always matched by a mode of differentiation, and we shall pay special attention to this fact when we analyze the cliques within the Bank Wiring Observation Room. There are forces making for difference as well as forces making for uniformity, and real behavior is a balance between the two.

NORMS

So far we have been behaviorists: we have looked at observable social behavior and sought to reach what generalizations about it we could, without making any assumption, one way or the other, that the ideas in men's minds have an influence on behavior. We have not said they do, nor have we said they do not. We have left the question alone, not because we thought it was trivial but because we did not have to face it. "As few as we may, as many as we must"—this is the best rule by which to judge the number of different factors that should be brought into a theory. The doctrine of economy is sound; we must not use concepts just for the sake of using them, but do as much as we can with as few as possible. Yet the time comes when further progress with the old machinery gets difficult, and this time has come for us. We can no longer

[5] For a brief account see T. N. Whitehead, *Leadership in a Free Society*, 32-53, and for full details see Whitehead's *The Industrial Worker*.

disregard ideas; we must bring them into our theory as a new element.

In this book we have never pretended to study all of the important aspects of social behavior, but only a few of them, and in order to retain as much economy as we can, we shall not study all ideas but only the special class of ideas that sociologists call *norms*. In the next chapter we shall find that one of the chief ways in which the members of a group are differentiated from one another is in the degree to which their activities approach group norms of behavior. We cannot come to grips with differentiation until we understand what norms are, and it is appropriate to take them up in this place, as a group's norms are peculiarly a product of the group as a whole, emerging from actual behavior and in turn reacting upon it.

What do we mean by norms? Sociologists and anthropologists are always saying that such and such behavior is, in a particular group, "expected" under such and such circumstances. How do they know what is expected? Sometimes the members of a group will state quite clearly what the expected behavior is, but sometimes it is a matter of inference. The process of construction by which social scientists determine the expectations of a group—and the process must be complex—seems to be taken for granted by the less sophisticated among them in their textbooks and popular works. Here we never take such things for granted, though we may not spend much time on them. Suppose, for example, three men are in a room. One goes out, and one of the two that remain says to the other, "I don't believe we've met. My name is Smith." Or, in another variation of the same scene, a man comes into a room where two others are already standing. There is a silence, and then one of the two says, "I'm sorry. I should have introduced you two, but I thought you had met. Mr. Jones, this is Mr. Smith." From observing several events of this kind, the sociologist infers that, in this particular group, when two men are in the presence of one another and have not met before, the third man, if he has met both, is expected to tell each the other's name, but that, should he fail to do so, each is expected to act on his own account and tell the other his name. The sociologist's inference may be confirmed when he reads in a book of etiquette current in this group,

"When two persons have not met before, their host must introduce them to one another." Inferences of this kind we shall call *norms*. Note that most norms are not as easily discovered as this rather trivial one, and confirmation by a book of etiquette or its equivalent is not always possible. The student should turn to *Management and the Worker* and run over the material from which the inference was reached that about 6,600 or, according to the type of equipment being wired, 6,000 completed connections were considered in the Bank Wiring Observation Room the proper day's work of a wireman. For example, Mueller (W2) said in an interview:

Right now I'm turning out over 7,000 a day, around 7,040. The rest of the fellows kick because I do that. They want me to come down. They want me to come down to around 6,600, but I don't see why I should.[6]

In few works of social science are the norms, whose existence the sociologist often appears to assume so lightly, traced back to their referents in word and deed as carefully as they are in the Roethlisberger and Dickson book. We have already seen what some of the other norms of the Bank Wiremen were, in such matters as squealing, chiseling, and acting officiously.

A norm, then, is an idea in the minds of the members of a group, an idea that can be put in the form of a statement specifying what the members or other men should do, ought to do, are expected to do, under given circumstances. Just what group, what circumstances, and what action are meant can be much more easily determined for some norms than for others. But even this definition is too broad and must be limited further. A statement of the kind described is a norm only if any departure of real behavior from the norm is followed by some punishment. The rule of the Bank Wiremen that no one should wire much more or much less than two equipments a day was a true norm, because, as we shall see, the social standing of a member of the group declined as he departed in one way or another from the norm. Nonconformity was punished and conformity rewarded. A norm in this sense is what some sociologists call a sanction pattern. But there are many other

[6] *Management and the Worker,* 417. Study the whole discussion, pp. 412-423.

statements about what behavior ought to be that are not norms and are often called ideals. "Do as you would be done by," is an example. In an imperfect world, departure from the golden rule is not followed by specific punishment, and this is precisely what gives the rule its high ethical standing. If a man lives by it, he does so for its own sake and not because he will be socially rewarded. Virtue is its own reward.

We have defined norms as the expected behavior of a number of men. This is justified: each of the Bank Wiremen was expected to wire about 6,000 connections a day. But some norms, though they may be held by all the members of a group, apply to only one of them: they define what a single member in a particular position is supposed to do. A father is expected to treat his children, a host, his guests, a foreman, his men in certain special ways. A norm of this kind, a norm that states the expected relationship of a person in a certain position to others he comes into contact with is often called the *role* of this person.[7] The word comes, of course, from the language of the stage: it is the part a man is given to play, and he may play it well or ill. A man's behavior may depart more or less from the role, and if the real behavior of enough persons in enough such positions over a long enough time departs far enough from the role, the role itself will change. For instance, our notion of the way a father ought to behave toward his children has changed greatly in the last century, as circumstances have made the patriarchal role of fathers on small, subsistence farms no longer appropriate for many fathers today.

One point must be made very clear: our norms are ideas. They are not behavior itself, but what people think behavior ought to be. Nothing is more childishly obvious than that the ideal and the real do not always, or do not fully, coincide, but nothing is more easily forgotten, perhaps because men want to forget it. A possible objection to the word *norm* itself is that we may easily confuse two different things: norm A, a statement of what people ought to do in a particular situation, and norm B, a statistical, or quasi-statistical, average of what they actually do in that situation. Sometimes the two coincide, but more often they do not. In the same

[7] See above, p. 11.

way, the word *standard* suggests, on the one hand, a moral yard-stick by which real behavior is judged and, on the other hand, in the phrase *standard of living,* a certain level of real behavior in the field of consumption.

CULTURE

By our definition, norms are a part, but only a part, of what social anthropologists call the *culture* of a group. Anyone who is interested in the various meanings that have been given to this famous concept should read the intelligent and witty discussion by Kluckhohn and Kelly. The definition they finally come out with themselves is the following: "A culture is a historically derived system of explicit and implicit designs for living, which tends to be shared by all or specially designated members of a group." [8] From this definition we might be led to believe that our norms are the same thing as culture, for designs for living suggest intellectual guides for practice rather than practice itself. The design of the ship is not the ship. But we should be mistaken. For Kluckhohn and Kelly, culture includes both theory and practice, ideal patterns and behavorial patterns, statements of what ought to be and modalities in what is done. Anthropologists are welcome to define *culture* as they wish, but we, interested in the relation between the two aspects of group life, must make it clear that our norms are statements of what ought to be, and only this. They are a part of culture, but not all of it.

THE RELATION OF NORMS TO BEHAVIOR

Our guiding principle throughout has been that unless things are kept separate in the beginning they cannot in the end be seen in relation to one another. We must not mix norms and actual behavior together in a shapeless mass if we are to examine the relations between the two, and the relations do confront us and demand analysis. It is clear, for instance, that norms do not materialize out of nothing, but emerge from ongoing activities. If the Bank Wiremen had not been doing the wiring job, and if their

[8] C. Kluckhohn and W. H. Kelly, "The Concept of Culture," in R. Linton, ed., *The Science of Man in the World Crisis,* 78-106, 98.

output had not reached the neighborhood of 6,000 connections per man per day (or about two equipments), it is hard to believe that this particular norm would ever have got itself established. If we think of a norm as a goal that a group wishes to reach, we can see that the goal is not set up, like the finish line of a race, before the race starts, but rather that the group decides, after it starts running, what the finish line shall be. Once the norm is established it exerts a back effect on the group. It may act as an incentive in the sense that a man may try to bring his behavior closer to the norm. But the norm can be a mark to shoot for only if it is not too far away from what can be achieved in everyday life. If it gets impossibly remote—and just how far that is no one can say—it will be abandoned in favor of some more nearly attainable norm. Society's preaching and its practice are elastically linked. Each pulls the other, and they can never separate altogether.

The really interesting question is, as usual, quantitative and not qualitative: not "Does behavior coincide with a norm?" but "*How far* does the behavior of an individual or a subgroup measure up to the norms of the group as a whole?" What, moreover, is the relation of this degree of coincidence to the sentimental process that we shall call *evaluation* or *social ranking*, by which individuals and subgroups are judged "better" or "worse" than others? What is the relation of evaluation to other aspects of the social system? These are questions we shall take up in the chapters that follow; the work we do now will help us then.

We have made an assumption without proof. In a chapter dealing with a single social unit, the Bank Wiring group, rather than the subgroups within this unit, we have talked about "the norms of a group as a whole." What do we mean? We mean that, the more frequently men interact with one another, the more nearly alike they become in the norms they hold, as they do in their sentiments and activities. But we mean still more than this. No doubt the norms accepted in a group vary somewhat from one person to another, and from one subgroup to another, and yet *the members of the group are often more nearly alike in the norms they hold than in their overt behavior*. To put the matter crudely, they are more alike in what they say they ought to do than in what they do in fact. Thus the Bank Wiremen were more nearly, though perhaps not wholly, alike in what they said output ought to be than in what they actually turned out. Perhaps the explanation of this rule, if it is one, lies in the fact that a person's subjective recognition of a norm, although under influence from other aspects of the social system, is under less immediate influence than his social activity itself, and thus varies less than his social activity. Being an idea, the norm come closer to having an independent life of its own.

Norms do not materialize out of nothing; they emerge from ongoing activities. This remark is true but needs to be amplified. The norms alive in a particular group do not all arise out of the activities of *that* group. Thus in the Bank Wiring Observation Room, the rule that about 6,000 connections should be wired in a day must have grown up in the main department from which the men came. The more general idea of restriction of output or, as labor sees it, "a fair day's work for a fair day's pay," is a part of the American, or Western, industrial tradition. That is, it is common to a large number of groups whose members have had some communication with one another. Again, the feeling that no man should act as if he had authority over someone else is an article in the democratic creed—and note that the creed is realized to some degree in American society and would not survive unless it were. Men bring their norms to a group; they work out new norms through their experience in the group; they take the old norms, confirmed or weakened, and the new ones, as developed, to the other groups they are members of. If the norms take hold there, a general tradition, the same in many groups, may grow up. The freight most easily exported is the kind carried in the head. In fact the environment determines the character of a group in two chief ways: through its influence on the external system, and through widely held norms.

ASSUMPTIONS OR VALUES

While we are speaking of the ideas that men bring to a group from the larger society of which the group is a part, we should not forget certain ideas that are closely akin to the norms: the unconscious assumptions the members of any society make or, as some sociologists would say, the *values* they hold. For instance, two such assumptions that the Bank Wiremen certainly brought with them to the Observation Room might be stated as follows: 1. A man who is paid more than another man has, in general, a better job than that man. 2. A man who can give orders to another man has, in general, a better job than that man. We can formulate these assumptions, but in everyday life they are not formulated, and for this reason we call them unconscious. Instead they are implied, over and over again, in actual behavior and in casual remarks. A man may in effect admit their truth even when he does not act upon them. He may turn down promotion to foreman because the job has too many "headaches," but he will concede that this job is somehow, on an absolute scale, better than his own. Perhaps the assumptions are so obvious that they do not need formulation—obvious, that is, to us who are also Americans, for the anthropologists have abundantly shown that what is obvious in one culture is not necessarily so in another. Note that these assumptions, including the two in our illustration, cannot be "proved." They are not propositions to be proved by logical processes, but premises from which logic starts, just as in geometry you do not prove that a straight line is the shortest distance between two points, you postulate it. From different premises different conclusions could be drawn. The social assumptions stand because a large number of people accept them and for no other reason. The Bank Wiremen brought many such premises with them to work. Some were and are a part of American democratic culture. Some may be found to contradict one another, which means that they are supposed to apply in different circumstances. And some may be unconscious assumptions of all human behavior. In their emphasis on cultural relativity, the anthropologists have almost—not quite—forgotten that there may be some premises held by all mankind.

TECHNICAL, SOCIAL, AND RELIGIOUS SYSTEMS

Norms are only one class of ideas. The student must remember this when he hears of concepts that sound like ours. W. Lloyd Warner, for example, describes society as made up of three "systems": the technical, the social, and the religious. He writes: "The type of behavior by which a group of individuals adjusts itself to, and partially controls, the natural environment is . . . its technical system; the system of adjustments and controls of the interactions of individuals with each other is the social organization; and the system of adjustments made by the group to the unknown or the supernatural is the religious system, which consists of beliefs and sanctions relating man to the gods and the gods to man." [9] We owe a debt to Warner and acknowledge it here. The germ of our external and internal systems lies in his technical and social systems. How closely the two pairs—Warner's and ours—correspond from point to point we cannot say, as Warner has only suggested his distinctions and not worked them out in detail. As for the religious system, it has, at the level of the group rather than the society as a whole, something in common with our norms. Though Warner speaks of the technical, social, and religious systems, as if they all had something in common, the fact is that they do not. The technical and social are parts of overt behavior; Warner's religious system is partly overt behavior and partly inferred from it, especially from what people say. It includes rituals and ceremonies, but it also includes myths, beliefs, and "absolute logics"; and in this latter group our norms belong. They are a part of Warner's religious system, but only a part. For example, cosmology— a people's scientific or pseudoscientific view of the physical world —is an element of religion, but is something other than a norm.

In summary, we have seen that the men in the Bank Wiring Room held certain sentiments, carried out certain activities, and interacted in a certain pattern, and that a part of these sentiments, activities, and interactions were conditioned by the social and physical environment and formed what we called the external system of the group. But the life of the group did not confine itself to the poverty of the external system. On the foundation of these initial relationships, new ones of a somewhat different kind spontaneously emerged, and these we shall call the internal system. For example, interaction between the men at work led to sentiments

[9] W. L. Warner and P. S. Lunt, *The Social Life of a Modern Community* (Yankee City Series, Vol. I), 21. See also W. L. Warner, *A Black Civilization,* 10; R. LaPiere, *Sociology,* 162.

of liking, which led in turn to further interaction and to activities, such as helping, that expressed these sentiments. In the same way, the sentiments or activities of the external system could, if one wished, be taken instead of interaction as the starting point of the process of development. We have seen that the elements of social behavior were linked to one another in the internal system as they were in the external, and that they were linked in such a way that the system grew, elaborated itself, attempted something new. At the same time, the activities of the internal system tended to be- come standardized, and norms of behavior were adopted or in- vented by the group.

We have been looking at the group as a whole; in the next chap- ter we turn to the subgroups within the group. But before we do, we need one reminder, which is well stated by Roethlisberger and Dickson, and which is of the first importance, though they leave it in a footnote of their book. It is this: "Perhaps a word of caution is necessary here. When it is said that this group was divided into two cliques and that certain people were outside either clique, it does not mean that there was no solidarity between the two cliques or between the cliques and the outsiders. There is always the dan- ger, in examining small groups intensively, of overemphasizing differentiating factors. Internal solidarity thus appears to be lack- ing. That this group, as a whole, did have very strong sentiments in common has already been shown in discussing their attitudes toward output . . ." [10] Both the whole and its parts must be borne in mind simultaneously.

[10] *Management and the Worker,* 510.

CHAPTER 6

The Internal System: Differentiation Within the Group

*The External System ... Mutual Dependence of Inter-
action and Sentiment ... Mutual Dependence of Sentiment and Activity ... Mutual Dependence of Activity
and Interaction ... Symbolism ... Personality ... Social
Ranking ... Social Ranking and Activity ... Social
Ranking and Interaction ... Social Ranking Apart from
Cliques ... Social Ranking and Leadership ... Reaction
of the Internal System on the External ... Feedback
... Adaptation*

WE SHALL always be saying something and then
taking it back, blocking out the main outlines of the composition
and then obscuring them with details. Since we can make only one
point at a time, this is the only possible way of going to work, but
the reader cannot be blamed if he finds it tiring. In the last chapter, we described a pattern of behavior followed by the Bank Wiring group as a whole. When we scrutinize the facts more fully,
we find that departures from the pattern are at least as evident
as agreements with it, and the departures are not meaningless:
they map out subgroups within the larger unit. Thus in one sense
most members of the group were friends and in another, some
members of the group were more friendly with one another than
they were with others. To the study of differentiation within the
group we shall now turn, and we shall try to show that the kinds
of generalizations we made about the Bank Wiring group in relation to other groups, such as the department from which the men
came, hold good also for the relation between any one subgroup
within the Observation Room and any other.

Let us state the problem in another way. 1. A group as a whole has certain characteristics. 2. Each subgroup has certain characteristics because it has, so to speak, "foreign relations" with other subgroups. 3. Each subgroup also has certain characteristics because it is not altogether a "sovereign power" but part of a "world order"—the group as a whole. The first aspect we considered in the last chapter; the other two we shall consider in this one, first studying the subgroups within the Bank Wiring group as a whole without taking account of the fact that they were all part of a larger unit, and then studying them further with this fact taken into account.

THE EXTERNAL SYSTEM

We will remember that there were two cliques within the Bank Wiring Observation Room, labeled by us clique A and clique B, and by the men themselves, the "group in front" and the "group in back." How shall we account for the appearance of the cliques?

As before, we begin with the external system. Just as interaction between members of the group as a whole was stimulated by their being shut up in the room together, so interaction in subgroups was encouraged even more by the physical geography of the room and the organization of work, that is, by forces originating in the environment. Thus the members of clique A were men who worked near each other at the front of the room, the members of clique B were men who worked near each other at the back. Moreover, clique A had as its nucleus soldering unit 1, including all the wiremen and the solderman of that unit; clique B centered around soldering unit 3. Again, clique A was almost identical with inspection unit A: it included inspector 1 (Allen) and most of the men whose work he inspected, and clique B, to a lesser extent, was associated with inspection unit B. Finally, the wiremen of clique A worked on connector units, that is, their activities in the external system were similar, while the wiremen of clique B, with the exception of Krupa (W6), worked on selector equipments. We shall have to ask ourselves later why the "fit" between the setup of the work and the membership in cliques was not perfect, why, for instance, soldering unit 2 never became the nucleus of a clique, and why Krupa, although a connector wireman, was to some degree a member of a clique otherwise made up of selector wiremen. But the fit, while not perfect, was obviously good.

When we speak of a number of men as forming a clique, we only mean that they form a subgroup within a larger unit; that is, their interactions with one another are more frequent than they are with outsiders or members of other subgroups. But the pattern of inter- action is not all we can see in clique behavior. To the interaction scheme we can relate certain schemes of sentiment and activity, and show how, through these relationships, the internal system builds itself up on the foundations of the external system in a way we have not considered so far.

MUTUAL DEPENDENCE OF INTERACTION AND SENTIMENT

Turn back to Chapter 3 and look at the charts showing friend- ships and antagonisms among the members of the group. Just as all the members of the group, thrown together in the room, were to some extent friendly, with the exception of Mazmanian (I3), so individuals within the group, thrown together by the geography of the room, the nature of their work, and common membership in soldering and inspection units, were friendly to an even greater extent. Winkowski (W1), Taylor (W3), Donovan (W4), Stein- hardt (S1), and Allen (I1), all working at the front of the room and in the same inspection unit, were all linked by friendships, and the same was true of soldering unit 3, but only one strong friendship, that of Hasulak (W7) for Steinhardt (S1), linked mem- bers of two different cliques. We can, then, sum up the relationship between interaction and sentiment both in the group as a whole and in the subgroups by saying once more that *the more frequently persons interact with one another, the stronger their sentiments of friendship for one another are apt to be.* The correlation between interaction and sentiment in the Bank Wiring group was not per- fect but it was significant.

As for antagonisms, good feeling in the Bank Wiring Room as a whole was associated with some antagonism toward members of the department, and it might have been expected that within the group the members of different cliques would have disliked one another. In point of fact the positive antagonisms did not grow up between members of different cliques but between clique members and men like Mazmanian (I3) who were social isolates. But speaking of friendships and antagonisms, we must always remember that their intensities within a group have relative and not absolute values. A group rent by backbiting factions will still join enthusiastically in presenting an unbroken front towards "foreigners." As in a healthy democracy, the conflicts may be loud but superficial, the unity silent but profound.

MUTUAL DEPENDENCE OF SENTIMENT AND ACTIVITY

Look now at the charts that show participation in games, controversies about windows, and job trading. Just as friendship within the Bank Wiring group as a whole expressed itself in the network of mutual help, so more particular friendships expressed themselves in certain activities, like job trading, that linked pairs of men together and in certain others, like games, that linked the members of a clique. The first four wiremen, with their inspector and solderman, took part in games together, and so did the last four and their solderman. Only Capek (W5) took part in games with both groups, and he did not do so often. These activities were not part of the setup of the work; in fact the company frowned on them. We can therefore say of differentiation within the group as we did of the group as a whole that *persons who feel sentiments of liking for one another will express those sentiments in activities over and above the activities of the external system.* In fact the sentiments would not persist unless the associated activities did too. Emotional relations between people do not exist in a vacuum but are sustained by countless, repeated events in which people take part together in work and play.

MUTUAL DEPENDENCE OF ACTIVITY AND INTERACTION

Moreover, these new activities rather obviously led to further interaction between the members of a clique. The men who interacted with one another frequently in the external system because they worked in the same part of the room or in the same soldering unit also interacted frequently in the internal system by taking part together in job trading, games, and conversations. This in fact is the point from which we started our analysis, for a clique, like any group, is defined as a body of men who interact with one another more frequently than they do with outsiders.

So far we have been dealing with the process that we called the mode of elaboration: the building up of new sentiments, activities, and interactions. Going on at the same time was another process called the mode of similarity and difference. Each clique developed its own style of behavior, in the games its members played, in their topics of conversation, in their controversies, and even in their horseplay. Most of the gambling games were carried on by clique A, most of the binging by clique B. Clique A did not trade jobs nearly so often as clique B, nor did it enter so much into controversies about the windows. Clique B ate more candy than clique A and bought a different kind. Its members also indulged in more horseplay. No doubt these distinctions will seem trivial to a social philosopher. Why should he trouble himself with different kinds of candy? All we can say is that in his own group it may, for instance, make a big difference to him whether or not he wears a necktie.

Above all, the two cliques differed in output. Hasulak (W7), Oberleitner (W8), and Green (W9), the selector wiremen and the nucleus of clique B, not only turned out somewhat less work, man for man, than the members of clique A but also claimed more daywork allowance and let actual output fall farther below reported output. We have seen that output differences could not be correlated with native differences in intelligence and dexterity, but they could obviously be correlated with clique membership. At any rate we can sum up the differences in the behavior of the two cliques by saying that *persons who interact with one another frequently are more like one another in their activities than they are like other persons with whom they interact less frequently.* According to this hypothesis, similarities in the behavior of members of a single subgroup and differences in the behavior of two subgroups are two sides of the same coin. If, moreover, the activities of the members of a subgroup are similar in the external system, and different from the activities of another subgroup, they will apparently tend to be similar and different in the same way in the internal system. Thus the selector wiremen resembled one another in their jobs and differed from the connector wiremen; they also resembled one another and differed from the connector wiremen in a whole series of other activities.

Like the others, the hypothesis we have just stated holds good only under certain circumstances. Or better, the relationship between interaction and similarity of behavior may be obscured by the influence of factors other than the two that come into the hypothesis, in this case such factors as authority and the kinds of activities people perform in the external system. Thus a gentleman of the old school and his valet interact frequently and yet their styles of behavior do not become very much alike. The servant continues to resemble other servants more than he does his master. The question is always one of degree. It is only when people interact as social equals and their jobs are not sharply differentiated that our hypothesis comes fully into its own. But even in the example we have considered, who shall say that through their long interaction the gentleman and his valet do not develop certain kinds of activities in which they resemble one another more than they do other gentlemen and other valets, just as the soldermen in the Bank Wiring Room adopted the activities of the wiremen for whom they worked? There may be some truth in the old proverb, "Like master, like man." An hypothesis may always hold good, and yet may vary greatly in the degree to which it makes its presence felt in any concrete human situation.

To return to the Bank Wiring Room, there is another matter that will bear watching. The differences between the two cliques in the activities they carried out may have been increased by the fact that the two were in contact. The behavior of the cliques was different not only because each enjoyed its own style but also because each wanted to be *different from* the other. An hypothesis worth considering is that, in these circumstances, *the activities of a subgroup may become increasingly differentiated from those of other subgroups up to some limit imposed by the controls of the larger group to which all the subgroups belong.*

SYMBOLISM

A chief obstacle to clear thinking in the social sciences is the fact that several different sets of words, or language systems, are available for the expression of a single idea. We must be careful not to think the ideas are different just because the words are different. Thus a great deal of behavior in the internal system may be called either expressive or symbolic, as we please. We may say that the behavior of each clique was an expression of, or we may say that it was a symbol of, the clique's distinctiveness. In order to cut down as far as possible the number of technical words we use, we shall in this book apply the words *symbol* and *symbolic* to physical objects, spatial relationships, and, of course, verbal symbols, but not to ongoing behavior. By this definition, a gift is a symbol of the friendship of one man for another, but the process of giving the gift is an expression of the friendship. And the spatial position of the connector wiremen at the front of the room was a symbol of their superior rank, but their behavior in that position was not. As a matter of fact, all such ways of speaking raise more questions than they answer. When we say that the behavior of a clique is an expression of its distinctiveness or its identity, we still have to explain what we mean by "expression" and "identity." Have we really said any more than this, "The more often a number of persons interact with one another, the more alike their behavior tends to become"? If this is what we mean, why not say it as simply as possible, without drawing long words across the trail of our thought?

PERSONALITY

We have seen that in the Bank Wiring Observation Room the fit between the external system and the internal was not perfect. Why, for instance, did not soldering unit 2 develop into a third clique? If the mechanisms we have described worked without interference from other factors, it should have. All we can say is that this failure was not due to chance, though we do not know as much about the interfering factors as we should like. Capek (W5) in soldering unit 2 was the most unpopular of all the wiremen. His character did not fit him for membership in any group in the room, and this fact, linked with his strategic position in the geographical center of the work layout, apparently prevented soldering unit 2 from becoming a clique and turned Donovan (W4) to clique A, Krupa (W6) to clique B. Like Capek, Mazmanian (I3) and Matchek (S2) were members of no clique, while Mueller (W2) and Krupa (W6) were clique members to only a small degree, participating in games with their cliques but isolated in other ways. In each case we have some information to explain why these men were isolates. Matchek had a speech defect; the others all had personality difficulties, but we must remember, saying this, that we are lumping together under *personality* at least the following factors: (*a*) a person's inherited biological tendencies, (*b*) the psychological tendencies induced by the social training given him in early life, and (*c*) the pressures brought to bear on him by his immediate social situation outside the group in question. The mechanisms of social elaboration will take effect only with those persons whose personalities enable them to become full members of the group being studied. It may be that persons like Capek and Mazmanian, social isolates in the Bank Wiring Room, would have become full members of a group of a different kind. There is no evidence that they were psychopaths.

SOCIAL RANKING

At the beginning of this chapter, we said that there were two ways of looking at the differentiation within the Bank Wiring Observation Room or indeed within any group. On the one hand, the subgroups were, so to speak, sovereign powers enjoying foreign relations with one another; on the other hand, they were all subject to a world order—the group as a whole. So far we have been considering the first aspect, the mere differentiation between the cliques in interaction, sentiment, and activity. We turn now to the second aspect. A further feature of the differentiation within the group cannot be understood apart from an important characteristic of the group as a whole.

This further feature is social ranking, and the important characteristic is the adoption by the group of the norms and unconscious assumptions discussed in the last chapter. As soon as two sub-groups are set apart from one another and conscious of their differences, at least one of the two is apt to feel that it is somehow better than the other. Not only are foreigners different from us, they also have no manners and filthy customs. How often we take a moral stand! How often the laws of sociology are the laws of snobbery! Sometimes the quarrel between the two subgroups ends in mutual recriminations, because there is no way of settling it, but sometimes there is a sort of way. In effect, though the process is perfectly unplanned and spontaneous, at least one of the parties demands that the norms and unconscious assumptions, accepted by the group as a whole, be used as a yardstick for evaluating its behavior more highly than that of the other party. The members of a group are more nearly alike in their norms of behavior than in their behavior itself, and a subgroup is ranked or evaluated as better or worse than another depending on how closely its behavior approaches the norms of the group as a whole. The higher the rank of the subgroup, the more closely its behavior "measures up."

In the Bank Wiring Room, clique A not only behaved differently from clique B in some ways but also felt that its behavior was better, that it was the superior clique. To understand this fact, we must begin by going back once more to the external system. Clique A was made up of men who worked on connector equipments, clique B, with the exception of Krupa (W6), who was hardly a member in good standing, of men who worked on selector equipments. As far as the skill required was concerned, the difference between the jobs was not great and was less in fact than in theory, but the job difference was linked with others much more significant. Connector wiremen had higher rates than selector wiremen and earned slightly higher wages; a wireman usually started in on selector equipments and, as he gained skill and seniority, moved to connectors; the connector wiremen, both in the room and in the original department, worked at the front of the room. In the Chicago community and in American society at large, assumptions are current to the effect that a job carrying higher wages, greater skill, and more seniority than another, even a job that is placed "in front of" another, is a "better" job. It is more highly valued. It may be that these assumptions are really corollaries of a still more profound one. By and large in organizations, the persons with higher wages, skill, and seniority than others are also in a position to direct or control the activities of others. This is even true of being "in front." The teacher stands in front of his class, the captain in front of his company, and each directs his group. These things are the outward and visible signs of control, and a high value is always given to control, to authority. At any rate, the arrangements of the external system of the Bank Wiring group combined with the unconscious assumptions of American society to make the connector wiremen feel that they had better jobs than the selector wiremen.

We shall now see how the feeling of the connector wiremen that their jobs were somehow better than those of the selector wiremen was connected with other elements of the behavior of the Bank Wiring group.

SOCIAL RANKING AND ACTIVITY

A feeling on the part of an individual and of the other members of his group that he is in some way better (or worse) than another individual, that he ranks higher (or lower) than the other, is by our definition a *sentiment*. The evaluation of a man relative to the evaluation of other members of his group we shall call his *rank* rather than his *status*, because, as we saw in Chapter 1, rank is only one of the elements of status as that word is usually defined. Evaluation is a sentiment released or stimulated by a comparison of a man's *activities* with those of other members of his group in accordance with some standard, the standard being provided by the *norms* and *assumptions* of the group. Unless there were some intellectual standard of judgment, it is hard to see how the comparison could be made. For a man to rank high in his group, it is not enough that he should evaluate himself highly; his group must also accept his evaluation, and the norms of the group provide the only possible basis for agreement. The reasoning that we have applied to an individual can also be applied to a subgroup. Thus the connector wiremen felt superior (sentiment) to the selector wiremen because their jobs (activity) were better in terms of some of the unconscious assumptions of American society.

Assuming the norms and assumptions of the group constant, let us look further at the mutual relationship between social rank and social activity. The wiremen of clique A (connector wiremen) thought that their jobs were better than those of the wiremen of clique B (selector wiremen), and they extended this feeling of superiority to all their activities. They believed their games were less boisterous and their conversations more refined. Moreover, their activities were superior not only by common American assumptions but also by the norms of the group. Thus they came much closer than the selector wiremen to meeting the standards of the group in the matter of output. The members of clique A put out close to two equipments per man per day; the members of clique B somewhat less. We can state as a hypothesis, then, that persons who set a high value on their activities in the external system will set a high value on their activities in the internal system. From this we can go on to the more fundamental hypothesis that *the higher the rank of a person within a group, the more nearly his activities conform to the norms of the group.* The hypothesis holds for subgroups as well as for individuals. The relationship is strictly mutual: the closer the person's activities come to the norm, the higher his rank will tend to be, but it is also true that, rank being taken as the independent variable, the higher the person's rank, the closer his activities will come to the norm, or, even more simply, *noblesse oblige.* To rank high in his group, a man must live up to all of its norms, and the norms in question must be the actual or sanctioned norms of the group and not just those to which the group gives lip service.

We must now consider the effect on the selector wiremen of the behavior of the connector wiremen. As far as their special jobs were concerned, the selector wiremen were not altogether ready to accept the judgment laid down by the other group. They resented the implication of inferiority, and with some reason. The differences between the two wiring jobs were slight, and the selector wiremen seem to have felt that their companions made too much of a few little things. In their relations with inspectors and supervisors, all the wiremen were on a par with one another, and in the organization of work the connector wiremen in no way directed or controlled the work of the selector wiremen. If in some ways the former could be made out as superior, in other ways all were equals.

At any rate, the selector wiremen were resentful, and as resentment, like all sentiment, seeks an outlet in activity, they expressed their feelings in activities that, in kind and in amount, they knew would be distasteful to the connector wiremen of clique A. The noisiness of their talks, games, and bickerings may have been adopted because they knew that clique A would not like this kind of behavior; their low output certainly was adopted for this reason. The activities of any one subgroup always tend to become somewhat different from those of another. Here a further factor of differentiation was the desire of one subgroup to pursue activities that would deliberately outrage the norms of the other.

If the members of clique B wished to irritate clique A, they certainly were successful. The next act in the drama found the connector wiremen hitting back—heckling clique B for its low output and damning its members as "chiselers." But, as Roethlisberger and Dickson point out, "The interesting thing about these tactics was that they served to subordinate clique B still further and as a result to strengthen their internal solidarity still more. So, instead of increasing their output, the members of clique B kept it low, thus 'getting back' at those who were displaying their superiority." [1]

Elsewhere Roethlisberger and Dickson write: "It may be concluded that the various performance records for the members of clique B were reflecting their position in the group. There was a clear-cut relation between their social standing and their output. But, it may be asked, did their low output determine their position in the group or did their position in the group determine their output? The answer is that the relation worked both ways: position in the group influenced output, and output influenced position in the group. In other words, these two factors were in a relation of mutual dependence." [2] In our language, the relation in question is the mutual dependence of sentiment (social ranking) and activity (output).

The connector wiremen kept trying to bring the output of the

[1] *Management and the Worker,* 521.
[2] *Ibid.,* 520.

selector wiremen closer to the standard; the latter kept trying to keep their output low just because they knew that this would anger the connectors. How far this process of attack and counterattack might have gone in other circumstances we do not know, but in the Bank Wiring Room there were forces that brought the vicious spiral to a halt and prevented the output of the selector wiremen from remaining indefinitely low. After all, both cliques were members of the same group and in a measure both accepted its norms. The output level of clique B can be looked on as the resultant of at least three forces: (*a*) the desire of the clique to differentiate its behavior, in the direction of irritation, from that of clique A, (*b*) its desire to conform to the output standard of the group as a whole, and (*c*) the economic interests of the selector wiremen, which must never be forgotten. If their output had gone too far down, they would have been fired. At any rate, the behavior of both clique A and clique B bears out our rule that the closer the activities of a subgroup approach the norms of the group as a whole, the higher will be its social rank. The social rank of clique B was lower than that of clique A, and the activities of its members were also further from the group norms.

According to the group norm, a wireman should not have turned out less than two equipments a day, but neither should he have turned out more. It is interesting that, while clique B was violating the norm in one way, Capek (W5) and Mueller (W2), the social isolates among the wiremen, tended to violate it in another. The selector wiremen were too low; Capek and Mueller, particularly the latter, were apt to be too high. They were connector wiremen, and therefore unwilling to identify themselves with clique B by turning out too little work, but neither were they members of clique A, so their output, instead of lying below, or close to, the group norm, tended to lie a little above it.

In the Bank Wiring Observation Room, there were two cliques, the one higher in social rank being also the one conforming most nearly to the norms of the group as a whole. The ways of men are infinitely subtle, and some situations are not as simple as this. Occasionally we notice that the persons who stand highest in a group do not conform with undue strictness to some of the group norms, and controls are not seriously applied to them. Well-established members will suffer only a little joking when they break a rule, whereas newcomers will be severely punished with ridicule and scorn. "Here is an apparent paradox: Admittance to the group may be secured only by adherence to the established definitions of the group, while unquestioned membership carries the privilege of some deviant behavior. This is, of course, not a paradox at all; for it is characteristic of social groups to demand of the newcomer a strict conformity which will show that he accepts the authority of the group; then, as the individual approaches the center of the group and becomes an established member, they allow him a little more leeway." [3] This is probably not the whole story, but we can recognize a new factor here, which we may call the factor of social security. Up to a point, the surer a man is of his rank in a group, the less he has to worry about conforming to its norms. This new factor will under some circumstances modify our earlier generalization, just as the factor of authority modifies our generalization that frequency of interaction and sentiments of liking are positively linked. Neither factor invalidates our hypotheses but must be added to them if they are to approximate the concrete reality more and more closely.

SOCIAL RANKING AND INTERACTION

The relationship between the sentiments of social ranking and and the scheme of interaction in the internal system can be seen in the matter of job trading. Job trading meant that a wireman exchanged jobs with a solderman, against the rules of the company. Most of the trades were made with Cermak (S4), the solderman for the three selector wiremen. In 33 of the 49 observed instances of job trading, he was a participant. The reason for the great excess was that wiremen from soldering units 1 and 2 (the connector wiremen) traded with all three soldermen, but no selector wireman ever traded outside his own clique. "The connector wiremen apparently felt free to change jobs either with their own soldermen or with the solderman for the selector wiremen, but the latter did

[3] E. C. Hughes, "The Knitting of Racial Groups in Industry," *American Sociological Review,* XI (1946), 517.

not feel free to trade outside of their own unit." [4] Now job trading involved interaction, and so we can suggest, as a tentative hypothesis, that *the higher a person's social rank, the wider will be the range of his interactions.* Note that we are talking about the range of interaction here, that is, the number of persons a man interacts with, and not just about the sheer frequency of interaction. Perhaps the wider contacts react to reinforce sentiments of superiority, but we have no immediate evidence for this. We must also notice, referring to the chart showing participation in job trading, that the two connector wiremen who traded jobs with Cermak (S4) were Mueller (W2) and Capek (W5), and that neither of the two were fully accepted members of clique A. Through their actions they may in effect have been saying to the selector wiremen: "Though we are not full members of clique A, we are still connector wiremen and, as such, superior to you."

Something of the same sort can be seen in the origination of interaction. The originator of interaction is the person whose activity, verbal or otherwise, is followed by the activity of one or more other persons. When the output of clique B remained below the group's norm of two completed equipments per man per day, the members of clique A started originating interaction, through criticism and heckling, for the members of clique B. The latter did not originate interaction for clique A, but reacted only by keeping output down. We can suggest, then, as a further hypothesis that *a person of higher social rank than another originates interaction for the latter more often than the latter originates interaction for him.* In later chapters we shall see this hypothesis borne out far more clearly than it is in the data from the Bank Wiring Observation Room. Note that when the members of clique A originated interaction for the selector wiremen, they were trying to increase the output of the latter, that is, they were trying to control the behavior of the selector wiremen, and it may be that the attempt at control is a more fundamental phenomenon than the sheer origination of interaction, but we are postponing to a later chapter any discussion of the great problem of control.

[4] *Management and the Worker,* 504.

SOCIAL RANKING APART FROM CLIQUES

In discussing social ranking we have so far concentrated on the relation between cliques, or rather on the relation between connector and selector wiremen, for not all the connector wiremen were fully members of clique A. Many of the points we need to make can be made by studying clique relations alone. Yet there were other differences in social ranking besides the difference between connector and selector wiremen, and they deserve brief mention.

Between wiremen and soldermen no such conflict existed as that between connector and selector wiremen. The external system made the soldermen too clearly inferior in rank. A solderman earned substantially less than any wireman, and in the organization of work, he had to "wait on" his wiremen, to "serve" them by soldering in place the connections they had made. That is, the wireman originated the activity that was followed by the activity of the solderman. In the unconscious assumptions of American society, a man who is paid less than another and who must respond to activity that the other originates, especially when the origination implies control, is inferior to the other. On every count, then, the soldermen were judged the inferiors of the wiremen, and this judgment the soldermen, unlike the selector wiremen when judged inferior by the connectors, accepted without reservation. And note that in the internal system, as in the external, the soldermen allowed the wiremen to originate interaction: a solderman traded jobs with a wireman only when the latter asked him to do so. *A person who originates interaction for another in the external system will also tend to do so in the internal.* This submission by the soldermen was the price of their admission to the cliques. For Steinhardt (S1) and Cermak (S4) were members, though subordinate ones, of cliques A and B respectively. Matchek (S2), with a speech defect, was not a member of any clique.

In relation to one another, the social rank of Steinhardt and Cermak was determined by the ranking of their cliques. As the solderman of clique A, Steinhardt was considered the social superior of Cermak, the solderman of clique B, and his superiority was demonstrated in his successful effort to pass on to Cermak the job of getting lunches from the company cafeteria, which was felt to be menial work. Once again, low social rank is associated with activity that is inferior according to some standard recognized by the group.

As for the relation between inspectors and wiremen, the former had in some ways the better jobs. They were paid more than the wiremen and, since they might accept or reject the work of the other men, their position was semisupervisory. In other ways the inspectors were in a weak position. Only two of them worked in the room—they were a minority group—and they were members of the separate inspecting organization—they were outsiders. Moreover, they responded, like the soldermen, to activities that the wiremen originated; that is, they inspected equipments only after the wiremen had finished making connections. As a group the wiremen were dominant in the room, and if the two inspectors wished to be accepted by the others they had to submit to the group norms, one of which required that no one should act officiously, like a supervisor. Allen (I1) made the adjustment successfully, became a member of clique A, and kept some of his superiority besides. In arguing with the supervisors, he took many more liberties than the wiremen dared to take. Mazmanian (I3) could not conform and was driven from the room.

SOCIAL RANKING AND LEADERSHIP

The same kind of analysis that has been given to the behavior of cliques may be given to the behavior of individuals in the Bank Wiring Observation Room. Let us look in particular at Taylor (W3). He was a connector wireman—an extremely skillful and dependable one. He was a key member of the superior clique, and he was, with Krupa (W6), one of the two men whose output conformed most closely and consistently to the accepted idea of a proper day's work. In every way, indeed, he embodied the norms the group had adopted as its own. He never broke a rate, "chiseled," "squealed," or took a superior tone. For this individual, as for a clique, conformity to the norms carried with it high social evaluation (mutual dependence of activity and sentiment). Taylor was the best-liked man in the room.

His high social rank had consequences that reacted to strengthen it. As the best-liked man, Taylor was the most helped man in the room (mutual dependence of sentiment and activity), in spite of the fact that he did not return the help, perhaps because giving help implied inferiority. Instead he offered much advice, which was often taken, to other members of the group, and got into many arguments, which he often won. That is, his high social rank allowed him to go some distance in controlling the behavior of the others. Turning now to the interaction aspect of his position, we can see that his activities in accepting help and taking control meant that much of the interaction, or, if we prefer, much of the communication, in the group focused on him (mutual dependence of activity and interaction). If other members of the group frequently originated interaction with him, he in turn frequently originated interaction with them. As we have seen, the higher the rank of a subgroup, the wider the range of interaction of its members. The same relationship holds even more strongly for a particularly high-ranking individual. At any rate, Taylor found himself at the center of a web of communications. His position in the web helped confirm his high social rank (mutual dependence of interaction and sentiment), but we must never forget that it could do so only if his incipient control was accepted, and such acceptance depends, as we shall see, not on any one man but on the constitution of the group as a whole. Furthermore, Taylor's rank within the group no doubt depended to some extent on his influence outside it. It is significant that he alone was much more successful than Winkowski (W1) and Oberleitner (W8) together in getting a supply of wire from the department.

In short, the Bank Wiremen were, in Taylor, beginning to develop a leader of their own, different from the supervisors given them by the company. To be sure, they were only just beginning, and Taylor's position had hardly become recognized. We do not know how far this development might have gone if the experiment had lasted longer. To the characteristics of leadership, surely one of the most important features of the small group, we shall return again and again in this book, showing what this word *leadership,* often defined in vague language, means in terms of the observed facts we call interaction, activity, and sentiment, showing also how a group tends to create its own leaders, and showing, above all, how the leader gets his power only by conforming more closely than anyone else to the norms of the group. He is not the most but the least free person within it.[5]

We looked earlier at the way personality factors—and we admitted that this word *personality* covers many different things—prevented some developments from taking place in the Bank Wiring Observation Room that might otherwise have taken place. But if personality can inhibit some social developments, it can encourage others. Leadership might not have appeared in the room if Taylor had not been the kind of a man he was. It is not enough that a group tends to create its own leader; a man who is capable of being a leader must also be available. Taylor could not have behaved in any other way than he did and still have remained the most influential of the Bank Wiremen, but what enabled him to behave as he did? His score on the intelligence test was only fourth highest in the room; he must have had qualities other than sheer intelligence. Apparently he was especially well informed, and it may be significant that he was very active, keeping up a steady stream of chatter and always holding himself ready to take part in a game or conversation. But Krupa (W6) was active too, although not in quite the same way, and came about as close as Taylor to observing the group's code of output. Why did not Krupa become a leader? The only answer seems to be that, though he lived up to some of the norms, he did not live up to them all. In particular, he sought leadership, he tried to dominate, and was obvious in doing so. Krupa sought greatness; Taylor had it thrust upon him, and the latter was the only road to greatness the group would tolerate. The reasons why Taylor was able to take this course and Krupa was not must lie far back in their biological inheritance and early family history.

[5] Cf. F. Merei, "Group Leadership and Institutionalization," *Human Relations*, II (1949), 28: "The leader is stronger than any one group member. (He gives orders—they obey.) He is weaker than *group traditions,* and is forced to accept them. He is stronger than the individual member, weaker than the 'plus' which a group is over and above the sum of the individuals in it. He is stronger than the members, weaker than the formation."

REACTION OF THE INTERNAL SYSTEM ON THE EXTERNAL

We shall now find that we have come full circle, back to the point we started from. This does not result from bad logic but from the nature of the thing being studied. There is no other way of describing an organic phenomenon in words. As Claude Bernard pointed out in the paragraph that stands at the beginning of this book, an appropriate symbol for any vital process is a snake that is biting its tail.

We have worked systematically, and in these intricacies the mind, unless it uses a system, is hopelessly at sea. We began with the environment of the Bank Wiring Observation Room: the Hawthorne Plant of the Western Electric Company and the groups, such as families, from which the wiremen came. And we showed how environmental pressures tended to produce a set of initial relations between the men in the room. If the men had not conformed in some degree to the output requirements and the organization of work set up by the company, and if the company had not paid the men what they considered a fair wage for the work they did, the group would not have survived. The company would have split the group up, or its members would have quit. The initial relations between the men we broke down into the elements of sentiment, activity, and interaction, and we showed that these elements were mutually dependent: a change in one would have brought about a change in the others. For these reasons, we called the initial relations the external system of the group: it was external because it was determined by the pressures of the environment and by the condition that the group was surviving in that environment; it was a system by virtue of the mutual dependence of the elements.

From the establishment of the initial relationships certain consequences followed. The manner in which the men were linked together in the external system released latent possibilities in them. New sentiments were expressed, different from those of self-interest that the men brought to the room, sentiments such as liking or disliking for individuals and groups within the room and the ranking of individuals and groups by the yardstick of an accepted set of norms. New activities were carried on, some of which the environment, in the shape of the Hawthorne management, had intended to prevent: helping, job trading, games, controversies, conversations, "binging." New patterns of interaction elaborated themselves: association in cliques, the beginning of a web of communication centering on a leader. In this development, moreover, the elements of behavior were mutually dependent as they were in the external system. These new relations we call the internal system, internal because it was not directly determined by environmental pressures, a system, again, by virtue of the mutual dependence of the elements.

But when we called one system external and the other internal we did not intend to imply that the two were separate. In fact they are continuous with one another, the internal arising out of the external by the processes we have described. The line between the two is arbitrary, drawn to help us analyze more compactly in words a circular or organic process, and the two are given special names simply in order that we may refer to them briefly in the future without repeating all that we say here.

We shall now assert that the internal system arises out of the external and then reacts upon it. What precisely do we mean by this? We began by considering the action of the group on the environment. The response of the group to the pressures of the environment was different from what it would have been if the external system alone had been in existence. We can best make this point clear in the matter of output, one of the most easily measured responses of the group. If output had been determined only by the organization of the work and by the motives of the workers, balancing the desire for more pay against the fatigues of more work, that is, if output had been wholly determined by the external system, it would have been greater than it was in fact. But output was not determined by the external system alone. It was also determined by the internal system, especially the norms of the group and the relationships of social rank linked with these norms. Every difference in individual output reflected a difference in social rank. Moreover, the internal system was determined in part by the external. The development of group norms, the division into subgroups, and the ranking of individuals and subgroups were all conditioned by the setup of work, that is, by such facts as these: the men were working together in one room, in certain spatial relations to one another; they were doing slightly different kinds of work; they differed from one another in pay rates and seniority. In short, the internal system, arising out of the external system, modified the response to the environment that would have been expected from the external system alone. But note that this modification was not large enough to prevent the group from surviving in its environment. In fact the company was satisfied with the group's output.

In order to illustrate the problems of analyzing organic wholes, we have already used analogies: a set of bedsprings and a gasoline engine. Let us now use two more, remembering that they are only analogies. The first is a physical analogy. We observe the concrete behavior of a group of men. This behavior we interpret as being the resultant of two kinds of forces: the pressures of the environment, which create the external system, and the internal development of the group, which creates the internal system. It would be correct to compare this method of analysis with Galileo's description of the path of a projectile as the resultant of two components: uniform motion in a straight line and uniformly accelerated motion downward—but for two crucial differences. In the first place, the physicist who makes Galileo's kind of analysis does in fact perform two separate operations. He measures the muzzle velocity of the projectile and the acceleration of gravity. What operations comparable to these do we have for separating the external system from the internal? Only when a new group has been formed to do a particular job have we a chance to watch the internal system growing out of the external. One of the charms of studying the Bank Wiring Observation Room, and one of the reasons for studying it ahead of other small social units, is that it comes close to being a group of this kind. In the second place, the two motions the physicist takes into consideration are independent of one another. However they be defined, the external and internal systems are not independent but mutually dependent.

FEEDBACK

A more illuminating analogy is an electrical one. We think of the current in an electrical circuit as flowing in a definite direction: from the positive side of the battery or generator through the circuit to the negative side. Many electrical circuits are, moreover, so arranged that, when the current reaches a certain point in the circuit, part of the current is, as the electricians say, "fed back" by some appropriate hookup to an earlier point in the circuit—earlier as defined by our assumption that the current is flowing in a definite direction. This kind of arrangement may be used to accomplish some useful purpose: it may allow the circuit to "build up" more rapidly to its full load or to carry its load without fluctuation. Even when every part of the circuit is fully energized, we still think of feedback and build-up as going on continuously. The circuit has attained a steady state, but we think of that state as being maintained by a continuous, circular, and dynamic process. We can also think of the behavior of a group as this kind of process, and if, in describing the process, we choose to begin with the external system, we can say that the internal system is continually emerging out of the external and continually feeding back to modify the external system or, rather, to build up the social system as a whole into something more than the external system we started with. Although the necessities of our method of exposition make one come after the other, the processes we call the external and internal systems go on together in reality. Sometimes we can follow the build-up. We can be on hand when the members of the Bank Wiring group are put in a room together for the first time, and we can then watch their social system begin to elaborate itself. More often, as when we study a group with a long social history behind it, we can see only the end result of the process. We can see only the equivalent of the fully energized circuit. And yet, in the group as in the circuit, we can still think of the processes of build-up and feedback as going on continuously.

Beneficent or vicious circles—"spirals" would be a better word— are characteristic of all organic phenomena. We can say that the feedback of the internal system may be either favorable or unfavorable to the group, making its action on the environment more or less effective, provided we have adopted a definite basis for judgment. From the point of view of the Hawthorne management, the feedback in the Bank Wiring group would have been judged unfavorable: it resulted in restriction of output. On the other hand, the members of the group itself, if they had thought along these lines at all, might have judged it to be favorable. They certainly said, in explaining their behavior, that if output increased continuously the piecework rates would be lowered, someone would be laid off, or something else unpleasant would happen. A familiar example of favorable feedback is provided in Moreno's research at the New York State Training School for Girls at Hudson. We will remember our discussion of sociometry on pages 40-42. Moreno was able to correlate certain other facts with the results of the sociometric test. He showed how those "houses" at Hudson that were most "introverted"—the members of the house expressed attraction for one another far more often than they did for outsiders —were also more efficient than other groups in doing their housework.[6] The mutual good feeling that accompanies close interaction may make the necessary practical work of a group go more easily: the group creates its own morale. On the other hand, the elaboration of new activities that is always part of the build-up of the internal system may, if these activities are merely "social," like the games and controversies of the Bank Wiring Room, take so much time from more practical activities that the action of the group on the environment may be rendered less effective.[7] As Barnard pointed out, in a passage we quoted earlier, the changes that take place in the behavior of individuals when they are brought together in co-operation may take a direction favorable to the co-operative system and act as resources to it or take an unfavorable direction and act as detriments. Probably most real social feedbacks are mixtures of the favorable and the unfavorable. We shall return to this point again and again.

[6] J. L. Moreno, *Who Shall Survive?*, 97-8.
[7] See A. B. Horsfall and C. M. Arensberg, "Teamwork and Productivity in a Shoe Factory," *Human Organization* (ex *Applied Anthropology*), VIII (1949), 21, 25.

ADAPTATION

In the Bank Wiring Observation Room, a more important process of feedback was taking place than any we have yet discussed, and we must touch on it briefly. Whatever its character, whatever its purpose, a group, if it is to operate successfully on its environment, needs some division of labor, some system of communications, some leadership, and some discipline. It should be wonderful to us, if the wonderful were not so often treated as commonplace, that the Bank Wiring group spontaneously produced each of these things, or rather began to produce them, for we can hardly see more than the tentative beginnings of the development. A division into cliques may not look like a division of labor, but it could have been seized on for that purpose. Often enough in other groups the division of labor has been founded on social distinctions. In the same way, the group evolved a scheme of interaction between individuals and a prospective leader, a scheme of interaction that would have been available, if needed, as a system of communication for co-ordinated action. And the social control—we shall consider this at length later—that the men imposed on themselves was at least as effective as the discipline imposed by the company. If it had wanted to undertake any new activity outside the wiring job—and such an undertaking may itself stem from social elaboration—, the group had a surplus of these necessary articles on hand and ready for use. It is this surplus that gives a social system room for adaptive evolution. Adaptation is the name we give to the parallelism between what successful operations on the environment may require and what the organism itself creates. Adaptation is as characteristic of the group as it is of other organisms.

CHAPTER 7

The Norton Street Gang

The Method of the Study . . . The Gang Members . . .
Organization of the Gang . . . Bowling . . . Leadership

WE TURN now to the second of our case studies
of small groups, a study by William Foote Whyte of a group he
calls the Norton Street Gang, which hung out on a street corner
in Cornerville, which is itself a slum district in Eastern City.[1] We
might have begun with this case, as it is in some ways our simplest
and most interesting one, but the Bank Wiring Observation Room
had the advantage, which this does not have, of letting us develop
most of our chief ideas. We wanted to put our chief ideas on record
as soon as possible.

As age goes in America, Cornerville is old. Originally settled and
built up by the people, mostly of English origin, who founded
Eastern City, Cornerville, from the middle of the nineteenth century onward, came to be inherited more and more by representatives of successive immigrant groups. So numerous were these immigrants that the state in which Eastern City lies came to have,
in the nation as a whole, one of the largest populations of persons
born abroad or of recent foreign descent. First came the Irish, but
they, like the people of English origin before them, as they rose
in the world above the level of common labor, moved out of Cornerville to more desirable dwelling places. By the beginning of
the present century, Italians, first from the north of Italy and later

[1] This study is a part of Whyte's book, *Street Corner Society* (1943). See
especially pp. 3-25, 255-68. Since the group is described in this small number
of pages, no further detailed page references will be made. Grateful acknowledgment is made to the author and the Chicago University Press, the publisher, for permission to quote from this book. All names, local and personal,
are fictitious.

from the south, had begun to supplant the Irish, though they continued to accept the leadership of Irish ward bosses. At the time Whyte's study was made, during the depression years of 1937-40, Cornerville was a crowded slum; its old houses, in bad repair, were occupied almost entirely by Italian immigrants and their children, poor and largely unemployed.

THE METHOD OF THE STUDY

If we are to judge how adequate any piece of sociological research may be, we need to know something about the way it was made. The observer in the Bank Wiring Room was somewhat outside the group. He was friendly with the men but did not participate in their activities. Whyte studied Cornerville by becoming part of it. He learned to speak Italian; he spent the better part of three years living in the district; he hung out with the Nortons on their corner, won the confidence of the leader and the rest of the gang, and became one of the gang in its games, its political campaigns, and its other activities. Moreover, Whyte explained at least to the leader of the group what his purpose was in coming to Cornerville—that he was making a sociological study. In fact he enlisted the leader's help in the work.

We shall proceed with the Norton Street Gang as we did with the Bank Wiring Observation Room. In this chapter we shall present in ordinary language the main facts about the group, bringing in as little interpretation as possible; in the next we shall make an analysis of these facts, using our conceptual scheme. But in this particular case the procedure meets some difficulties. In writing *Street Corner Society*, Whyte was concerned with many things besides the Norton Street Gang itself. He was concerned with showing the relation between the gang pattern of behavior, of which the Nortons were a typical example, and such matters as the rackets, the politics, and the avenues of social mobility—"getting ahead" —in Cornerville. Our more modest interest is in the small group itself; and yet the pages that Whyte devotes especially to the Nortons are few and come in widely separated parts of his book. At the very beginning he concentrates on this gang, going into great detail about its competition in bowling, and near the end he describes the behavior of the gang leader. Any disjointedness in our description of the Nortons will be the result of our taking part of Whyte's material out of the context he gave it. Moreover, the importance of some of the facts we include will become clear only when we reach the analysis in the next chapter.

THE GANG MEMBERS

The Norton Street Gang, so named because its members hung out together on a Norton Street corner, included in the spring of 1937 thirteen young men: Doc, Mike, Danny, Long John, Nutsy, Frank, Joe, Alec, Angelo, Fred, Lou, Carl, and Tommy. As children, all of the men had lived in the same neighborhood in Cornerville and gone to the same school. Many had belonged to an earlier adolescents' gang. The homes of most of them were still in Cornerville. Even Fred and Lou, whose families now had houses in a suburb of Eastern City, still returned to Norton Street to hang out with the gang. But home takes little time in the life of a corner boy. "Except when he eats, sleeps, or is sick, he is rarely at home, and his friends always go to his corner first when they want to find him. Even the corner boy's name indicates the dominant importance of the gang in his activities. It is possible to associate with a group of men for months and never discover the family names of more than a few of them. Most are known by nicknames attached to them by the group."

The year 1937 was one of depression, and the depression had hit Cornerville hard. All the members of the gang were in their twenties, Doc, Nutsy, and Mike the oldest at 29, Tommy the youngest at 20, and yet only two of them had steady jobs. Carl and Tommy worked in factories; the rest were unemployed or could get only temporary work. Danny and Mike ran a crap game; Doc was on and off the WPA. The fact of unemployment had an important bearing on the formation of the group, as all of the men were of an age at which, in good times, they would have had work to take them away from the corner. They might also have married and settled down outside of Cornerville.

Doc was the leader of the gang. He had been born on Norton Street in 1908. His mother and father were the first Italians from southern Italy to settle on the street. "In a large family, Doc was the youngest child and his mother's favorite. His father died when he was a small boy. When he was three years old, infantile paralysis shriveled his left arm so that it could never again be normal, but by constant exercise he managed to develop it until he was able to use it for all but heavy work." Doc had been leader of the kids' gang that preceded the Nortons. Nutsy had been leader earlier, but then Doc beat Nutsy up in a fight, and, as Doc said, "After I walloped him, I told the kids what to do." From then on the only serious threat to his position had come from Tony Fontana, a smalltime professional fighter. At one time he started to "get fresh" with Doc, to push him around and talk big. Doc hit him, but as Doc told Whyte later, "He wouldn't fight me. Why? Prestige I suppose. Later we had it out with gloves on the playground. He was too good for me, Bill. I stayed with him, but he was too tough. . . . Could he hit!" Apparently Tony did not want to assume the responsibility of leadership. This defeat did not hurt Doc's position, so long as Tony did not carry through his threat to dominate Doc in front of the gang.

The kids' gang broke up when the members were seventeen or eighteen years old. Doc himself worked for a while in the Norton Street Settlement House. He had always been interested in painting, and had a gift for it, and through the settlement house he got a job in a shop that manufactured stained-glass windows. Then the depression deepened; the stained-glass firm failed, and Doc, unemployed, came back to the corner. In the early spring of 1937 the Norton Street Gang began to gather around him. Nutsy, Frank, Joe, Alec, Carl, and Tommy had long been friends of Doc's, and they joined up. Angelo, Fred, and Lou followed. Danny and Mike were drawn to Norton Street both by their friendship for Doc and by the location of their crap game, next door to "the corner." Long John followed Danny and Mike.

ORGANIZATION OF THE GANG

A gang in Cornerville—and there were many like the Nortons—soon falls into a strict regime. Besides its own corner, it often has a regular evening meeting place, a cafeteria or a tavern, where the

gang goes at about nine o'clock for coffee or beer before going
home. "Positions at the tables are fixed by custom. Night after
night each group gathers around the same tables. The right to
these positions is recognized by other Cornerville groups." A corner boy never gets far away from his own corner and his own
routine. His lack of wider social experience contributes to, and is
also a result of, his close association with a small group of friends.
Even when away from the corner, the gang has its favorite kind
of amusement, and, following this pattern, the Nortons set aside
one evening a week for bowling.

Certain kinds of behavior the gang values highly. One is athletic
skill: a man should be a good boxer, bowler, baseball player. Close
to athletic skill is toughness: ability to dish it out and take it. But
a man does not have to be a crook to be tough, and some kinds
of behavior are beneath a corner boy. Doc said of his kids' gang:
"We were the best street in Cornerville. We didn't lush [steal from
a drunk] or get in crap games. Sometimes we stole into shows free,
but what do you expect?" As for women, it is expected that a man
will "make" a girl if he can. This is the thing to do, but it is quite
different from going steady with, or marrying, a girl who is "no
good." A man who does this may still remain a member of the
gang, but he is apt to be laughed at as a "sucker." In bad times
as in good, if you have a few extra dimes you are expected to
give them to your friend when he asks for them. You give them
to him because he is your friend; at the same time the gift creates
an obligation in him. He must help you when you need it, and
the balance of favors must be roughly equal. The felt obligation
is always present, and you will be rudely reminded of it if you
fail to return a favor. This web of mutual aid and mutual duty
spreads across the whole gang, and Whyte shows interestingly how
the pattern is extended from the gang to politics and the rackets.

Whyte provides a diagram, reproduced in Fig. 12, of the organization of the Nortons in the spring and summer of 1937. The
diagram looks simple, but in fact it shows two things at once. In
the first place, the lines between the members of the gang are lines
of "influence." In actual behavior this seems to mean that if Doc
felt the group ought to take a particular line of action, he was apt
to talk the matter over first with Mike and Danny and perhaps

Long John. If the decision reached Long John it went no further: he influenced no one. But if it reached Mike, he was apt to pass it on to Nutsy, and through Nutsy it reached Frank, Joe, Alec,

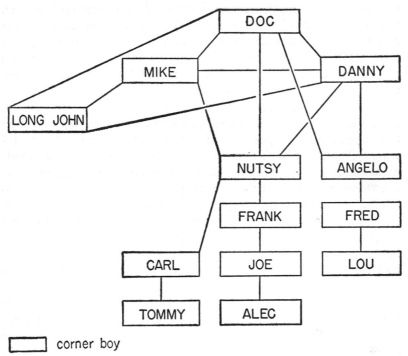

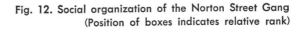

Fig. 12. Social organization of the Norton Street Gang
(Position of boxes indicates relative rank)

Carl, and Tommy. Or Doc could influence Nutsy directly. As for influence in the opposite direction, if Tommy, for instance, had an idea that the gang ought to take a certain step, the idea was apt to get to Doc through Carl and Nutsy. The diagram sums up hundreds of instances in which communication between the men in the group took place in these channels. In the second place, Whyte says of the diagram that the positions of the boxes indicate relative status. Thus Doc was the person with highest status, or social rank. Mike and Danny were at about the same level, just below him; Tommy and Alec were at the bottom.

Doc was the acknowledged leader of the Nortons, Mike and Danny serving as his lieutenants; the rest of the men were followers. These three were older than any of the others except Nutsy. Mike and Danny also ran the crap game. While this prevented them from associating with the rest of the gang as frequently as Doc did, it gave them distinction. The men who hold a game are businessmen; the shooters are suckers, and a sucker, even when he knows he is one, is not highly regarded in Cornerville. Furthermore, Doc, Mike, and Danny were, in their social contacts, less restricted to the gang itself than any of the others. They were well and favorably known to other groups in Cornerville and dealt as equals with other leaders. Doc indeed commanded enough influence to run, though unsuccessfully, for representative in the state legislature. The three were celebrated both for their fighting ability, though none of them was called upon to display it, and for their powers of self-expression. "Doc in particular was noted for his skill in argument." He was seldom drawn into a discussion, but when he was, he was able to outmaneuver his opponent without humiliating him.

Long John was in a special position, in that he had little influence over the rest of the gang—the others did not follow him—and yet he was close to the leaders: Doc, Mike, and Danny. He was always taken along when they went anywhere, and so shared to some extent in their prestige. At the same time, he used to gamble away in the crap game any money he might happen to have, and this made him a sucker.

BOWLING

As we have learned from the Bank Wiring Observation Room, some kinds of behavior that may look trivial to outsiders—for instance, the kind of candy a man eats—are on occasion good signs of social rank or, to use the commoner phrase, social status in a group. In order to illustrate what he means by social status, Whyte describes in great detail a favorite activity of the Nortons—bowling. Through the winter and spring of 1937-38, Long John, Alec, Joe, and Frank bowled together several nights a week, and on Saturday nights the whole gang gathered at the alleys for team and individual matches. These became the climax of the week's sporting events; on other days the men would discuss at length what had happened on the last Saturday night and what would happen on the next. Doc chose a five-man team to bowl for the Nortons against other gangs and clubs. He first chose Danny, Long John, and himself, that is, three men who were important members of the Nortons for reasons other than skill at bowling. Mike was not included; he had never been a good bowler and was just beginning to bowl regularly. The two other members of the team were not taken from the follower group among the Nortons. Instead Doc named Chris Teludo, Nutsy's older cousin, and a man named Mark Ciampa. Neither of these men was a member of the Nortons at other times, but both were good bowlers. These five, Doc, Danny, Long John, Chris, and Mark, bowled for the Nortons. Only when a member of the regular team was absent was one of the followers called in, and on such occasions he never distinguished himself.

"The followers were not content with being substitutes. They claimed that they had not been given an opportunity to prove their ability. One Saturday night in February, 1938, Mike organized an intraclique match. His team was made up of Chris Teludo, Doc, Long John, himself, and Bill Whyte. Danny was sick at the time, and Bill was put in to substitute for him. Frank, Alec, Joe, Lou, and Tommy made up the other team. Interest in this match was more intense than in the ordinary 'choose-up' matches, but the followers bowled poorly and never had a chance." The followers, as a team, never again challenged the first team.

Yet in individual competition some of the followers could on occasion make excellent bowling scores. Frank, for one, was a natural athlete and a semiprofessional baseball player, although he once admitted to Whyte, "I can't seem to play ball when I'm playing with fellows I know. . . ." He often practiced bowling, and sometimes bowled well, but never well enough to be considered for the first team. It may be worth mentioning that at this time Frank worked with Alec in the pastry shop owned by Alec's uncle.

He had little steady employment and little money, became dependent on Alec for most of his expenses in group activities, and held a very low rank in the group.

In the same way, Alec often bowled well. In fact "he made the highest single score of the season, and he frequently excelled during the week when he bowled with Frank, Long John, Joe Dodge, and Bill Whyte, but on Saturday nights, when the group was all assembled, his performance was quite different." One evening he boasted to Long John that he could lick every man on the first team. Long John had an answer to that: "You think you could beat us, but under pressure you die." Alec was furious, although he recognized the group's opinion of his bowling. But Long John turned out to be right. Shortly after this conversation, Alec had several chances to prove himself, but each time it was an "off night" and he failed. The rest of the followers, except Tommy, were never good enough to make boasts. Tommy was a good bowler, but he did most of his bowling with a younger group.

Toward the end of April 1938, Doc had the idea that the end of the season should be celebrated by an individual bowling match among the members of the group. "He persuaded the owner of the alleys to contribute ten dollars in prize money to be divided among the three highest scorers. It was decided that only those who had bowled regularly should be eligible, and on this basis Lou, Fred, and Tommy were eliminated." This was the first time a full-dress competition had even been planned, and there was much speculation about the order in which the bowlers would finish. Doc, Danny, and Long John published their predictions. They agreed that the men on the first team would get the highest scores; that is, the three of them, together with Mark Ciampa and Chris Teludo, would all be in the top five. Next, they thought, would come either Bill Whyte or Mike. They placed Alec, Frank, and Carl close to the bottom, and conceded Joe Dodge last place.

Chris did not show up for the match. Alec let it be known that he was going to show the boys something, and after the first four boxes he was leading by several pins. "He turned to Doc and said, 'I'm out to get you boys tonight.' But then he began to miss, and, as mistake followed mistake, he stopped trying. Between turns, he went out for drinks, so that he became flushed and unsteady on his feet. He threw the ball carelessly, pretending that he was not interested in the competition. His collapse was sudden and complete; in the space of a few boxes he dropped from first to last place." At the end of the match, the bowlers ranked by score as follows:

1. Whyte	6. Joe
2. Danny	7. Mark
3. Doc	8. Carl
4. Long John	9. Frank
5. Mike	10. Alec

Note that there were only three departures from the published predictions of Doc, Danny, and Long John. Whyte and Joe Dodge did much better than the leaders expected, Mark a little less well. We are not trying to explain the departures from the predictions, but it may be worth pointing out that both Whyte and Mark were in somewhat ambiguous social positions. Whyte was in origin an outsider. Though close to all the boys, he was closer to the leaders than to the followers, and Doc was his particular friend. Mark was not a member of the gang and associated with it only at the bowling alleys.

After the match, Doc and Long John discussed the results with Whyte. The conversation went as follows:

LONG JOHN: I only wanted to be sure that Alec or Joe Dodge didn't win. That wouldn't have been right.

DOC: That's right. We didn't want to make it tough for you [Whyte], because we all liked you, and the other fellows did too. If someone had tried to make it tough for you, we would have protected you. . . . If Joe Dodge or Alec had been out in front, it would have been different. We would have talked them out of it. We would have made plenty of noise. We would have been really vicious. . . .

Whyte asked Doc what would have happened if Alec or Joe had won. His answer was: "They wouldn't have known how to take it. That's why we were out to beat them. If they had won, there would have been a lot of noise. Plenty of arguments. We would have called it lucky—things like that. We would have tried to get them in another match and then ruin them. We would have to put them in their places."

Though Whyte had been ahead from almost the beginning of
the match, he had been subjected only to good-natured kidding.
As he says, "In a very real sense, I was permitted to win." At the
same time not even the leaders had expected him to win, and he
was not allowed to get a swelled head. He was hailed as "The
Champ" or even as "The Cheese Champ." Rather than admit he
had won by a fluke, he pressed his claims as a first-rank bowler.
So Doc arranged to have him bowl a match against Long John.
If he won, he would have the right to challenge Doc or Danny.
The four went to the alleys together. Urged on by Doc and Danny,
Long John won a decisive victory.

Alec was only temporarily crushed by his defeat in the group
match. "For a few days he was not seen on the corner, but then he
returned and sought to re-establish himself. When the boys went
bowling, he challenged Long John to an individual match and defeated him. Alec began to talk once more. Again he challenged
Long John to a match, and again he defeated him. When bowling
was resumed in the fall, Long John became Alec's favorite opponent, and for some time Alec nearly always came out ahead. He
gloated. Long John explained: 'He seems to have the Indian sign
on me.' And that is the way these incidents were interpreted by
others—simply as a queer quirk of the game.

"It is significant that, in making his challenge, Alec selected Long
John instead of Doc, Danny, and Mike. It was not that Long John's
bowling ability was uncertain. His average was about the same as
that of Doc or Danny and better than that of Mike. As a member
of the top group but not a leader in his own right, it was his social
position that was vulnerable.

"When Long John and Alec acted outside the group situation,
it became possible for Alec to win. Long John was still considered
the dependable man in a team match, and that was more important
in relation to a man's standing in the group. Nevertheless, the
leaders felt that Alec should not be defeating Long John and tried
to reverse the situation. As Doc told Whyte:

Alec isn't so aggressive these days. I steamed up at the way he was going
after Long John, and I blasted him. . . . Then I talked to Long John.
John is an introvert. He broods over things, and sometimes he feels inferior. He can't be aggressive like Alec, and when Alec tells him how he

can always beat him, Long John gets to think that Alec is the better bowler. . . . I talked to him. I made him see that he should bowl better than Alec. I persuaded him that he was really the better bowler. . . . Now you watch them the next time out. I'll bet Long John will ruin him.

"The next time Long John did defeat Alec. He was not able to do it every time, but they became so evenly matched that Alec lost interest in such competition."

Clearly the group, and particularly the leaders, had a definite idea what a man's standing in bowling ought to be, and this idea had a real effect on the way he bowled. Good bowling was not a matter of sheer individual ability, if indeed individual ability meant anything. Alec and Frank showed that they could bowl well at times, but they could not keep it up. As in all games that demand muscular co-ordination, a man is badly handicapped in bowling if he "tightens up." His ability to control the ball and make a difficult shot depends enormously on his confidence that he can do it. The mere heat of the contest will not carry him through. If he is competing on a five-man team, the bowler must wait his turn at the alleys, and he has plenty of time to brood over his mistakes. Then, when it is his turn, he will be in danger of tightening up.

The custom, almost universal in American sports, of heckling one's opponents is also a factor in bowling skill. The heckling is general; the tone varies greatly but is always recognizable. There is the gentle kidding of the man you really wish well, and there is heckling of another kind. A strike—knocking down all the pins with the first ball—takes great skill, and the Nortons felt that it was a matter of chance when a man got a strike. They judged a bowler not by his strikes but by his ability to get spares: to "pick" the pins remaining on the alley after the first ball. Now when you have only one or two pins left standing, and your opponents are shouting, "He can't pick it up," then you most need the confidence that will take the tension out of your muscles and give you smooth control. You will have the necessary confidence if you have made good shots in the past and are accustomed to getting good scores. Above all, you will have confidence if your teammates have made plain by comments, past and present, their belief that you can make the shot. Then their opinion of you tells. On the one hand, your bowl-

ing ability helps to form their good or bad opinion of you, though
it only helps, as many other factors—indeed your whole social behavior—will sway their judgment. On the other hand, their opinion
is crucial in determining how well you bowl.

We have seen how opinion affected the results of individual competition among the Nortons. The force of opinion showed itself
also when the gang chose up sides for an intragang team match.
"When Doc, Danny, Long John, or Mike bowled on opposing sides,
they kidded one another good-naturedly. Good scores were expected of them, and bad scores were accounted for by bad luck
or temporary lapses of form. When a follower threatened to better
his position, the remarks took quite a different form. The boys
shouted at him that he was lucky, that he was 'bowling over his
head.' The effort was made to persuade him that he should not be
bowling as well as he was, that a good performance was abnormal
for him. This type of verbal attack was very important in keeping
the members 'in their places.' It was used particularly by the followers so that, in effect, they were trying to keep one another down.
While Long John, one of the most frequent targets for such attacks, responded in kind, Doc, Danny, and Mike seldom used this
weapon. However, the leaders would have met a real threat on the
part of Alec or Joe by such psychological pressures."

The very process of choosing up sides for these intragang team
matches showed what the Nortons thought of one another's ability
at bowling. Two men chose sides to make five-man teams. "The
choosers were often, but not always, among the best bowlers." Two
poor bowlers might do the choosing, so long as they were evenly
matched; but in all cases the method was the same, a method
familiar to Americans. "Each one tried to select the best bowler
among those who were still unchosen. When more than ten men
were present, choice was limited to the first ten to arrive, so that
even a poor bowler would be chosen if he came early. It was the
order of choice which was important. Sides were chosen several
times each Saturday night, and in this way a man was constantly
reminded of the value placed upon his ability by his fellows and
of the sort of performance expected of him."

Finally, the standing of a man in the eyes of other gangs contributed to his standing, even in bowling, within his own gang.

"In the season of 1938-39 Doc began keeping the scores of each man every Saturday night so that the Nortons' team could be selected strictly according to the averages of the bowlers, and there could be no accusation of favoritism. One afternoon when Bill Whyte and Doc were talking about bowling performances, Bill asked Doc and Danny what would happen if five members of the second team should make better averages than the first-team bowlers. Would they then become the first team? Danny said:

Suppose they did beat us, and the San Marcos would come up and want a match with us. We'd tell them, those fellows are really the first team, but the San Marcos would say, 'We don't want to bowl them, we want to bowl you.' We would say, 'All right, you want to bowl Doc's team?' and we would bowl them.

Doc added, 'I want you to understand, Bill, we're conducting this according to democratic principles. It's the others who won't let us be democratic.'

LEADERSHIP

At the end of his book Whyte makes some general observations about the leader of a gang in Cornerville. He does not say in so many words that they all apply to Doc, the leader of the Nortons, but it is likely that they do, as the Nortons were the gang Whyte knew best. At any rate, we shall assume that they apply to Doc.

The leader is the man who, on the whole, best lives up to the standard of behavior that the group values. If the group is interested in boxing or bowling—and any group of young men in America sets great store by athletic skill—, the leader must be a competent boxer or bowler. At the same time, he naturally promotes those activities in which he excels, and his high social standing helps him, as we have seen, to excel in them. He also lives up to the demands of mutual aid better than the rest of the group. "The man with low status may violate his obligations without much change in his position. His fellows know that he has failed to discharge certain obligations in the past, and his position reflects his past performances. On the other hand, the leader is depended upon by all the members to meet his personal obligations. He cannot fail to do so without causing confusion and endangering his position. . . . When he gives his word to one of his boys, he keeps it."

In order that he may always be solvent in the matter of favors, the leader is careful not to be under obligation to one of his followers in large amounts or for long. If he himself does borrow, he is apt to borrow from one of his lieutenants or, better, from an outsider. Here his social contacts outside the gang, much more frequent than those of his followers, will help him, as will the very fact of his leadership. In Cornerville politics, for instance, a man who wants the support of the gang will go to the gang leader, and to the gang leader will also go the petty favors in which support is repaid. It follows that the leader always gives more in money and favors to his followers than he ever receives from them, and that he is enabled to do so just because he is a leader: he has more patronage to dispense. He pays them in money; they repay him in the coin of accepted leadership.

When the leader is not present, the gang tends to fall apart into smaller groups. Among the Nortons, as Whyte's diagram shows, these subgroups were two in number: Nutsy's followers and Angelo's. "When the leader appears, the situation changes strikingly. The small units form into one large group. The conversation becomes general, and unified action frequently follows. The leader becomes the central point of discussion. A follower starts to say something, pauses when he notices the leader is not listening, and begins again when he has the leader's attention."

Thus communication flows toward the leader. It flows toward him in general conversations; it also flows toward him in private ones. The followers come to him with their problems and confidences. Thus he is better informed than anyone else about what is going on in the gang. When a quarrel arises among the boys, he knows what its sources are and is in a better position to settle it than any other man. Since his opinion is the most important single factor in determining a man's standing in the group, each party to a quarrel comes to him with its version of the story, and may appeal to him to act as judge and compose the differences. Here again he must live up to the standards of the group or risk his position. He must be scrupulously fair, even when his closest friends are concerned—and not all men in the group are equally close to him.

If communication flows towards the leader, it also flows away from him. He is the man who makes the decisions, who starts action going, and he is expected to do so. Other men may offer suggestions, but these must reach him and receive his approval before the gang will take them up and do something about them. Moreover, his decisions will pass through definite channels: the leader secures group action by dealing first with his lieutenants. Doc explained once: "On any corner you would find not only a leader but probably a couple of lieutenants. They could be leaders themselves, but they let the man lead them. You would say, 'They let him lead because they like the way he does things.' Sure, but he leans upon them for his authority."

Finally, the leader's position depends on his being "right," being right meaning simply that his decisions have usually turned out to be acceptable to the group. "One night when the Nortons had a bowling match, Long John had no money to put up as his side bet, and he agreed that Chick Morelli should bowl in his place. After the match Danny said to Doc, 'You should never have put Chick in there.' Doc replied with some annoyance, 'Listen, Danny, you yourself suggested that Chick should bowl instead of Long John.' Danny said, 'I know, but you shouldn't have let it go.'" Even against his own advice, Danny had relied on Doc to make the right decision. Ability to carry the followers with him is the source of any leader's authority.

CHAPTER 8

The Position of the Leader

Influence of the Environment . . . The Internal System:
The Group as a Whole . . . Differentiation within the
Group: Mutual Dependence of Activity and Sentiment
. . . Mutual Dependence of Sentiment and Interaction
. . . Mutual Dependence of Interaction and Activity . . .
Reaction of the Internal System on the Environment

IN ACCORDANCE with our regular procedure, we shall now go back and, using our conceptual scheme, make an analysis of the Norton Street Gang, or rather the facts about the gang that Whyte gives us. We are not especially interested in describing the surface facts of group life, however picturesque they may be. As a necessary evil, they are described because from them all profounder investigation starts, but they are endless and vary from group to group. Instead we are interested in establishing the similarities between groups that underlie the surface facts. These similarities, we believe, can only become clear to us if we have a single way of analyzing group behavior and apply it regularly to every new group we encounter. We must train ourselves so thoroughly in a method of thinking about group life that its use will become second nature. For this purpose, practice is what we need, practice in applying our conceptual scheme. We practiced on the Bank Wiring group; in this chapter we shall practice on the Norton Street Gang; in time we shall know how to take hold of any new group we meet, in or out of this book.

Although we shall apply our method in the same way to every new group, we shall not expect to emphasize the same points every time. That would only lead to dreary repetition, whereas we want to introduce one or two new ideas in each chapter. The same features tend to reappear in every group, but not all elaborated to the same degree. The most conspicuous feature of the Bank Wiring Observation Room was the development of the cliques and its relation to the organization of work. Leadership was only rudimentary. In the Norton Street Gang, leadership was well developed, and we shall, in our analysis, pay most attention to its characteristics.

INFLUENCE OF THE ENVIRONMENT

We begin, as always, with the environment and its influence upon the group. The Bank Wiremen were originally brought together by a business organization. This was not true of the Nortons, but other characteristics of their environment conspired to increase and maintain interaction among them. As we have seen, their families had long lived in the Norton Street neighborhood of Cornerville; they themselves had gone to school together; they had belonged to an earlier gang of adolescents, and all but two of the men still lived in Cornerville. To this extent, the environment had thrown them together until their interaction had become habitual, and the effect of the environment in increasing interaction is the starting point for the formation of a group.

Not only did the environment throw the Nortons together; it also tended to discourage their frequent interaction in groups other than the gang. Cornerville was a slum; its tenements were old and crowded. There was not much room for family life and not much charm in it. The Nortons, moreover, were children of immigrant parents. Their fathers and mothers had come to America as adults; they themselves had been born in America, or had arrived here at so early an age that they remembered nothing of the old country. Since the Italian pattern conflicted with the American at many points, the old folks had little to offer the youngsters that could help them fit into American life. What they needed to learn they could learn only away from home. Most young men want to get away from their families, but for all the reasons we have cited the Nortons spent even more time than other young Americans hanging around with their age-mates. They went home, for the most part, only to eat and sleep.

The gang members might have gone to the Norton Street Settlement House. After all, it was there to provide a better recreation center than a street corner and to help young Italians adjust to American life. But forces were at work that limited the effectiveness of the settlement house. The standards of behavior of its administrators were those of middle-class American society, of the "good people" of Eastern City. For the young men of Italian descent who were willing and able to work to attain these standards the settlement house could do much. It could, and did, start them on the road to success and full assimilation. But such men were a minority. If Cornerville's standards were not altogether the old Italian standards, neither were they altogether those of the good people of Eastern City. The leaders of the Cornerville boys' gangs naturally conformed to Cornerville's standards: that was one condition of their leadership. They did not feel at home in the settlement house, which, failing to attract the leaders, failed also to bring in their followers. In effect, the settlement house wanted the boys to come in on its own terms, not theirs.[1]

The boys' gang is a natural phenomenon of adolescence, at least in America. It springs up in every community. What makes the adult gang seem somehow wrong to many people is that it prolongs an adolescent pattern well past adolescence. Many of the Nortons were in their late twenties, yet they still spent most of their time on the corner. For this the depression could be blamed and the lack of opportunity for the advancement of young Italian-Americans. Most of the Nortons had no particular work-training or skill, nor had their families position and influence. They were poor men to begin with, and as such were almost bound to become unemployed in a depression. In good times they might have had jobs and got married.

But even if there had been no depression, the Nortons would still have had trouble escaping from the corner. Whyte shows that social advancement within Cornerville takes place largely in the channels offered by local politics and the rackets, which are closely tied in with the corner-boy pattern of behavior. Advancement outside of Cornerville, in the world of business and the professions,

[1] See *Street Corner Society*, 98-104.

requires that a man cut himself loose from his old friends and way of life—something that not every young man, in Cornerville or out, finds it easy to do.[2]

The environment, then, tended to throw the members of the gang together and keep them together. It also had an influence on what they did and did not do. The Nortons were unemployed, which meant that certain kinds of activity were not open to them, and they were reduced to "hanging out" on the corner. Certain other kinds of activity they were particularly apt to take up, by reason of the norms they brought to the group from Cornerville society at large. Cornerville people were mostly members of the lower class; the gang members were young men, and there were many corner gangs in Cornerville besides the Nortons. The norms of behavior the members of the gang valued highly—skill in games and athletics, toughness, willingness to share one's money and other advantages with a friend—were all characteristic of a lower-class, youthful society, organized in gangs. To take one example, these norms made it particularly likely that the Nortons would pursue an activity such as bowling.

But there was nothing in the environment of the gang to compare with the Western Electric Company, and nothing as specific as the organization of work, determined by the company, in its influence on differentiation within the group. The *external system* of the gang consisted only of frequent interaction among the members, the absence of certain kinds of activity, and some tendency to take up certain other kinds, such as games of athletic skill. Much the larger part of group behavior was highly spontaneous; that is to say, it was not directly conditioned by the environment. For this reason we may speak of the Nortons as an *autonomous group*,[3] provided we remember that autonomy is always a matter of degree and that no group wholly escapes environmental influences. We shall want to ask, as we compare the Nortons with the

---

[2] See *ibid.*, 94-108.

[3] This name is borrowed from the journal entitled *Autonomous Groups Bulletin*, R. Spence and M. Rogers, eds. The difference between the Nortons and the Bank Wiring group resembles the differences between the *psychegroup* and the *sociogroup* in H. H. Jennings, "Sociometric Differentiation of the Psychegroup and the Sociogroup," *Sociometry*, X (1947), 71-9.

next group we study, whether a group's autonomy has any effect on the character of its leadership.

THE INTERNAL SYSTEM: THE GROUP AS A WHOLE

Standing on the generalizations made in earlier chapters, we shall do no more here than point to a few parallels between the internal systems of the Nortons and the Bank Wiremen. As before we shall proceed by successive approximations, first blocking in the main outlines of the group as a whole, and then differentiating more carefully the behavior of subgroups and individuals.

The Nortons hung out together. This was their way of saying that they interacted frequently with one another. Repeated social contacts define a group. And this frequent interaction was associated with sentiments of liking for one another: the Nortons were friends. There are no "natural" sentiments between people, not even between mother and child, apart from such repeated contacts, though some of us still talk as if there were. No doubt some members of the group interacted with one another with a particularly high frequency and were particularly friendly. For instance, Doc, Danny, Mike, and Long John saw a great deal of one another —note how often everyday phrases like this denote sheer interaction without specifying the activity that accompanies the interaction— and they were also especially close friends. But when the gang was assembled at one of its regular haunts, every member must have interacted with every other, and all were friendly to some degree. We must always remember the wise remark by Roethlisberger and Dickson that in carefully analyzing the differentiation within the group it is easy to lose sight of its over-all unity. Both differentiation and unity are always present.

Moreover, frequent interaction within the group implied infrequent interaction outside it. This, again, was more true of some members of the group than of others. Some of the Nortons had hardly any associates outside the group. They always saw the same old gang. This poverty of social contact was much less characteristic of the leaders. And, as usual, infrequent interaction with outsiders was associated with unfavorable sentiments towards them.

The Nortons felt themselves to be "better" than other Cornerville gangs.

Sentiment does not exist in a vacuum but needs the sustenance of activity. One way in which friendship expressed itself among the Nortons was in lending a man money and doing him other favors in time of need. Note how an activity like this has a three-fold significance: a loan is a sacrifice of immediate self-interest on the part of the man making the loan; it is also an expression of friendship, and it is expected in the norms of the group. Besides these exchanges which, like helping in the Bank Wiring Observation Room, linked individuals together, the group seized on other activities that it carried out as a unit: merely hanging on the corner and talking, going to a cafeteria for coffee and more talk, playing games such as bowling, and taking part in political campaigns. Finally, to complete the circle, these activities supported inter-action, as they were stimulated by it.

In the dynamic relations between interaction, sentiment, and activity, we can follow the process of elaboration, or "build-up" in the internal system. We can also see the process of standardization. The Nortons fell into a routine, and a rather rigid one at that. At certain hours they hung out on the corner, at others they went to a cafeteria for coffee. It was always the same cafeteria; they always sat down at the same table and at the same seats. On Saturday nights the gang went bowling. Anyone who knew the group could tell where it was almost certain to be found at any moment. In elaborating their activities, the Nortons also made them customary. It is a mistake to think that the environment is the only agency that imposes custom on society, as the seasons impose some customs on a farmer. Society makes and imposes its own routines. Nor is there anything mysterious about the process. The best way to understand why routines exist is to ask what would happen if they did not. Suppose you are a gang member and are not present to take part in some activity of the group. To that extent you fail to inter-act with the other members, and to that extent you are no longer a member of the group. But one of our fundamental assumptions is that interaction with others is rewarding to a person and failure to interact, or social isolation, hurtful. So when you fail to interact with your own group, you have been hurt, especially if, like many of the Nortons, you have no other group to which you can turn. The routine of a group therefore implies a control: once it is established, you depart from it at your social peril. Conversely, and this is perhaps a more difficult point to grasp, even a hint of peril helps establish the routine. If, fearing the consequences of departure from the group's routine, you act so as to abide by it, you have by that action helped to establish the routine. Custom and control grow up together. Which comes first we cannot say, but the interplay between the two may bring it about that a group left to itself will maintain fairly rigid routines. These dynamic balances are the steel of society.

The same kind of argument can be used in analyzing the relation between custom and expectation. If you are a gang member, you know that the gang will probably be hanging out on the corner at a certain time, and that if it is not there, it must be at one of a very few other places. The established routine enables you to find your friends, to act sensibly and coherently without wasting time, and this kind of action is rewarding. Many wise men have pointed out that people are lost without some framework of expected behavior. But the need for routine does not account for its appearance. Except in fairy tales, useful articles do not appear just because they are needed. The interesting point is that by acting on your expectations you, and others like you, are helping to create the very thing you all need. The fact is that if the gang turns out to be where you expected it, and you join it there, you have by your action helped to create the routine on which your future expectations, and those of others, will be based. This plunge into the problem of custom and control will be followed later by a whole chapter on the subject.

DIFFERENTIATION WITHIN THE GROUP: MUTUAL DEPENDENCE OF ACTIVITY AND SENTIMENT

The Nortons, like all groups, evaluated a man's behavior by certain norms. He was expected to be strong and skillful at games and athletic sports, particularly those in which the group was interested; he should be openhanded and ready to meet his obligations; he should be able to "dish it out and take it"; he should be no sucker, and so on. Though the group may not have stated its norms thus explicitly, they nevertheless governed its judgments. The more closely a man in his activities conformed to these standards, the more popular he was and the higher his social rank.

We might, following Whyte, have spoken of *status* instead of *rank*, but *status*, as ordinarily used by sociologists, refers to several different kinds of fact, while we want a word that refers to one kind only. We have spoken of this before, but perhaps a reminder is needed now. When a sociologist says that a man has high status in an organization, he may mean any or all of the following: (*a*) the man is close to the center of the web of communication in the organization; (*b*) he is carrying on a particular kind of activity or maintaining a certain level of activity; and (*c*) by reason of his position in the web of communication and the kind of job he does, he is highly ranked or valued. Thus in a certain manufacturing firm, the General Manager reports to the President, is in charge of manufacturing, and has high prestige. We do not want to lump all three aspects of his position together under the name of *status*, but to separate them and see the relations among them. And of the three aspects, we give the name of *rank* to the evaluation or prestige aspect—in our language, the sentimental aspect.

In the Bank Wiring group we saw that the persons and subgroups coming closest to achieving the group norms were also those holding highest social rank. Although we could see this relation most clearly in the matter of output, because output was measured, the relation also seemed to hold for such activities as conversation: the group that talked with least noise and most sophistication had the highest social rank. The activities of the Nortons were somewhat different from those of the Bank Wiremen, but the underlying relation between activity and sentiment remained the same, and the relation could again be seen most clearly where the quality of the activity could be easily measured—in this case, by bowling scores. It was perhaps for this reason that Whyte spent so much time on the Nortons' behavior in bowling. At any rate his data, especially the results of intragroup competition, make it plain that the men who got the better scores in bowling, Danny, Doc, Mike, and Long John, all had higher social rank among the Nortons than the men who got the lower scores, Joe, Mark, Carl, Frank, and Alec. And just as the relation between rank and output in the Bank Wiring Observation Room was one of mutual dependence, so was the relation between rank and bowling among the Nortons. Ability in bowling certainly helped give a man a high social rank, but high social rank also helped give a man ability in bowling. He was expected to do well; he had confidence, and the leaders supported him.

On the face of it, we might have expected that a man would do very much better in some activities than in others; that is, if he were a good bowler, he might be slow to return a favor. But in fact the kind of relation that existed between rank and bowling scores also held for most of the men in their other activities. The leaders were good bowlers; they were also good boxers. They were particularly careful to return favors, so careful indeed that the followers got more money from the leaders than they ever returned. The leaders were also fair and just in their decisions. And just as Taylor (W3), the most popular man and incipient leader among the Bank Wiremen, came closer than the others to realizing *all* the norms of the group, so did Doc, the leader and most popular man among the Nortons.

The point is that a good record in one activity is not enough to give a man high social rank. Among the Bank Wiremen Krupa (W6) lived up to the norms of the group in the matter of output but not in other ways, and among the Nortons Alec was comparable to Krupa. In individual matches and when the leaders of the group did not gang up on him, he could do very well in bowling, but in other activities he did not conform very closely to group standards. He was boastful; he was aggressive in trying to improve his social ranking. He spent more time chasing girls than the other Nortons did, and, what was worse, showed that he was capable of leaving friends in the lurch when on the prowl.[4] If his behavior had improved in these respects, his social rank might then have risen, and his scores in intraclique bowling competition might have been allowed to go up. As it was, his rank remained low. On the basis of all this data, we can say again, as we said in our study of the Bank Wiremen, that *the closer an individual or a subgroup*

[4] See *Street Corner Society,* 25-35.

comes to realizing in all activities the norms of the group as a whole, the higher will be the social rank of the individual or subgroup.

In both the Bank Wiring Observation Room and the Norton Street Gang social rank and the degree to which a person lived up to the norms of the group were positively correlated. But we can see more clearly in the latter than in the former some of the mechanisms by which this association was maintained. So far we have talked as if the sentiments according to which the members of a group are ranked in some order were shared by all the members of the group. We have talked as if all would agree on the ranking. Though this is true enough for a first approximate description of group behavior, it also becomes clear from Whyte's data on the Nortons that the *sentiments of the leaders of a group carry greater weight than those of the followers in establishing a social ranking.* The sentiments of the leaders are transmitted to the followers, and when the leaders have established a ranking, they take action to preserve it. Thus when the leaders of the Nortons felt that Long John was getting lower scores in bowling than their opinion of him warranted, they tried by encouragement to improve his scores, and when Alec was getting too high a score, they proceeded by heckling to bring it down. But the leaders were not alone in keeping persons of low social rank in their places. The followers shared in some degree their leaders' opinions, and if one of the followers bowled too well for his rank, the rest turned on him. They kept each other down.

MUTUAL DEPENDENCE OF SENTIMENT AND INTERACTION

In an earlier chapter, talking of the mutual dependence of interaction and sentiment, we began by pointing out that persons who interact with one another more frequently than they do with people whom we choose to consider outsiders also have stronger favorable sentiments for one another than they have for the outsiders. In a first approach to an analysis of group behavior, this statement is good enough, but if the relation between interaction and sentiment were no more complex than this, differentiation within the group would not go as far as we know it does. Among the Bank Wiremen, the members of the group tended to "go to" Taylor (W3) in order to help him or to get his advice, and Taylor was the most popular man in the room. Among the Nortons the pattern was a little more complicated, since lieutenants were interposed between the top leader and the followers. If Lou, for instance, had a suggestion for the gang as a whole, or if he had a problem on which he wanted advice, the suggestion or the problem might go to Doc directly. But it might also go to Doc, if we can believe Whyte's diagram showing "lines of influence" in the group (Fig. 12 above), by way of Angelo and Danny. In the same way, if Carl had an idea he might take it directly to Doc or indirectly through Nutsy and Mike. And Doc, as we know, had the highest social rank in the gang, Danny and Mike ranking next to him. We can say then that *the higher a man's social rank, the larger will be the number of persons that originate interaction for him, either directly or through intermediaries.* Men that are not highly valued must seek others rather than be sought by them.

But the word *interaction* implies a two-way process. If interaction flows toward the person of high social rank, it also flows away from him. The leader is the man who starts action going for the group. If Lou, among the Nortons, had an idea about what the gang ought to do, it went to Doc either directly or by way of Angelo and Danny. The chain of interactions might end there: Doc might not take up the idea. But if he did take it up, he would, after consultation with his lieutenants, pass it down the line again, and the gang would act. Or Doc might have an idea of his own and pass it down in the same way. We can say then that *the higher a man's social rank, the larger the number of persons for whom he originates interaction, either directly or through intermediaries.* We must, moreover, always remember that these relations are mutual: if interaction flows toward a man because he has high social rank, it is also true that he has high social rank in part because interaction flows toward him. The interaction pattern confirms his rank.

Some theorists have tried to define the position of leader by saying that he is the man who originates interaction for several persons at once, as when an officer gives an order that is carried out by his assembled soldiers.[5] Thus Lou, in passing his idea to Doc,

---

[5] See E. Chapple, with the collaboration of C. M. Arensberg, "Measuring Human Relations," *Genetic Psychology Monographs*, XXII (1940), 3-147. The

might interact with Angelo singly, Angelo with Danny singly, and Danny with Doc singly; whereas Doc, if he adopted the idea, might pass it on to all his subordinates at once. So he might, but he would not necessarily do so. In groups of many kinds, the leader does not have to give his commands to all his followers at once. Speaking to each lieutenant by himself, he can still control the organization. It is better to define the leader, as far as interaction is concerned, by his position at the juncture of channels of interaction rather than by the condition, which does not always hold, that he originates interaction for many others at the same time.

But if it is true that the higher a man's rank the larger will be the number of persons who originate interaction for him, how can he find time for so many interactions? The problem is a real one, as all executives know, and it is handled by having the interactions pass through intermediaries, so that the leader at any level interacts at high frequency with only a few lieutenants. In Chapter 4 we spoke of the *span of control*. A small span of control—that is, a small number of subordinates reporting to any single leader—is a necessity for effective two-way communication in any group. But the fact that a certain kind of behavior is needed is no explanation why it should appear, especially in a group like the Nortons whose chain of command developed spontaneously and was not set up, like that of a business organization, with effective communication in view.

The fact is that in any group another tendency exists besides the one by which interaction flows toward a leader, and the actual relation between sentiment and interaction represents a balance between the two tendencies. Doc, Danny, Mike, and Long John—the leader of the Nortons, with his chief lieutenants and friends—interacted with one another at high frequency. They saw a great deal of one another; they went around together. And the same was true of the followers. They were divided into subgroups, Angelo's friends and Nutsy's. That is, a subgroup, instead of being made up as it was in the Bank Wiring Observation Room of men who held similar jobs, was made up of men who were friendly with, and interacted with, a single subleader. But within each subgroup, and perhaps within the body of followers as a whole, interaction was fre-

phrase they use for interaction with several persons at once is "originating interaction in set-events."

quent. We can say then that *the more nearly equal in social rank a number of men are, the more frequently they will interact with one another.* Or, as some sociologists would say, interaction is most frequent where social distance is least.[6] As usual, this process works in both directions. A lowering of a man's rank will change his associates, but a change for the worse in his associates will change his rank. It is a matter of social experience that a person will avoid associating often with someone of lower rank because, unless he is very secure socially, he is, by his action, putting his own rank in danger.

The hypotheses we have stated may look irreconcilable but are not wholly so. At one and the same time both propositions may be true: that any single person interacts most often with his equals, and that the higher a man's rank, the larger the number of persons that originate interaction for him. Indeed the balance between the two tendencies has an important effect on the organization of a group. It means that *if a person does originate interaction for a person of higher rank, a tendency will exist for him to do so with the member of his own subgroup who is nearest him in rank.* For this reason, interaction from a follower to a leader will, if the leader has lieutenants, tend often to go to a lieutenant first rather than to the leader directly. Channels of interaction will become established, and the leader will not be overburdened with interaction. The relative frequency of interaction with immediate superiors and interaction with the top leader must differ from group to group according to a number of circumstances, two of which are the size of the group and the severity of its environment. The smaller the group, the more easily interaction can go directly to the top leader. The more severe the environment in which the group must survive—ships and armies are examples again—, the more likely it is that interaction will be strictly channelled.

Let us turn back now to the top group among the Nortons: Doc, Danny, Mike, and Long John. All interacted frequently with one another, and all but Long John were leaders in their own right. Leaders, in short, tended to interact with other leaders, and it was this process that held the gang together. When Doc was not on the

---

[6] For social distance see R. E. Park, "The Concept of Social Distance," *Journal of Applied Sociology,* VIII (1924), 339.

corner, the gang tended to fall apart into its constituent subgroups. When Doc appeared, the interaction of the subgroup leaders with him pulled the group together again. Long John was in a special position. As we have seen, he was close to the leaders; wherever they went they took him along, and as an intimate of men of high rank he had a kind of rank of his own. But he was not a leader in his own right; the channels of influence led from him to no other man, and his activities did not conform in every respect to the norms of the group: he was a good enough bowler, but he was apt to gamble away his money in the crap game and was therefore considered a sucker. Long John's position among the Nortons was similar to that of the decayed aristocrats within the class structure of a nation. These aristocrats have high social rank, and they often maintain social intercourse with the men running the productive and administrative enterprises of the nation, but they can no longer, like their ancestors, lead such enterprises themselves. The *nouveaux riches*, on the other hand, are men who are important in the organizations of society but have not yet been granted high rank or admitted to social interaction with other leaders, partly because they have not yet acquired the proper style of behavior. When we say that the position of Long John or of a decayed aristocrat is "ambiguous" or "vulnerable," we imply that in establishing a man's high social rank a number of factors are important, not any single one: his leadership, his association with other leaders, and the degree to which in his activities he lives up to the norms of his group. If his high rank is to be unshakable, he must score high in *all* these factors. If he is deficient in any one, his rank is to that extent insecure. It was because Long John's rank was insecure that Alec, eager for social advancement among the Nortons, singled him out as the man to beat in bowling.

Finally, the leaders among the Nortons, and especially Doc, had wider contacts with members of other gangs in Cornerville, and especially with their leaders, than did any of the followers, and this fact contributed to the leaders' high social rank. In this respect Taylor (W3) among the Bank Wiremen seems to have been a little like Doc. He was successful where other wiremen failed in going outside the room and getting a supply of good wire. He must have known the right men to ask. We can say then that *the higher a man's social rank, the more frequently he interacts with persons outside his own group.* As a matter of fact this rule is only a special form of the more general one that social equals tend to interact with one another at high frequency. The equals of the leader of a Cornerville gang are the leaders of other gangs. No wonder that interaction should be frequent between such men. If we had been looking at the organization of Cornerville as a whole, instead of concentrating on the Nortons, we should have found a network of interaction linking the gang leaders and perhaps we should also have found above the leaders a still higher set of leaders—politicians and racketeers—to whom the gang leaders were subordinated.

We should not, incidentally, forget that Doc, Mike, and Danny were older than any of the other Nortons except Nutsy.[7] It was not age in itself that made them leaders but the things age was apt to bring: skill in activities the gang admired, wide acquaintance with other leaders, and above all the habit of originating interaction for younger men. In adolescent society—and gang behavior is a prolongation of adolescent behavior—the older person is even more apt to be dominant over the younger than he is in other age groups. In acquiring leadership the dice are loaded in favor of the older men.

The Nortons, in short, developed on a small scale the same sort of pyramid of command—followers interacting with lieutenants, who interact in turn with leaders of a higher level—that we find on a larger scale in business and military organizations. The pyramid can be seen clearly in Whyte's diagram showing lines of influence among the Nortons. The pyramid was not as regular as it is in the larger organizations, but even in them the actual channels of interaction are not as regular as the official channels shown on the organization chart. Moreover, the pyramid was not designed with an eye to establishing effective communication for achieving group purposes. True, it had that result, but the result was not foreseen. Instead the pyramid evolved spontaneously, that is, through the dynamic relations between the norms of a group, its activities, sentiments, and interactions. The fact is that the organization of the large formal enterprises, governmental or private, in modern society

[7] See *Street Corner Society*, 13.

is modeled on, is a rationalization of, tendencies that exist in all human groups.

MUTUAL DEPENDENCE OF INTERACTION AND ACTIVITY

The position of the leaders of the gang in the chains of interaction within the group and between the group and others like it enabled the leaders to carry on the special activity of controlling or supervising the behavior of the gang. Since interaction flowed toward them, they were better informed about the problems and desires of group members than were any of the followers and therefore better able to decide on an appropriate course of action. Since they were in close touch with other gang leaders, they were also better informed than their followers about conditions in Cornerville at large. Moreover, in their position at the focus of the chains of interaction, they were better able than any follower to pass on to the group the decisions that had been reached. Note that they exercised their control in both, so to speak, external and internal affairs. They decided what the gang was to do, whether, for instance, to hang out on the corner or go bowling, and they tried to maintain the established social ranking of the followers, by supporting Long John and keeping Alec down. Yet whatever the advantage their position gave them, their decisions were carried out only so long as these decisions were accepted. The high social rank of the leaders established an initial presumption that their decisions would in fact be accepted, but the decisions still had to conform to the norms and meet the desires of the group. In a dispute between followers, the leader's judgment had to be fair; a suggested course of action had to result in satisfaction to the group, or his next decision might not be followed. The social rank of the leader helped bring it about that his decision was followed, but a decision, if successful in the eyes of the followers, in turn confirmed his rank. We are here beginning a discussion of the leader's authority that will occupy us at length later.

REACTION OF THE INTERNAL SYSTEM ON THE ENVIRONMENT

Just as the pressure of the environment on the Nortons was not so specific in determining differentiation within the group as it was for the Bank Wiremen, so the group organization had no such obvious impact on the environment as was illustrated by the restriction of output among the Bank Wiremen. Nevertheless the gang did have an effect on its environment, an effect worth noticing if only for logical completeness. Certain stores, restaurants, and bowling alleys were patronized; money was spent in them. The norms of the gang were in part induced in the members by the social environment; in part the norms of Cornerville were created and re-created in gangs like the Nortons. Whyte shows clearly how both politics and the rackets in Cornerville have their foundations in the attitudes and organization of the Cornerville gangs. In particular, the gangs develop leaders, with whom the politicians and racketeers must deal in getting support for their activities, and who are apt themselves to become politicians or racketeers. Doc, as head of the Nortons, was widely known to other leaders and groups in Cornerville and on the strength of his popularity entered a campaign for representative in the state legislature, from which he was, however, forced to withdraw.

In summary, this chapter has been an introductory sketch of leadership in a small group—an autonomous group, if we want to call it that: not too closely constrained in its internal development by its surroundings. The leader is the man who comes closest to realizing the norms the group values highest. The norms may be queer ones, but so long as they are genuinely accepted by the group, the leader, in that group, must embody them.[8] His embodiment of the norms gives him his high rank, and his rank attracts people: the leader is the man people come to; the scheme of interaction focuses on him. At the same time, his high rank carries with it the implied right to assume control of the group, and the exercise of control itself helps maintain the leader's prestige. This control he is peculiarly well equipped to wield by reason of his position at the top of the pyramid of interaction. He is better informed than other men, and he has more channels for the issuing of orders.

[8] For further illustrations, see H. H. Jennings, *Leadership and Isolation* and T. M. Newcomb, *Personality and Social Change,* the latter summarized in T. M. Newcomb, "Some Patterned Consequences of Membership in a College Community," in T. M. Newcomb and E. L. Hartley, eds., *Readings in Social Psychology,* 845-57.

He controls the group, yet he is in a sense more controlled by it than others are, since it is a condition of his leadership that his actions and decisions shall conform more closely than those of others to an abstract norm. Moreover, all these elements, and not just one or two of them, come into leadership; all are related to one another and reinforce one another for good or ill.

CHAPTER 9

The Family in Tikopia

MARRIAGE is the most successful of human institutions. We do not mean to imply, against the evidence, that all mariages are happy, but that marriage must fulfill a universal human need, if we can judge from the fact that the nuclear family, consisting of an approved association between a man, at least one woman, and their children, is found as a recognizable unit in every known society.[1] All the theories of primitive group marriage—that the men and women of a horde had promiscuous sexual relations with one another, and that the children were brought up by the horde as a whole rather than by particular couples—all these theories, part of the picture of primitive communism popular at the turn of the century, have faded in the light of fuller field work among primitive peoples and better understanding of the institutions that were taken as evidence for an original group marriage. Some at least of our collateral kinsmen, the higher apes, have recognizable

[1] G. P. Murdock, *Social Structure,* 2.

families.[2] It may be that men have lived in families as long as men have been men. Any book that pretends, as this one does, to study the general characteristics of the small group cannot afford to leave out of consideration this most nearly universal of human groups.

We hold also that mankind is a unity. This does not mean we subscribe to the theory that "human nature is the same the world over" in the sense of actual behavior being everywhere the same. For instance, a Japanese, when insulted, might behave differently from one of us. He might be less belligerent at the moment but much more concerned about "losing face." Cultures differ profoundly from one another. No one today needs to hammer at this point; it has been made almost too well. Instead, mankind is a unity in the sense that men the world over placed in the same situations, or as a psychologist might say in the same "fields," will behave in the same way—and we must always include as a part of the field the traditions handed down in a society from past generations. When we know the situation, the behavior always "makes sense." The Japanese and the American behave differently when insulted because the situations in which they are placed and which may look alike superficially are not in fact the same. Yet when we have said that they are not the same, we have not ruled out the chance that they may have some points in common. The "fields" are complex and may vary widely, partly because the behavior of individuals, which is determined by the fields, itself helps determine them. This is the great fact that an organic philosophy must face. But our theory is that if we applied the same kind of analysis to all the societies of men, we should find that they were different because they possessed in different degrees characteristics that are present in all. So far in this book we have analyzed groups within our own society. If our theory is correct, and if we are interested in the general characteristics of the small group, we should try to apply our method of analysis to at least one group in a society different from our own.

[2] See C. R. Carpenter's account of the social relations of the gibbon, reprinted in part in C. S. Coon, *A Reader in General Anthropology*, 2-44.

KINSHIP IN PRIMITIVE SOCIETIES

We need to study the family; we need to study a group in a society different from our own. There are good reasons for combining
the two tasks in a study of kinship in a primitive society. "Primitive," to be sure, is not a good word for the peoples investigated
by social anthropologists, though we use it because it has become
customary. Primitive societies are not always primitive in the sense
of "simple." Some primitive institutions are more complex than
their analogues in what we complacently call the higher civilizations, and there may be greater differences between primitive societies than there are between some primitive societies and the
higher civilizations. Primitives are better called nonliterates; but
besides their failure to develop written languages, they have another characteristic in common. In these societies more activities
are carried on by organizations, membership in which is determined by kinship, than in any modern Western society. Civilization,
in fact, is a process that takes activities away from the family and
gives them to other institutions.

This is one reason why the study of the family should begin with
primitive kinship; but there are other reasons. Primitive societies
are apt to be relatively isolated from one another—stress should be
put on the "relatively"—and therefore they can be studied, at least
up to a point, as self-contained units. Many of them seem to have
persisted for fairly long periods of time with much less change than
we are used to in modern Western history. Living near the subsistence level, without a complex technology, each family tends to
find itself in much the same circumstances as its neighbors. Therefore the forces inherent in family organization have had time to
work themselves out undisturbed; the pattern tends to repeat itself
from family to family; family custom is well established. Many
characteristics of family behavior that an observer might miss if he
encountered them in only one family are forced on his attention
if they occur in family after family and are enshrined in the norms
of a tribe. The effect is cumulative; the subtle points become salient.

In studying primitive kinship, we are crossing the line that divides sociology from social anthropology. But does any line, except

an academic one, exist? The unity of mankind implies the unity of the sciences of mankind. If we agree that there is only one sociology, a sociology of human organization, we can hardly admit any division between sociology and social anthropology. A social anthropologist is a sociologist of primitive peoples, a sociologist, an anthropologist of civilizations. The anthropologists are indebted to some of the ideas of the earlier sociologists, and the other side of the exchange has been even more rewarding. In many of the social sciences, ideas worked out by anthropologists have been adopted and found fecund, and anthropologists, self-trained in the bush, have gone on to make excellent studies of civilized communities using the techniques of gathering material and analyzing it that they learned among the primitives.[3] This book, for one, leans heavily on their findings and ideas.

THE WORK OF RAYMOND FIRTH

We are not equipped to undertake a general study of primitive kinship, and that, moreover, is not our way of going to work. We like to concentrate on a case, and an admirable one is ready to our hand in Raymond Firth's study of kinship in Tikopia, a small island of Polynesia.[4] (To pronounce, accent the *i*'s rather than the *o*.) Firth's work there, done in a stay of twelve months in 1928-29, ended in one of the best studies ever made of the way kinship works in a primitive society. Although hundreds of societies in all parts of the world have been described, few anthropologists have supplied us with anything like Firth's report, opulent in its description of the concrete events of everyday primitive life. His is the sort of record necessary to support any close analysis of group be-

[3] Especially the work of W. L. Warner and his associates in the so-called Yankee City Series, and of the men trained by Warner, such as C. M. Arensberg and S. T. Kimball, *Family and Community in Ireland;* A. Davis, B. Gardner, and M. Gardner, *Deep South.*

[4] Raymond Firth, *We, The Tikopia* (1936), *Primitive Polynesian Economy* (1939), *The Work of the Gods in Tikopia* (1940), and several articles. See also his *Primitive Economics of the New Zealand Maori* (1929). The first book is our chief source. Grateful acknowledgment is made to George Allen and Unwin, Ltd., publishers of *We, The Tikopia,* and to Routledge and Kegan Paul, Ltd., publishers of *Primitive Polynesian Economy,* for permission to reproduce quotations and charts from these books.

havior such as we are trying to make here. Anthropologists, like other people, tend to see and report only the kinds of fact that their theories, consciously held or not, train them to see. It is true that theories based on inadequate material lead to a recognition of the inadequacies and thus to better field work and eventually to still better theories, but in the meantime the primitive societies are dying. Tikopia may have changed greatly as a result of the war in the Pacific. We do not know. But in any event Firth studied just in time one of the last Polynesian communities rather little changed by contact with whites.

There are many interesting things in Firth's account of Tikopia besides a study of kinship, but we shall concentrate on that. At the same time, we must remember, first, that kinship is only one aspect of a society and cannot be understood without reference to others, particularly geographic and economic factors, and second, that in describing our earlier groups we could leave out the background, relying on our general familiarity with American society, but in describing the Tikopia family we must give the necessary facts both about the family and about the society in which it is embedded. In this chapter we shall simply try to report, without comment, the mere facts, summarizing as briefly as we dare the great wealth of material Firth presents, while bringing out what seem to us the important points. Our duty here will simply be to keep faith with our author. In the next chapter, we shall as usual analyze the facts in terms of the conceptual scheme we have been developing. Here we may be able to state some generalizations we have not reached so far. We shall use many suggestions of Firth's, but the responsibility for the theory as a whole must, of course, be ours.

THE ISLAND OF TIKOPIA

The island of Tikopia (Fig. 13) lies approximately in latitude 12° 30′ S, longitude 168° 30′ E. The nearest neighboring island is Anuta, seventy miles away and even smaller than Tikopia. Tikopia itself is small, an oval three miles long by a mile and a half wide, lying with its long axis northeast and southwest. It is a model South Sea isle. The land is lush, green, and rugged, the sea, deep blue, changing to violet, green, and white on the reef. There is a coral reef; there are beaches; the trade wind blows. Like many other islands in the South Seas, its core is the crater of an ancient

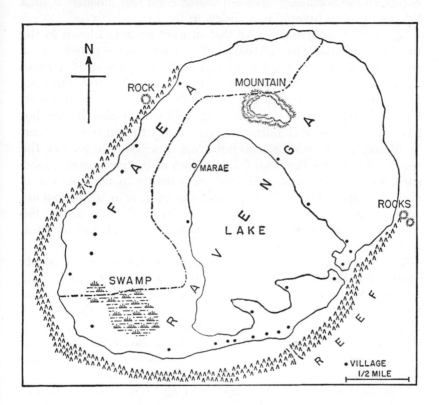

Fig. 13. Chart of the island of Tikopia

volcano, rising at its highest about 1,200 feet above the sea. The hollow center of the crater is now filled with a deep lake, and though everywhere the crater walls are much wasted by centuries of rain and growing vegetation, one of them, the southeast, has broken down entirely to leave a narrow opening from the sea to the lake. The northeast end of the island is particularly rough and steep· the southwest, on the other hand, has a small flat plain of alluvial soil, good for taro gardens, though part of it is lost in a swamp. The coast, except to the northeast, is surrounded by beaches somewhat cut up by cliffs, and outside the beaches, again except on the northeast, lies the fringing coral reef, flooded at high tide and broken by only two outlets to the sea.

The climate of Tikopia, like that of most oceanic islands in the tropics, is pleasant though damp. The temperature remains as a rule between 80° F. and 85° F. and rarely goes above 90°. From April to September the trade winds blow steadily from the east; the sky is often overcast and the air chilly. For the rest of the year, the winds are variable from the north and west. Calm, baking hot days are broken by cloudbursts, and toward the end of the year, in March, fierce gales sometimes reach hurricane force. On the small pieces of flat land and on the slopes of the crater walls, most species of tropical roots and food trees native to the South Seas grow well, particularly the taro and the yam, akin to the potato, among the roots, and among the food trees, the breadfruit, the coconut, and the sago palm. These, with the fish of reef and sea, provide the food of Tikopia.

The Tikopia—the name is given both to the place and to its people—number some twelve hundred persons. Politically, the island is in the extreme southeastern part of the British Solomon Islands Protectorate, but ethnographically it lies on the extreme northwestern edge of Polynesia, that land of many archipelagoes which curves in a great arc from Hawaii on the northeast to New Zealand on the southwest, inhabited before the coming of the white man by famous seafarers much like one another in appearance, language, and culture. For all their geographical closeness to the squat, dark, and crinkly-haired peoples of Melanesia, the Tikopia have the true Polynesian look: tall, long-limbed, with light brown skins and wavy hair worn long. They are a healthy people, little affected by the white man's diseases.

Europeans have been touching at Tikopia since 1606, but no white man yet lives in the island, and though it is nominally part of a British protectorate, contact with the outside world was small before the war. Tikopia owes its isolation to the fact that it has little to offer to the white planter or trader. About half the people have been baptized, chiefly in one of the two districts into which the island is divided, and a native teacher from one of the Banks Islands in Melanesia lives there, married to a Tikopia woman. A mission vessel visits the island about once a year. A few Tikopia have visited other islands, but there is no labor recruiting. Some simple European tools—knives, crowbars, wire, adzes, fishhooks—are used and appreciated. Tobacco is grown in small amounts, and certain varieties of banana and sugar cane, the manioc and the pawpaw, not native to Tikopia, have been introduced. But on the whole the changes coming from the white man have been small. The Tikopia use no money; they still wear their ancient bark cloth and live in huts thatched with sago palm. They carry out their traditional rites of initiation, marriage, and mourning. They are still governed, as they were in the past, by four chiefs, or *ariki,* one for each of the four patrilineal clans. And, most unusual of all, large numbers of the Tikopia still worship their ancient gods in the full splendor of the ancient ceremonies. There are no Typees any more, no Polynesian communities left undisturbed by the West, but tiny, isolated Tikopia remains in this century as little touched as any other.

VILLAGES

The Tikopia lived in "villages" of low huts thatched with palm leaf, each village near a spring and back of the beach, conveniently placed for the work of both sea and land. There are no settlements inland, if any part of an island so small may be called inland, nor on the steep northeast end of the island, and few on the swampy southwest end. Thus the population is concentrated on the northwest and southeast shores, not far from the two gaps in the reef that can be navigated by canoes. Villages vary greatly in size, but the average population of a village is about fifty persons.

Each house in the village has, to go with it, a cookshed, a canoe shed, a path to the beach, and a small plot of land, which is hereditarily owned by the family group and has known boundaries. In the recognized subdivisions of a village, kinsmen are apt to be neighbors of one another and to accept the leadership of an elder belonging to some senior lineage within the clan, who must give permission before any new house is built. Though the land of certain villages is wholly in the hands of members of one clan, more often village lands and houses belong to several clans, one of them usually dominant. We shall speak later of the Tikopia lineage and clan, whose constitution we cannot understand until we have studied the family.

The villages are sometimes very close to one another, yet each is a recognized entity and has its own name, often that of the ranking lineage within it. One of the centers of attraction linking villagers together is the spring, the waters of which are piped in hollow tree trunks down to a pool used by all. Neighbors work together in the ordinary small give and take of life, but the village as a whole works together too. The village fleet of canoes puts out to sea in one body for the fishing and, in the torchlight search for flying fish, sweeps the sea in concert. The villagers may also work together in the drives to catch fish trapped on the reef by the falling tide. Moreover, the young people of each village gather together for dances on nights when wind or moon do not favor fishing. Outsiders may come to these dances, but they come as outsiders and not as of right.

Even when children play together those from different sections of the same village mingle freely, but children from another village are apt to be treated as strangers, or to be admitted to the little group on sufferance. A child visitor, especially if he be not from an adjacent village, looks ill at ease, tends to keep by his father or the person with whom he comes; if he joins the local children at play he is apt to find himself left on the fringe of the group; other children call to him less frequently than they do to each other, and he may be reduced to sitting down by himself and watching the rest. It is fair to assume that these attitudes form a basis to some extent for analogous behavior in adult life.[5]

Three main kinds of link unite the members of a Tikopia village: (1) neighborhood and village co-operation, from the small exchanges of everyday life to fishing, dancing, and deference to the leading chief of the locality, even if he be not of one's own clan; (2) ties of descent through male ancestors, descent also determining the ownership of house and land and the duty of obedience to a particular chief; (3) diffuse ties of kinship through intermarriages old and new. These links tend to support one another in the vil-

[5] *We, The Tikopia,* 56.

lage, where, for instance, one's neighbor is apt to be one's kinsman too. But sometimes they are divisive, as when members of different clans live in the same village.[6]

DISTRICTS

Besides the division into villages, Tikopia is split into two main districts, Faea and Ravenga, corresponding to the concentrations of population on the northwest and southeast, the leeward and windward, shores. The districts are equal in numbers, containing about 600 persons each. The lands of any single clan are scattered all over the island and are not necessarily confined to one district, but each chief lives and is dominant on one side rather than the other. When people from different sides meet, each party is apt to be a little suspicious of the other, to sit apart and put on a formal style of behavior. When its members are at home, each side is a rival of the other, ready to spread any story that runs the other down. Each is said to be a little different from the other in its mode of life, in the kinds of activities it excels in, and even in the temperament of its members. Faea, the northwest or leeward side, is the predominantly Christian side.

THE TIKOPIA ECONOMY

The Tikopia make their living by fishing and farming. The fishing is of two main kinds: deep-sea or offshore and reef. When wind and sea serve, the village canoes put to sea together, but once at sea they usually operate independently. Like fishermen everywhere, the Tikopia get their catches on recognized banks, where the water is shoal, and these are not owned like land ashore but open to all users. A skilled fisherman may find a new bank, fix its position by bearings on the shore, and try to keep it secret; but if his catches are good he will soon be followed. Fishing for flying fish is somewhat different from other offshore fishing; the village canoes do not work individually but make a concerted sweep, and since torches must be used to attract the fish, the canoes cannot go out in daylight or bright moonlight. In the offshore fishing, the canoes spend

[6] *Ibid.*, 64.

all night or all day at sea, and then come in to give the crews a rest.

Fishing gear is individually owned, but canoes are held in the names of the heads of kinship groups. This does not mean that a man without a canoe is barred from fishing. He may, for example, go out with an older brother, if the brother is the owner of a canoe, or he may be welcomed in the boat of another household. He may even borrow a canoe, if the owner does not want to go out himself. The crew of each canoe is made up of four or five men, and brothers are particularly apt to be shipmates, though arrangements are loose. In dividing the catch, the fish are shared equally among the crew. The titular owner of the boat, if he has not gone along, may also be assigned a few fish, and other fish, particularly a big one like a shark, may go to the chief if he is known to be gathering food to support a ceremony or a large working party.

Offshore fishing is carried on by men; combing the reef is done by both men and women, and they wander wherever they will, no proprietary rights in the reef being recognized. As the tide ebbs, fish caught on the reef will try to escape through shallow channels to the sea. In the narrows of these channels nets are placed from time to time and drives organized to pen the fish into the nets. In favorable spots, stone walls have been built as fishweirs to make the narrows even narrower, and these are used freely both by the men that built them and by others. The workers at a drive share in the catch, but a few extra fish may go to the owner of the net if he is not present.

The food plants cultivated by the Tikopia are, in order of their quantitative importance, taro, breadfruit, coconut, banana, pulaka (a form of taro), sago palm, and yam. Taro is under the protection of the senior clan and its deity; breadfruit, coconut, and pulaka come under the other clans, banana under a lineage of one of the clans. The clan chief (*ariki*) conducts the principal ceremonies devoted to the well-being of his foodstuff; he himself tills ritual plots, and he has powers of control over this food throughout the island, both on his own lands and on those of other clans. If, for instance, the *ariki* responsible for the coconut feels that too many coconuts are being taken off the trees and not enough left as a provision for the future, he may lay a *tapu* [7] on the coconut, and then no one on the island will pick any.

Banana, breadfruit, coconut, and sago trees bear perennially, and the land on which they stand cannot be used for other crops. The taro and yam, however, are root crops, seeded every year, and since the cultivation of the taro is the more difficult of the two, it will serve as a specimen of Tikopia farming. The brushwood on a plot is first cut off with knives, and the ground tilled to a depth of about nine inches with a simple digging stick. In planting, the stick is driven into the ground, the hole enlarged, the seed top of the taro put in, and the earth pressed down around it. The seedlings are placed from a foot and a half to three feet apart. Then grass and the cut brushwood are laid around them as a mulch, for the young taro must be kept moist if they are not to suffer from the sun. Later the plots are weeded as many as three times by the women of the household. At the last weeding the grass and brush are thrown away, as the taro needs them no longer. Taro matures in four or five months, and a man usually has several plots in different stages of advancement. Harvest consists of digging up the taro as it is needed. It is never stored, because it rots if left uncooked for more than two or three days.

Every scrap of land in Tikopia, except the swamp and the rocky ridges, is under cultivation, either in gardens (taro, etc.) or in orchards (coconut, etc.). In the gardens no set rotation of crops is followed. Each man does what his experience and judgment suggest. Much of the soil is naturally rich, but after it has been planted with taro or yams a plot must usually lie fallow for several years until the brush has once more grown high. The Tikopia, unlike many primitive farmers, do not clear land by burning, since they need the cut shoots for mulch. It should be clear by now that living on a South Sea island is not matter of lying under a banana tree and waiting for the ripe fruit to fall into one's mouth. At sea and ashore, the Tikopia work and work hard. They do not work under pressure, and much of their work is fun, but they earn their bread

[7] This is of course our English word *taboo,* but since it is Polynesian (and Tikopian) originally, we had better write it in a form that represents the Polynesian pronunciation.

by the sweat of their brows just the same, and he who does not work does not eat.

The group of people co-operating in the tillage of a plot of taro or yams is usually made up of pretty close kinsmen. Firth records one such group. When the Ariki Kafika, chief of clan Kafika and premier chief of the island, was planting taro one day, he had six persons working with him: his wife, his son, his son's wife, his grandson, another kinswoman, and Pa Porima, a ritual elder (sub-chief) of the Kafika clan. Firth calls this group typical.[8] If a man asks a kinsman who is not a member of his household to work by his side in planting taro, he will reward him, a day or two after the job is done, by sending him a basket of food.

LAND TENURE

The study of such a co-operating group leads us into the problem of land tenure. The land in orchards and gardens is divided into small plots, marked off from one another by boundary stones or by rough hedges made by cutting the undergrowth and laying it in a line. Paths are often bordered by man-high live hedges. Tikopia is a patrilineal society, which means, among other things, that owner-ship of land is hereditary in the male line: land descends from a father to his sons. "Ownership" is the best word to use, provided we remember that Tikopia ownership is not just the same as ours. The usual practice is for the sons to divide the orchards and gardens on the death of their father; but sometimes they continue to hold them jointly, and then the oldest brother will have the final decision on the use to which the land will be put. This practice means that a given piece of land is always owned by a single household or a small group of households, subject, as we shall see, to certain rights of eminent domain exercised by the clan chief. A family, like the clan of which it is a part, may hold land in several parts of the island, though most of it is apt to be near the family's own village. Since he does not have at his disposal the records of a registry of deeds and must fall back upon the oral traditions of the Tikopia, an anthropologist can offer no certain explanation of this scattering

[8] *Primitive Polynesian Economy,* 134.

of land holdings, but he may guess that it is the result of the acci-
dents of inheritance and division between brothers in the past.

When a woman marries, her father gives her a few plots of land.
These she does not own; her husband and later her sons may till
them, but when her sons marry they lose their rights in the land,
which reverts to their mother's brothers.

Besides belonging to households, land also belongs to lineages, in
the sense that if all the male descendants of a given household die
out, their land reverts to their nearest male kinsman on the father's
side. This is the accepted theory, but as a matter of fact quarrels
over the land may arise in these circumstances between distant
patrilineal kinsmen and nearer kinsmen on the mother's side. The
patrilineal rule is not rigid enough to prevent such disputes.

Except through the successful use of force or the decision of a
chief, there is no transfer of land. In the past, when the daughter of
a chief had married an immigrant from another island, the chief
sometimes ruled that a part of his land would go to the male children of the immigrant, who of course had no land of his own in
Tikopia, instead of descending, according to the usual rule, to the
chief's own sons.

Ownership of land and use of land do not necessarily coincide.
Anyone, wandering through an orchard, may take a breadfruit or a
coconut if he wishes it. He does not ask permission of the owner,
but he does send him a small present of food with an announcement
of what he has done. Usually the owner does not object; if he does
not wish his trees treated in this way, he wraps fronds around the
trunks to signify that they are under *tapu.* Then no one except a
close kinsman or a thief will meddle with them, but a certain
amount of thievery does take place.

A similar rule holds for gardens. A man may not plant, and of
course would have no interest in planting, perennial trees like coconut and breadfruit on land not his own, but if he wants to plant a
patch of taro on another man's plot he does so. He is more apt to
do so if he is a close kinsman of the owner, but even this rule is not
always observed. As before, the owner may, if he wishes, put the
plot under *tapu.* Obviously these practices could not be followed
unless there was, on the whole, enough land in Tikopia for everybody, and it is true that in the past the people have used various

means, including infanticide, for keeping the population within the means of subsistence. The Tikopia are well adjusted to their environment.

According to the situation, then, the Tikopia may speak of a piece of land as being "of" an individual, of a group of brothers, of a ritual elder (the head of a lineage), or of a chief. Each can do certain things with the land on certain occasions. The chief is the recognized overlord of the lands held by members of his clan. Disputes about boundaries and ownership are settled in the last instance by him. He may also have a good deal to say about the use of the land. We have seen that each of the four *ariki* is ritual guardian of one of the principal food crops. He can lay a *tapu* on it if he feels that the supply is getting low. One of his great interests in the lands of the clan is that they shall provide him with enough food to keep up the ceremonies for which he is responsible. A ceremony is like any other big job of work: a chief cannot carry it through unless he feeds a large number of participants. The Tikopia say that the lands of a clan are really those of the chief, but Firth points out that the statement might just as well be reversed:

Without a following the chief could not work [the land]; nor would he gain by continual encroachment and oppression. Supported in all public affairs by the food contributions of his clan members, it would be distinctly against his best interests to restrict their sources of supply very greatly. . . . The power of the chief, absolute though it is in theory, is continually held in check in the interests of his people. In matters of land ownership the position of either party is defined by a system of rights and obligations, delicately adjusted and widely spread out through the various social institutions.[9]

THE HOUSE

We need to know something about the Tikopia economy, but the institution we have closest at heart is the family, or better, the household. And the study of the household begins with the house itself as a physical object. It is rectangular and low, in order that it may not be blown down or unroofed in the gales, and it has a low-pitched gable roof, the gable ends coming within a foot or two

[9] *We, The Tikopia*, 384.

of the ground, so that the doors must be entered on hands and knees. Its roof and side walls are thatched with sago palm leaf. The house is placed with its long axis parallel to the beach, which is usually not far off, and between the house and beach stands the canoe shed. There are no doors on this side of the house—a protection against the winds that beat in from the sea. Instead, the doors are placed on the ends of the house and on the landward side. On this side, too, is the cookshed.

On the inside, the house is dark and smoke-grimed; the posts that support the roof are rubbed shiny by many human backs. There is no furniture except mats of plaited coconut leaf. Gear not in use is stowed overhead on shelfbeams at one end of the roof. In terms of social use, the interior falls into three parts (Fig. 14). The central area is called *roto a paito*, "the middle of the house," and is common ground for all members of the household. Here meals and beds are laid out, and equipment in active use is put down. The seaward side of the house, that is, the side with the blank wall, is called *mata paito*, "the eye of the house." Here, under the eaves, are laid a set of trapezoidal mats which cover the graves of ancestors buried within the house. In respect for the dead, people do not turn their backs towards this side; when they are ready to sleep they lie down with their heads this way; the seats of the men of the house are next to these mats. The opposite side is called *tuaumu*, "the back of the oven," though cooking is actually done outside in the cookshed. Here are the fires, and here the women and children sit, facing towards *mata paito*.

The doorways toward the cookshed are used by women and children. On one end of the house there are two more doors, one common to all and the other, next to *mata paito*, used by the men only. On the other end of the house, under the shelf beams, is a single door, used by the head of the house and by no one else. Only senior male members of the household may use the house posts as back rests, and each post is assigned to a particular man.

Each house has its own name, often identical with the family name of the man occupying it. When he inherits it, he will no longer be called by his personal name but by his house name. Thus the head of the house called Notoa might himself be called *Pa Notoa*, literally "Father Notoa." The word for *house* as a phys-

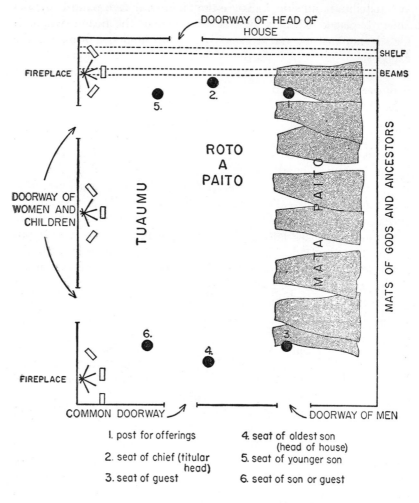

Fig. 14. Tikopia house: Ground plan

1. post for offerings
2. seat of chief (titular head)
3. seat of guest
4. seat of oldest son (head of house)
5. seat of younger son
6. seat of son or guest

ical object is *te paito,* and this is also the name given to the lineage, the patrilineal kinship group larger than the family and smaller than the clan. For this reason, Firth speaks of this group as a "house," just as we might speak of the British royal family as the House of Windsor.

THE HOUSEHOLD

The household in Tikopia usually includes more than one nuclear family. Sometimes two brothers, with their wives and children, live together, each taking a section of the floor. More often a man will have his unmarried brothers and sisters, or his father and mother, living with him. Seldom, on the one hand, do more than two nuclear families live together, since the rule is that brothers divide their land at the death of their father, especially if all are married. On the other hand, only about ten dwellings in Tikopia are occupied by single persons—young orphaned men, old bachelors, and spinsters. Usually the need for co-operation in getting and preparing food makes it convenient for a single person to join another household. The Tikopia are great visitors, and besides the permanent residents a number of persons are apt to be running in and out of the house: near neighbors and kinsmen of every age and every grade of relationship.

The activities of the household follow a daily routine. As Firth says, primitives may be divided into two classes: those that wash and those that do not. The Tikopia fall into the first class. For most persons the day begins with a bath in the sea or the lake, the sexes bathing separately but in full view of one another. When the bathers come back to the house, they find that someone who stayed behind, a child, an old person, or a nursing mother, has rekindled the fire and laid out small kits of cold food. Soon after breakfast, the able-bodied members of the household go out to their work, which varies with the season, the weather, and personal tastes. So long as he brings back food, there is not much objection to a person doing what he pleases in the way of work. If both husband and wife are going fishing, they usually work separately, the wife combing the reef and the husband fishing from the reef with rod and line or from a canoe at sea. But working parties in the gardens consist of men and women together: the head of the household, his wife, some of their children; and if other hands are needed, a kinsman or a neighbor is asked to come along too.

Most work ends about midday. The members of the household come home, and the preparation of the one big meal of the day begins. Tikopia cookery, whose basic technique consists of wrapping food in leaves and then burying it with hot stones, is long and complicated, and a number of persons are needed for the work: a single man or woman would hardly be able to get a hot meal. The cooking itself is mostly left to the women, but the men must do certain kinds of hard muscular labor, such as grating taro or coconut and pressing out coconut cream. In a vivid passage that gives the homely but crucial details so often left out of anthropological reports, Firth describes one household at work on the midday meal.

Breadfruit pudding is being prepared in Nukutaukara, the house of Pa Maniva. The breadfruit are roasted on the oven-stones by two women, his unmarried daughters (his wife being dead), while in the dwelling-house a son, Rakeimuna, grates coconut and proceeds to express the cream. The breadfruit when cooked are peeled by the women in the oven-house and brought in steaming hot, wrapped in *pilaka* leaf. The father cuts them up and puts them into a wooden bowl, assisted by one of the daughters, while Mairunga, another son, cuts a pestle and begins to pound the food. After some minutes the father takes a spell at this work, and later the son takes the pestle back, the mashing of the fruit demanding considerable energy. Mairunga calls after a time, "Are the breadfruit ended?" His sister in charge of them answers, "Yes." Then turning to the cream producer he asks, "Finished or not?" "Wait a while," his brother replies. Soon both jobs are ended and the two men combine, the one squeezing his cream over the pudding while the other continues his pounding. The father meanwhile is tearing up *pilaka* leaf to hold the portions. A younger son, who has taken no part in the more energetic operations, passes him half a coconut shell, which he covers with banana leaf and then uses as a spoon to scoop out the food. Mairunga, his pounding over, now licks the pestle clean, while other members of the family hand round portions on their leaf platters. The meal is then begun.[10]

Preparing the big noon meal takes about two hours. Every household cooks its own meal and eats it by itself. After the meal, people

[10] *We. The Tikopia,* 100-1.

scatter once more to their various pursuits, but the pace of work is not as quick as in the morning. The women, perhaps, make mats or bark cloth, craftsmen ply their trades, children play, and many men just sit about and talk. As the evening draws on, social life becomes more intense, and people gather on the beach for games and general conversation. When it is dark, and wind and sea are propitious, the village fleet puts out to sweep for flying fish until dawn or moonrise. If the moon is bright and the surf heavy on the reef, the village dance is started instead. Only the young and unmarried take part. This is the time and opportunity for love-making, and every so often a girl drifts off to meet a lover in an empty house or shed.

INTERPERSONAL RELATIONSHIPS

Now that the main activities of the household have been described, we can turn to the relationships between the persons in it. But here a warning is in order. In anthropological studies it is particularly easy to confuse ideal behavior with actual behavior. Often the ethnographer, ignorant of the native language, is not looking at what happens in the society but is working with informants, who have a tendency to say, as all but the best of us should in similar circumstances, what behavior ought to be rather than what it is. Moreover, the ethnographer is apt to sum up information about many groups in a description of a single ideal or typical group, for instance, "the Tikopia family." He describes, as if it occurred in a single family, behavior that in fact tends to repeat itself in different degrees from family to family. As a result, we do not know how many individual persons and families depart from the type or how far they depart. From both these dangers Firth protects us as far as reasonably possible. He learned the Tikopia language (he was already familiar with other Polynesian languages); he studied the natives' behavior by participating in their activities; and though he describes relationships in the household as forming a typical configuration, he is careful to say that individuals and families depart from the typical, and he gives us enough reports of real events to enable us to form our own judgment.

Many of the relationships between Tikopia kinsmen are like our own and yet unlike; they possess enough of that difference within sameness which raises a smile and invites a joke, but our purpose, to give a mere summary of observed behavior while leaving its interpretation to the next chapter, is best served by keeping a straight face.

HUSBAND (MATUA) AND WIFE (NOFINE)

Except for incest taboos that are more or less like our own—marriage with a kinswoman closer than a second cousin is frowned upon—a Tikopia man has no restrictions on his choice of a wife. As in many primitive societies, there is much promiscuity before marriage but little or none, for the wife at least, afterwards. No marriage ceremony is performed as such; instead marriage is a drama of capture or abduction: the groom steals the bride from her father's house in theory, and sometimes in fact, without the father's prior knowledge. When the woman becomes pregnant, the couple settle down in a permanent and recognized union, and then begins a series of elaborate gift exchanges between the man's family and the woman's. The husband does not observe any restrictions while his wife is pregnant, but a prominent ceremony is performed at the birth of the first child, the outward sign of the founding of a family. The nuclear family is always a recognizable unit. Even when two families live together in one household, each has its own section of the floor, and "when visits are paid to other households it is this little group that moves together." [11]

Wives are expected to be faithful to their husbands; in fact, during his stay on the island, Firth heard of only one case of adultery. But some married men do go about among the young girls, though they are laughed at as old lechers for doing so. Polygyny—marriage to more than one woman—once allowable everywhere though commonly practiced only by persons of rank, is now restricted to the pagan side of the island. Husbands and wives are sometimes jealous of one another and fight with one another in Tikopia as elsewhere. As elsewhere, too, a wife may go

[11] *We, The Tikopia*, 130.

back to her own family when she can no longer stand her husband's treatment of her.

We have seen that husbands and wives usually go out together to work in the gardens and orchards and then come back home to co-operate in preparing the materials for the noon meal and cooking it. In other matters they work separately, though each contributes to the common enterprise. They engage in different kinds of fishing. The wife makes the bark cloth, fills the water bottles, sweeps the house, and sees that there is food on hand to offer to a casual visitor. The husband makes the fishing nets and carries out all the woodworking. Though care of the children is primarily the responsibility of the wife, the husband must sometimes take a hand, as must all kinsmen. As for authority:

The man is held to be the head of the house, but mutual deference is the norm aimed at. Each partner issues orders in his or her own sphere, orders which the other is free to ignore or object to if desired. If the husband scolds the wife, then she should bow her head to the words, not contradict and exasperate him. But conversely, if she should scold him he should bow likewise; it is right, the natives say, that each party should "listen to" the other when rebuked. The husband is of course in a superior position since the house usually stands on the ground owned by his family; it is then "his" house rather than hers in the last resort. The strength of the wife lies in her ability to return at any time to her own family, and this she can use as a weapon, the mere threat of which may be sufficient to make a querulous or unjust husband see reason.[12]

Terms of endearment comparable with our "dear" and "darling" are not used between a Tikopia husband and his wife. Nor do they use each other's personal names, but address one another, just as other people address them, by the house name of the husband, to which an appropriate prefix is added. Thus a Tikopia may say *Pa Kafika* and *Nau Kafika* much as we might say Father and Mother Kafika. There is no personal joking between husband and wife; that is reserved for other relatives.

[12] *Ibid.,* 135.

FATHER (TAMANA), MOTHER (NANA),
SON (TAMA), AND DAUGHTER (TAMAFINE)

A newborn child is cared for by its mother, aided by the women of her own and her husband's family. But after the first few weeks the husband is expected to take a hand too, and if, for instance, the wife wants to go fishing, the husband who cannot find a good excuse must look out for the baby. When husband and wife are working together in a garden or orchard, the baby is brought along and put down in a shady place. Older brothers and sisters also take their turns in its care, and enjoy doing so. Later on, the children of a village, both boys and girls, tend to run around naked in little gangs of contemporaries.

At this time, too, a boy begins to accompany his father, and a girl her mother, in the separate tasks of men and women. Each is assigned small unskilled jobs and begins to learn something of Tikopia techniques. All older persons may boss youngsters around, and an older brother dictates to a younger much as a father does to his son. A child also begins to learn some of the good manners of Tikopia society: respect for older men and a reasonable degree of silence when they are speaking; a girl learns to avoid the ceremonies at which women are not to be present. But discipline is seldom severe; there are many words and few blows, and a child can always escape to a kinsman's house until the storm of a parent's wrath has blown over.

The Tikopia word *arofa* (the familiar Hawaiian *aloha*) means any strong emotion, but especially friendship, sympathy, and parental affection, in contrast to *fifia* (desire). Parents feel, or say they feel, *arofa* for their children, but they also say that the grades of affection for different children are different. A younger child is more loved than an older one, a daughter, at least by the father, more than a son. One informant, himself the father of a big family, told Firth:

The married pair who have many children, great is the affection for their youngest, and for the girls, but as for the eldest, there is not affection—they are affectionate to him but lightly, because he is the eldest, the household has begun to obey him. Therefore affectionate are the parents to the youngest. In this land the youngest, last appearing, great is the affection for him. They spoil their youngest.[13]

Some of the Tikopia are sensitive observers and acute analysts, and they have an adequate language for expressing what they know about personal relationships. Firth tries to reproduce, as well as he can in translation, the characteristic rhythms and emphases of Tikopia speech.

The father's lesser affection for his oldest son and the latent friction between the two are most marked among families of rank, where the oldest son inherits the authority and much of the property of his father. In most families the sons, when they marry, leave the family home and set up households for themselves—except the youngest son, who stays and takes care of his parents in their old age. But in families of rank, where leadership and the possession of a particular house go together, the oldest son is apt to move back at his father's death.

A parent is thought to show greater affection to children of the opposite sex. As Pa Fenuatara told Firth:

In this land the man favors his female children, the mother favors her male children. The woman, great is her affection for her male children, the man, great is his affection for his female children; it is done from affection. When a man in this land dies, he divides his goods, he gives a small portion to his male children and a large portion to his female children. The woman marries, she secretly takes away her goods from the relatives and gives them to her husband. The point of her taking these things secretly is because her brothers object to her having gone and married.[14]

Note that Pa Fenuatara speaks of goods, movable property, rather than land. The Tikopia also say that a father does not like his daughter to marry, though the reason they give is not the father's affection for her but his desire to keep in the household a person who does a great deal of important but dull work. After her marriage, the brothers continue to suspect that their sister is coaxing gifts out of their father, thus alienating heirlooms from the male line.

[13] *We, The Tikopia,* 165-6.
[14] *Ibid.,* 167.

The affection of children for parents is not so marked as that of parents for children, though it may on occasion be strong. The authority of the father is the key to this side of the relationship. He is said to be the "head" (*pokouru*) of the son, who must "listen" (*fakarongo*) to him. In everyday circumstances the authority of the father is limited. He voices decisions, while his wife qualifies them and the children comment freely. But when he wants to assert himself he is always the master. A son calls his father by his house name and not his personal name. He does not use "bad speech" or tell dirty stories in his presence. The rule of good manners is "to observe gravity towards the father; not to go and make sport with him." [15] Any bodily contact is avoided. A son may not touch his father's head—it is *tapu* to him—and striking one's father is a high crime that can be expiated only by suicide. Firth sums up by saying: "Towards the father a mingling of affection and respect appears to be the norm, each component being a matter of social injunction as well as of individual feeling." [16] The behavior of a child toward his or her mother is of the same general kind but not as sharply distinctive. When the oldest son takes over the leadership of a kin group at his father's death, his mother comes under his rule.

A father must of course provide food for his son and protect him when he is young and helpless. He must also provide all things necessary to bring the son to man's estate. He must, for instance, lay up the goods that are distributed as gifts on the son's behalf at the initiation ceremonies and at marriage. The son, for his part, must feed his parents in their old age and mourn for them in appropriate fashion after their deaths.

BROTHERS (TAINA)

Brothers work side by side in the gardens under the leadership of their father; they are shipmates in fishing canoes; they are close associates from early infancy; sometimes as adults and heads of families they live together in the same house. When both are young, an older brother is apt to take charge of a younger one, protect

[15] *We, The Tikopia*, 185.
[16] *Ibid.*, 182.

him, patronize him, and boss him around, and throughout life the eldest, particularly in chiefly families, acts as spokesman and leader of the group of brothers. He is called *te urumatua, uru* being a common word for "head" which also comes into an expression for the father, or *te uru o fanau,* "the head of the family." But on the whole the relation between brothers is one of comradeship rather than superiority and subordination. Brothers joke and tell dirty stories to one another, as they never would to their father.

BROTHER (TAINA) AND SISTER (KAVE)

Brothers and sisters have their own spheres of interest within the household, but they come together and co-operate in many activities, and particularly in the work around the oven. Their relationship is, in general, free and easy. A brother freely criticizes a sister and orders her around, and so does a sister a brother. Each takes the criticism and the orders as he or she pleases. But they are not quite so unrestrained as are brothers among themselves. A brother does not make obscene jokes in his sister's presence or mention her love affairs in any way. If, however, a man gets a girl with child and shows no intention of marrying her, her brothers rather than her father take action against him. Incest between brother and sister is spoken of with horror; it is against the formal rules of the society, and it rarely occurs in fact. The Tikopia theory is that since sexual relations between them are unthinkable, there is no objection to intimacy between brothers and sisters in the everyday affairs of life. A brother and sister may sleep side by side on the floor of the house, covered by the same blanket. And when a girl has married, her brother is her natural helper and protector.

GRANDPARENT (TUPUNA) AND GRANDCHILD (MAKOPUNA)

No distinction is made in terms of reference between male and female grandparents or between those on the father's and those on the mother's side, and the same is true of grandchildren. Since at least one of a man's sons is apt to bring his bride home to live in his father's house, and the other sons are apt to live near by, grandparents may see more of their sons' children than of their daughters' children. In these circumstances the grandmother is all too free with advice to her daughter-in-law as to the best way to bring up the youngsters. But what the maternal grandparents lose by living farther away they make up for in frequent visiting. And the special fondness of a man for his daughter is easily extended to her children. A daughter begs gifts from her father on the ground that they will benefit his grandchildren.

Grandparents love to have grandchildren come and stay with them, and sometimes almost quarrel with their own children over keeping the youngsters. They pet the grandchildren and tend to spoil them. The rule that respect must be shown for all older people is still theoretically in effect between grandson and grandfather, but practically it is relaxed. The proscription of joking and lewd talk, the avoidance of bodily contact and personal names are a little less severe. A grandfather will tell his grandson some of his ritual lore, the genealogies and legends of his house and clan. We must also realize that as a man grows older and his physical energies decline, by the time, that is, that his grandchildren are growing up, he is apt to be relinquishing his activity and authority in practical affairs.

FATHER'S SISTER (MASIKITANGA) AND BROTHER'S SON (TAMA)

The behavior and attitudes one adopts toward a father's brother or a mother's sister are, with a lesser intensity, much like those one adopts toward a father or a mother, and we shall say no more about them. But the relations of a man to his father's sister and his mother's brother cannot be dismissed so easily. A young child may see a good deal of his father's sister. So long as she is unmarried, she is probably living in the house or next door, and takes a hand in caring for the infant. But when she marries, she goes off to live elsewhere, and though she comes back as a visitor, the contact is not so close as it was. The father's sister is *tapu,* much as the father is. A child does not use her personal name or talk scurrilously in her presence. He never curses her or strikes her. In some circumstances, especially when she is the last member of her brother's generation alive, she may have a certain amount of control over his children, and will be addressed as *Nau E,* "mother," or even as *Pa E,* "father." One of Firth's informants described her

as "the double of the father" and "just the same as the father." [17]
When a chief or ritual elder is getting old and is afraid that he may
die before his son is old enough to understand the *kava*, the names
of the ancestors and the gods, he may tell them to his sister so
that she may transmit them to the child. We have seen that a brother has special obligations to help his sister, and these must have
an effect on her relations with his children.

MOTHER'S BROTHER (TUATINA) AND SISTER'S SON (IRAMUTU)

The patrilineal theory is strong in Tikopia so far as descent of
name, rank, and property is concerned, but it does not prevent a
man's having close relations with members of his mother's family.
They are always interested in him and often visit him. Just as a
woman goes home to her family when she can no longer abide her
husband's treatment of her, so a child runs away to his mother's
family when he is in trouble with his father and wants to escape
punishment.

The link between a child and his mother's family centers on his
mother's brothers, who call him *iramutu* but more often *tama tapu*,
"sacred child." We shall speak of "the" mother's brother as a single
kinship personality. Although the mother may, of course, have several brothers, the behavior of one of them toward *tama tapu* is
much like the behavior of all the rest. The mother's brother is a
boy's friend, teacher, and helper. When the baby is born, he takes
it in his arms and recites a spell over it. Later, when a boy first
goes deep-sea fishing at night in a canoe, his mother's brother takes
charge of him and shows him the ropes. In fact if he is a master
of any such craft as fishing or canoe building, he will begin to teach
the boy something about it.

Like most primitive societies, Tikopia holds a formal ceremony
to show that a boy has become a man, and it includes the painful
operation of superincision of the boy's penis. To this initiation the
mother's brothers bring the frightened lad, tell him what to do,
strip him, hold him, and reassure him, while one of them makes
the cut. For weeks afterward the boy, now officially a man, goes
about visiting his mother's brothers, who entertain him and give

[17] *We, The Tikopia,* 210.

him as much food as he can eat. Then again, when a boy goes for
the first time to the sacred dances at Marae, a mother's brother
shields him from the curiosity of the crowd and, holding his arms,
goes through the motions of the dance until the youngster can
perform them himself. When *tama tapu* is sick, the mother's brother
comes to offer his back as a support or to hold the invalid in
his arms. And so on. On each of these occasions the child's father
rewards the mother's brother, his own brother-in-law, with gifts
of food.

In all the great occasions of life, then, the mother's brother acts
as an older friend of *tama tapu* and helps him over the rough places.
When he must be hurt, the mother's brother will do it as quickly
and gently as possible. When a man needs someone to hold his
hand, the mother's brother is always ready. But he would not behave in this way on the great occasions if he did not do so in the
everyday encounters. Though the mother's brother may live some
distance away, *tama tapu* is always running in and out of his house.
Emotionally the relationship between them is friendly, free, and
easy. Though the mother's brother, as a male of the older generation, is deserving of some respect, yet he is treated much more
familiarly than the father. One may use his personal name, touch
him, tell him lewd jokes, and talk to him about anything under
the sun. But it may be worth noting, incidentally, that the relationship is not cemented in Tikopia, as it is in many primitive societies,
by a custom of marriage between a man and his mother's brother's
daughter.

It should be clear by now that a mother's brother is a practical
and emotional necessity to a Tikopia man. Yet we shall certainly
ask ourselves: "What if his mother has no brother? What does a
man do then? This difficulty is met through a classificatory system
of kinship, of which we shall speak later at greater length. According to this system, more distant male kinsmen on the mother's
side of the family and of her generation, for instance, a mother's
mother's brother's son, are called *tuatina,* just as the true mother's
brothers are, and the relationship between a man and these distant
tuatina is like that between him and his true *tuatina,* though not
so intense. From day to day, the link is closest with the true mother's
brothers, but should none of them be available for any reason there

are always more distant ones to take their place. And on the great occasions, such as the initiation ceremonies, all the *tuatina*, near and distant, appear in a body.

Firth says of the *tuatina-tama tapu* relationship:

The mutual trust between these two rests on a solid foundation of inti-macy. In infancy the child soon comes to recognize its mother's brothers. Says Pa Fenuatara, "It knows its true mother's brother, because he comes constantly to it, he looks constantly on it, therefore it also marks him." This statement, like so many others of the Tikopia, expresses their pragmatic point of view in kinship. Just as they acknowledge no obliga-tion on the part of a son to have anything to do with a mother who has deserted him in infancy, so they hold that the tie between mother's brother and sister's son is a function of the degree of their reciprocal social intercourse. The concept of "natural" feelings between kin does not enter the Tikopia scheme of values, though it has not wholly dis-appeared from our own sociological analyses.[18]

CROSS-COUSINS (TAINA OR KAVE)

Anthropologists give the name cross-cousins to the children of mother's brother and of father's sister, and parallel cousins to the children of mother's sister and of father's brother. They make this distinction because natives themselves so often make it. The Tikopia call parallel and cross-cousins by the same names, male cousins being "brothers" (*taina*) and female cousins "sisters" (*kave*). But they add the word *fakalaui* when speaking of parallel cousins and *fakapariki* when speaking of cross-cousins. The former means an attitude devoid of restraint, the latter, an attitude of restraint. The relationship of a man with his parallel cousins is like his relation-ship with his brother; the relationship with his cross-cousins is a little different. An attitude of restraint is part of it, but the restraint does not go very far. The personal name is not *tapu*, and everyday relations are easy enough. At the same time, one does not enter a cross-cousin's house without being invited, and one is respectful toward him, especially when he is the child of a father's sister. As one Tikopia put it:

My cross-cousin is weighty indeed. I do not speak evilly to him. He also does not speak evilly to me. Because he is the son of the father's sister.

[18] *We, The Tikopia*, 216-7.

One does not strike the father's sister, one does not speak evilly to her. Good speech only is made to her. The basis of the father's sister is the father. I do not speak evilly to my father, nor do I speak evilly to his sister, my aunt. I again do not speak evilly to the child of my father's sister. It is in this fashion because she is of weight.[19]

Behavior is equally restrained toward both types of cross-cousin: father's sister's child and mother's brother's child. In theory one might expect that, since a man is close to his mother's brother, he would also be closer to his mother's brother's child than to his father's sister's child. But we must also look at the relationship from the latter's point of view. If I am a Tikopia, my mother's brother's child sees me as his father's sister's child, and if, for this reason, he is restrained in his attitude toward me, I can hardly avoid being so to him. We have seen that cross-cousin marriage is not looked on with favor in Tikopia and seldom occurs. It is on just the same footing as marriage with parallel cousins.

BROTHERS-IN-LAW (MA)

We shall take up the relationship between brothers-in-law as an example of the ties between affinal kin (persons related by marriage), but we may first say a few words about the behavior of a man toward his father-in-law and his mother-in-law. The Tikopia say that a father always objects to the loss of a daughter in marriage. He loves her and she is economically important to the household. Perhaps because it is assumed that his consent to her marriage will be given reluctantly, it is never asked. She is stolen away from his house suddenly and, in theory, secretly, though he may know perfectly well what is going on and take care to be looking the other way. The first visit of the son-in-law to the father-in-law after this elopement is a time of great embarrassment to the latter. The son-in-law shows him elaborate respect, but the conversation is formal—the Tikopia call it "crooked discourse." People shy away from any mention of the marriage, the weather being a safe topic with the Tikopia as with us. Afterward the son-in-law will go to the orchards of his wife's family, bring back food, and present it to the parents-in-law.

[19] *We, The Tikopia,* 220.

As for the mother-in-law, so celebrated a personage in many societies, including our own, special taboos are not carried out in behavior toward her, as they are in some other primitive groups; but when a woman encounters her son-in-law or father-in-law on a path, she will draw clear and pass in a wide circle around him.

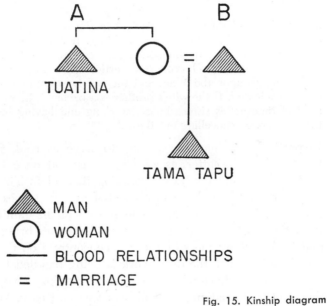

Fig. 15. Kinship diagram
to illustrate the relationship between brothers-in-law

And a mother-in-law, in Tikopia as elsewhere, is not reluctant to offer her daughter-in-law advice on the proper way to bring up the grandchildren.

Turning now to brothers-in-law, let us look first at a conventional kinship diagram (Fig. 15). Consider the two brothers-in-law, A and B. A, the woman's brother, is linked to B through his sister and also through his sister's son, his *tama tapu.* And B is linked to A through his wife and through his son, who has A as his *tuatina.*

We have already seen how a brother and sister, and how a *tama tapu* and a *tuatina*, are linked. On a number of occasions, *tuatina*

helps, guides, and sustains *tama tapu* and is rewarded by gifts made
to him by the boy's father. But the co-operation between brothers-
in-law goes far beyond this. It is wholly proper for the head of a
family to call on any kinsman for aid in economic and ritual tasks
—and every task is both economic and ritual—that strain the capacity of the household, and a brother-in-law is specially apt to
be asked to help.

It is understood that brothers-in-law in the ordinary way render each
other assistance in economic undertakings. If one wants help in breaking up ground for cultivation, felling a tree, setting a net, or building a
house; if he wishes to borrow some article or to augment his food supplies, he calls upon the other, and the call is rarely denied; indeed it is
often anticipated. If the wife's brother is a bachelor, he may spend quite
a lot of time at his sister's house, working and having his meals there,
the one service cancelling out the other.[20]

In particular, a man is expected to serve as cook for his wife's
family when the latter, as a group, must put on a big ceremony
and provide food for those attending it. And in Tikopia, as elsewhere, the cook is the man abused if anything goes wrong. This
practice allows the women who have left the family to visit it
from time to time, since their husbands always bring them along,
and it also allows the wife's kin to concentrate on their ritual and
social duties, since the dirty work is being handled by others.

Between brothers-in-law, then, there is close co-operation, but
the emotional relation is not always free and easy. We have seen
that the Tikopia use the word *fakalaui* to mean an attitude devoid
of restraint and *fakapariki* to mean an attitude of restraint. In the
same way they recognize two classes of kinsmen and kinswomen:
tautau laui and *tautau pariki*, literally those with whom one's relation is "good" and those with whom one's relation is "bad." The
Tikopia do not mean "good" and "bad" in a moral sense here. They
do not expect one to "be on bad terms with" one's *tautau pariki*.
They mean, rather, that freedom in behavior and emotional expression is the rule in the first case and restraint in the second.
Examples of *tautau laui* relationships are those between brothers,
between mother's brother and sister's child, and, to some extent,

[20] *We, The Tikopia*, 304.

between grandparent and grandchild. Examples of *tautau pariki* relationships are those between father and son, between father's sister and brother's child, and, above all, all affinal relationships, including that between brothers-in-law.

In these affinal relationships, the men and women concerned must not use each other's personal names, but rather the appropriate kinship terms or the house names. In the same way, a husband in America in the old days would speak to his spouse as "wife" or "Mrs. Jones" but not, at least in public, as "Mary." In speaking to an affinal relative, a Tikopia is apt to use a "polite dual" form instead of the singular, just as some European peoples use the second person plural to address someone formally. One does not take objects from in front of a relative-in-law; one does not walk directly in front of him; one is not naked in his presence, and one does not tell him a joke, especially a lewd one. One avoids all cursing and even the appearance of anger. The relationship is close in one sense, but restrained and formal in another.

CLASSIFICATORY KINSHIP

This is not a treatise on social anthropology, but we need to say something about classificatory kinship terminology, as the anthropologists call it, in order to understand behavior toward distant kinsmen in Tikopia. A disproportionate amount of attention has been given to kinship terminology, largely because it includes the facts about kinship that are most easily collected, sometimes the only facts that are collected. Any native can tell the ethnographer rather quickly what names are applied to kinsmen. Watching and describing behavior toward kinsmen takes longer. We shall not discuss the different systems of kinship terminology, suspecting that systems which look rather unlike one another may be so because, in effect, a close decision went one way rather than another.

In all societies, kinship terminology is partly specific, partly classificatory. That is, a few of the terms apply to only one person; most apply to any member of a class. Thus an American calls only one person *mother*, but there are usually several persons he calls *uncle* or *cousin*. Systems of kinship terminology differ according to the way kinsmen are classed together.[21] Thus an American calls his father's brothers and his mother's brothers, and for that matter his aunts' husbands, by the same word *uncle*—he classes them together; members of many other societies, including Tikopia and the European societies from which America derives, do not or did not do so. In medieval England, for instance, only the father's brother was called *uncle;* the mother's brother was not called *uncle* but *eme.* Furthermore, a common practice of classification is that rather distant kinsmen or persons not kinsmen at all are called by names applied to close kinsmen. This is not so characteristic of our society, in which ties with distant kin are weak, as it is of some others, but even in our society a Catholic calls his priest *father,* and not so long ago *cousin, uncle,* and *aunt* were used to refer to persons who were not real relatives but were intimate enough with the family to behave like relatives. They were kin by courtesy. In the same way, when he went to Tikopia, Firth became a "son" of two of the chiefs, and other people on the island adopted behavior toward him appropriate to his new position.

It should be obvious from what has just been said that kinship terminology and kinship behavior are mutually related. On the one hand, behavior helps determine terminology. Thus the Catholic calls a priest *father,* not only because this is the custom, but also because the priest, in his capacity as a spiritual authority, behaves in some degree like a father. Again, we Americans call father's brother and mother's brother both *uncle* because we do not, apart from the personal characteristics of particular uncles, distinguish between them in behavior, but a Tikopia does behave differently toward the two persons and he calls them by different names. On the other hand, kinship terminology helps determine behavior. Any person that a Tikopia man calls *tuatina* will behave toward him in some degree like a true mother's brother, especially if the man has no true mother's brother of his own. And when Firth was called *son* by a chief, the chief's real sons proceeded to call him *brother* and to some extent treated him as such. The name established the proper pattern of behavior.

[21] The American kinship system is technically an "Eskimo" one; the Tikopian is a "Guinea" one. For an excellent discussion of kinship terminology, see G. P. Murdock, *Social Structure,* 184-259.

The Tikopia have two sets of kinship terms, one used in talking about kinsmen (terms of reference), the other used in talking to kinsmen (terms of address). We have given the terms of reference and need concern ourselves with them only, since the principles on which the two sets work are much the same. There are fifteen basic terms, only two of which, the words for *husband* and *wife,* refer to one person and one only, and this is not even true of *wife* when a chief has more than one. All the other terms are applied to members of a class. Thus grandparents are called *tupuna,* and the class includes real grandparents, both male and female, all relatives on the father's and on the mother's side of about the same age as the grandparents, and all ancestors, real or classificatory, more distant than grandparents—there is no word for great-grandparent. A father is called *tamana,* as are all his brothers and all male kinsmen of about his age on his side of the family. A mother's brother is called *tuatina;* so is a mother's mother's brother's son, and so, for that matter, are all male kinsmen of the mother's in her generation. And so on. The details may be left to specialists.

The Tikopia have supplementary words that they can use, if necessary, to make distinctions between persons called by the same basic term. Thus they can distinguish different degrees of closeness of kinship and speak, for instance, of "near" or "distant" *tamana,* that is, to use the language of anthropology, true or classificatory "fathers." They can also distinguish between persons who may be equally close but belong to different sides of the family, between, for instance, a grandfather on the father's side and a grandfather on the mother's side. They certainly make distinctions in behavior between persons called by the same name. Thus the rules of appropriate behavior are much less scrupulously observed for a distant *tamana* than for a near one, though the two relationships bear, so to speak, a family resemblance. And for near affinal kin, observance relaxes with the passage of time and the growth of familiarity. In the ordinary affairs of life, one associates most often with one's near kinsmen. Only when one is badly ill, or when one is organizing a big ceremony or economic undertaking, do many of one's more distant kinsmen come to visit. But if the appropriate near kinsmen, a mother's brother, for instance, is not available by reason of a quarrel, illness, or death, there is always a more distant one who can step in and play the required part. The link between kinship nomenclature and kinship behavior is always close, and it is doubtful whether distant kinsmen would be called by the same names as close ones, if they did not at times act as such. At any rate, Tikopia is a small place, and no one need lack for relatives. Everyone is in some way or other, and usually in many ways, related to everyone else.

"HOUSE" AND CLAN

Our chief interest in Tikopia is the household and its immediate connections, but we need to say something about larger kinship units, if only to tuck in loose ends. In the affairs of life, large and small, a Tikopia helps, and is helped by, the members of four kin groups: his father's, his mother's brothers', his wife's brothers', and his sisters' husbands'. This does not prevent his belonging to one of these groups, his father's, more particularly than to the others. We call Tikopia society patrilineal because a man receives his land, his house name, his rank, and his ritual duties from his father and his father's kinsmen. No land whatever can descend through a woman. The patrilineal bias is strong enough to make the Tikopia disapprove of the remarriage of a widow: she ought to stay and look after her children, who will naturally remain with her husband's kinsmen. But there is no custom like the *levirate,* the requirement, observed in some societies, that the widow marry her late husband's brother or some other one of his close kinsmen. Sometimes a widow remarries in the face of popular opinion, but if she does, she leaves her children behind her; she does not take them to the house of her new husband. The same patrilineal tendency that brings disapproval of the widow's remarriage brings approval of the widower's.

When a man has left behind him sons who have settled down near him and have left descendants themselves, the group thus formed is recognized by the Tikopia and called *paito,* which we have seen is also the name for the house as a physical object. Firth calls this group a *lineage.* There is no special time when the appearance of a "house" is first admitted. Whenever people begin to think of the descendants of a particular man as forming a unit, a body of men, they begin to speak of the unit as a "house." It follows that new "houses" are always appearing in Tikopia, old houses splitting as they get too large, some old houses dying out for lack of heirs, others just maintaining themselves, and so on.

The development of a house follows naturally from the co-operation between brothers in the immediate family; and from the leadership of the oldest brother comes the custom that the headship of the *paito* descends by primogeniture in the senior male line. Not that the rule is as strict as it was in some European kingdoms. If, at the death of the last head, the heir presumptive is too young or too inept, he is passed over, with the consent of the *paito* as a whole, in favor of some less senior but more competent man; but when the latter dies in turn, the headship is apt to revert to the senior line. If any member of the house dies without male descendants, the head will reassign his land to other members. Certain canoes are held in the name of the head for the use of members of the house. These formal duties are carried out against a background of everyday informal co-operation between patrilineal kinsmen.

People in Tikopia differ in social standing, and social standing is closely associated with duties in religious ritual. The higher a man's rank, the closer his link with the principal gods and ceremonies. Two main classes of *paito* are recognized: the houses of chiefs and the houses of commoners, though the original ancestors of many commoner houses came themselves from chiefly families. And among the houses of commoners, two subclasses are recognized: those led by "ritual elders" and those not so led. A ritual elder has special duties in the great ceremonies, but they are not so important as the duties of a chief.

As we have seen, there are four chiefs, each the head of what the Tikopia call a *kainanga*, a word which has no other referent in the Tikopia language and which Firth translates as "clan." [22] Just as the members of a house trace their descent from a common an-

---

[22] G. P. Murdock, in setting up a terminology that doubtless will become standard, gives the word *clan* only to those groups which are formed by a unilinear rule of descent and which also have residential unity. He would call the Tikopia *kainanga* a *sib*. See G. P. Murdock, *Social Structure*, 47, 68. But since we are reporting Firth's work we had better stick to Firth's terminology.

cestor in the male line, so the clan consists of those houses that trace their descent from a still more distant common ancestor.

Unlike the clan in some primitive societies, the clan in Tikopia has nothing to do with the regulation of marriage. It is neither exogamous (a clansman must marry outside it) nor endogamous (a clansman must marry inside it). Nor is the clan united by living together in the same territory. There is a tendency in Tikopia for a man's sons to live near him, or, as anthropologists would say, there is a tendency for residence to be patrilocal, but the rule is not absolute, and what is true of the family must be all the more true of the clan. The members of any one clan are found living in all parts of the island, though perhaps in greater concentration in one part than another. But if it lacks residential unity, each clan has its own name, its own traditions, its own chief, and its own lands, which are the sum of the lands of its members.

Fellow clansmen play together as a team in many of the traditional games of Tikopia, but, above all, clansmen co-operate in the service of their chief, the *ariki*. He has an arduous part to play in the yearlong cycle of ceremonies called "The Work of the Gods." Besides serving as one of the high priests himself, the chief must feed the other men who attend and perform the ceremonies, and he must present gifts to the other chiefs and their clansmen. The material for food and gifts, and the labor in the ritual itself and in the preparation of meals, the chief depends on his clansmen to provide. In fact he distributes again to his clansmen, while they work for him, the food they themselves have brought him. In short, the chief organizes the enterprise, while the clansmen provide the material and labor that are organized.[23]

The duties of a chief are not confined to ritual, or, rather, ritual and practical affairs may hardly be separated. Whenever some piece of work must be undertaken that is too much for the resources of a single household and the help it can command from its immediate kinsmen, the chief organizes the working party. For instance, certain fishing canoes are said to be "sacred," and they belong to the chief, who maintains them for the use of his clansmen. The building and repair of such a canoe is a task beyond the capacity

[23] For an example of similar behavior in another society, see G. C. Homans, *English Villagers of the 13th Century*, 357.

of an ordinary household, but the chief, requisitioning the labor and the food of his clansmen, can provide the necessary lumber, tools, and willing hands, pay the expert carpenter, perform the appropriate ritual over the canoe, and feed the workers.

We have already seen that the chiefs are the guardians of the principal crops of the island and can largely control the way the land is used. A chief is also the ultimate overlord of all the land of the clan. He settles disputes about boundaries and inheritance when the contestants themselves cannot reach an agreement; in fact he keeps the peace in the land.

In short, the chief rules the clan much as its head rules the *paito*. Succession to the chieftainship follows the same customs. But the chief is powerful only if he is responsible; he can govern the clan because he governs with its consent. Firth writes of the chiefs:

The performance of the great part of the ritual practices with which they are traditionally vested, and which is not challenged by the commoners and their clansfolk, does not give them an appreciably higher standard of living, nor allow them to accumulate large stocks of goods without the obligation of disbursing them again through similar channels. It does place in their hands the power to direct much production, and here the checks upon them are provided to a considerable extent by their individual conformity to a theory of responsibility and to the opinion of the body of the commoners.[24]

[24] *Primitive Polynesian Economoy*, 172.

CHAPTER **10**

A System of Interpersonal Relations

*The External System: Mutual Dependence of Sentiment
and Activity . . . Mutual Dependence of Activity and
Interaction . . . The Internal System: Introduction . . .
Mutual Dependence of Interaction and Sentiment:
Relations Between Equals . . . Relations Between Su-
perior and Subordinate . . . Relations Between Three or
More Persons . . . The Mother's Brother . . . The Mother's
Brother in the Trobriands . . . The Matrix of Kinship . . .
Mutual Dependence of Sentiment and Activity, of
Activity and Interaction . . . Kinship Extension . . .
Norms and Social Rank . . . The Functional Theory . . .
Reaction of the Internal System on the External . . .
The Modern Urban Family*

IN THE Tikopia family we face our hardest job of
analysis. The family is a group that has had a continuous history
for hundreds of thousands of years. It is not, like the Bank Wiring
Observation Room, a group formed just the other day, whose history can be rather easily reconstructed. The family is also a group
whose members differ from one another not only in personality but
also in age and sex. The groups we have studied so far were made
up of men only, and these men were of about the same age. Now
we must face the delightful questions that women always raise.
We are, moreover, for the first time in this book, studying a group
that, instead of buying its food, clothing, and housing, provides the
necessities of life by working directly on the physical environment.
The Tikopia family is, to a great extent, a self-sufficient unit. Finally, we have in our earlier studies confined ourselves, with the
single great exception of leadership, to subgroup relations: the

similarities and differences between subgroups. The Tikopia family must be treated as a web of relations between individuals, or, better, between social personalities.

The difficulty of studying a group that has a long history behind it, produces its own subsistence, and consists of persons differing both in age and in sex is balanced by one great advantage. The Bank Wiring Group and the Norton Street Gang were single groups. We had no way of telling from the material we presented whether there were others like them. But when we talk about the Tikopia family we are in effect talking about many similar groups. To be sure, the family we have described is only a "typical" family, and we do not know just what "typical" means, nor how far individual families differ from the typical. Nevertheless, so far as families are similar, we must assume that this similarity is not a matter of chance, but that similar forces are producing similar results in all families. To this extent the generalizations we reach will be better founded than our earlier ones.

Whatever our difficulties may be, we shall not go far wrong if we plod ahead, applying our method of analysis. The more intricate the problem, the more necessary, if we are to make head or tail of it, is the use of a method. Any method is better than none, since even a poor method, regularly applied, will tend to throw a glaring light on its own deficiencies. But if we are to plod, we had better go back to the beginning and go over once more the elements of our conceptual scheme. We deal with an *environment*, the physical environment in this case; with *individuals*, who may differ in many ways, but certainly differ biologically, in age and sex; with *materials and tools*, employed by individuals in working on the environment; and with the elements of the social behavior of individuals: *activity, sentiment, interaction,* and *norms*, norms being inferences from what people say about the way they ought to behave. *Time* also is always an element, though we do not always take it into explicit account.

THE EXTERNAL SYSTEM:
MUTUAL DEPENDENCE OF SENTIMENT AND ACTIVITY

We will remember that, by our definition, the external system of
a group consists of the elements of social behavior and their mutual relations, so far as these elements and their relations provide
one solution to the problem: How shall the group survive in its
environment using a certain body of materials and tools? To set it
going, so to speak, a group needs motives for co-operation, a set
of activities it is to carry out, and a scheme of interaction among
its members. So far we have studied groups that were part of a
complex society, and we have considered the sentiments entering
into the external system to be those that the members bring to the
group in question from other groups in the larger society. The desire for wages to support a family is a typical example of such a
sentiment. But Tikopia is an isolated island; it is not a part of a
larger society, and its members cannot bring sentiment to the group
from other groups outside. Nevertheless there are sentiments that
can be treated as part of the external system of the Tikopia family,
and these are the biological drives of men. They are analogous to
other sentiments brought into a group from outside in that a member of a Tikopia family brings them to his group at birth and they
are later modified or canalized by the action of the group upon
him.

In the family, the first of these biological drives is sexual desire.
In modern America there is no danger of our underrating it. Indeed
we exaggerate its power, perhaps because so many of us have forgotten what it is to be hungry. Take a young man who has gone
for days without food or women, and give him his choice between
a dry cracker and a lovely girl. He will not choose the girl every
time. But we shall grant that sex is important, though not an everyday necessity of life, and if it had not been for the peculiar characteristics of the sexual desires of man, he would hardly have developed the family. For man is still, wherever he goes, a tropical mam-
mal, and like his cousins, the anthropoid apes, he feels sexual desire
at all seasons of the year, and not, like the deer, at one season only.
With a different sexual constitution, he might not have produced an

institution in which a man and a woman live together permanently.

Another biological characteristic of man, crucial in the formation of the family, is the slow maturation of his young; for several years they are too weak and ignorant to fend for themselves. The species would never have maintained itself for as long as it has if its members had possessed no drive to feed, protect, and teach their children.

Sexual desire and the need to care for the children must have been important factors in the founding of the first family hundreds of thousands of years ago. As for the need for food and drink, and the fear that they may not be obtained, men and women might conceivably have satisfied these sentiments by their own individual actions. But so long as children must be fed and women are somewhat, though not entirely, handicapped in gathering food while they are bearing and rearing children, these sentiments contribute to the establishment of the family as a group: the husband must help feed both wife and children. Perhaps there are other sentiments that enter the external system of the Tikopia family and other families, especially if the need for companionship is in any sense biological. But the drives for sex, food, and child care are quite enough to set the system going.

A warning is badly needed here. On the plea that this is not a psychology textbook, we are going to dodge the great debate on instinct. All of these drives are, at one and the same time, biological and social, inherited and acquired; and no one has yet been able to make them out as wholly one rather than the other. In fact, the issue may be meaningless. The drives are always modified and channeled, and heavily so, by the action of the group on the individual, who learns, as he grows up, modes of behavior that are both biologically and socially appropriate. Only so far as they have a biological component do they come into the external system, as we use the term. In a later chapter we shall consider briefly the process by which inherited drives are channeled by social training, but for the moment we must acquire a high tolerance for half-truths, though they ache for wholeness.

The biological drives are satisfied by the co-operative activities of men and women, the form of the activities being determined, in greater or lesser degree, by the environment and the available tools and techniques. Let it never be said that in describing systematically the relations between the elements of behavior we are afraid of the obvious; and so, with straight faces, let us point out that even the satisfaction of sexual desires demands co-operation between a man and a woman in accordance with a technique. This is hardly less obvious in the activities of rearing children and providing food and shelter.

MUTUAL DEPENDENCE OF ACTIVITY AND INTERACTION

If there is one thing we must do in order to understand the characteristics of families, it is to forget, for the moment, that they are families and ask ourselves what they have in common with all human groups. We must emancipate ourselves from the unconscious assumption that just because the family is a group in which a man and a woman co-operate in sexual relations and child rearing it is somehow unique. A family is a group with jobs to do, and therefore its behavior illustrates the principles of all co-operative action. In particular, the scheme of activities in the family is mutually dependent with the scheme of interaction among the members. That is to say, the same process takes place in the family as takes place in any organization: a division of labor and a chain of command are set up. The total activity of the family is broken down into specialties: child rearing, fishing, making cloth, carrying water, etc. There may be more than one possible way of making the breakdown, just as there may be more than one way of dividing a company into departments, but once made, the nature of the breakdown and the man-power requirements of the different specialties determine the frequency of interaction between different members of the family. Some tasks are carried out by the group as a whole, and in these tasks all members of the group interact. Some are carried out by subgroups, and in these the members of the subgroup interact with one another rather than with other family members. And some tasks are carried out by individuals. The co-ordination of the different activities is, moreover, effected by interaction between leaders and their followers. Finally, when we say that the scheme of activity and the scheme of interaction are mutually dependent, we mean that if either one changes, the other will, in general, change also. In the family the method of organization is handed down from generation to generation; in an industrial firm it is deliberately planned to meet special needs, but in both cases the kinds of result achieved are the same.

The activities of sex, child rearing, and providing food and shelter are all important in determining the constitution of human families. But one difference between the first two and the third is particularly important to us. It may well be that if sexual relations and child rearing were the only activities carried out by families, the variations in family types would be less great than they are observed to be. Sexual and child-rearing practices do differ among the many societies of men, but they are for obvious reasons less under the influence of changes in environment and technology than are the economic activities. It is these latter that chiefly determine, so far as the external system is concerned, the different types of family and particularly the different types of relation between the nuclear family and larger kinship groups, and to these economic activities we shall pay special attention in our analysis of the Tikopia family.

As for the size of the interacting group, we must note that in Tikopia the basic kinship unit in economic affairs is not the nuclear family but the household, which usually includes several kinsmen besides a man, a woman, and their children. One of the activities that determines, within wide limits, the constitution of this unit is cooking. There is only one big meal a day; it takes a long time to prepare, and many different kinds of work must go into it. All members of the household interact in getting it ready, and each contributes something to the common task. A Tikopia is at a great disadvantage if he lives alone, and almost no one does.

Again, work in the orchards and gardens is done in working parties of a half-dozen persons or less, that is, the number that can be furnished by the household. The technique is not complicated, but a certain amount of sustained effort is needed, and the work goes more easily when a small group co-operates. Persons of both sexes can contribute their labor. The husband and wife usually work together, with some of their children, both boys and girls. Sometimes members of other households are pressed into service, but the activity is of a kind that a single household of average size can easily carry out by itself.

Let us turn now to the division of labor within the household, and especially to the division between women and men. In the early weeks of a child's life and to a lesser extent later, he is cared for by his mother and the other women of the household. This means a particularly close association, at an important time in his life, between the child and his female relatives. Someone must take care of the children; breast feeding makes it natural that women should do so; but their duties in child rearing prevent them from undertaking some other kinds of work, which must accordingly be left to the men. As the child grows older, the father or one of the older brothers may take care of him, especially if the women are busy away from the house. This responsibility a man could not assume if his duties absolutely compelled him to be absent from the household for the whole working day. The Tikopia man, with his loose schedule and large supply of leisure, is in a much better position than, for instance, the Eskimo man to associate with his children in their early life. Quantitative differences like these go far to establish the differences between types of family.

Other activities are associated with the women's paramount duty of caring for the children. They keep the house swept; they make the bark cloth, while the men provide the bark; they comb the reef in time spared from other work; the younger women fetch water from the spring. Other jobs, like the long and arduous sea fishing, are left to the men alone because, for one reason, the women, with the many other tasks they have to accomplish, can give no time to them. The usual fishing canoe seems to carry a crew of four or five men, made up of the father and his sons, or the sons alone, with perhaps a kinsman or two from other households if needed. This heavy, nightlong or daylong work, means, of course, intense, prolonged interaction between the men of the family apart from the women. The division of labor between men and women in Tikopia is much like that in other societies, in most of which the women are assigned jobs, such as water carrying, cooking, gathering fuel, and making clothing, that do not take them far from the house, whereas the men are assigned jobs, such as herding, fishing, hunting, and lumbering, that draw them farther afield.[1]

[1] G. P. Murdock, *Social Structure,* 213.

We must now speak of command, that is, the relation of the scheme of interaction to the process by which different activities are co-ordinated. At times in Tikopia the nature of the work to be done does not require a centralized authority. In the preparation of the noon meal, the necessity for, and proper timing of, the different pieces of work is pretty clear to everyone, and the same may be true of work in the gardens, once the decision to plant a particular crop in a particular place has been made. But some degree of unified command must be required in the canoes, as in all ships: you cannot sail by popular vote. And so far as there is a single authority in the household it is the father. He gets plenty of suggestions from his children, and even more from his wife, but if he wants to assert himself he is the boss, and the others listen to him. In particular, he is the boss of the men and the men's work, while his wife is the boss of the women and the women's work. These two originate the interaction that controls and co-ordinates the activities of household. In the absence of the father, or in his old age when he retires from management of the household, the oldest son is put in charge.

Now let us sum up what we have learned. The practical activities of the Tikopia household are adapted to a certain scheme of interaction among its members. The household itself is large enough to carry out these activities, and in some of them, notably agriculture and food preparation, all the members work together. In others, men interact more frequently with other men, and women with other women, than either of the sexes interacts with the other. In still others, young children interact more frequently with their mother and the other women than they do with the men. All this concerns the size of the interacting group and the relative frequencies of interaction within it. As for the chains of interaction by which the different activities are co-ordinated, the father has the over-all control. He gives the crucial orders and the others obey. His chief lieutenants are his wife, in the women's department, and his oldest son, in the men's. The point is that in the family, as in any organization, there is an over-all task to be accomplished, in this case the survival of the family, specialized tasks that contribute to the main one, a division of labor in carrying out the specialties, and a chain of command to insure co-ordination. Effective work on the environment could not be carried out at all, or could not be carried out so well, without these arrangements. They are not a matter of deliberate planning, as in formal organizations, but they are present just the same. They must be. The family has jobs to do and therefore must exemplify, as much as other groups, the general principles of co-operative organization. The other characteristics of the family cannot be understood without reference to these.

What we have just said is open to a possible misunderstanding, which we had better try to clear up and, in so doing, amplify the remarks about organization made in Chapter 4. To say that the division of activities in a group and the scheme of interaction among its members are mutually dependent is not the same as saying that the nature of the activities themselves always demands or makes inevitable one single scheme of interaction and one only. At times, it is true, the characteristic activities of a group do seem to have some effect of this kind. The Bedouins of Arabia make their living almost wholly from their herds of sheep and camels, and herding in this arid land requires the co-operation of relatively large numbers of men, who must often, in order to find pasturage, go far away from the place where the tents are pitched. The women, who must stay close to the tents to take care of the young children, cannot in this environment combine child rearing with gathering food. The result seems to be a kinship organization in which the men are tied together with exceptional closeness in kin groups larger than the nuclear family and are much more dominant over the women than they are in a society like Tikopia.[2] In Arabia, then, the nature of the economic activities, in a particular environment, seems to determine to a large degree the nature of the social organization, but this kind of situation may be rare. More often, a number of different forms of the division of labor may be about equally effective in securing useful results from the environment. Thus in an industrial firm manufacturing a complicated piece of machinery, it may be difficult to determine whether lower costs are obtained by manufacturing in a separate shop each part that goes into the machine and then assembling the whole in still another shop, or by manu-

[2] See E. D. Chapple and C. S. Coon, *Principles of Anthropology*, 315-19.

facturing every part and assembling the whole machine in one single shop. Each method has advantages and drawbacks. With the first, management obtains the efficiency of high specialization and mass production; with the second, the efficiency of close co-ordination of the whole process. In a somewhat similar way, two different kinds of social organization dominated different parts of rural England in the Middle Ages, one organization marked by small, nuclear families combined into big villages, the other marked by what anthropologists call joint families—groups of brothers, their wives, and their children living together—but without villages. The two organizations seem to have carried out the same kinds of agricultural activity in about the same kinds of environment, but without recognizable differences in efficiency.[3] In short, the division of activities and the scheme of interaction must be mutually dependent—there must be organization—, but the activities in themselves do not always make inevitable any one particular form of organization. Variation is possible within wide limits.

Although we are not chiefly interested in the local group, or village, in Tikopia, we can, if we wish, apply to it the same kind of analysis of the mutual dependence of activity and interaction. A village does not exist in a vacuum. It is a unit because its members do certain specific things in co-operation with one another. They live side by side, but the mere living is not what makes the village. Its members are united by two main activities, along with some others. They use the waters of the same spring, and a great deal of social interaction goes on around the pool where these waters are stored; the canoes of the village put out to sea together, and conduct a co-ordinated sweep in the torchlight fishing at night. In one sense, these activities require the existence of a village as a local group larger than the family. In another sense, the village is created by the tendency of members of kin groups to settle down near one another, and is then seized on for these other purposes.

THE INTERNAL SYSTEM: INTRODUCTION

We will remember that the internal system includes the mutual relationships between interaction, sentiment, and activity as these

[3] See G. C. Homans, *English Villagers of the 13th Century*, 109-32.

relationships elaborate themselves upon those of the external system and then react upon the external system. But in analyzing the process of elaboration and reaction—or build-up and feedback—in the Tikopia family we encounter a difficulty that was not present in, for instance, our analysis of the Bank Wiring Observation Room. As an aid to thought, we have used in describing society the metaphor of a complex electrical circuit. (Remember that this is only a metaphor; we are not implying that society *is* an electrical circuit.) If we think of such a circuit as a process having a beginning and an end, we say that the arrangements of the circuit may be such that a part of the energy is fed back from a later to an earlier stage in the process in order to accelerate the build-up of the circuit to some point of equilibrium and to maintain the equilibrium when attained. If we stick to our metaphor, we can say that in the Bank Wiring Observation Room we could follow the actual process of social build-up and feedback. We know how the company tried initially to set the relations between the men in a certain frame, and how, on the basis of these relations, the men elaborated new ones that fed back to prevent the company's plan from being fully realized.

In analyzing the internal system of the Tikopia family we are in no such fortunate condition. The family has a long history behind it; the process of build-up took place long ago. All parts of the circuit are, so to speak, carrying their full load. But just as in an electrical circuit the arrangements and energies that brought the circuit up to equilibrium must still be present in the equilibrium when attained, and we can still analyze the circuit intellectually as a linear process, now that all parts are fully energized, so perhaps we can use in analyzing the Tikopia family the same method we used in analyzing the Bank Wiring group, though in Tikopia the process by which the internal system continually elaborates on the external and reacts upon it has reached a steady state and is not, so far as we can tell, leading to further social development.

Our usual method, in analyzing the internal system, is to take up in turn the three relations: interaction-sentiment, sentiment-activity, and activity-interaction. But the method should be familiar enough by now to excuse our skipping over some of it. The fact is that we shall pay more attention to the first of these relations than to the others, because under this heading we can most easily examine the system of interpersonal relations revealed by Firth's description of Tikopia kinship.

MUTUAL DEPENDENCE OF INTERACTION AND SENTIMENT: RELATIONS BETWEEN EQUALS

Firth's own discussion of sentiment is a good place from which to start a study of the mutual dependence between interaction and sentiment. He says:

The use of the term "sentiment" in this book implies not a psychological reality but a cultural reality; it describes a type of behavior which can be observed, not a state of mind which must be inferred. Inflections in the voice, the look of the eyes and carriage of the head, intimate little movements of the hands and arms, reactions to complex situations affecting the welfare of parent or child, utterances describing the imagined state of the internal organs—such are the phenomena which are classed together under the head of sentiment, the qualifying terms of "affection," "sadness," etc., being given on the basis of distinctions recognized by the natives themselves and embodied in their terminology. Such distinctions, broadly speaking, correspond to those distinguished in our own society.[4]

This is a good working definition of sentiment, which we will accept with one comment. The behavior we include under the word "sentiment" must of course be observed, or we should not, as scientists, be entitled to make generalizations about it. Nevertheless, people in our own society, as in Tikopia, do in fact refer this kind of behavior to "states of mind" and "imagined states of the internal organs." Moreover, sentiment in this sense can be more easily inferred from such behavior as "inflections of the voice, the look of the eyes and carriage of the head, intimate little movements of the hands and arms"—in short, from what psychologists call "expressive behavior"—than it can from certain other kinds of behavior such as, for instance, baiting a fishhook.

In making our analysis of the mutual dependence of interaction and sentiment in the family, we must begin with two main types of relationship: between brothers, and between a father and his

---

[4] *We, The Tikopia*, 160. See also p. 128.

son. In Tikopia the former is the prototype of the "good" or *tautau laui* relationship, the latter of the "bad" or *tautau pariki* relationship.

We have seen that in the external system of Tikopia society, in such activities as fishing and gardening, brothers from early childhood interact frequently with one another. And in Tikopia, as in other groups and societies, the more frequently persons interact with one another, the greater in general is their affection for one another. This rule accounts for the first great elaboration of the internal system on the relations established in the external. It accounts in part for the continued existence of groups and also for the division between groups, since it implies that if interaction is infrequent, affection will be weak. A large part of our earlier chapters has been a commentary on this rule. The Tikopia, Firth says, formulate it for themselves and say, in effect, that familiarity may conceivably breed contempt but certainly breeds attachment.[5]

If the rule holds, increased affection should further increase interaction, perhaps up to some point of equilibrium, since no social development can go on indefinitely unchecked, but at least beyond the amount required by the external system. Certainly the Bank Wiremen, as they became friendly, increased interaction beyond the amount that the job demanded. Firth does not say in so many words that this is true of brothers in Tikopia, but his whole discussion of their behavior implies that they associate intimately with one another not only in productive activities but also in wholly "social" ones. Moreover the close association of brothers is the basis for the appearance of larger kinship units, the house and the clan. Our contention is that society is always providing a surplus, so to speak, of interaction, sentiment, and activity, and then finding a use for the surplus.

The rule that association breeds affection holds only when other things are equal, that is, only under certain circumstances, and Firth helps us to see what these circumstances are. Not only do brothers interact frequently with one another; they also have scant authority over each other. No one of them gives orders much more often than any of the others, or, as we say in our technical lan-

5 *We, The Tikopia*, 203, 205.

guage, no one of them originates interaction much more frequently than any of the others. This is not as true of the oldest brother, especially in chiefly families, as it is of the rest; but for the most part the authority of the father is dominant, and so long as it is, brothers are equal before it, and the leadership of the oldest is in abeyance. Brothers not only interact often but interact as equals, and this double polarity has its counterpart in the emotional relation between them. They feel friendly; they also feel at ease in one another's presence, free to say anything, from a joke to a curse, without fear that it will be taken amiss. Indeed this lack of constraint may be one of the conditions that allow brothers to be friendly. We can now amplify a hypothesis stated earlier in simpler form and say that *the more frequently persons interact with one another, when no one of them originates interaction with much greater frequency than the others, the greater is their liking for one another and their feeling of ease in one another's presence.*

The characteristic relation between brothers is repeated with less intensity in other relations of Tikopia kinship. The tie between parent and child has some tincture of it, especially when the child is young. So have the ties between a child and his grandparent and between a child and his mother's brother, though these relations are modified by differences in age and generation. So has the relation between brother and sister, modified by the difference in sex. In the practical affairs of life, the two associate frequently, though not as frequently as brothers, and neither has authority over the other. They are friendly and free in their relations, though, again, not as free as brothers. In so far as they are persons of the same generation but of different sexes, they are appropriate sexual partners, and yet, in the eyes of the Tikopia, sexual relations between them are unthinkable. That is, there is an element of conflict in the relation between brother and sister, for a psychologist would say that the horror of incest is itself a sign that incestuous tendencies exist but are repressed.[6] Repressed or not, the conflict seems to show itself in the fact that in conversation brother and sister stay away from sexual topics. But it is easy to make too much of this.

[6] For a good discussion of incest taboos, see G. P. Murdock, *Social Structure*, 260-322.

The close association between brother and sister, like the association of all the members of the family, is the basis for their affectionate regard for one another.

Such is the relation between brothers in Tikopia. Who shall say it does not hold for brothers elsewhere, and indeed for men who are not brothers? It has much in common with the link between connector wiremen, between selector wiremen, between the leaders in the Norton Street Gang, and between the followers in that gang. We must forget that we are dealing with the family and generalize for all social groups. In fact a relationship of this kind, under the name of the brotherhood of man, is our norm for all mankind, although a cynic will remember that one element of the relationship is the submission of the brothers to a common authority.

RELATIONS BETWEEN SUPERIOR AND SUBORDINATE

In the relationship between the Tikopia father and son, something appears that we have encountered before but have not yet analyzed. The two interact frequently in the external system, and since association breeds affection, affection is an element in their relationship, especially in the attitude of the father toward the son. But another element enters in, which does not affect the tie between brothers. In all the practical duties of life, the son is under the direction of the father. We can say, in our language, that the father originates interaction for the son, provided we always remember that the crucial point in establishing the attitudes we are describing is not the mere fact that the father originates interaction but that the son's response to the origination is in accordance with the father's wishes: his orders are obeyed. At any rate, the fact of authority seems to turn the relationship into an ambiguous or, as the psychoanalysts would say, an ambivalent one. One loves one's father; yet in a way one resents his control. Behavior toward him, instead of being free and easy, is constrained. At best one's attitude is admiration; at worst it is open hatred; its norm is respect. And interaction between father and son, instead of increasing like interaction between brothers, tends to be kept down to the amount required by the external system. The two interact frequently but only, so to speak, on business and not socially. For this kind of behavior we can offer no explanation except perhaps the following: it is not so much that the son positively avoids the father as that the son seeks out opportunities for association with persons with whom he can be at ease.

Once again, there is nothing "natural" about the relationship between father and son. It is not inherent in being a son to a father, but depends on the particular circumstances in which father and son associate with one another. It is true that the relationship tends to reappear in societies all over the world in which the family is an important productive unit and the father is its boss. For a good description, in a society otherwise quite different from Tikopia, reread in Chapter 2 the account by Arensberg and Kimball of the relations between father and son in the Irish farm family. The fact of reappearance proves that the relationship is not merely "cultural." It does not maintain itself just because it is taught to children and adopted by them as the appropriate "pattern of behavior," though of course it is so taught and adopted. It reappears wherever the situation, the "field" reappears, but where the situation is different, the relationship also is different. In a society in which the nuclear family is not an important productive unit and the father is not boss of the son the relations between them are, as we shall see, quite different from what they are in Tikopia.

In fact, we recognize that the relationship between father and son in Tikopia is much like that between superior and subordinate everywhere. Good examples are the ties between sea captain and seaman, between officer and soldier. In these ties, as in the tie between father and son in Tikopia, the emotional tone is one of mixed admiration and constraint, rather than friendliness, on the part of the subordinate; and interaction tends to be cut down to the amount required by the external system. The splendid isolation of sea captains, which is apt to turn them into Blighs and Ahabs, is conspicuous, as is the social gap in armies between officers and men, and even between different grades of officers, especially when the gap, which we feel must always exist in some measure, is reinforced by actual or imputed class divisions. Some modern psychologists would say that the subordinate extends to the superior those attitudes he has already learned to adopt toward his father in the small family.

No doubt he does, and it is interesting that a sea captain is always "the old man"; but we must also note that the subordinate does so when his situation vis-à-vis his superior has something in common with his situation vis-à-vis his father. The "fields" of action are alike, whatever the past experience of the actors.

Note that if the authority of one man over another is associated with a low frequency of mutual "social" interaction, an increase of interaction will imply a decline in authority. Thus the inspectors in the Bank Wiring Observation Room were accepted as friends of the wiremen only if they gave up all signs of bossy behavior. Familiarity does breed contempt in this sense, and the advice given to military officers that they will impair their authority if they "go around with" their men is not altogether unwise. If, moreover, a superior does for any reason interact with a subordinate outside of the external system, the former is apt to be the one to originate interaction, just as he does in the external system. A sea captain may prefer not to meet one of his crew in a beer hall, but if they do meet he is apt to be the one to take the initiative in ordering beers for both.[7] Few men are flexible enough to work out a two-stage emotional relationship, one for the times when authority must be exercised and another for everyday relaxed routine. What is appropriate in one set of conditions tends unfortunately to be followed in all, and, in ships and armies especially, the authoritarian relationship is carried over into situations where it is no longer obviously necessary.

Although the relationship between superior and subordinate is to some degree the same in every group, it varies greatly in intensity from group to group according to various circumstances, including the relation of the group to its environment, the ability of the subordinate to escape from authority, and the extent to which the superior is chosen by the members of the group. The relationship between sea captain and seaman lies at one end of the spectrum. The ship is an isolated physical and social unit. If it is to accomplish its purposes in a dangerous and capricious environment, a number of complex activities must be carefully co-ordinated, and

[7] For this observation the author is indebted to S. A. Richardson. See his Harvard B.A. Honors thesis, "The Social Organization of British and United States Merchant Ships" (1949).

the authority of the captain must be unquestioned, especially in the emergencies that may arise at any time. The authority of the captain extends, or did extend in the old days, to every aspect of the seamen's lives; while at sea they cannot escape from it. And they certainly do not choose their commander: democracy ends when the last line is cast off the pier.

The relationship between Doc and the rest of the Nortons lies close to the other end of the spectrum. This group was certainly not carrying out complex activities in a dangerous environment; the men could escape from the group if they found Doc's authority intolerable, and Doc was, in effect, if not by formally democratic procedures, chosen by the members of the group to be their leader. The closer the situation approaches the former end of the spectrum, the more completely the interaction between superior and subordinate is kept down to the amount characteristic of the external system and the greater is the divinity that hedges the superior. In favorable circumstances, especially if he lives up to the norms of the group as a whole, respect for him will be great; in unfavorable circumstances, hostility toward him will be great in like measure. The father in Tikopia, head of a unit carrying out important activities in a somewhat uncertain environment, exercising authority over his sons in most of the activities in life, and certainly not chosen by them to be their leader, is closer to the sea captain than to Doc. The variations from group to group in the relationship between superior and subordinate are quantitative; in some groups the tie is hardly different from the tie between equals, in others very different indeed.

In summary, we may say that *when two persons interact with one another, the more frequently one of the two originates interaction for the other, the stronger will be the latter's sentiment of respect (or hostility) toward him, and the more nearly will the frequency of interaction be kept to the amount characteristic of the external system.* Or we may say, alternatively, that the strength of sentiments of friendliness and freedom from restraint between two men varies directly with the frequency of interaction between the two and inversely with the frequency with which one originates interaction for the other. The tie between father and son in Tikopia, like the tie between brothers, has its parallel elsewhere in

the kinship system, though at lesser intensities. Examples are the tie
between mother and daughter, and between chief and clansmen.

RELATIONS BETWEEN THREE OR MORE PERSONS

Now that we have established the general character of these two
relationships—between equals, and between a superior and a subordinate—and have pointed out that these relationships appear not
only in the family but wherever in social groups certain kinds of
situations exist, we can go on to more complicated problems, where
we have to consider not just the relationship between two persons,
such as two brothers or a father and his son, but between three or
more. A general rule, special forms of which we shall try to illustrate, is the following: *the relationship between two persons, A and
B, is partly determined by the relationships between A and a third
person, C, and between B and C.* This rule can be extended to any
number of persons, and thus a matrix or system of relationships is
formed. Firth notes "how impossible it is to separate completely
the discussion of one set of kinship ties from that of others in the
same system; they are like a set of forces in delicately poised equilibrium; if one is disturbed, others must respond in adjustment
also." [8] But let us look at some examples.

Consider first some triangular relationships in the nuclear family.
In Tikopia the ties between father and daughter and between
mother and son are warmer and closer than those between father
and son and between mother and daughter. Freud would tell us
that the explanation lies in the Oedipus and Electra complexes. The
son is unconsciously in love with his mother and is therefore the
sexual rival of his father. And the daughter is comparably motivated. We do not deny that sexual interests help determine this
configuration, but we have some reason for asserting that something else comes into it also. For in societies organized differently
from Tikopia, the relationship between father and son is, as we
shall see, rather different from what it is there, although the un-

[8] *We, The Tikopia*, 218. Early statements of this principle in the social
sciences were those of Simmel and Radcliffe-Brown. See K. H. Wolff, ed. and
trans., *The Sociology of Georg Simmel*, 135, 145-67, and A. R. Radcliffe-Brown,
The Social Organization of Australian Tribes (Oceania Monographs, No. 1), 98.
See also R. H. Lowie, *Social Organization*, 67-8.

conscious sexual rivalry between the two presumably remains the same. We are emphasizing in this book those characteristics that all groups, whether made up of men alone or of men and women together, have in common, and therefore we must see to it that whatever nonsexual factors are important in determining family organization get their due share of attention. In particular we may point out that in the division of labor in the Tikopia household sons come under the control of the father more than they do under the control of the mother, and that the reverse is true of daughters. And we have seen the effect of authority in constraining sentiment and limiting interaction. No barrier like this exists to cut down affection between father and daughter or between mother and son. If, moreover, we postulate a certain need of human beings for affection and association, we may assume that if this need is thwarted in one direction, it will seek satisfaction all the more strongly in another. Thus one reason why the father-daughter tie is close is that the father-son tie is distant. And comparable forces determine the mother-son tie. We cannot understand the relationship of two parties without reference to the relationships of both to a third party. Finally, the different attitudes of father and mother toward sons and daughters may be one factor making the relationship between brothers and sisters something less than entirely intimate. At any rate we may suggest the hypothesis, which follows from two of our earlier ones, that *the higher becomes A's frequency of originating interaction for B compared with his frequency of originating interaction for C, the stronger becomes his feeling of affection for C compared with his feeling of affection for B.*

Just as the Tikopia father is more affectionate toward his daughter than toward his son, so, as we have seen, he is more affectionate toward his younger than his older son. In the chiefly families, the oldest son inherits important duties and privileges from his father, and no one likes to realize that another is going to supplant him in high place, although the conflict inherent in the relationship may be mitigated by the fact that the oldest son is in the normal course of events the first of the brothers to leave the father's house. But if we turn from chiefly families and the problem of succession and look at everyday behavior in the ordinary household, we can see another reason why the father and his oldest son should not be close. The father has authority over all his sons; the oldest son exercises some authority, though not as much, over all his brothers. Here are two persons exercising potential control over the same group of persons, and we may say perhaps that *so far as A and B both originate interaction for C, the relationship between them is one of constraint, and interaction between them tends to be kept at a minimum.* At any rate, the relatively close link—remember that all these problems are quantitative not qualitative—between a father and his younger sons cannot be understood without reference to the rather different link between father and oldest son. There is more than one triangle in the drama of society.

A simpler but perhaps less exact way of phrasing the hypothesis we have just formulated is that two persons avoid occasions for conflicts of authority. An effort is made to maintain what military men call unity of command. This is one of the bases for the avoidance of frequent contact between mother-in-law and son-in-law, for which there is some evidence in Tikopia, and which is a spectacular feature of many primitive societies. In popular lectures on anthropology this avoidance is always good for a laugh because it corresponds, with a heightened emphasis, to something in our own kinship system. No doubt it has a sexual component. As a woman, a man's mother-in-law is a potential object of sexual interest for him. They avoid one another so that there will be no danger of her becoming an actual object of his interest and one particularly apt to arouse the jealousy of his wife. But the avoidance also has what we may call an organizational component.[9] The mother-in-law has long exercised, and is used to exercising, authority over her daughter. Now her daughter has married and has come under the authority of a husband. Two persons now wield control over the same person, and avoidance—that is, decrease of interaction— lessens the chances that conflict between the two will result. In other relationships between affinal kin—for instance, between mother-in-law and daughter-in-law and between father-in-law and son-in-law—similar possibilities of conflict exist in greater or lesser degrees.

[9] G. P. Murdock's explanation of mother-in-law avoidance as a result of sexual factors alone seems a flaw in an otherwise excellent book. See *Social Structure,* 280.

Remember that the effect of the rule we have just stated, as of our other rules, may not be apparent under all circumstances. Thus two executives who are good friends in the other occasions of their lives may share the services of a secretary without any sign of conflict between them. But our contention is that, so far as both exercise authority over the same person, the tendency to conflict is latent and can only be overcome by stronger forces, such as the friendship of the two men in other situations and perhaps the narrow field in which authority is exercised. Secretarial work includes, after all, a narrower range of activities than those in which her husband and her mother wield authority over a woman in Tikopia, and this lessens the chances of conflict.

In Tikopia grandfathers are closer to their grandchildren than they are to their sons. The relation between father and son is one of respect and distance, as is the relation between the latter and his own son. In these circumstances, grandfather and grandson are, so to speak, allied in opposition to the man in the middle, especially as the grandfather does not wield much direct authority over his grandson: when the latter begins to grow up, the grandfather has begun to retire from active management of family affairs. The two can be good friends; much of the respect due to mature men can be relaxed in dealing with a grandparent; the interaction between them increases even though there is no practical need for it to do so. Or, as Firth says:

It may be suggested that the freedom between grandparent and grandchild is to some extent a reflex of the constraint between parent and child. The latter is to be correlated with the authoritarian position of the parent and his or her capacity for active control of affairs. With the waning energies of the grandparent there is a tendency for authority in practical affairs to be resigned, and so there is no hindrance to the growth of an easy familiar relation with the grandchildren.[10]

More generally, *if the relationships between A and B and between B and C are both marked by constraint and relatively infrequent interaction, the relationship between A and C may be easy, affectionate, and marked by frequent interaction.*

In Tikopia the relationship in public between husband and wife

---

[10] *We, The Tikopia,* 208.

is respectful and formal, whatever may be their intimacy in private. In fact, the modern American notion that husband and wife should be intimate companions, or pals, if not entirely romantic and built on novel reading, can be realized only in a very different kind of family from the Tikopia family or, for that matter, the old-fashioned farm family in this country. In a family that is also a vital unit of economic co-operation, sexual intercourse is only one of many activities drawing husband and wife together, and in all the others the husband is the boss and his wife is his chief lieutenant. Her position must be upheld in the eyes of others. *So far, then, as A originates interaction for B, and B for other members of a group, the emotional attitude of A toward B will be one of respect and constraint.*

THE MOTHER'S BROTHER

Our focus is the household, and we are under no obligation to make an analysis of all the ties between kinsmen in Tikopia. But one in particular is an admirable illustration of some of the points we have been trying to make. This is the relationship between mother's brother (*tuatina*) and sister's son (*iramutu* or *tama tapu*). A boy's mother's brother is on particularly friendly and intimate terms with him. His mother's brother works and plays with him often, teaches and helps him in many of the difficulties of life, and, above all, holds his hand in all crises from birth to death and is rewarded by the boy's father for the trouble taken. The facts have been recorded in the last chapter.

The mother's brother is a classic figure of anthropology. He is always turning up in some important capacity. It is not always the one he assumes in Tikopia, but even this one, in its main outlines, reappears in societies so far distant geographically and so different technologically from Tikopia that we can probably rule out the possibility of cultural diffusion. For instance, the special role of the mother's brother has been lost in our present society, but in the Middle Ages, among the peoples of northwestern Europe from whom our own social traditions spring, a close relationship linked mother's brother and sister's son. Tacitus, describing the German tribes of the first century A.D., says that they held this tie to be closer

than the tie between a father and his son and that they made use of
it in taking hostages.[11] That is, a tribal statesman would, if he
could, keep a man's sister's son in custody in order to keep the
man himself on his good behavior. In the Iceland of the saga time
(ninth and tenth centuries A.D.) the custom of sending children
away from home to be brought up by foster fathers was common,
and a study of the examples in the sagas shows that a boy was
often fostered by his mother's brother.[12] Again, in the great martial
legends, this relationship is always prominent. Roland is sister's
son to Charlemagne in the *Chanson de Roland;* Beowulf is sister's
son to Hygelac; and in a less heroic vein, Criseyde is sister's daughter to Pandarus in Chaucer's *Troilus and Criseyde.* In *Chevy Chase,*
one of those Border ballads that, as Sir Philip Sidney said, move
our hearts as with a trumpet, the Earl of Douglas, dying, calls for
"his sister's son, Sir Hugh Montgomery," and the latter takes re-
venge on Percy for Douglas' death. In every instance, the assumption is that mother's brother and sister's son (or sister's daughter)
are devoted to one another. We cannot take legends as direct evidence of the kinship ties in a society. At the same time, few themes
can have been taken into legend that were not intelligible in the
existing social order. Unless they had been intelligible, they would
have bewildered or bored their hearers. Literature is not society,
but it is a reflection of society.

To pass from heroic legend to humbler matters, that proverbial
figure the "Dutch uncle" may originally have been the mother's
brother rather than the father's. When you "talk to someone like a
Dutch uncle" you talk to him as man to man, without reservations
or constraint, and this is the way a mother's brother behaved towards his sister's son in many societies, including the old Germanic,
or "Dutch." Finally, we have seen that Middle English and other
old Germanic languages resembled many primitive languages in
having a special word for mother's brother. In English it was *eme,*
whence perhaps come our family names *Eames* and *Ames;* in German it was *oheim.* Kinship terminology tends, perhaps with some
lag, to follow kinship behavior, and *eme* has now disappeared,
uncle being used for all uncles, maternal and paternal, as well as

[11] C. Tacitus, *Germania,* Ch. 20.
[12] See especially the saga of Gisli Sursson.

for aunts' husbands, just as behavior has ceased to discriminate among them.

This example is enough to show that the characteristic relationship between mother's brother and sister's son appeared in societies other than Tikopia. It appears, in fact, in all societies where the other ties in the web of kinship make this one appropriate, where it is congruous with the rest of the pattern. The technique of making a living was somewhat different in medieval Europe from what it is in Tikopia, but the two societies have some characteristics in common. In both, the family is the chief productive unit and the father is its boss; in both, the inheritance of name and property is patrilineal; in both, the relationship between father and son is distant and respectful. In the *Chanson de Roland*, indeed, the devotion of mother's brother and sister's son for one another is linked with positive hostility between father and son. This masculine triangle, rather than the soft modern love triangle, is one of the themes of the great legend.[13] These similarities between societies far separated in time or space, similarities that are often almost overpowering in their extent, cannot, we contend, be explained by cultural diffusion, that is, the process by which one society picks up a new pattern of behavior such as a new technological process by contact with another society.[14] If the emotional relationships in a family in one society resemble the emotional relationships in a family in another, the reason must be that similar organizational forces are at work in both. We have tried to show what some of these forces are. If, moreover, the organizational forces change, the emotional patterns will change too. The relation between mother's brother and sister's son that we have described is an inevitable part of a certain system of interpersonal relations. In the evolution of our own kinship system from the medieval peasant family to the modern urban

[13] For further information see M. Bloch, *La société féodale*, I, 191-221; G. C. Homans, *English Villagers of the 13th Century*, 192; W. O. Farnsworth, *Uncle and Nephew in the Old French Chansons de Geste* (Columbia University Studies in Romance Philology and Literature); C. H. Bell, *The Sister's Son in the Medieval German Epic* (Univ. of California: Publications in Modern Philology, X, No. 2).

[14] For a society in which the system of interpersonal relations in the family corresponds almost point for point with that of Tikopia, see M. Fortes, *The Web of Kinship among the Tallensi*.

family, the mother's brother-sister's son relation has changed as the other relations in the system have changed.

What is this particular system? To work it out in only a little detail, let us go back to Tikopia. The tie between a child and his father is one of respect, rather than close affection, especially on the child's part, and though the two are closely associated at work, there is no great efflorescence of interaction between them. At the same time, the tie between the child and his mother is warm and close, and in his babyhood she has been his closest associate, his comforter and protector. The child's mother's brother, moreover, is intimately linked with his sister, the child's mother. To be sure, he is not as intimate with her as he is with his brothers, but he is quite intimate enough, and he helps and supports her. What could be more natural than that the child should extend to his mother's brother some of the sentiments he feels toward his mother, or that the mother's brother—for we must look at the relationship from his point of view too—should extend to the child some of the senti- ments he feels toward his sister? The mother's brother is a kind of male mother, taking over some of the care of the child when his mother's usefulness ends. To put it analytically, *if the relationship between A and B is of a particular kind, and the relationship be- tween B and C is close and warm, the relationship between A and C will tend to resemble the relationship between A and B.*

This rule subsumes as special cases not only the relation between a child and his mother's brother (put the child as A, his mother as B, and his mother's brother as C), but also the relations between a child and his father's sister or father's brother. The relation be- tween a child (A) and his father (B) is distant and respectful, while the relation between father and father's sister (C) is com- paratively close. Therefore the child will extend to his father's sister some of the sentiments he feels toward his father. She is a kind of female father. In like manner, a child's behavior toward his father's brother is much the same as his behavior toward his father, and he refers to the two older men by the same kinship term (*tamana*).

We have hardly exhausted the factors that determine the link between mother's brother and sister's son. We must not forget the rank of the mother's brother and the kind of activities he performs.

In the household itself, a boy as he grows up is left without any intimate who is also an adult male, that is, a person who belongs to the class of highest social rank in the community. And there are occasions in life when the boy needs and appreciates an intimate friend who is also a superior and can therefore be an adviser, teacher, comforter, and protector. We must, moreover, never forget the mother's brother's point of view. He is fond of his sister, and his connection with his own sons precludes intimacy with them. Perhaps he needs an emotional outlet to some young man over whom he need not wield authority. No doubt the analysis might be carried further, and yield new truths. At any rate, the particular character of the relationship between mother's brother and sister's son can be explained only by its position in a whole system of interpersonal relationships. Sentiment between the two is warm; interaction is frequent, and goes far beyond any amount required by the external system, and this interaction serves further to increase their affection.[15]

THE MOTHER'S BROTHER IN THE TROBRIANDS

We modern Americans are in no danger of thinking of the tie between mother's brother and sister's son as being "natural," in the same way that we think of the love of mother for son as being natural. We do not even recognize that this special tie exists in our society at all, though we may have more experience of it than we admit. Therefore we are especially well able to look at the tie from the outside, and analytically, and we can take advantage of this objectivity to clinch some of the ideas we have been advancing, by studying briefly a society in which the mother's brother plays a very different part from what he does in Tikopia.

Bronislaw Malinowski, who was Firth's guide and teacher, owed to a fortunate accident his years of residence and intense field work in the Trobriand Islands off the northeast coast of New Guinea. World War I broke out while he was in the field; the Trobriand

---

[15] Many of the ideas in this analysis of the mother's brother-sister's son relationship are ultimately derived from A. R. Radcliffe-Brown, "The Mother's Brother in South Africa," *South African Journal of Science*, xxi (1924), 542-55. But the present author has been unable to find and read a copy of this paper.

Islands were then German territory, and he had to stay there. He recorded his observations, and his reflections upon them, in a set of famous anthropological monographs.[16] Perhaps no primitive society has been more thoroughly studied than that of the Trobrianders.

The Trobrianders, like the Tikopia, make their living by fishing and gardening. But we must remember that the techniques of production seldom require any one single type of human organization to carry them out; they only set limits to the possible range of types. At any rate, the Trobrianders are Melanesians, whereas the Tikopia are Polynesians, and their ways of organizing themselves are somewhat different. Trobriand society is matrilineal. Descent is traced through the mother; indeed the part the father's semen plays in the conception of a child is not known. A Trobriander belongs to his mother's kin group, and rank and property come to him by reason of descent from his mother. Matriliny in the Trobriands does not mean that women have general authority over men, nor that the nuclear family—father, mother, and children—does not live together as a recognized unit. But in other ways matriliny produces a family situation rather different from the Tikopia one. The father plays an important part in the care and instruction of the young child, but as the latter grows up, he is expected to work under the direction of his mother's brothers in the cultivation of yams in their gardens, whence part of the crop will go as a gift to his mother. He does not continue to work under the direction of his father, as he does in Tikopia. But the father is not left without a job. He must till his own gardens with the aid of *his* sister's sons. When a man reaches maturity he is expected to leave his father's house and village and live in the village of his mother's kin, where his wife will join him when he marries. In short, the basic unit in production is made up in the Trobriands of a man and his sister's children, whereas in Tikopia it is made up of a man and his sons. There seems to be no reason why the two kinds of organization should not be equally efficent.

[16] The principal ones are: *Argonauts of the Western Pacific, Crime and Custom in Savage Society, Sex and Repression in Savage Society, The Sexual Life of Savages, The Father in Primitive Psychology, Coral Gardens and Their Magic.*

What interests us especially is that, as the Trobrianders and the Tikopia differ in the composition of the basic productive unit, so they differ in the attitudes they take toward the father and the mother's brother. In the Trobriands, the attitude of a boy toward the mother's brother is one of respect, not close affection, and interaction with him is kept down to matters of business, whereas the father, who lives with the boy, sees him all the time, and exercises little or no authority over him once he has begun to grow up, is the boy's close friend and companion.[17] Indeed, if the boy's father is a chief and thus in a position to indulge his affection, he may try to keep the boy in his own village and not send him back, as custom requires, to the village from which his mother came. Then the chief's own sisters' sons may begin to fear that the chief's property and rank, which ought by the matrilineal rule to go to them, will be diverted to the chief's son.

In short, the system of relationships is the mirror opposite of the Tikopia system, if we look at it from the point of view of kinship; that is, a Trobriander takes the same kind of attitude toward his father that a Tikopia takes towards his mother's brother. But the system is almost exactly the same as the Tikopia if we forget about biological kinship, as we have urged we should, and look at the working group instead. From this point of view, a man's tie with the male of the older generation who is his chief boss is, in both systems, one of respect and low social interaction, whereas a man's tie with the male of the older generation who is closest to him but not his boss is one of affection and intimacy. The crucial factor is the locus of authority in the external system. As this shifts, the emotional relationships in the internal system rearrange themselves accordingly. There is no neater example of the influence of the external system on the internal.

One word of warning is needed here. Nothing we have just said should be taken as implying that all patrilineal societies have exactly the same system of kinship relationships as the Tikopia, nor that all matrilineal ones have the same system as the Trobriand.

17 *The Sexual Life of Savages*, Ch. I, secs. 1, 3; IV, 4; V, 3; VII, 3, 6; *The Father in Primitive Psychology*, 13, 85. For a similar pattern, see F. Eggan, "The Hopi and the Lineage Principle," in M. Fortes, ed., *Social Structure*, 132-40.

The anthropological distinction between patriliny and matriliny is too sharp to represent the real state of affairs. In every society, influences from the father's side and from the mother's side bear upon the nuclear family. The actual system of emotional ties depends on the relative strength of these influences under given circumstances; and in the range of human societies, almost every shade of variation could no doubt be found between a Tikopia, or even more extreme, patrilineal system on one side, and a Trobriand, or even more extreme, matrilineal system on the other. Kinship systems differ from one another quantitatively and not qualitatively. To use a mechanical analogy, they vary with the varying tensions along the many strands of a complex web of interpersonal relations.

THE MATRIX OF KINSHIP

We have not drawn every sublety out of the ties of Tikopia kinship, but we had better not pursue the analysis any further. The returns are diminishing. If the number of persons in a group being studied is n, the number of relationships between them is $n(n-1)/2$; that is, any increase in the number of persons brings about a much more rapid increase in the number of relationships. As soon, therefore, as we follow out the ties of Tikopia kinship beyond the nuclear family, the number of ties we must take into consideration soon becomes very large indeed. Moreover, the tie between any two persons cannot be fully understood apart from the ties of these two with all the other persons in the system, or matrix, nor apart from the ties of these others to one another. For these reasons the full analysis of a system of interpersonal relationships, carried out in ordinary literary language, is apt to become unmanageable. Most novelists seem to know this and do not try to make their analyses complete. Henry James did try, and as a result made some of his books impossibly dull because impossibly intricate, yet even James hardly devised any system of relationships more intricate than the one Tikopia, or any other group, spontaneously evolves. But if there is any man so bold as to make the attempt, let him pursue for himself the further analysis of Tikopia kinship, using his own social sense, the facts that Firth supplies and the method in which we have drilled him.

It is the method of analysis, not the actual analysis of any particular relationship, that is our chief concern; or rather it is the analytical hypotheses reached by the method. For there is the possibility, which it may be presumptuous of us to raise, that in the study of human affairs, as in other sciences, the complexity we encounter in the phenomena arises less from the number of "laws," which, though no doubt numerous enough, may yet be comparatively few, than from the intricate interaction of these laws in particular systems of behavior.[18] Thus Newton's laws of motion were three in number, and yet they served to account for the behavior of a very large number of superficially different mechanical systems, from a pendulum to the planets.

Though the system of interpersonal relations is complex, it still has a head and a tail. We can at least make a start in analyzing it. Certain ties seem particularly crucial; the others crystallize or fall into order around them. These in Tikopia are the ties between father and son, between brother and brother, and between mother and son. By the rule that no pair relationship is independent of the whole matrix of relationships, these ties help to determine the others. The grandfather-grandson tie, for instance, could not have been what it is if the father-son tie had been different. Nor would such a link between families as the closeness between mother's brother and sister's son have developed if the pressures that we have observed within the nuclear family had not existed. Our analysis can begin with the nuclear family and spread out at least some distance from it.

The matrix of interpersonal relationships is itself part of a larger system. This is what we mean when we say that none of the ties is natural. As we have seen from our comparison of Tikopia and Trobriand kinship, the nature of the bond between, for instance, father and son is not inherent in the blood relationship, but rather in the way the two work together in carrying out the practical tasks of everyday life. The crucial question seems to be: Is the father the boss of the son? In short we have discovered in Tikopia the same kind of process at work as the one we have already encountered in

18 For this idea in biology, see Sir D. Thompson, *On Growth and Form* (1948 ed.), 289, 784.

the Bank Wiring Observation Room. If, in doing the necessary work on the environment, one man gives orders to another, or if one interacts frequently with another while following the directions of a third, and so on—then, on the basis of these relationships a further set of relationships will elaborate themselves or emerge. We must assume that certain latent sentiments are released in the members of a group, with the possibility of setting off novel developments in interaction and activity, whenever an initial coordination among the members has been achieved. Or, in our language, the internal system builds itself up on the basis of the external. We shall see later how it reacts upon the external system.[19]

None of the relationships of Tikopia kinship is natural, nor is any, we submit, strange. They are not just the kinship bonds we know, yet we can imagine ourselves behaving as the Tikopia do in the Tikopia situation. We do not behave just as people do in novels, but the skill of the great novelist lies in making us feel that, if we were placed in the situation he has contrived, we should behave as his characters do. Their behavior is, as we say, believable. We can even go further than this. Our kinship bonds are not those of Tikopia, yet they are different not in kind but in degree. There is something of the Tikopia father in our life with father, and certainly the mother-in-law problem of the primitive finds an echo in all our hearts. The fact is, as we have insisted so often, that the kinship system of one society differs as a whole from the kinship system of another because each of the relationships of one differs from each of those of the other in the degree in which it exemplifies a set of underlying rules, the ones we have formulated or others.

[19] G. P. Murdock points out (*Social Structure*, 192, 199) that technical changes diffuse from one primitive society to another much more easily than changes in social organization, such as emotional ties between kinsmen. Our analysis helps to account for this fact. The internal system, related as it is to the external, cannot easily change directly but only indirectly, so far as new techniques stimulate a new form of external system in the group. Moreover, a new technique may not have this effect. The new process may be carried out by the same old organization of production: the same division of labor, the same loci of authority, etc.

MUTUAL DEPENDENCE OF SENTIMENT AND ACTIVITY,
OF ACTIVITY AND INTERACTION

We find ourselves under no obligation to give the same amount of space, with each of our "cases," to each of the relationships of mutual dependence in the social system. We repeat ourselves often enough without going that far. In the present chapter we are emphasizing interpersonal ties, as in other chapters we have emphasized intergroup ties, and we have given much space to them under the heading of the mutual dependence of interaction and sentiment. We need say only a few words about the other relationships of mutual dependence.

By the mutual dependence of sentiment and activity in the internal system, we refer, among other things, to the fact that any emotional attitude we take toward someone tends, like any other drive, to get itself expressed in activity, which may in turn arouse sentiment in the person to whom it is addressed, and so lead to reciprocal activity. The activity may be a gesture, a change in tone of voice, a caress: it may be evanescent and informal. It may also be much more visible, much more formal: an especially careful form of language, the giving of a gift, an offer to help in a piece of work. This kind of activity may go far beyond the amount initially required in the external system and lead to new interactions between the persons concerned.

In Tikopia the range of activities open to a man in his relationship with another is much affected by his sentiments toward the other. Persons in the "bad" or *tautau pariki* relationship—father and son, for example—are much more restrained or formal in their mutual behavior than are persons in the "good" or *tautau laui* relationship—brothers, for example. Brothers are free to take any liberties with one another in word or deed without fear that what they do will be misunderstood or resented. Like friends in our society, brothers in Tikopia can vilify one another in the most loathsome curses without the slightest danger that their words will be taken literally. This freedom of brothers in Tikopia to tell jokes, including dirty jokes, to one another may be misunderstood by persons who have only a little knowledge of anthropology. For the "joking relationship" is a classic of that science. In some societies persons in a certain kinship relation to one another are expected to joke with one another. It may be that a joke is always a response to a conflict—the conflict between the ideal and the real if no other is present—but this does not mean that persons who joke with one another are always in some sort of conflict with one another. In some societies they may be. We ourselves use a joke to pass off a temporary difficulty; other peoples use joking to cover an embarrassment of long standing; the practical joke may serve to release aggression that is allowed no other outlet. And so on. But in other societies joking may mean something quite different. Thus the relationship between brothers in Tikopia is marked, not by conflict, but rather by its absence, and as a result the brothers feel free to express any emotion whatsoever, from humor to passing anger. Joking occurs in many different situations, and the situations must not be confused just because they arouse similar responses.[20]

KINSHIP EXTENSION

The relationships of mutual dependence between sentiment and activity, and between activity and interaction are specially important in developing a feature of primitive society that anthropologists call kinship extension. We recognize this as one of the ways in which modern American society contrasts most greatly with primitive society. Our own society has a single kinship unit, the nuclear family, whereas a society like Tikopia extends kinship ties far beyond the bounds of the nuclear family; in special links with kindred by marriage and in the formation of house and clan, until at length the whole island becomes a body of kinsmen. How shall we explain this process? We should be false to our whole approach if we admitted that the natives were just different from ourselves. There must be better reasons than that for kinship extension, and they must be expressible in terms of our conceptual scheme.

Let us use the relationship between Tikopia brothers as an illustration. When all are unmarried, all members of one household, and all working under the direction of their father, a strong sentiment of freedom and friendship between them is built up. Then, one by one, brothers marry and, for the most part, found house-

[20] See *We, The Tikopia.* 190.

holds of their own near the old home. Yet their friendship does not for this reason die away. It might, indeed we feel quite sure it would, die away gradually if nothing were done to keep it up, but the fact is that something is done. Brothers come back to visit their old home, an easy task if they live nearby. That is, their sentiments lead them to continued interaction, which itself helps keep the sentiment alive. Their sentiments also lead them to new activities. Brothers may make presents to one another, and these take the place of the more informal expressions of friendship that were natural in the old days. Perhaps a man feels guilty when the old tie is in decline, feels that he has neglected his brother, and tries to make up for his neglect in some highly visible expression of friendship, such as a gift.

So far there is nothing strange in the process. We are familiar with it in our own society. In New England as in Tikopia, brothers and sisters give one another presents and visit one another often, particularly on ritual occasions. The chief of these occasions is the Christmas or Thanksgiving dinner, which brothers and sisters attend with their spouses and children. Since the members of any one nuclear family may belong to as many as four dining groups—the husband's father's, the husband's mother's, the wife's father's, and the wife's mother's—the problem of fitting in all the dinners and digesting all the food and drink is a big one. But Yankees are tough and it is solved somehow. Kinship in New England may be stretched farther than it is in some other parts of the United States, but even in New England the group that dines together seldom includes all those persons who trace common descent from an ancestor more than three generations back. As the group increases in size, and feeding everyone around a single table gets more and more difficult, the kin group is likely to break up, no longer held together except by genealogy.

Why does the New England kin group break up and not the Tikopian? The difference lies in the kinds of activities that kinsmen perform as an expression of their sentiments. It is pleasant to get Christmas presents, but an accident of the strangest kind if they are of any use. They are mere tokens. A Christmas dinner may be good fun, but one can live without it. Suppose, however, that a man gives his brother a present of food that is a welcome replenishment of his larder, or offers him help without which he could not carry out a practical task like building a canoe. Then the interaction is kept up as no single Christmas dinner can possibly keep it up; then the sentiments are reinforced instead of being gradually allowed to die, and in this way kinship ties are maintained. Nor is there any reason why they should not be extended as new generations increase the population of the kindred. Co-operation between brothers will be perpetuated in the same kind of tie between the brothers' sons as once existed between the brothers themselves. And if the senior first cousin takes the lead in co-operative activities, as the oldest brother did in the group of brothers, the Tikopia house will be organized. Kinship sentiment leads to activities expressive of sentiment and to increased interaction among kinsmen. A surplus, so to speak, of interaction and activity is produced. If it is used by the family and the larger group for doing work that could not otherwise be done or could not be done so well, then kinship sentiments, interactions, and activities are kept up from generation to generation, or in the ordinary phrase, kinship is extended to wider and wider groups. It is not extended unless it is used. Never do interpersonal relations exist in a vacuum. Kinship is more widely extended in Tikopia because it is more widely used than it is in our society, where tasks beyond the capacity of the nuclear family are carried out by organizations not based on kinship.

NORMS AND SOCIAL RANK

We have based our analysis of Tikopia kinship on Firth's description of the actual behavior of kinsmen. But Firth shows us also that, besides behaving in certain ways, the Tikopia are quite able to say what behavior ought to be in the various kinship relations. In fact the norms are probably better established among the Tikopia than in some of the other groups we have studied. Kinship in Tikopia has a long history behind it, and there are probably more families on the island that resemble one another fairly closely than there are groups like the Bank Wiremen in the Western Electric Company, or gangs like the Nortons in Cornerville. The older the pattern is, and the more often it is repeated, the more easily it is recognized and enshrined in group norms.

No doubt we are right in emphasizing behavior first. What the members of a society consider normal behavior must be created and re-created on the model of actual behavior. When some event has occurred enough times, its continued occurrence comes to be expected. As the lawyers know, law is built on precedent. We can hardly believe that norms were established in any other manner in the days before professional philosophers were born, and even the ideals of the philosophers may only represent the behavior of the advanced individuals of their time. We shall never go far wrong if we assume that behavior is the primary phenomenon, the formulation in words of the rules for proper behavior, secondary. But like everything else in a social system, norms once developed have important effects on the other elements of behavior. Norms are taught to the youngsters, and when so taught are called by anthropologists the culture of the group. Norms are in force even for the disapproved kinds of social behavior. There is a right way of carrying on black magic—an item in what the anthropologists refer to as "covert culture." And there is honor among thieves. Moreover, the development of norms is a decisive step in social control. A norm states what a person is expected to do in given circumstances. Usually he is so placed that he also wants to do what he is expected to do. But whether or not he wishes of his own accord to perform the right action, he performs it nevertheless, because the relations of the social system are such that departure from the norm will bring him some form of punishment. The connection between individual motivation, norms, and social control is not an easy thing to describe, and we shall spend much time on it in the next two chapters. All we can say here is that Firth was fully aware of the problem as it arose in Tikopia society. Thus he says of the father-son relationship: "Towards the father a mingling of affection and respect appears to be the norm, each component being a matter of social injunction as well as of individual feeling." [21] And again, "Another obligation, one of the most definite of all, is that of mourning the parent in the appropriate manner at his or her death. Here the social group takes charge, and the child has no option but to express these sentiments of *arofa* which as we have shown are usually felt

[21] *We, The Tikopia,* 182.

in actuality, and which the society has determined shall be demonstrated." [22]

In earlier chapters we saw the close connection between social norms and social rank. The persons that come closest to realizing the group norms hold the highest social rank. We need not repeat here all that we have already said on this subject, but at the same time we should not allow the fact that in Tikopia we are dealing with families rather than groups of other kinds to prevent our realizing that the connection between rank and social norms holds on the island as it does elsewhere. The chiefs, of course, rank highest in Tikopia, and the ritual elders next, but even the other adult men form, in relation to the women, a superior group, just as the connector wiremen's clique was superior to that of the selectors. The men monopolize some of the most difficult and important activities of the society, notably sea fishing, and this contributes to their rank. But the relationship also works in the other direction, and menial tasks are assigned to certain persons just because they hold low social rank. Thus in Tikopia the young women must fetch water from the spring, just as, in the Bank Wiring Observation Room, the solderman assigned to the selector wiremen had to fetch the lunches. The men carry out many of the most difficult undertakings, and they exercise ultimate control over many others. Their rank depends on their authority, and their authority on their rank. In any social relationship, moreover, where authority is not too strong a factor, the interaction of other members of the group tends to flow toward the adult men. This is a component in the tie between mother's brother and sister's son: the latter looks up to and turns towards the man of higher rank. Tikopia, finally, has a religion of its own, and in all societies, ours included, the basic norms of the group, among which the norms of kinship behavior stand high, are closely linked with religious beliefs and the worship of the ancestors, the Founding Fathers who passed on the social norms to the living generation. It is not surprising, then, that the higher a person ranks, the more closely he is connected with religion. In Tikopia the ritual significance of the adult men is shown by their position in the house, where they sit next to the graves of the ancestors.

[22] *Ibid.*, 186.

Their position is a symbol of their superior rank, just as the position of the connector wiremen at the front of the room was a symbol of their superior rank in the Bank Wiring group. The ritual elders, as their name implies, take a larger part in religious observances than the commoners, and, finally, the four chiefs have the responsibility of keeping up the major ceremonies—"The Work of the Gods." The Brahmins of India are not the only priests that are also members of an upper class.

THE FUNCTIONAL THEORY

Although sociology and social anthropology make one science, we are still, in studying Tikopia, within the official domain of social anthropology. The theories of "functionalism" were first developed in anthropology; they have something to teach us, and they come in conveniently here. Anthropologists who were working in societies small enough to be viewed as wholes observed (a) that all or most of the elements of a society were related to one another, articulated with one another in such a way as (b) to meet the needs of individuals and, (c) in so doing, to contribute to the survival of the society in its environment. Of the two leaders of the functional school—Malinowski and Radcliffe-Brown—the former put more emphasis on the needs of individuals, the latter on the survival of the group. But surely the two things are not independent: group survival is inconceivable without some degree of satisfaction of individual needs. At any rate, the anthropologists saw, for example, that the ceremonies of a primitive tribe were not unconnected with the rest of tribal life. The ceremonies would have been different if the myths, the family groups, or even the routines of productive work had been different. They also saw that the performance of the rites, by its effect on the sentiments of individuals, contributed to the natives' ability to carry out the activities of daily life on which the survival of the group depended. The rites released pent-up emotion, gave confidence, and reinforced the motives for co-operation.[23] The anthropologists then said that religion had a "function" in meeting individual needs and contributing to the survival of a society.

[23] See B. Malinowski, "Magic, Science, and Religion," in his *Magic, Science and Religion and Other Essays*, 1-71.

With this example behind us, we can give Radcliffe-Brown's definition of *function:*

The *function* of any recurrent activity, such as the punishment of a crime, or a funeral ceremony, is the part it plays in the social life as a whole and therefore the contribution it makes to the maintenance of the structural continuity. The concept of function as here defined thus involves the notion of a *structure* consisting of a *set of relations* amongst *unit entities,* the *continuity* of the structure being maintained by a *life-process* made up of the activities of the constituent units.[24]

The idea of society as an organized whole or structure and the related idea of function, worked out by such men as Durkheim, Radcliffe-Brown, Malinowski, and Talcott Parsons, are among the great contributions of social anthropology and sociology to modern social science. We build on these ideas everywhere in this book, but they run into some difficulties, which must be faced. In the first place, the functionalists have not always made clear what they mean by the "elements" or "unit entities" that are related to one another in the social structure. Sometimes they have said that the unit entities were *institutions* and, to take the example we used above, that "the religious institutions of a society help maintain or support the economic institutions." Unfortunately the word *institution* has been given at least two meanings, and the functionalists do not always specify which meaning they are using. Is religion an institution, or is the church one? For us, who shy away from *institution* just because it is ambiguous, religion is a certain kind of activity, while the church is a specialized organization, a department, so to speak, of a society. Religious activities may be, but are not always, carried out by a specialized organization, and the two things had better not be confused in a single word. Our classification of the elements of social behavior is an effort to avoid this kind of difficulty.

In the second place, the meaning of *survival* or *continuity* is not always clear. The anthropologist is living with a primitive tribe.

---

[24] A. R. Radcliffe-Brown, "On the Concept of Function in Social Science," *American Anthropologist,* New Series, Vol. 37 (1935), 396. In the rich literature on functionalism, the student might also begin with B. Malinowski, "The Functional Theory," in *A Scientific Theory of Culture and Other Essays,* 147-176, and the article "Culture" in *Encyclopedia of the Social Sciences.*

However enfeebled it may look to him, it is obviously, at the moment, surviving. He is not able to change its characteristics to see whether it would survive if these were any different. He is not in the position of a biologist in a laboratory, experimenting with a cat's nervous system in order to determine what changes impair its "survival value," that is, the contribution the nervous system makes to the cat's capacity to survive. If we turn to history for help, it is astonishing how few societies have failed to survive. No doubt some primitive societies have disappeared, and all their members have died out, like the last of the Mohicans. But by far the more usual situation resembles the decline and fall of the Roman Empire. What fell then was not a society but a governmental organization, an empire, whereas the society of Italy, for instance, survived the barbarian invasions and has maintained its continuity unbroken from the Roman era to the present day. When sociologists talk about survival, they are apt to mean the survival of a society rather than that of a governmental organization, yet it might seem hard to establish any but the most elementary inferences about the contribution a social institution makes to the survival of a society when so few societies have *not* survived. How can you be sure what contributes unless you have some idea what does not contribute? The meaning of social survival can be made much more precise for small units and organizations within a society than for the society itself, and when we have invoked the idea of survival in this book we have tried to limit ourselves to these small units. In our own nation, small groups are breaking up every day, larger organizations dying from bankruptcy and other maladies. We have plenty of evidence with which to analyze their fitness to survive. But, since a society may decline a long way before it dies, the notion of the survival of a society as a whole is too indefinite to be useful, unless we specify pretty carefully the level at which the society is supposed to survive. If we have done that, we may meaningfully ask how a certain kind of interrelatedness between the elements of society helps to maintain that level of life. The more carefully we phrase this kind of question, the more closely our answer will approach a study of social equilibrium of the kind we describe in the next chapter.

In the third place, there is an assumption in a statement like the one of Radcliffe-Brown's we have just cited that, because some recurrent activity is organically interrelated with the other activities of society, it *therefore* makes a contribution to the continuity or survival of society. Thus the magical rituals of a certain society may be closely related to its economic activities. Magic may be be performed at every step in farm work, on the theory that it will make the crops large. But this relatedness does not necessarily mean that magic will contribute to the survival of the society. It may stimulate people to work hard by giving them confidence that their efforts will be successful, but it may also, to take an obvious possibility, consume time that could be better spent in farm work itself. That magic, or any other activity, makes, on balance, a contribution to the survival of a society is not an assumption that can be made in advance; it is a hypothesis to be investigated, for the interrelatedness of the elements of social behavior may be dysfunctional as well as functional.

Finally, some members of the functional school, Radcliffe-Brown much more than the others, tend to see in the part a social activity plays in preserving the continuity of a society an adequate explanation of the activity's appearance. In the words of the old philosphers, they are content to point out the final cause of a phenomenon and neglect the efficient. But no element of an organic system appears just because it is needed; it appears because forces are at work tending to produce it. "In Aristotle's parable, the house is there that men may live in it; but it is also there because the builders have laid one stone upon another." [25] The really interesting characteristic of Nature is the way her efficient causes play into the hands of her final ones. We are going to see, and in fact have seen, that the organic nature of society goes far beyond anything conceived by the functional anthropologists, that functional relations—and dysfunctional ones too—not only do emerge but cannot help emerging, that, in the small group at least, they tend to produce a positive surplus, a margin of safety in the qualities the group needs for survival, and that this surplus may be used, not simply

[25] Sir D. W. Thompson, *On Growth and Form*, 6. His whole discussion of efficient and final causes is interesting.

to maintain the existing adaptation of the group to its environment but to achieve a new and better adaptation. We are interested in survival, but in evolution too. The functional anthropologists were content to point out such things as the interrelatedness of religious and economic activities in a primitive tribe and to show that the former contributed to the effectiveness of the latter. We have tried and will try to go further, to trace the simplest analytical relations between the elements of behavior, and to show that inherent even in these is the possibility of organic growth, the emergence of some of the most general characteristics of society: morale, leadership, control, extension of the range of social contact—all needed for survival, but for development too. Society does not just survive; in surviving it creates conditions that, under favorable circumstances, allow it to survive at a new level. Given half a chance, it pulls itself up by its own bootstraps. How can we account in any other way for the emergence of a civilization from a tribe?

A sociologist must sometimes forget that his chief subject is human society, and remember that he is also a student of society in general, a society of cells, or electrons, as much as one of men. Then he will begin to wonder whether this emergent surplus that may be used for development is not the secret of that capacity for evolution so characteristic of organic life.[26] In a way he is fortunate in his focus on human society, for he is often studying from within an organism in the very act of emergence, rather than one that has already emerged and reached the fixed form of an anthill or an animal body. But human society, while letting him view the process, also prevents his becoming enthusiastic about the results. He sees that unfavorable as well as favorable characteristics emerge, that for many groups the environment may simply be too severe or too lacking in stimulus to let the development go very far, and that, finally, a development favorable at one stage may in the end create the conditions, inside and outside the group, that bring the development itself to a halt.

[26] See *On Growth and Form*, 591 for an example from biology. By the sheer geometry of cell division, an organism consisting of a growing number of cells tends to create a skin or integument surrounding the cells, and this skin may then be used to contribute to the survival of the organism. See also *ibid.*, 451, 889, 1019.

REACTION OF THE INTERNAL SYSTEM ON THE EXTERNAL

In our study of the external system, we have considered the final causes of some features of group life. That is, we have assumed that a group has to have certain characteristics, varying with the environment in which it is placed, if it is to survive in that environment. We have assumed, for instance, that the Tikopia family has to have some division of labor and some chain of command. To the extent that we have "explained" the existence of these features of group life by the assumption that the group could not survive without them, we have been functionalists. But in our study of the build-up and feedback of the internal system, we have considered, or have begun to consider, for we have not carried our analysis very far, the efficient causes of these features. That is, we have shown some of the processes that create or modify the group characteristics we assumed at the beginning, the processes that enable the group to survive or to move by evolution to survival at a different level from the one we took for granted at first. In this way we have brought our analysis around in a circle, as we threatened to do when we used as an analogy the problem of describing the operations of a gasoline engine. The circularity is not, we believe, a matter of bad logic, but arises from the difficulty of describing in words an organic phenomenon. That the difficulty is a real one is suggested by the quotation from Claude Bernard with which this book opens.

But let us look a little more closely at the build-up and feedback of the internal system. In all the groups we have studied we have seen how the group creates its own morale. Persons would not have become members unless they were to some degree willing to co-operate, but their membership in a group releases forces that make them more willing to co-operate in furthering the group's purposes, though not always in furthering those of the external human environment. In the Bank Wiring Observation Room we saw that the social relations developing between the men reacted so as to change the methods of work that the company had laid out and largely to defeat the intentions of its wage incentive plan. In the Bank Wiring Observation Room we also saw the tentative emergence of leadership, and in the Norton Street Gang we saw leadership fully developed. The gang had no immediate need for the elaborate organization it created, and yet if it had needed to carry out complicated operations on the environment, the organization would have been available, and could, so to speak, have been seized on to contribute to the group's survival. In both groups, too, a tough social control or discipline emerged, and this we shall speak of in the next chapter. Morale, leadership, and discipline all, we hardly need to say, have potential survival value for a group.

From this review, let us turn back to Tikopia. We assumed at the beginning that, if the Tikopia family was to survive, it had to have some leadership and some division of labor. Then we saw that the relation between social norms and social rank tends to put the chiefs, ritual elders, and, in fact, all adult males in the society in a position where they can exercise leadership for their respective groups. We also saw, or began to see, that the division of labor is effected by the assignment of different tasks to persons of different social rank. Moreover, the sentiments of affection that grow up between members of a family positively help the family to carry out its activities well. They provide new motives. But the feedbacks are not all favorable, and the social distance between father and son, or, more generally, between persons of different social rank, may be a source of possible conflict and failure of communication. In fact, the characteristics of leadership, so important in the development of larger social units out of smaller ones, may, when the society becomes sufficiently large, create some of the gravest social problems. The problems of modern Western society may be seen as problems of leadership.

As the young men and women leave the Tikopia household, the links of sentiment and interaction between them do not disappear, but provide a means of assembling a labor force sufficient for tasks beyond the capacity of the immediate household. A surplus of human co-operativeness is available not just for survival but for improved activity on the environment. If the surplus is actually used, the links of kinship, instead of gradually dying away, are reaffirmed, perpetuated, and, as families grow, extended to ever larger groups of kinsmen.

The forces at work within the family extend the links not only between blood kinsmen but between affinal kin, and if these links are seized upon and used they are perpetuated. If a young man is uncertain and afraid in the various crises of his growth to maturity, he can go to his mother's brother for help. The pressures in the family push him in that direction, and, in turn, the help that his mother's brother gives him serves to cement the relationship.

The need for making gifts supplies a further incentive to work, over and above the need of providing for one's own family. Thus a boy's father will work to repay his brother-in-law, the boy's mother's brother, for the kindness he has done the boy. But gift giving does more than supply new incentives. Every society must have a method of distributing to its members the material goods produced by it. In Tikopia the distribution is largely direct: the man who catches the fish eats it. But much distribution follows the channels of kinship obligation in all groups from household to clan. The gifts he receives from his clansmen enable a chief to amass large supplies of provisions and thus to feed and keep together a working party whose members would otherwise have had to scatter to feed themselves.

Besides these direct feedbacks, we can see in Tikopia some indirect feedbacks that contribute to the survival of the society by controlling tensions that might otherwise be disruptive. Let us take as one example the position of a married woman. Tikopia is strongly patrilineal. When a woman marries, she goes to live in the neighborhood, or actually in the house, of her husband's family. In an alien world, she is a novice, a stranger, and outnumbered. Her hand needs strengthening. The affection and protection of her brother, the respect that her brother's children show her, the tie between her own children and her brother, who is their *tuatina*, and the co-operation of brothers-in-law—all these things have the effect of supporting her in a difficult position. The support is not planned; it makes no sense to talk of planning here; but the support is furnished nevertheless and follows from the other relationships established between kinsmen. In organic systems, many things emerge from interrelatedness, including further interrelatedness.

We can sum up by saying that much work in Tikopia is at one and the same time (*a*) effective in enabling the group to survive in its environment, and (*b*) carried out as an expression of social sentiments. The external and the internal systems are fully merged. They are not in other groups we have studied, but then, none of these groups has had so long a time to effect the merger. Remember always that though we describe, and must describe—the limitations of language being what they are—the build-up and feedback as if they followed one another in a time sequence, we are, nevertheless, always dealing in fact with cycles or circuits of mutual dependence, each part of which is energized and active at all times.

THE MODERN URBAN FAMILY

This book has no need for one kind of comprehensiveness. It has no need for special chapters on "Industry," "The Community," "The Family," etc., in the manner of some textbooks. Its subject is the group in general, and its thesis is that the subject is obscured if we study groups with different names as if they illustrated different principles of organization. Our attack is analytical, not taxonomic. But at the end of a long discussion of the Tikopia family, we inevitably compare it with the family we know best: the modern American, middle-class, urban family. The two are very different, and yet if our notions are correct, the very differences should be capable of explanation by a single set of analytical hypotheses. The two represent different solutions of the same field equations.

That "something is wrong" with the modern family is established to the satisfaction of many by the figures on divorce. In America, one marriage out of four ends in divorce. But if something is wrong, we can correct it not by bawling out Mom and a Generation of Vipers but by trying, first of all, to understand what has happened. For us, the process of analysis begins with the external system. The growth of civilization has meant that activities have been steadily taken away from the family and turned over to other organizations. Or better, other organizations have arisen by a process of differentiation within kinship. Today, about the only activities left to the family are the sexual relations of husband and wife, the care of young children, cooking, and the maintenance of a household. Farming, fishing, clothmaking, education, and religious ritual have all gone from it; even cooking and childcare may be on the way out.

We have learned from Tikopia (if we did not know it already) that the emotional ties between persons do not exist in a vacuum but are a function of the activities they carry on together and of the way these activities are organized. In Tikopia, as in old-fashioned families everywhere, the emotional tie between husband and wife is firmly founded on the activities they contribute to the common enterprise. Today, the jobs that a married couple carry out together are much fewer. The partners choose one another on grounds of romantic love, because the social system offers nothing else to guide their choice, but when the dream of romantic love has faded, as fade it must, they have to rely upon sexual relations and mere companionship to form the foundation of their marriage. Yet sexual relations alone are a weak basis for an enduring bond, as modern novelists suggest by showing how short a time this kind of liaison lasts, and if the man and the woman are to be companions, they must find activities to be companions in. In the old-fashioned family, the activities did not have to be contrived; they were given. When, moreover, trouble arises in the area either of sex or of companionship, it is apt to lead to disaster, for there are no other links between husband and wife to take up the strain.

Because the activities of the family are no longer complex enough to require centralized control, the father has lost his job as boss and has lost at the same time much of the respect that was once gladly yielded to him. From being a sort of god, he has become a mere equal and familiar, if not a joke. The check that he earns in an outside organization and deposits in a bank for the support of the family has no such emotional impact as the exercise of direct and necessary command. His chief lieutenant, his wife, has lost her divinity too, though in a lesser degree, since she still must take control of the household. In this fact lies the germ of truth in the charge that Americans are ruled by women. When the family was also a farming enterprise, as most families were two generations ago, the father was the boss because he ran the farm; when the family is no longer a farm but remains a household, father is out of a job in the family, and the authority of Mom rises relatively if not absolutely. For the old formality and respect between hus-

band and wife is substituted familiarity and a fragile companionship. Finally, as the ties between members of the family are impoverished, the ability of the group to control its members declines. In the old days, it was certain that the family itself would
not break up whatever happened. Now there is no such certainty,.
and its emotional correlate is our famous insecurity. Helped, in
one sense if not in another, by the psychiatrists and the novelists,.
husband and wife are self-conscious about their relationship. One
ought to be able to take one's wife for granted. But can one?

Much the same kind of thing is true of the ties between parents.
and children. In the old-fashioned family, the boy gradually learned
the tasks of an adult by carrying them out under the eye and orders of a father or a brother, as the girl learned them from her
mother. The emotional relationship was founded on prolonged and
shared activities. Today sons are far more resentful of the father's
authority than they were in the past, although the father's authority has declined. This is no paradox; the two facts follow from
one another. Authority is resented when it is exercised rarely and
in circumstances in which the need for authority is not obvious.
The resentment has consequences for the rest of society: many a
revolutionary was once a rebellious son. And as parents are more
self-conscious about their relations to one another, so they are more
self-conscious about their relations to their children. They devour
millions of volumes of advice on child care, none of which make
the point that it is more important to have some system and confidence in carrying it out than the best system in the world and
anxiety. Anxiety is catching; the child catches it. If the books tell
you to bring up your child like a Navaho, do so, provided that you
can be as sure of yourself as a Navaho parent.

In the old-fashioned family, the activities carried on were the
ones approved in the norms of the whole society. A man got his
social rank by being a good farmer, a woman by being a good
housewife, and thus every man and woman had a chance for self-
respect and the respect of others. This unity has broken down as
society has become less familial. The husband is valued by society
in accordance with his position in organizations outside the family,
but this position does him little good at home, where he is a mere
pal or buddy. The wife finds that good housekeeping no longer

pays off in the admiration of her fellows, and that the women's activities in which excellence is rewarded are carried on outside the family. No wonder that housework—cleanliness, good cooking, fine needlework—, which was once defined as a glory, is now, though less in amount, defined as drudgery. No wonder that there is a splendid demand for labor-saving devices in the kitchen, though their upkeep may take as much time as they save. It is not that the modern woman wants a career, but that she wants a different kind of career.

The kinship extensions so characteristic of old-fashioned society all over the world have dissolved as there have been fewer occasions to use them. They persisted only while they fed back to the external system. The nuclear family first left the household and then even the neighborhood of other kinsmen. It did so because it was able to, and because a young couple felt the charm of getting away from the aunts and the old folks. Then the servant disappeared; the problem of baby sitting arose, and the neglected kinship extensions could not be revived immediately. No grandmothers, maiden aunts, or cousins, now seen to be useful and not just peculiar people, were around to take some of the burden of child care off the mother. The result is that the mother has moments of resenting her child, while feeling at the same time overanxious and solicitous about him, and these are the roots of Momism. As for the child himself, left alone with his mother or, at best, his mother and a brother or sister, he develops intense emotional ties with a few persons rather than more relaxed ties with many. Where the old-fashioned child played with grandmothers, aunts, and contemporary cousins, the modern one must put all his emotional eggs in one basket, and when it falls he is in bad trouble. The old people are shipped off on government pensions to homes for the aged, where they live as querulous outcasts, no longer having the security that comes from living with one's friends and doing, to the very end of one's life, some work to help them.

If the kin fails the family, so does the neighborhood. The occupational and geographical mobility of the father is so great that stable ties with neighbors, which might take some of the loneliness away from the family, are not formed.

And through all this, the society's norms of familial behavior change much more slowly than familial behavior itself. In much of our most eloquent literature, in all of our religion, even in the Holy Family itself, the picture of father, mother and children that is offered as the approved one is a picture of the old-fashioned farm family, which *was* the family for thousands of years. No wonder we feel guilty when our behavior does not live up to the model so strongly taught us as the right one. And yet the novelists, psychologists, and sociologists, while pointing to the impaired validity of the old ways, have themselves worked out no new norms for the relationships between husband and wife and between parents and children. The new norms will emerge, but the immediate result is further confusion.

Finally, we are beginning to see that the character of the adult individual is a result of the kind of training—the kind of social training—he has received since childhood. This training is carried out by groups, of which the family is the first both in order and in importance, but the child must in time escape from the family to the body of his contemporaries. As the family disintegrates, and the transition from family to neighborhood group becomes more difficult, the personalities trained in these groups are apt to have an impaired capacity for maintaining a steady state under stress. The family may be breeding men and women who in their turn will be less able than were their own parents to raise children in psychological health. The feedback, which was once favorable, may become vicious.

The family will not go wholly to pieces. Marriage is still the most successful of human institutions. A new equilibrium will be reached, supported by new norms. The decline of the servant may revive the extended kin. The family may no longer be what it used to be—after all it used to be everything—but this will not prevent its being an essential, successful, and perhaps more flexible instrument. In the work of attaining that new equilibrium, we are helped, if intellect helps at all, not by denunciation but by understanding, and here, for the family of low integration, as for the family of high integration, the same patient analysis of the relations of mutual dependence in the internal and external systems, in which we have been drilling ourselves, will always be found useful. We have only been sketching its possibilities.

Social Control

THIS STUDY now enters a new phase by taking up a question we have long postponed: How and why do the members of a group comply with the group norms or obey the orders of the group leader? The process by which conformity is achieved we call social control if we are thinking of compliance with norms, or authority if we are thinking of obedience to orders. We shall see that the two are closely allied. So far we have taken control and authority for granted; we have simply assumed that both were effective in any group we have studied, but in the long run we cannot afford to take anything for granted.

We can put our question in another way. So far we have been making an analysis of custom. Sentences like: "The connector wiremen talked on intellectual subjects"; "Doc was the leader of the Nortons"; "In Tikopia a son's attitude towards his father is ambivalent, a mingling of friendship and respect"—these sum up recurrent events in the relations between persons. Social scientists might never have been able to make a start in studying society if it had not been for these recurrences. Society might have been too fluid to grasp. But as it was, custom stared the sociologists and anthropologists in the face; they began to describe it and found they could make progress. The pattern, the structure in custom began to appear. In the study of large social units—societies—sociologists will do well if they ever get beyond the analysis of structure, but in the study of the group, which is a unit small enough to let us get all the way around it, we may be able to go on and ask, with some hope of getting an answer, "Why does structure persist?" We can rephrase our original question, "How and why do the members of a group comply with its norms?" and ask, "What makes custom customary? Why do recurrences recur? Why is it that in the welter of human behavior there are persistencies for us to talk about?"

One assumption we make at once: no custom is self-sustaining. The idea that obedience to custom is automatic—an idea once firmly held of savages, though we know from experience that it is not true of our own society—has been destroyed even for the savages by Malinowski in a book that will have much influence on this chapter.[1] A regularity of behavior persists, similar events recur in similar circumstances, only because departure from regularity is met by resistance. Nor is the resistance mere inertia. We all discern in human behavior some blind resistance to change, but the amount of sheer change that does take place in society suggests that the inertial force is not very powerful. Custom is not just "natural"; it is a miracle, and its persistence demands more than inertia alone.

The fact is that if a social system consists of a number of elements in a complex state of mutual dependence, a change in one or more of the elements will have effects on the other elements that may counteract the change, just as a pull on one of the strands in a web of elastic bands will be met by increased tension on the others. Our whole approach has been designed to help us see a social system as a configuration of dynamic forces. Sometimes the configuration is in balance, and a steady state of the system is maintained; sometimes it is out of balance, and continuing change occurs. In fact our analysis will lead us from a study of social stability to a study of social development. But in both cases, our emphasis is on the dynamic forces. Statics, in sociology as in mechanics, is a special case of dynamics. It is not structure but the forces producing structure that interest us.[2]

[1] B. Malinowski, *Crime and Custom in Savage Society*, 10. We have also much to learn from K. Lewin, "Frontiers in Group Dynamics," *Human Relations*, I (1947), 5-41.

[2] See the brief discussion in Sir D. W. Thompson, *On Growth and Form* (1948 ed.), 288.

Before we try to answer our question more fully, a few preliminaries must be got out of the way. We have stated the problem as
one of submission to norms; we have also stated it as one of regularities in behavior. But we have emphasized again and again that
norms and actual behavior seldom coincide. Perhaps the two come
closest together in a primitive society when the norm in question
is felt to be particularly important; but Malinowski shows that even
among his Trobriand Islanders, one of the most nearly universal
human rules, the rule against incest, is occasionally disobeyed.[3]
Such aberrations horrify, but they do occur. Therefore we should
restate our question as follows: How is it that regularities persist
in the *degree* to which members of a group live up to its norms?

SOCIAL CONTROL AND THE SOCIOLOGY OF LAW

The study of social control is at once more and less comprehensive than the sociology of law. By law, social scientists generally
mean those explicitly formulated rules of behavior that are enforced
by a legal organization distinct from the other organizations of a society. This definition raises two questions for us: Are we going
to include in our discussion of social control both the social rules
that are explicitly formulated and those that are not? And we are
going to include both the rules enforced by a legal organization—
judges, prosecutors, and police, under those names or others—and
the rules enforced in other ways? Let us take up the questions in
order.

When we speak of a law we ordinarily think of a statement in a
statute book or its equivalent. The distinction between law in this
sense and what William Graham Sumner called "folkways" is important when the enforcement of law is the province of a legal
organization and the enforcement of folkways is not. But legal
organizations appear only in large societies, and we are studying
small groups. We shall draw no line between a law and a folkway;
for us both are norms, and departure from either is met by punishment: as some sociologists would say, both are sanction patterns.
We may admit that some norms are much more important than
others, and that a group may hold some much more explicitly than

[3] *Crime and Custom in Savage Society,* 83.

others. Some are stated outright; others the observer must infer, accepting all the risks of inference. Much of our knowledge of norms comes from hearing remarks like "That's not fair," or "That's not right," made about a particular event. What would have been the fair behavior, the right behavior in the circumstances is a matter of inference. Yet, directly or indirectly, the evidence for norms is always verbal, and we shall make nothing here of the different degrees of verbal explicitness or the different degrees of importance. For the moment, a law against forgery and a convention requiring respect for one's father will be, as norms, on the same footing.

A student of social control will go hopelessly wrong if he thinks of it as always lying in the hands of policemen, district attorneys, judges, and their like. Historically this kind of control, which we shall call external control, appears late. As societies grow in size, activities like religion, war, and law enforcement are delegated, first to individual specialists, and then to specialist organizations, but the original basis of control always persists. Many small societies show an admirable obedience to law without having anything like law officers. Even in our own society, external control is concerned with relatively few, though perhaps important, crimes, and in dealing with them can be effective only when supported by controls other than the formal law. The history of law enforcement, of the Prohibition Amendment, for example, is the history of the degree to which informal controls have backed up, or failed to back up, the formal. These informal controls, which we shall also call internal, are the subject of this chapter. We have paid some heed to the judicial functions of the leader of a group, but we shall pay none at all to the law as a separate organization.

AN EXAMPLE: THE CONTROL OF RECIPROCITY

Now let us plunge into the detailed study of social control by taking up some particular instances of it, which means going back over the cases in the first part of this book. They were put there to be used, if necessary, over and over again in several different connections. Let us choose a norm that is one of the world's commonest: if a man does a favor for you, you must do a roughly equivalent favor for him in return. Unlike economists, we do not need to go into the question of what constitutes equivalence or price—how many yams are worth a fish in one society, how many votes are worth a job in another. Equivalence varies from favor to favor and from group to group. Let us take the different equivalencies as given for a particular group, and ask ourselves what controls tend to maintain the observance of the norm, so far as it is observed. Whyte has this to say about fair exchange in Cornerville:

The code of the corner boy requires him to help his friends when he can and to refrain from doing anything to harm them. When life in the group runs smoothly, the obligations binding members to one another are not explicitly recognized. Once Doc asked me to do something for him, and I said that he had done so much for me that I welcomed the chance to reciprocate. He objected: "I don't want it that way. I want you to do this for me because you're my friend. That's all." It is only when the relationship breaks down that the underlying obligations are brought to light. While Alec and Frank were friends, I never heard either one of them discuss the services he was performing for the other, but when they had a falling out over the group activities with the Aphrodite Club, each man complained to Doc that the other was not acting as he should in view of the services that had been done him. In other words, actions which were performed explicitly for the sake of friendship were revealed as being part of a system of mutual obligations.[4]

We all feel that, in the end, social control is a matter of the sentiments of individuals. The question we always ask ourselves is: "Does a certain course of action taken by an individual bring reward or punishment to him so that he continues or ceases to take this course?" But whatever we may, from our knowledge of our own sentiments, infer about the sentiments of others, we shall, as mere observers of behavior, find it difficult to determine whether a certain course of action has rewarded or hurt another man. We shall be lucky if we hear him say he has been hurt. In studying social control, what we do in fact is observe the consequences of a certain course of action and then observe whether or not an individual persists in this course. If he does not persist, we assume that the consequences have hurt him. We shall, in this book, continue to use the conventional language of reward and punishment, provided we always remember that we do not, for the most part,

[4] *Street Corner Society*, 256.

observe the sentiments directly but rather correlate the results of a man's action with his continuance of, or failure to continue, that kind of action.

The best way of determining which controls tend to secure obedience to a norm is to ask what would happen if the norm were not obeyed. Whyte says in effect that many controls, rather than any one control, tend to maintain equivalence in the exchange of favors. In the first place, if B does not return A's favor, A may not do him another favor at another time: a decrease in the activity rate of B will be matched by a decrease in the reciprocal activity rate of A. So far as either man needs the help of the other in furthering any purpose he has in mind, either within the framework of group life or without, the control tending to maintain the equivalence of favors is automatic; it is built into the process of exchange. This is the economic control, the control based on individual self-interest, or, in our language, the control inherent in the external system.

But the economic control is never the only one at work in a group. Whyte makes the point, and our whole conceptual approach is designed to underline it, that the reciprocal activities of the two men are not something apart from the sentiments they feel for one another. Equivalence of exchange is also an expression of friendship. This means that any departure from equivalence between the two men will bring about a decrease in their favorable sentiments toward one another; and vice versa, that any departure from favorable sentiments between the two—between Frank and Alec, for example—will bring about a breakdown of equal exchange. In the market exchanges studied by economists, interpersonal sentiment is not a factor; at least it does not come into the equations of economics, however important it may be in ordinary business. But in the everyday reciprocities between the members of a group, interpersonal sentiment is always a factor. So far as being liked by another is a reward for a man, and being disliked a punishment, the control of equivalent exchange is again automatic, in the sense that departure from equivalence brings some degree of punishment. The punishment may not be great enough to prevent a breakdown of exchange, but punishment of some kind follows the breach of the norm. Note that we emphasize *departure* from equivalence of exchange, not the absolute amount of the favors done by either party.

We know, moreover, that any decline in favorable sentiment between two persons implies a decrease in their frequency of interaction. So far, therefore, as associating with another person is a
reward for a man, and being avoided by him a punishment, any
departure from equivalence in exchange will, through its effect on
the sentiments, bring a further control into play. But Whyte, in the
passage we are studying, does not mention this process, and we
ought not to emphasize it.

So far we have considered only the control inherent in the relation between two persons and have neglected the fact that both are
members of a group larger than two. On this subject Whyte writes:

Not all the corner boys live up to their obligations equally well, and this
factor partly accounts for the difference in status among them. The man
with low status may violate his obligations without much change in his
position. His fellows know that he has failed to discharge certain obligations in the past, and his position reflects his past performances. On
the other hand, the leader is depended upon by all the members to meet
his personal obligations. He cannot fail to do so without causing confusion and endangering his position.[5]

To analyze what Whyte has said here, we must first go back to
his remark that repayment of obligations is part of "the code of the
corner boy." That is, it is one of the norms of the group, and we
have seen the relationship between the social rank of an individual
and the degree of his obedience to the norms of the group. So far,
therefore, as his social rank is rewarding to a corner boy, any failure
to meet his obligations will hurt him and, we presume, tend to
prevent his falling short another time. His failure may also, as we
have seen in the case of Frank and Alec, come to the notice of the
leaders of the group, and they are the persons whose opinions carry
most weight in determining social rank. If the defaulter is a
man whose standing is already low, it is probably not so much his
failure to meet his obligations that hurts him—he is behindhand to
start with—as it is any departure from his existing level of failure.
Even this departure may not hurt him much, and it is a fact that
persons of low rank in a group are the persons least well controlled
by the group, though they must accept the risk of total exclusion if

[5] *Street Corner Society,* 257. See above p. 169.

they deviate too far from its norms. If the defaulter is a man whose standing is high, it is again any departure from his existing level of reciprocation that hurts him, and it hurts him more than the man of low rank, who has not so much to loose. Accordingly we find Whyte, excellent observer that he is, showing that a leader will take care that no follower reaches even an equality of payments with him. We may also take the relation in the other direction and guess that if, for other reasons, a man's social rank is falling, his willingness to repay his obligations will decline too. In short, the mutual dependence between social rank and performance in a certain activity, in this case, the return of favors, constitutes an automatic control of the activity.

ANALYSIS OF THE EXAMPLE

No doubt we could carry further our study of the control of reciprocal exchange. We have taken into account only a few pertinent items in the behavior of corner boys. But perhaps we had better stop. We have become tedious by carefully describing the familiar. After all, we have studied the Nortons in earlier chapters, and though we have not all been corner boys, we have all at some time behaved much like them. Another reason for stopping is that our purpose in this chapter is not to make a systematic study but to clarify our ideas. What clarification have we gained?

In the first place, we have discovered no new form of behavior that we could specifically point out as control. Instead, we have found ourselves examining the following: (*a*) a rule of behavior, that is, in our language, a norm; (*b*) activities, taking the form, in our example, of favors done by persons for others, (*c*) sentiments in the form of friendship or antagonism between men, (*d*) sentiments in the form of social evaluation, or ranking, of individuals by other members of a group, and (*e*) interaction between members of a group, including interaction between followers and leaders. This list carries its own lesson: there is nothing new to us here. These are the same old elements of behavior we have been meeting at every turn. We asked what would happen to a man if he departed from parity in returning favors, and we found that his departure would, by virtue of the links between the elements of the social system, bring about in each of the elements changes that would hurt him. In the small group, social control is not a separate activity, but is inherent or implicit in the relations we have already shown to exist among the elements of behavior.

In the second place, we have perhaps discovered that the effectiveness of control lies in the large number of evils a man brings down upon himself when he departs from a group norm. His punishment does not fit the crime but is altogether out of proportion to it. When one of the Nortons fails to return a favor, he is in danger of losing the right to ask a favor another time, and this hurts him whether or not he is a member of the group: it is an injury to individual self-interest. But as a member of the group he is also in danger of losing his friendship and association with other members and his ranking within the group. The larger the number of elements of social behavior that are linked together in mutual dependence with one another, and the more complex the linkage, the greater is the likelihood that a change in one of the elements will bring changes in the others tending to reverse the original change. Or better, the more fully a group becomes a social system, the greater its control over an individual member. In the end, the whole social system, in its external and internal aspects, is involved.

Wise men have often noticed how powerful control can be in the small group, what a high degree of conformity often exists, though legal machinery is lacking. The reason for this should now be obvious. The intelligent leader of a group will give less heed to inflicting punishment for the infringement of norms than to fostering the conditions under which the group can discipline itself. He will not neglect punishment, but it is ineffective unless supported by informal controls.

Nor does control depend on the social system alone. Suppose, for instance, that one of the Nortons moves away from Cornerville. He can get the pleasures of social life from groups nearer his new home, but he comes back to hang out with the Nortons because he is used to them. For him, any loss of rank within the gang may not act as a control bringing his behavior more nearly into conformity with group norms, but may rather tip the scales far enough to drive him out of the group altogether. The effectiveness of the control a group exercises over its members is influenced by the social and physical opportunities open to the members for escaping from the group. For any individual in relation to the group, control depends not just on the links of mutual dependence in the social system but also on the state of the system in relation to its environment.

These insights have often been attained. We are only trying to make them more explicit than usual. Thus Malinowski writes of his Trobrianders:

It scarcely needs to be added that "law" and "legal phenomena," as we have discovered, described and defined them in a part of Melanesia, do not consist in any independent institutions. Law represents rather an aspect of their tribal life, one side of their structure, than any independent, self-contained social arrangements. Law dwells not in a special system of decrees, which foresee and define possible forms of nonfulfillment and provide appropriate barriers and remedies. Law is the specific result of the configuration of obligations, which makes it impossible for the native to shirk his responsibility without suffering for it in the future.[6]

Or, more tersely, "Law and order arise out of the very processes which they govern.[7]

In a marvelous essay on "The Psychology of Control," Mary Parker Follett has the following suggestive passages:

Those biologists, psychologists, and philosophers I have mentioned in this paper, whose most fundamental thinking is concerned with integrative unities, tell us of the self-regulating, self-directing character of an organism as a whole. They mean that the organizing activity *is* the directing activity. The interacting *is* the control, it does not set up a control, that fatal expression of some writers on government and also some writers on business administration. . . . We get control through effective integration. Authority should arise within the unifying process. As every living process is subject to its own authority, that is, the authority evolved by or involved in the process itself, so social control is generated by the process itself. Or rather, the activity of self-creating coherence *is* the controlling activity.[8]

[6] *Crime and Custom in Savage Society*, 58-9.
[7] *Ibid.*, 123.
[8] H. C. Metcalf and L. Urwick, eds., *Dynamic Administration: The Collected Papers of Mary Parker Follett*, 202, 204.

The insight is obviously the same as Malinowski's, and is important. But a science, though it grows through insight, cannot be founded on it. Therefore we have tried to nail down this idea with deliberate analysis.

In the third place, we may learn something about social control from the very way we have gone about studying it. We have asked, in effect, what happens to the other elements of the social system if there is a small change in one of them, such as a man's activity in returning favors. In so doing we have been unconsciously following the procedure of some of the older sciences. The classical physicists get their insight into the conditions of stability or equilibrium in the systems they study by asking questions just like ours. Here, for instance, is a gyroscope spinning steadily about an axis that maintains a constant alignment in space. How does the physicist achieve insight into the stability of this system? He asks, among other questions, what happens if he pushes the axis slightly out of its present alignment. He considers a small change because a big change might produce entirely new conditions of equilibrium, whereas he is interested in the present ones. To put the problem in a more general form, let us say that the physicist has described the system he is studying by setting up a number of equations showing the relations between a number of variables, x, y, z, and so forth. He gets his insight into stability of the system by asking what change will occur in the values of y, z, and the other variables if a small change takes place in the value of x. In the preceding part of this book we have been setting up in our crude and unmathematical way some statements about the relations between the elements of a social system. In the present chapter we get our insight into social control by asking what happens to the other elements if there is a small change in one of them. Note that in this process we learn nothing new. We learn nothing from asking: "What will happen to y if there is a small change in x?" that was not already implied in the answer to the question: "What is the relation between x and y?" [9] This is what we meant by saying that in studying social control we had as yet encountered nothing that we had not known

[9] A mathematician will note that we have left out of consideration the constant of integration.

before. To use a term of mathematics, the understanding of social control comes from looking *differentially* at the relations of mutual dependence in the social system.

ACTUAL AND VIRTUAL CHANGES

Many people look upon mathematics as something mysterious rather than as a language, which can say elegantly many things that English can also say after a fashion. They miss a great deal, especially the beauty and the delightful departures from common sense that are part of the mathematics of classical mechanics and thermodynamics. It will do them no harm to encounter some mathematical ideas here. When a physicist asks: "What happens to y when a small change takes place in x?" he is studying an *actual* change, and uses the symbol dx for the actual small—as small as you please—change in x. But if he asks, "What would happen to y if a small change took place—as it does not in fact take place—in x?" he is studying what we should call a hypothetical change, but what mathematicians call a *virtual* change, and he uses the symbol δx for the virtual infinitely small change in x.[10] Thus we might use the symbol di to indicate an actual change, as small as you please, in the interaction between two persons, and δi to indicate a virtual change. (Actually we should be more apt to use di/dt, the time rate of change of the interaction.) We shall not use mathematical expressions, but we ought to understand that the ideas could be stated in mathematical language.

In attempting to understand the processes of social control, we shall consider, and have considered, both actual and virtual changes: what does happen if a man departs from his existing level of obedience to a norm, and what would happen if he did so, although in fact he does not. In everyday social life, virtual changes are the more important of the two, for through them intelligence takes part in control. Without intelligence—if we can conceive of human society as existing at all without intelligence—violations of social norms would be commoner and greater than they are in fact. The members of a group are obedient to its norms not only be-

[10] See, for example, M. Planck, *Treatise on Thermodynamics*, A. Ogg, trans., 119.

cause they have actually disobeyed and been punished in the past, but also because they see what would happen if they did disobey. They may not think of the relationships of the social system in the same way that we do, but they are nevertheless effectively aware of the relationships and are therefore able to anticipate the consequences of breaking a rule. Consider, for instance, a woman trying to decide whether to send a friend a Christmas present. She wonders whether she will get one if she does not give one, but this calculation does not carry much weight. Her domestic economy will survive the loss of a Christmas present. More serious is the question how her friend will take her default. If the friend does not get the present, will she assume that their friendship is less than it was, and will that in turn affect the association between the two? Will they see as much of one another as they used to? Finally, will the friend say anything to others that might affect the woman's reputation and social standing? The woman will probably end by giving the present, unless she is rising socially and her friend is not. In this case, she may wish to break off their association, and she may not fear any attacks on her reputation from a person of lower rank than hers. In short, in reaching her decision, she takes account, however crudely, but probably far from crudely, of the relations of mutual dependence in the social system. With her intelligence, she "sees" the relations, and to this extent intelligence is always an element in social control.

Let us have no great expectations. The result of this chapter may well be disillusion. It may be that the study of social control will not add anything to what we have known so far—except the knowledge that it does not add. But this is something, if the disillusion brings increased clarity of ideas. It is certainly disillusioning to find that an understanding of social control comes from examining differentially the relationships of mutual dependence that we have already examined in another way, but we may recall Ernst Mach's words about a similar problem in physics. Speaking of the general equation of equilibrium in mechanics, he writes:

Let it be remarked in conclusion, that the principle of virtual displacements, like every general principle, brings with it, by the insight which it furnishes, *disillusionment* as well as elucidation. It brings with it disillusionment to the extent that we recognize in it facts which were long before known and even instinctively perceived, although our present recognition is more distinct and definite; and elucidation, in that it enables us to see everywhere throughout the most complicated relations the same simple facts.[11]

SOCIAL CONTROL AS A PROCESS OF DISTRIBUTION

Another source of disillusion is the fact that we can describe the process of social control in at least two somewhat different language systems. We can describe control in the language of reward and punishment, or we can describe it in the language of the distribution of goods, provided that in this case we consider both tangible goods, such as money, and intangible goods, such as the enjoyment of high social rank. Let us go back to the Nortons and think first of the distribution of money in the group. The favors continually being exchanged among the Nortons often consisted of small money payments. Since the followers were apt to repay their obligations less fully than the leaders, money tended to flow in the group from the leaders to the followers, and therefore money must have come into the group more through the leaders than the followers and gone out more through the followers than the leaders. Note that in the small group as in the society at large, the mere possession of money is not the important fact. The wealth of a rich man consists not in dollars but in his ability to control the flow of dollars. Power, not money, is crucial.

Let us turn now to an intangible good such as social rank. Unlike money, which came originally from outside the group, social rank among the Nortons was, so to speak, produced inside the group and flowed from the followers to the leaders. The followers granted the leaders high rank. Thus the latter received from the group more of the goods produced inside the group than did any of the followers and gave to the group more of the goods produced outside. If we want to close the system, there is still one factor that remains unaccounted for. Why was it that the leaders received more money from the outside than the followers? They received more precisely because they were leaders, because, for instance, they could deliver the votes of the group in a political campaign. They were leaders

[11] E. Mach, *The Science of Mechanics*, T. J. McCormack, trans., 88. See also 430.

in part because of their high social rank, which derived, in part again, from the excess of outgo over income in their individual exchanges of favors with followers. Thus the circle is closed, and thus the system of distribution of money and rank—to take only two kinds of goods among many—can be treated in a simplified way as an economy. It is surprising how much the economy of a street corner gang, when analyzed in this way, resembles that of a business enterprise. To this idea of the generalized economy of organizations C. I. Barnard returns, over and over again, in *The Functions of the Executive*.[12] Note that in using the language of distribution we have discovered nothing about social control that we did not know already. At the same time, the study of the distribution of goods, including intangible goods, may be a good way to approach the problem of control.

Let us now sum up briefly what we have learned:

1. Since there is seldom absolute conformity with any norm, control, for an individual, is not brought into play by his disobedience to the norm but by his departure from his existing degree of obedience to the norm.

2. There is nothing new about control, no separate element that we have not already found coming into social organization.

3. The separate controls, that is, the relations between a man's disobedience to a norm and the various consequences of that disobedience, are nothing more than the old relations of mutual dependence considered differentially.

4. Control as a whole is effective in so far as a single departure from an existing level of obedience to a rule activates not one but many separate controls.

5. That is, any departure activates the system of relations so as to reduce future departures.

ANOTHER EXAMPLE: THE CONTROL OF OUTPUT

At the risk of again laboring the obvious, let us take another example, one which may illustrate something we have already implied. In the Bank Wiring Observation Room a rule existed that a wireman ought to turn out about 6,000 completed connections

12 See especially Chapter XI, "The Economy of Incentives."

or about two equipments a day. This was a norm: the members of the group said that output should be this much, but we know that the output of individual wiremen departed more or less from the norm. What forces assured obedience to it, so far as it was obeyed? Let us try to answer this question, taking into account, for simplicity's sake, only the connector wiremen of clique A and the selector wiremen of clique B, and disregarding the complexities brought in by the presence of the soldermen and inspectors.

For the members of the dominant clique, the same kind of controls were at work as those that tended to hold the Nortons to the rule of reciprocity. For example, Taylor (W3) came closest to realizing the output standard of the group. He also had the highest social rank, received most interactions from other men, measured in the number of times he was helped, and was the most influential member of the group. Any long-continued departure in his activity rate from the norm of the group would have brought about a decline in all of these other things. So far as he enjoyed his social rank, his associations, and his influence, a change in his output rate would have hurt him. In the relations of each of these elements to all the others in a system lies the fact of control. The specific activities and norms of the Bank Wiring Observation Room were different from those of the Norton Street Gang, but in the relations between generalized activity, generalized norms, and the other elements of the social system, the controls at work on Taylor were exactly the same in kind as those at work on Doc. Our analytical concepts were introduced to bring out these underlying similarities.

Let us turn now to the selector wiremen of clique B. Their output was decidedly below the group norm, and in this sense their behavior was less well controlled than that of the connector wiremen. Yet, with the exception of Green (W9), who had not been a wireman before he came into the room and whose output tended to increase while he was learning his new job, the output of the connector wiremen did not vary much from its admittedly low level.[13] Relative to that level, their behavior was controlled. What controlled it? The selector wiremen were men of shorter service

[13] *Management and the Worker*, 424.

and slightly lower pay than the connector wiremen; they worked on slightly different kinds of equipment and were placed at the back of the room. According to the norms of the connector wiremen, these facts made the selector wiremen social inferiors. But the differences were slight, and the selector wiremen were unwilling to accept inferiority. Between the two groups, there grew up some antagonism that showed itself in a differentiation of activity and a relatively low frequency of interaction. The selector wiremen were different from the connectors in their games, conversations, and so forth, and they were also different in output. Moreover, they were different in a certain direction: in every item of activity they fell below the norms of the connector wiremen. Their conversations were too loud, their output too low. In doing all this, they were further lowering their rank in the eyes of the connector wiremen, but they were also getting back at the connectors, and that was a satisfaction. The latter proceeded to ridicule them for their low output, which further stimulated the antagonism, and so on.

We have spoken of social control as a matter of reward and punishment, and this is true but not true enough. Anyone who has had to administer discipline knows that punishing a person does not always bring his behavior closer to a norm, but sometimes has exactly the opposite effect: his resentment of the punishment, his knowledge that his behavior has infuriated the person inflicting the punishment, and any number of other reasons may drive his behavior still further away from the norm. In ridiculing the selector wiremen for their output, the connector wiremen were trying to punish them, and in keeping their output low, the selector wiremen were getting back at their self-appointed judges. But why, we may ask, did they not make their output still lower, and thus irritate the connectors still more effectively? Output neither got closer to the group norm nor went further away from it. We can answer this question only with an assumption. The selector wiremen formed a subgroup within the Bank Wiring Observation Room but they were also a part of the group as a whole. If they resented being defined as inferiors, and got back at the connector wiremen by keeping their output low, they still accepted the norms of the group and did not want to "chisel" so much that they would be wholly ostracized by the others. They may also have feared what would happen to their pay and their chances for advancement if they kept their output too low. Their level of activity in output must have been the one that secured for them the greatest excess of reward over punishment—the greatest total satisfaction—possible under the social circumstances, both internal and external. If their output had fallen below its actual level, we assume that they would have lost more by increased ridicule, lowered social rank, decreased interaction with other members of the group, and the threat to their economic interests than they would have gained from the pleasure of asserting their independence and driving the connector wiremen to fury. If, on the other hand, their output had gone up, they would have lost more by decreased irritation of the connector wiremen and a decreased assertion of their independence than they would have gained in other ways.

We can see once more that the analysis of social control leads to all the relationships of the social system, in both its internal and its external aspects. But we need to see more than this. If any of the elements that entered the social system of the Bank Wiremen had had a different value, if, for example, the job of a selector wireman had been more different from that of a connector wireman than it was in fact, and if as a result the selector wiremen had been reconciled to accepting an inferior position, as the soldermen were reconciled to inferiority in relation to the wiremen, then the point at which control became effective might have been different, and the output of the selector wiremen greater or less than it was in reality.

Control is the process by which, if a man departs from his present degree of obedience to a norm, his behavior is brought back toward that degree. We have emphasized the degree of obedience rather than absolute obedience, yet so far we have not tried to define the degree except by saying that is the man's present one. We should now be able to see that control can be effective only when that degree of obedience is the one that produces the greatest amount of satisfaction of the man's sentiments possible under the existing state of the social system, so that any departure whatever from that degree brings a decrease in satisfaction, a net punishment. If a greater amount of satisfaction is possible for him at some other degree, then the mechanisms that would otherwise produce control will serve instead to drive the man away from his present degree of obedience and toward the new degree. That is, these mechanisms may bring the man's behavior absolutely closer to the norm or farther away from it, but in either case his behavior will depart from his previous *degree* of obedience to the norm.

At this point we need to remember something we said earlier. Although our assumptions about reward and punishment may make exposition easy, they can hardly be justified on other grounds. After all, it is going to be exceedingly difficult to prove for any group that a certain kind of behavior produces the greatest satisfaction possible under the circumstances. But our ideas do not rest altogether on assumption; they also rest on observation. There are situations where a man's departure from his existing level of obedience to a norm brings about changes in the other elements of the social system such that his behavior tends to return to that degree; and there are other situations where a departure from his existing degree of obedience to a norm does not produce a return but a further departure. We can observe this without making any assumption about the amount of his satisfaction, and we shall call the first situation, the one in which control is effective, a state of *equilibrium*.

RESTRICTION OF OUTPUT

We have treated the social control of output in the Bank Wiring Observation Room as if it had effects only within the room, but obviously it also had effects on the environment in which the group was placed, and it was partly conditioned by that environment. For the Western Electric Company, the group norm in the matter of output, and the controls that maintained that norm, meant "restriction of output." Not that output in the group was considered low; it was, on the contrary, considered entirely satisfactory. But output was not as high as it would have been if fatigue had been the only factor limiting production. We are under no obligation to go into the question of restriction of output in industry; but we may, on the strength of the insights we have gained, make a few general remarks. Groups are surely going to develop group norms

—and controls to check departures therefrom. Among other norms, working groups, in agriculture and in industry, will often develop output standards. Thus our measure of land area, the acre, is based on the amount of land accepted as the proper amount to be plowed by one draft of oxen in one day under the conditions of medieval farming. And an industrial group will often develop an output standard for its job. For industrial management, therefore, the problem of increasing output is seldom one of increasing the output of individuals but is usually one of raising the standards of groups. Moreover, the group must accept the standard; it must become a real group norm before group controls will come into play to support it.[14] The important question is not whether there will be norms of production—there often will—but whether these norms will be accepted by all members of the working community. In traditional agricultural communities, all members of the community, both the bosses and the farm hands, accept the output standards. In most American industry there is no such agreement between the management and the workers. The reasons for this are many. If, for instance, the Bank Wiremen were asked what would happen if they raised output beyond the accepted standard of about two completed equipments a day, they had various answers ready. The slower men would get bawled out; someone would be laid off; hours, and therefore take-home pay, would be reduced; a piecework rate would be cut, so that the men would have to do more work to get the same amount of money; or, more vaguely, "something" would happen. In their life in the Western Electric Company, the men had, it is true, experienced none of the results they feared; and restriction of output, by keeping production costs high, may encourage rather than prevent industrial change. But who shall deny that these results of increased output have been experienced by some American workingmen, if not by the Bank Wiremen? If the student is not satisfied with the explanation the wiremen gave of their own behavior, he should read the whole discussion in *Management and the Worker* of the problem of restriction of output.[15]

[14] *Management and the Worker,* Chap. XXIII.
[15] *Ibid.,* 524-48.

Let us now sum up once more what we have learned about social control:

1. Control is the process by which, if a man departs from his existing degree of obedience to a norm, his behavior is brought back toward that degree, or would be brought back if he did depart. The remaining statements hold for both actual and virtual departures.

2. There is nothing new about control, no separate element that we have not already found coming into social organization.

3. The separate controls are nothing more than the old relations of mutual dependence taken differentially.

4. Control as a whole is effective in so far as an individual's departure from an existing degree of obedience to a norm activates not one but many separate controls.

5. That is, any departure activates the system of relations so as to reduce future departures.

6. Punishment does not necessarily produce control. The state of a social system in which control is effective we shall call a state of equilibrium of the system.

EQUILIBRIUM

Lacking any elaborate mathematical treatment of sociology, we have no doubt been crude in our handling of the idea of equilibrium, but an idea need not be refined if it is not to be used with refinement, and we shall use equilibrium with very little refinement indeed. At any rate, there is nothing inherently mysterious about the idea of equilibrium. The effort of a group to decrease the amount by which a member departs from his existing degree of obedience to group norms, and the effectiveness of this effort under some circumstances, but not all, are surely facts of experience and observation. Indeed, we can watch this kind of process more closely in sociology than in other sciences because we are in the midst of it every day. We have given it the name of equilibrium only because that name has been given to analogous processes in fields as far separated as mechanics and economics. (Note that we say *analogous* processes: they have points in common but are not the same in every field. We never imply, for instance, that a social system *is* a mechanical system.) But perhaps because *equilibrium* is a long word and seems to imply changelessness in a world where change is the rule, the idea has been misunderstood and its usefulness denied. We must give a little more time to it.

A classic definition of equilibrium in a physical science is the so-called LeChatelier theorem in physical chemistry:

The effect on any physico-chemical equilibrium, produced by an attempt to alter any one of the factors which influence it, can be qualitatively predicted by means of a theorem formulated by LeChatelier which may be stated as follows: If an attempt is made to alter any one of the factors (*e.g.* the temperature or pressure of the system or the fugacity of any constituent of the system) which influence any physico-chemical equilibrium, then a shift in the equilibrium will take place in such a direction as to decrease the magnitude of the alteration which would otherwise occur in that factor.[16]

Instead of saying that "a shift in the equilibrium will take place," it might be better to say that the system *is* in equilibrium when the shift described *does* take place, but this may be a mere quibble. At any rate, if we substitute social "factors" for physico-chemical ones, we shall perhaps agree that if there is a change in any one of the factors that enter a social system (*e.g.*, the degree to which a member's activities coincide with a norm), the system as a whole reacts, under some circumstances, so as to decrease the magnitude of the change that would otherwise take place in that factor. When

[16] E. W. Washburn, *An Introduction to the Principles of Physical Chemistry* (1915), quoted in G. C. Homans and C. P. Curtis, Jr., *An Introduction to Pareto*, 273n. For a more rigorous and mathematical formulation of this theorem, see P. A. Samuelson, *Foundations of Economic Analysis*, 38. He points out, as we have, that the tendency to decrease the magnitude of change is greater, the greater the number of interrelations between the elements of the system. Also important is his statement on p. 262. "The equations of comparative statics are then a special case of the general dynamic analysis. They can indeed be discussed abstracting completely from dynamical analysis. In the history of mechanics, the theory of statics was developed before the dynamical problem was even formulated. But the problem of stability of equilibrium cannot be discussed except with reference to dynamical considerations, however implicit and rudimentary. We find ourselves confronted with this paradox: in order for the comparative-statics analysis to yield fruitful results, we must first develop a theory of dynamics." In sociology we cannot understand structure until we understand control.

the system behaves in this way, that is, when control is effective, we say that the system is in equilibrium.

In sociology, the classic definition of *equilibrium* is Pareto's. His words are: "This state is such that if some modification were artificially made in it, unlike that which it undergoes in reality, a reaction would at once take place that would tend to bring it back to the real state." [17] Pareto was trained to be a civil engineer, and as a young student in the Polytechnic School in Turin, he wrote a thesis on the equilibrium of elastic solids. (It is interesting that Clerk-Maxwell, the great formulator of the field equations of electromagnetism, wrote a paper on exactly the same subject while he was a student at the Edinburgh Academy.) Pareto later did much work in establishing the equations of equilibrium in economics. His statement of sociological equilibrium is, then, part of a long tradition. The definition of equilibrium in classical mechanics is given in terms of virtual changes, the changes that conceivably might occur but do not, and Pareto begins by speaking of them, under the name of artificial changes. We have seen that virtual changes are important in maintaining social equilibrium, in the sense that a man refrains from violating a group norm because he foresees what would happen if he did. But Pareto goes on in a footnote to bring in the actual changes. He says: "There are changes analogous to artificial ones: these are the accidental changes coming from an element that appears, acts for a short time on a system, producing in it a slight deviation from the state of equilibrium, and then disappears." If we were able to apply LeChatelier's theorem to the facts of social control, we shall also, perhaps, be able to apply Pareto's definition of equilibrium.

After so many definitions we can hardly tolerate one more, but we had better wind up this discussion by giving, for our own purposes, our own definition of *equilibrium:* A social system is in equilibrium and control is effective when the state of the elements that enter the system and of the mutual relationships between them is such that any small change in one of the elements will

[17] V. Pareto, *Traité de sociologie générale,* P. Boven, trans., §2068. Also translated into English by A. Livingston under the title *The Mind and Society.* For a more careful definition, see L. J. Henderson, *Pareto's General Sociology,* 111-2.

be followed by changes in the other elements tending to reduce the amount of that change.

We have argued that equilibrium, as we and others have defined it, is a mere description of the way some social groups behave under some circumstances. Serious objections to the idea have nevertheless been raised. For instance, in his excellent book on the relations between Negroes and whites in the United States, Gunnar Myrdal has an appendix, "A Methodological Note on Facts and Valuations in Social Science." And in it he writes:

The presence of this same static and fatalistic valuation in the hidden *ethos* of contemporary social science is suggested by some of the terminology found throughout the writings of many sociologists, such as "balance," "harmony," "equilibrium," "adjustment," "maladjustment," "organization," "disorganization," "accommodation," "function," "social process," and "cultural lag." While they all . . . have been used advantageously to *describe* empirically observable situations, they carry within them the tendency to give a do-nothing (*laissez-faire*) valuation of these situations. How the slip occurs is easily understandable: when we speak of a social system being in harmony, or having equilibrium, or its forces organized, accommodated, or adjusted to each other, there is the almost inevitable implication that some sort of ideal has been attained, whether in terms of "individual happiness" or the "common welfare." Such a situation is, therefore, evaluated as "good" and a movement in this direction is desirable.[18]

Myrdal has much to justify him. The concept *equilibrium* has sometimes carried the connotation that social conservatism is desirable, especially when the concept is applied to large units, societies as wholes, where it cannot easily be tied down to observed facts. Yet the concept has been found useful in many sciences from mechanics to economics, and we shall try to use it, much as it has been used in those sciences, as an aid in analyzing the behavior of small groups. We shall try not to allow hidden emotional evaluations to creep into our discussion by this entrance, but we may not succeed, so let no one say he was not warned! Myrdal says that the mere use of the word *equilibrium,* and of another one, *organization,* that is scattered through these pages, may encourage conservative thinking both in the author and in the reader. So beware! For

[18] G. Myrdal and others, *An American Dilemma,* II, 1055.

dangerous as it is, we shall use the concept anyhow. Myrdal would not have had to stretch his list much further to show that there is no concept that may not let in an evaluation. If we are evaluators—conservative or radical—we will evaluate, and nothing shall stop us. It would be intolerable to let this melancholy fact divorce us from conceptual thought. So we shall work with *equilibrium* and may even learn in time to find its terrors delicious.

Perhaps a very characteristic remark of Pareto's may be quoted here. He says that social equilibrium is analogous to the dynamic equilibrium of a material system—such as a spinning gyroscope or the solar system—and he adds in a footnote:

That is what a certain good soul did not understand when, for reasons best known to himself, he imagined that economic equilibrium was a state of immobility and therefore to be condemned by every loyal worshipper of the god Progress. A number of persons talk just as wildly when they take it into their heads to judge the theories of pure economics. The fact is that they do not give themselves the trouble to study the material they want to discuss, and they think they can grasp it by a hasty and careless reading of books they understand backside-to, for their minds are loaded with preconceptions, and they do not apply their attention to cold scientific research, but think only of favoring their social faith. In this way they lose golden opportunities for keeping their mouths shut and not revealing their ignorance.[19]

DEDUCTIONS FROM EQUILIBRIUM

The difficulties of this chapter arise from the fact that, as we have insisted, we are adding nothing to what we know already. Our new ideas are matters of form and not of content. We are attempting to gain clarity by looking at our material in a new way, and in carrying out this purpose we must try our patience with a last reformulation. Not every state of a social system is a state of equilibrium, nor does every social system "seek" equilibrium—we have implied nothing of the sort. Only when the state of the elements that enter the social system and the state of the relations between them is of a certain kind does equilibrium exist. But note carefully that this is as much as to say that if equilibrium exists, the state of the system must be of a certain kind. Although the two sentences

19 V. Pareto, *Traité de sociologie générale*, §2072n.

are equivalent, it is worth while to write them both so that the point may be brought out plainly. Suppose that we are studying a group and have means of knowing that equilibrium exists in the group—we observe that control is effective—we can then ask ourselves what state of the system makes equilibrium possible. We can begin to study what the classical physicists would call the "conditions of equilibrium" in the system, although we may not, in sociology, be able to make much progress. In earlier chapters, we reached many statements about the relations of mutual dependence between activity, sentiment, and interaction; we were careful to explain that none of the statements held good unless "other things were equal," and we tried to show what the meaning of that celebrated phrase was. One of these "other things," one that conditions many of our statements, is equilibrium. For instance, interaction increases friendship only in a group that is a "going concern." We can see interaction producing altogether different results in a group that is breaking up. Then people "get on each other's nerves." Again, the attitude of subordinates toward a superior is apt to be distant and respectful only if his orders really are obeyed, and, as we shall see in a later chapter, obedience to orders is one aspect of group equilibrium. If the superior's orders carry little authority, the attitude toward him is quite different from the one we have described. We cannot always say that a social system is in equilibrium, but if, for any reason, we can, we have in those words laid a heavy restriction on the amount of variation possible in the system. The relations of the system are that much more fully determined. This is true of systems other than the social system and sciences other than sociology. As Lawrence Henderson put it:

Another characteristic of many ideal systems that is, in general, indispensable in order that conditions shall be determinate is the establishment and use of some definition of equilibrium or some criterion of equilibrium, whether in the case of statical equilibrium or in the case of dynamical equilibrium. For the abstract conceptual scheme this is as a rule the decisive feature that goes farthest to establish determinate conditions.[20]

[20] L. J. Henderson, *Pareto's General Sociology*, 85. For simple examples of the use of equations of equilibrium to establish determinate conditions in a system, see E. Mach, *The Science of Mechanics*, 561-78.

We have used Pareto's definition of equilibrium; perhaps we may also use his statement on the matter in question. He points out that between the elements of a social system two kinds of mutual dependence may exist: first, a direct mutual dependence, such as our mutual dependence between interaction, sentiment, and activity, and second, an indirect one, "arising from the condition that equilibrium is maintained." Then he goes on to say:

In order that we may better understand the difference between the mutual dependence of the first and that of the second kind, let us consider a certain society. Its existence is already one fact; we have, besides, the various other facts that are produced in this society [such as the facts we have classified under the headings of interaction, sentiment, activity, and norms]. If we consider together the first of these facts [the existence of the society] and the others, we shall say that *all* are mutually dependent. If we separate the existence of the society from the other facts, we shall say that the latter are mutually dependent among themselves (mutual dependence of the first kind), and that they are also mutually dependent with the first fact (mutual dependence of the second kind). We can say, moreover, that the fact of the society's existence results from the other facts that we observe in society, that is to say, the latter determine the social equilibrium. We can add that if the fact of the society's existence is given, the facts that are produced in this society are no longer wholly arbitrary, but must satisfy certain conditions; that is to say, if equilibrium is given, the facts that determine it are not wholly arbitrary.[21]

Although the elements we have used in analyzing the social system are not the same as Pareto's, we have followed the method he suggests in this passage. We began by describing the first kind of mutual dependence—the mutual dependence of interaction, sentiment, activity, and norms—and now, in the last few pages, we have turned to the second kind of mutual dependence—the mutual dependence between these interrelated elements and the existence of equilibrium in the group. It should be clear that Pareto's treatment of equilibrium has much in common with the functional theory, discussed in the last chapter. Indeed the idea of survival or continuity, which comes into the functional theory, can be made rigorous only if survival is redefined as equilibrium. When this is done, we can see that both Pareto and the functionalists are asking: "Suppose

[21] V. Pareto, *Traité de sociologie générale*, §2088-89.

we have reason to know that a social system is in equilibrium, what deductions can we then make about the other conditions that must exist in the system?"

PUNISHMENT AS A RITUAL

In order to state the problem in its full generality, we have so far developed only a very simple theory of social control. The further complexities we might go into are endless, but we shall only introduce one. Just as we have made no distinction between law and custom, so we have made none between punishments that are not recognized as such and those that are. Take the case of avoidance as a punishment. Interaction often tends to be infrequent between persons whose activities are different. And when the activities of a member of a group depart even more than usual from the group norms, interaction with him will be even less frequent than usual. Avoidance, that is, decrease of interaction, is a common result of breaches of a norm. We do not talk to, we have nothing to do with, we shrink from people of whose behavior we disapprove. So far as his existing amount of interaction with other members of a group is a pleasure to a man, any decrease in that amount is, in effect, a punishment. But except in the extreme cases of ostracism or "sending to Coventry," avoidance is not often recognized as a formal punishment. It is, so to speak, just one of those things that happen.

But even the smallest groups develop practices that are recognized as punishments for specific offenses. An example in the Bank Wiring Observation Room was the practice of "binging"—hitting a man a blow with the edge of the hand on the upper arm. Binging was a game. Two men "binged" one another to see which could hit the harder. But it was also used as a punishment. If a man disapproved of something another had done, such as working too fast, he would threaten to bing him. And if the offender admitted his guilt, he let himself be binged. Sometimes he thought that he had been binged too hard, that the punishment did not fit the crime, and he wanted to hit back.[22]

Punishment of this kind has some of the effects of ritual, in the

[22] *Management and the Worker*, 421-23.

sense that it affects not only the offender but all members of the group that witnesses it or knows about it. "We may say without paradox"—this is Durkheim speaking—"that punishment acts chiefly on the law-abiding citizens, for, since it serves to heal the wounds given to collective sentiments, it cannot fulfill this role unless the sentiments exist and are alive." [23] Let us try to make this insight more clear. Someone commits a breach of a social rule, a norm. Three classes of persons are then, in general, affected: (*a*) the offender, (*b*) the person or persons directly offended, and (*c*) the other members of the group to which both offender and offended belong. Different processes of control may affect the three classes in different degrees. In what students of the law call civil actions, (*a*) and (*b*) are the classes most concerned; in criminal actions all three are concerned, and this is true of the social control of everyday life in small groups, where the distinction between civil and criminal law is probably not useful.

Let us consider especially the action of the offense on the members of the group as a whole. So far as the group knows about the offense—and for us offenses that remain secret need not be treated as offenses at all—the departure from the norms of the group will arouse sentiments in the group, the stronger the more important the norm violated, and, as is usual with sentiments, they will seek some expression in activity. The activity in question is the punishment of the criminal. When, moreover, the punishment is of a special kind, linked with the breach of a specific norm, the punishment, with its release of sentiment, will tend to reawake in the minds of the group members the importance of the norm. Thus a breach of a norm sets in motion controls that tend, when the group is in equilibrium, not only to bring the offender back toward conformity with the norm, but also to keep the norm alive in the minds of the other members of the group. The offender is chastized and the norm vindicated. So far as norms are an element in the group equilibrium, and we have argued that they are, social control in this further way tends to pull the group back to the point from which the offense moved it. Much legal behavior is ritual in the sense that, although it may not have much effect on the lawbreaker, it continually re-

[23] See E. Durkheim, *The Division of Labor in Society,* G. Simpson, trans., 108.

affirms the law. The majesty of the law is a religious majesty, and our courts are churches.

We are not going to develop a theory of religion for the group, but the notion of social control we have just touched on resembles one theory of ritual. The central ritual of a society—for example, the Mass in the Roman Catholic Church—symbolizes the central body of beliefs of the society. Belief includes the norms of behavior, and the performance of ritual reawakes, in the persons who witness it and take part in it, a sense of the value of the norms. To the extent that the norms are one element in the group equilibrium, ritual helps to maintain equilibrium.[24] It is also true that in primitive societies, and to a great extent in civilized ones too, important ceremonials are performed when an individual or a group is going through a crisis. The individual may be undergoing some change of status, for instance, a change from the single to the married state; the group may be undergoing some change in the activities it performs, for instance, a change from the harvest season to the plowing season. If, therefore, we add the idea that ritual is often an expression of the sentiments aroused by change or crisis, and that it has the effect of bringing the group back to equilibrium after change or of easing the group's transition to some new point of equilibrium, the similarity of the theory of ritual to our enlarged theory of social control is clear.[25]

If the enlarged theory is correct—and we insist only on the limited theory worked out in the first part of the chapter—it illustrates once more the capacity of the social organism to develop its own self-regulating activities: control is emergent. It also implies that the maintenance of a given equilibrium is helped rather than hurt by a few small departures from the group norms. Crime—not too much of it—is needed; it keeps the controls in good working order. A control is not effective unless it is tested. This sounds paradoxical, but there are parallels in the other sciences that deal with organisms. In 1900 the French physiologist Charles Richet wrote:

The living being is stable. It must be so in order not to be destroyed, dissolved, or disintegrated by the colossal forces, often adverse, which

[24] There are several important discussions of this theory. A good one appears in W. L. Warner, *A Black Civilization*, Chap. XI.
[25] See E. Chapple and C. Coon, *Principles of Anthropology*, Chaps. 19-23.

surround it. By an apparent contradiction, it maintains its stability only if it is excitable and capable of modifying itself according to external stimuli and adjusting its response to the stimulation. In a sense it is stable because it is modifiable—the slight instability is the necessary condition for the true stability of the organism.[26]

SUMMARY

It is hard to believe that social scientists could have worked out many generalizations about the behavior of men in groups, if there had been no persistencies in this behavior, and we have been no different from other social scientists in this respect. When we formulated, in the earlier chapters of this book, the relationships between the elements of social behavior, we took persistence or custom for granted. But in the long run nothing can be taken for granted, and in the present chapter we have asked what makes custom customary. Custom persists so far as the behavior of men is controlled, so far, that is, as a departure from custom has results that tend to restore customary behavior. How, then, is social behavior controlled? We have tried to answer this question by pointing out, with examples, what would happen if a member of a group departed from his existing level of obedience to the norms of the group. In carrying out this work we discovered nothing new in social behavior that we could specifically point to as control. Instead we discovered that we were merely looking differentially at the relations of mutual dependence we had already formulated. That is, we discovered what would happen to the other elements of the social system, by reason of the mutual dependence of the elements, if a small change took place in one of the elements, namely a change in the degree to which an individual's activity measured up to the norms of his group. The individual's behavior is controlled because the results of his departure from the norm are, on balance, unpleasant to him, and because the mutual dependence of the elements of behavior means that a relatively small departure will have relatively large results. When control is effective in this sense we say that the social system is in equilibrium. Not all states of a social system are equilibrium states. Instead of bringing an individual's behavior back

[26] Quoted in W. B. Cannon, *The Wisdom of the Body,* 2nd ed., 21.

toward his former degree of compliance with a norm, punishment may under some circumstances drive it still further away from that degree. But if we have independent reason to believe that a social system is in equilibrium, we may then be able to make some deductions about the other conditions that must obtain in the system, which is as much as to say that, when a social system is in equilibrium, not all conceivable states of the system can be actual states.

CHAPTER 12

The Individual and the Group

*The Group and Mental Health . . . The Social Contract
Theory . . . The Social Mold Theory . . . Reconciliation
of the Theories . . . Malinowski's Theory of Magic . . .
Radcliffe-Brown's Theory of Magic . . . Reconciliation
of the Theories . . . Culture and Personality . . . The
Problem of Liberty*

A SOCIAL system has at least one characteristic
in common with a biological system such as a living being: it is an
organized whole made up of units that are themselves organized.
The individual, or, to use a better word, the person, is in this respect
analogous in the group to the cell in the body. In its full scope, the
problem of the relation between the individual and the group is
enormous, embracing the whole of social psychology. We do not
have the space, even if we had the equipment, to study the whole
field here, and we shall have to content ourselves with making a few
points especially important for our purposes. In particular we shall
ask ourselves if it makes sense to say either that the individual determines the character of the group or that the group determines
the character of the individual.

THE GROUP AND MENTAL HEALTH

As the body is not healthy unless its cells are healthy, so the converse is true: the cell does not prosper unless the body does. In the
same way, sick individuals make a sick society, and a sick society,
sick individuals. In fact, as we shall see, the two problems are inextricably interrelated. If there is one truth that modern psychology
has established, it is that an *isolated* individual is sick. He is sick in
mind: he will exhibit disorders of behavior, emotion, and thought;

he may, as psychosomatic medicine teaches, be sick in body besides. Perhaps it is better to say that he will have an impaired capacity for maintaining his personal equilibrium under the ordinary shocks of life. This does not mean that, for health, he must be a member of any particular group: not every group will be good for him. It does mean that unless he is a fully accepted member of *some* group —a family, a group of friends, a group of fellow workers—he will be in trouble. And perhaps we need not require him to be a fully accepted member of a group at any particular time but only to have been a member at *some* time. A person who has always been isolated may be less able to bear continued isolation than a person who has once known something very different.

To escape isolation, a person must be able to become a member of a group, and this is not just a problem of finding the group. The capacity for relating one's self easily to other men and women is not inborn but a result of experience and training, and that experience and training is itself social. It begins early, in the family, where the child learns the basic imperatives of his society. Our account of social control in the last chapter was inadequate because it implied that a person always calculates, consciously or unconsciously, the various painful consequences of a breach of a norm, whereas many persons, perhaps most persons for at least part of the time, feel a direct and immediate hurt if they violate a norm, aside from any calculation of the other consequences of the offense. If virtue is its own reward, sin is its own punishment. Such persons are governed by the imperatives of conscience and duty; they must accept the agony that lies in the inevitable conflicts of norms and try to create the moral intelligence to resolve them. Modern psychology holds that conscience, which is the representative in the individual of the norms of the group, is not inborn but induced in the individual as a part of the process of social education. For some norms the process begins early. Freud talks about the effect of the emotional relations between father and son in our Western societies in forming the ego-ideal of the son. (Ego-ideal is Freud's name for conscience.) It is a precipitate in the child of the father's personality. But if the process is most important in the family, where the chief social imperatives are learned, it must still go on in any other group that has strongly held norms. In fact social training, though it begins in the family, may become disastrous if it goes on too long there. The youngster must, as he grows up, escape from the intense but narrow emotional ties of the family and become a member of some group of his contemporaries, where he can learn the kind of morality just as necessary as conscience for adult life: the morality that is not an absolute imposed by a superior power, like the father, but a convention, akin to the rules of a game, accepted by a body of equals as the first condition of their co-operation.[1]

The doctrine of modern psychology that the capacity of the adult to maintain his personal equilibrium under the ordinary strains of life is the result of training begun early in childhood, and that this training is social, implies that the groups in which successful training takes place must have certain characteristics. If the family is under stress for any of the reasons considered in Chapter 10, if it is isolated in the community so that the necessary transition of the child from the family to the group of contemporaries is made difficult, or if the community is so shattered that groups of contemporaries do not form easily or form in utter opposition to society at large, then social training will suffer. The sickness of society will end in the sickness of the individual, but the sickness of the individual will then react on society. He will come to maturity with a lowered capacity for co-operation with others. He will be less easily able to found a family or build a community, that is, he will be less able to provide the conditions in which his children can grow up to be resilient adults. The circle may easily turn vicious, may indeed in many parts of Western society be vicious now. The group, then, sustains the individual, but he cannot become a member of a group unless he has some capacity for membership. This capacity for group life is itself learned in groups: if they are unhealthy the training will suffer. These are tremendous facts. No study of the group can fail to cite them, but here we can do no more than that. A large literature on the problem awaits the interested reader.

[1] See especially S. Freud, *Three Contributions to the Theory of Sex,* and *The Ego and the Id;* J. Piaget, *The Moral Judgment of the Child.*

THE SOCIAL CONTRACT THEORY

The question of social training and mental health is only part of a much larger one: What is the relation between the individual members of society and the society itself? It has come up again and again in human thinking; in sociology it is one of the main issues in the study of social control and cultural education. Let us begin our study of it by going back a little way into the history of sociological theory.

What is the relation between the individual members of society and society itself? Two main positions have been taken on this issue. The older position is the "social contract" theory, which goes back in the end to the great Greek thinkers, but which was classically stated by Thomas Hobbes in the seventeenth century. Hobbes is speaking of the "Leviathan," the subject of his book, and he writes: "In him [the Leviathan] consisteth the essence of the commonwealth; which, to define it, is *one person, of whose acts a great multitude, by mutual covenants one with another, have made themselves every one the author, to the end that he may use the strength and means of them all, as he shall think expedient, for their peace and common defence.* And he that carrieth this person is called SOVEREIGN, and said to have *sovereign power;* and everyone besides, his SUBJECT." [2]

We realize that we cannot take Hobbes' language quite literally, and he probably did not mean us to do so. At no time can a number of hitherto independent individuals have met together to form a commonwealth, or society. If they did, they must have been the rat-like animals that were our ancestors, for our recent biological history has been consistently social. The implications of the metaphor are something else. For Hobbes, society consists of a union of individuals, each with his own character independent of the society. The individual is primary; society is an expression of, a resultant of, the characteristics of individuals. This does not mean that society once formed does not have, through its sovereign, great power over individuals. It does mean that the character of society is determined by the character of individuals. Of course we are greatly simplifying, and laying hold of only one aspect of Hobbes' theory.

[2] *Leviathan,* Part 2, Chap. 17. The italics and capitalization are Hobbes'.

THE SOCIAL MOLD THEORY

This kind of theory, expressed or implied, reigned from Hobbes' time to the end of the nineteenth century. In fact it had reigned long before Hobbes. Classical and medieval social theory was shot through with the notion of social contract. After Hobbes, the eloquence of Rousseau gave it wide currency, but toward the end of the nineteenth century a new note began to appear, especially in the thinking of the French sociologist Émile Durkheim. He came close to turning Hobbes and Rousseau inside out. Where they had assumed that the individual was primary and society a mere resultant of the characteristics of individuals, Durkheim came near to saying that society was primary and individuals mere resultants of the characteristics of society. He thought of society putting its stamp on individuals, like a mold forced over hot metal, and so we may call his theory the "social mold" theory.

Let us follow the ideas that led Durkheim to this conclusion, as they are stated in one of the most famous, but not perhaps one of the best of his books, *The Rules of Sociological Method.* Its fame and its weakness have the same origin: its tone is *doctrinaire.* Durkheim made the point that whenever a number of individuals come together in a group something new emerges, the nature of which depends not just on the individuals but also on the fact of their mutual relations. "Every time that any elements whatever, in combining, release new phenomena by the fact of their combination, it is necessary to think of these phenomena as situated not in the elements but in the whole formed by their union." [3] This insight led Durkheim to his famous statement that society is an entity *sui generis:* the group is an entity as truly as the individual, and of a different kind.

Though Durkheim might have avoided eventual disaster if he had inserted two short, but important, words in his sentence and said that "these phenomena are situated not *only* in the elements but *also* in the whole formed by their union," yet his essential insight was sound and wise, and we have followed it in this book. But he went further than this, further, perhaps, than the facts al-

---

[3] *Les règles de la méthode sociologique* (1927), xv (Pref. to 2nd ed.).

low. He was an expert in the sociology of law; he saw, as we all see, that any society, any group, develops a set of rules, norms of behavior, and that these norms act as a constraint on the individual so far as departure from the norms is followed by punishment. Durkheim then proposed that the province of sociology should be limited to those facts of social behavior that result from the pressure of society on the individual. He developed a celebrated definition of "social facts" that runs as follows: "Here is an order of facts that present the following very special characteristics: they consist of ways of acting, thinking, and feeling, exterior to the individual, that possess a power of coercion by virtue of which they impose themselves upon him. In consequence, they should not, since they consist in representations and actions, be confused with organic phenomena, nor with psychic phenomena, which only exist in and by means of the individual consciousness." [4] Durkheim was saying, in effect, that since the beliefs (representations) of society and obedience to its norms are imposed by society on individuals, these beliefs and controls should be considered as different from individual thought and action. Trying again to delimit the field of sociological phenomena, he wrote: "Since their essential characteristic consists in the power that they possess of exercising, from the outside, a pressure on individual minds, it must be that they do not derive from individual minds and that, accordingly, sociology is not a corollary of psychology." [5]

At last Durkheim had pushed his views too far. Intellectually, the descent into hell is easy. One false step, and logic will do the rest. Durkheim's logic was French and admirable, but it was mistaken, and he failed to recognize the facts that would have corrected it. Gripped by his logic, he could not see the facts. The disease is one to which all we intellectuals are subject. But let us analyze. (1) Durkheim said that a phenomenon must belong either to one class or to another, which might have been sound logic pro-

---

[4] *Les règles de la méthode sociologique,* 8.

[5] *Ibid.,* 124. We have stated Durkheim's argument too simply. Among the forms of behavior that society impresses on the individual, he had in mind not only beliefs and obedience to norms but also such things as suicide rates. Each society has a characteristic suicide rate, so that here again, he felt, the characteristics of society as a whole are imposing a pattern of behavior on individuals. See E. Durkheim, *Le suicide.*

vided he had defined his classes appropriately. Unfortunately he got himself into the position of holding that an item of human behavior must be either psychological, that is, a phenomenon of individual consciousness, or social, that is, not a phenomenon of individual consciousness. He would not allow that it could be both. To the classic peril of being impaled on the horns of a dilemma, we moderns should add a new one: being split by a false dichotomy. (2) Durkheim thought in terms of cause and effect, and not of mutual dependence. If norms of action are imposed on the individual, then they are the cause of his behavior, and the cause is different from the effect. "He is asserting for a special case that since y is a function of x, x cannot be a function of y. This is absurd and . . . one of the most dangerous fallacies that a sociologist can fall into. It is a well established fact that Durkheim's concrete sociological entities . . . not only act upon but are acted upon by individual consciousness." [6] (3) As for failures to recognize fact, Durkheim thought always of the single individual over against society, so that it was easy for him to focus on the constraint exercised by the society over the individual and to neglect the mutual dependence of society and individual consciousness. The fact is that society is made up of many individuals. The norms of society arise from the mutual relations of these individuals, but once the norms have been established, then if a single individual departs from them he will be punished, and new members of the society will be taught to obey them. In this sense they will constrain the individual consciousness. (4) Durkheim thought of the "social" element in behavior as consisting solely of the norms of a society and the constraint they exercise over the individual. He emphasized a legal system, whether formally organized or not; he might also have emphasized education. He did not perceive that the social element may enter in more than one way, so that there are several terms in the relation between an individual and society.

RECONCILIATION OF THE THEORIES

A better statement than Durkheim's, though still a crude one, might be the following. (*a*) An individual brings to his group cer-

[6] L. J. Henderson, *Pareto's General Sociology*, 72.

tain characteristics of mind and certain sentiments (needs). These sentiments are at once biologically inherited and socially instilled. (*b*) His group has a method of co-operation for satisfying these sentiments, which makes natural and appropriate certain forms of behavior in certain situations. (*c*) But while these forms of behavior may be natural and appropriate, the group has also reached the idea that they *ought* and *must* be adopted in these situations. (*d*) If an individual does not behave in these ways, the relations in the group are such that he will be punished. Moreover, the norms, or if we prefer, the culture, will be taught to new members of the society, which brings us back to statement (*a*), that the needs of an individual are at once biologically inherited and socially instilled. These terms form a continuing cycle. In describing the relation between an individual and his society, the social contract theory emphasized (*a*) and (*b*); Durkheim with his social mold theory emphasized (*c*) and (*d*). This is what we mean when we say that, according to the social contract theory, the behavior of individuals determines the characteristics of society, and that, according to the social mold theory, the characteristics of society determine the behavior of individuals. Both are wrong and both are right because both are incomplete.

Let us illustrate from our Tikopia case. We assume that the Tikopia have certain sentiments that lead them to want food, clothing, housing, and so forth. To secure these goods, they co-operate in groups, the most important of which is the family, headed by the father. The configuration of emotional relationships in the family, partly conditioned, through the authority of the father, by the method in which the family is organized to do its practical work, makes appropriate and natural a special emotional tie between a boy and his mother's brother. Tikopia, moreover, does not consist of a single family. There are many families of roughly similar organization, and there have been many others in the past. Under these circumstances it is inevitable, not only that a boy should have feelings of a certain kind for his mother's brother, but also that a general norm or expectation should grow up, stating what the mother's brother-sister's son relation ought to be. As Firth says in a remark we quoted earlier, the relation is "a matter of social injunction as well as of individual feeling." Furthermore, the relation itself and the norm defining the relation are linked with other items of the social system so that, whether or not the relation is felt by a single individual to be natural and satisfying, he will nevertheless be hurt if he does not live up to the norm in some degree. If, for instance, a boy does not show towards his mother's brother the sentiments that society expects of him, he may not be helped by his mother's brother in one of the crises of his life. Finally, the norm is taught to children in Tikopia—it is an item in the culture—and for this reason they are all the more apt to find the mother's brother-sister's son relation appropriate. Even the demands for food, housing, clothing, and so forth are instilled into the youngsters by the teaching of their society, at least in the sense that certain kinds of food, housing, and clothing are marked out as appropriate goals. Yet in spite of these self-reinforcing features, we suspect that if the organization of the Tikopia family changed, in response perhaps to a change in the environment itself or the techniques available for exploiting it, the actual mother's brother-sister's son relation, and ultimately the norm defining the relation, would, among other things, change too. In this complex cycle, Durkheim would have emphasized the norms, and the control exercised by the society over individual behavior. He would have said that individual behavior was determined by the society, and would have neglected the relations of mutual dependence in the cycle.

MALINOWSKI'S THEORY OF MAGIC

A more recent and complicated example of the contrast between the social contract theory and the social mold theory is provided by a controversy between two great anthropologists, Malinowski and Radcliffe-Brown, the latter a disciple of Durkheim's. The subject of the controversy—the theory of magic—is far from our interests, but the opponents argue so well and the issues come up so clearly that we cannot afford to let the controversy alone.[7]

We begin with Malinowski's views on magic among primitive peoples, specifically among the Trobriand Islanders, whom he studied so long. He holds that any primitive people has a body of tech-

[7] For a fuller analysis, see G. C. Homans, "Anxiety and Ritual," *American Anthropologist*, XLIII (1941), 164-72.

nical knowledge, comparable to modern scientific knowledge, about the behavior of nature and the means of controlling it to meet man's needs. This knowledge the primitives apply in a thoroughly practical manner to get the results they desire: a crop of yams, a catch of fish, and so forth. But seldom are their techniques so powerful that the results are certain. For example, when the tiller of the soil has done the best he can to see that his fields are properly sown and weeded, a drought or a blight may overwhelm him. In these circumstances the primitives feel a sentiment that we call anxiety—the desire for a result, linked with the fear that it will not be gained—, and they perform magical rites that, they say, will bring them good luck. These rites give men the confidence that allows them to attack their practical work with energy and determination.

That anxiety and ritual go together, Malinowski makes clear in a decisive observation. The largest of the Trobriand Islands, like many islands in the South Seas, consists of a ring of land surrounding a central lagoon. He writes:

An interesting and crucial test is provided by fishing in the Trobriand Islands and its magic. While in the villages on the inner lagoon fishing is done in an easy and absolutely reliable manner by the method of poisoning, yielding abundant results without danger or uncertainty, there are on the shores of the open sea dangerous modes of fishing and also certain types in which the yield varies greatly according to whether shoals of fish appear beforehand or not. It is most significant that in the lagoon fishing, where man can rely completely upon his knowledge and skill, magic does not exist, while in the open-sea fishing, full of danger and uncertainty, there is extensive magical ritual to secure safety and good results.[8]

This theory is almost physiological. We know that in circumstances creating fear the body mobilizes for action of some kind: flight or defense. The autonomic nervous system sets free substances that speed up the heart, dilate the vessels of the skin, and allow blood to clot more easily—all changes that help the organism to take and maintain physical action.[9] It seems natural, then, that if

[8] B. Malinowski, *Magic, Science and Religion and Other Essays*, R. Redfield, ed., 14.

[9] See especially W. B. Cannon, *Bodily Changes in Pain, Hunger, Fear, and Rage*.

some practical action allaying the fear is impossible, a substitute must take its place. The aroused energies must be worked off; the body must *do* something. Since in the nature of things the substitute cannot be adapted to securing a practical result, it may be magical, that is, expressive or symbolic.

Malinowski sums up his theory as follows:

We have seen that all the instincts and emotions, all practical activities, lead man into impasses where gaps in his knowledge and the limitations of his early power of observation and reason betray him at a crucial moment. Human organism reacts to this in spontaneous outbursts, in which rudimentary modes of behavior and rudimentary beliefs in their efficiency are engendered. Magic fixes upon these beliefs and rudimentary rites and standardizes them into permanent traditional forms.[10]

In mentioning belief and standardization, Malinowski is adding to what we already know of his theory, and we had better be clear what the additions are. He begins with the anxiety situation and the actions that express the anxiety—the substitute actions taking the place of the unknown or impossible actions that would have brought fish or other food. He then adds the fact that primitives *say* that the expressive action is in fact a practical action, that it brings good luck. This belief, Malinowski would say, is a rationalization: it is an explanation after the fact. The primitives want it to be true, so it is true for them. Furthermore, in the course of time, the expressive action becomes standardized in a symbolic form. A norm is developed specifying what magical rites shall be performed in what circumstances. Note, finally, that although the magic does not bring the practical results the primitives claim for it, it does have practical results they are not aware of. The performance of magic gives them the confidence and determination they need to carry on productive work. This, Malinowski would say, is the *function* of magic.

RADCLIFFE-BROWN'S THEORY OF MAGIC

Radcliffe-Brown, an anthropologist as famous and important as Malinowski, levels his criticism, in a little pamphlet called *Taboo*,

---

[10] B. Malinowski, *Magic, Science and Religion and Other Essays*, 69-70. See also B. Malinowski, *Foundations of Faith and Morals* and *Coral Gardens and Their Magic*.

at the latter's theory of magic. He too backs up his argument with an example: the ritual surrounding childbirth in the Andaman Islands, an Indian Ocean group inhabited by a very primitive negrito people. As Malinowski did his field work in the Trobriands, so Radcliffe-Brown did his in the Andamans,[11] and just as we allowed the former to state his case in his own words, so we had better, in all fairness, allow the latter to do so. He writes:

In the Andaman Islands when a woman is expecting a baby a name is given to it while it is still in the womb. From that time until some weeks after the baby is born nobody is allowed to use the personal name of either the father or the mother; they can be referred to only by teknonymy, *i.e.*, in terms of their relation to the child. During this period both the parents are required to abstain from eating certain foods which they may freely eat at other times.[12]

The superficial circumstances are different, but the underlying similarities between Andaman childbirth and Trobriand sea fishing should be clear. In both situations people are not sure of getting desired results. Childbirth is always a dangerous process, in which tragedy may appear without warning. It is dangerous today; it was supremely dangerous under primitive conditions. The woman may feel great anxiety, and the husband may be worried about his wife. In the Andaman example, moreover, as in the Trobriand one, rites are performed. The fact that in the Andamans the rites are negative and consist in avoidances and the keeping of taboos is a detail. In both cases, finally, the people concerned say that the rites ward off the danger and bring good luck.

We might suppose that Malinowski's interpretation fits both situations. But Radcliffe-Brown says it does not, and we must quote him:

The alternative hypothesis which I am presenting for consideration is as follows. In a given community it is appropriate that an expectant father should feel concern or at least should make an appearance of doing so. Some suitable symbolic expression of his concern is found in terms of the general ritual or symbolic idiom of the society, and it is felt generally that

[11] A. R. Radcliffe-Brown, *The Andaman Islanders.*
[12] A. R. Radcliffe-Brown, *Taboo*, 33. Teknonymy is the practice by which, for instance, a woman would not be called "Mary," but "John's mother."

a man in that situation ought to carry out the symbolic or ritual actions or abstentions.[13]

If he had analyzed the rites of childbirth in the Andamans, Malinowski would have said that a father, or the normal father, feels concern and shows that feeling in action. Radcliffe-Brown says that he is expected to show concern. The former emphasizes individual feeling, the latter, the pressure of society to produce the appearance of feeling in the individual. And Radcliffe-Brown goes on to make another criticism of Malinowski's theory. The latter had argued that the rite is a response to anxiety; Radcliffe-Brown says that the rite creates anxiety. While a woman in the Andaman Islands is expecting a child and for some weeks after its birth, both parents must abstain from eating certain foods, dugong, pork, and turtle meat, that they may properly eat under ordinary circumstances. Moreover, says Radcliffe-Brown, "If the Andaman Islanders are asked what would happen if the father or mother broke this taboo, the usual answer is that he or she would be ill, though one or two of my informants thought it might perhaps also affect the child. This is simply one instance of a standard formula which applies to a number of ritual prohibitions." From these facts Radcliffe-Brown advances to the attack of Malinowski's anxiety theory:

I think that for certain rites it would be easy to maintain with equal plausibility an exactly contrary theory, namely, that if it were not for the existence of the rite and the beliefs associated with it the individual would feel no anxiety, and that the psychological effect of the rite is to create in him a sense of insecurity or danger. It seems very unlikely that an Andaman Islander would think it dangerous to eat dugong or pork or turtle meat if it were not for the existence of a specific body of ritual the ostensible purpose of which is to protect him from those dangers. Many hundreds of similar instances could be mentioned from all over the world.[14]

In short, Malinowski would emphasize the anxiety aroused by the approach of childbirth itself, while Radcliffe-Brown emphasizes the anxiety aroused by the rites of childbirth: the fear of what

[13] *Ibid.*, 41.
[14] *Ibid.*, 35, 39.

would happen if the rites were not properly performed. And just as Malinowski would say that the function of the rites is to relieve individual anxiety and to give confidence, so Radcliffe-Brown would say that their function is to contribute to the survival of the society by making a solemn occasion of a vitally important activity such as childbirth.

RECONCILIATION OF THE THEORIES

The theories of the two anthropologists look diametrically opposed. Yet there may be a higher synthesis in which the differences are resolved. Other distinguished investigators have talked past one another and presented their ideas as alternatives when in fact they are complements.

A first difficulty is resolved if we make a clear distinction between anxiety itself and a situation in which anxiety would appear if something were not done to relieve it. There are many occasions —fishing, childbirth, what you will—when we might expect the members of a primitive band to feel anxiety. They want very much to get a result and are not sure of getting it with the means at their command. Lay aside the question whether the primitives are born with a tendency to be anxious or learn from other members of the group to be anxious on certain occasions. On either assumption, much that we know of physiology suggests that in the absence of practical actions—actions that will make the desired results certain—some action will be taken anyhow. The stimulus-response arc will be closed by the expressive behavior we call magic. Malinowski's observation that magic is associated with fishing only when conditions are dangerous and a catch is doubtful, and the fact that magic increases in wartime even among civilized peoples, both seem to bear out this analysis. Magic and anxiety-provoking situations are linked.

So much seems certain, but to stop here is to neglect the complexity of human behavior. A situation may be one that we might expect to provoke anxiety, and yet anxiety will not appear. The fact is that if primitives perform magic in dangerous situations, they do not feel anxiety but confidence in the success of their enterprises. Let us be quite clear. Primitives do not perform magic *in order to* relieve their anxiety. Instead they believe that magic helps get practical results in the same way that baiting a hook and lowering it overboard gets practical results. And yet, believing what they do, they gain from the performance of magic not only a release for their physiological drive for action but also an assurance that they will get what they want. What Thomas and Znaniecki have observed of the Polish peasant seems to be true of most primitive peoples: "The fact is that when the peasant has been working steadily, and has fulfilled the religious and magical ceremonies which tradition requires, he 'leaves the rest to God,' and waits for the ultimate results to come; the question of more or less skill and efficiency of work has very little importance." [15]

What has all this to do with the controversy between Malinowski and Radcliffe-Brown? Radcliffe-Brown argues, in effect, as follows: "My adversary says that natives feel anxiety in dangerous situations, such as sea-fishing or childbirth, and perform magical rites as a result. I say that they feel no anxiety in these situations but are made anxious only by the danger that the magical rites themselves may not be properly performed. Thus the Andaman father and mother think that they will be sick if they do not keep the food taboos of childbirth." But this argument does not do justice to Malinowski, pardonably perhaps, because he himself did not make the issue altogether clear. Rightly understood, he does not say that the natives feel anxiety in dangerous situations but that they would do so if the rites of magic were not performed. And the facts that Radcliffe-Brown cites, instead of supporting a theory opposed to Malinowski's, follow directly from it. To say that magic relieves anxiety, as Malinowski did, amounts to saying, as Radcliffe-Brown did, that if magic is not performed anxiety appears. This is especially clear when we treat the explanations, the rationalizations, the natives provide for their feelings and actions as secondary phenomena and take as the primary phenomenon the relation between a dangerous situation and the performance of magic.

We can add one point that neither anthropologist talked about though both must have been familiar with it. In the primitive and peasant mind, where everything participates in everything else, the

[15] W. I. Thomas and F. Znaniecki, *The Polish Peasant in Europe and America*, I, 174.

link between anxiety and ritual is broad. The assumption is that unless all the rules of society are observed nature will not yield her fruits. Incest or murder in the camp will lead to a failure in the crops just as surely as a breach of magical ritual will. In the shape of war, pestilence, or famine, God will visit their sins upon the people. Accordingly when, in a village of medieval Europe, the peasants, led by the parish priest, went in procession about the boundaries of the village in the Rogation Days to bless the growing crops, they offered up prayers at the same time for the forgiveness of sins.[16] The association of ideas is characteristic: nature and morality are mutually dependent.

A second difficulty in the controversy between Malinowski and Radcliffe-Brown is resolved by a correct understanding of the relation between the individual and the group. Even if the Trobriand fisherman and the Andaman mother and father were isolated individuals, we should expect the rites they perform to become, in time, standardized. But they are not isolates; they are members of groups with histories. If ritual has been performed in a certain way over a period of time, the expectation grows up that it will go on being so performed. The performance is incorporated into the norms of the group and is taught to the children. It becomes linked with other items of the social system in such a way that nonperformance will bring some form of punishment. For instance, the man who is careless about magic will not be a man of full social rank.

Malinowski emphasizes magic as a means of coping with the emotions of individuals; Radcliffe-Brown emphasizes it as conformity to the expectations of the group. This issue justifies our bringing their controversy into our study of the relation between the individual and the group. But surely both individual sentiment and obedience to group norms come into the performance of magic. There may be an occasional Andaman father who does not really worry much about his wife but observes the taboos of childbirth to keep up appearances. We know American fathers who hang around the hospital because they think they are expected to. And there are other fathers, in the Andamans and in America, who do

[16] G. C. Homans, *English Villagers of the 13th Century,* 368.

worry, who find the rituals that the group provides for the expression of their worry entirely appropriate, and for whom no problem of conscious conformity arises. We may feel that a society is healthy when the impulses of individuals and the expectations of the group coincide. Both are always present and related mutually to one another.

Once we have seen the difficulties to which Durkheim's theory can lead, when applied uncritically by his followers, we must not be hard on him. In arguing that, in order to reach an explanation of social behavior, only the stamp put on the individual by his society need be considered, he was overthrowing a ruling idea, the social contract theory, and a Lenin does not reform a monarch; he kills him. To overcome the inertia of the intellect, a new statement must be an overstatement, and sometimes it is more important that the statement be interesting than that it be true. Justice Holmes used to say that the systems of the great theorists perish but their insights remain. Durkheim did not leave a completed system, and in his casual remarks we find that he really recognized those awkward facts which, in the effort to be clear and rigorous on main issues, he allowed himself to overlook. In such passing insights lies the principle of growth. We will remember that he defined *social facts* as "ways of acting, thinking, and feeling, exterior to the individual, that possess a power of coercion by virtue of which they impose themselves upon him." But as a footnote in the second edition of his *Rules of Sociological Method*—in short, as a late afterthought—he adds this:

The coercive power that we attribute to it is so much less than the whole of the social fact, that it can just as well present the opposite character. For at the same time that institutions impose themselves on us, we cleave to them; they give us duties, and we love them; they constrain us, and we find our satisfactions in their functioning and in this constraint itself. Moralists have often pointed out this antithesis between the two notions, the "good" and the "right," which express two different but equally real aspects of the moral life. There may, moreover, be no collective practices whatever that do not exercise on us this double action.[17]

Pursuit of this insight leads to the analysis we have made.

[17] *Les règles de la méthode sociologique*, (1927), xx.

At the end, let us summarize the theory of magic we have reached by comparing the theories of two great anthropologists. Magic is apt to be performed in situations of danger, such as sea fishing or childbirth, when people cannot be sure that results they greatly desire will in fact be gained. As the body mobilizes for action in these situations, magic takes the place of the unknown or impossible actions that would have made certain the desired results. Magic releases tension, and since people believe that the rites, like any other technique, actually help them in a practical way, magic gives them the confidence they need to carry on necessary work. Before the worry that might otherwise paralyze them has a chance to spread, magic drains it off. But the proof that anxiety is latent is the fact that, when the rites are not properly performed, anxiety reappears. And although magic is an expression of the emotions of individuals in the face of danger and uncertainty, it is also performed as a matter of obedience to social norms. Society, demanding the performance of ritual and specifying the dreadful consequences of nonperformance, creates, in part, the anxiety that magic alleviates. Magic, moreover, has a function in helping the group to survive, both by giving confidence to individuals and by solemnizing, for the group, activities of essential importance. The social contract theory, which holds that social behavior results from the characteristics of individuals, and the social mold theory, which holds that individual behavior results from the characteristics of society, are both correct, both incomplete, and complementary to one another.

CULTURE AND PERSONALITY

In recent years, more recent than the controversy of Malinowski and Radcliffe-Brown, the students of the relation between culture and personality—between the "way of living" of a society and the character of the individuals that make up society—have got into difficulties like those which the social mold theory encounters. The difficulties are persistent, and reappear in new forms in every intellectual generation. The students in question are interested in social education—the process by which the members of a society are taught its culture—rather than in social control, but they still think of society as putting a stamp on the individual. Yet they have added much to our understanding of society, and we may now be able to appreciate the contribution their theory makes to ours.

So far as we have gone, our theory does not pretend to form a closed body of doctrine. In order, so to speak, to set the group going, we have assumed that individuals have sentiments that they bring to the group from somewhere outside it, but we have not tried to explain why these sentiments, the sentiments that enter the external system, are what they are. Sometimes, as in the Western Electric Company, the members bring their sentiments to the group in question from other groups in a larger society. Sometimes, as in the Tikopia family, the sentiments of the external system are the physiological needs of the members, who bring these sentiments to the group by being born into it. But in both cases we have taken the sentiments for granted. Now we must go a little further, and here the students of culture and personality make their great contribution. They would say that in some measure every group teaches its members to have the sentiments it then proceeds to satisfy. Perhaps this is more obviously true of the family in a primitive society than it is of other groups. Embroidering on the physiological needs of its members, it teaches them the cultural needs that, if all goes well, it can hope to satisfy within its borders. To take a simple example, the general needs for food, clothing, and shelter may be biologically determined, but the society teaches its members what particular kinds of food they should gather and eat, what kinds of clothes they should make and wear, and what kinds of houses they should build. In a society made up of many groups of different kinds, the process is more complicated, needs created in one group being met in others. Here, the circularity of the process creating and satisfying needs holds only for society as a whole, and not for any one group, though the family, which teaches children some fundamental needs early in life—early because they are fundamental, or fundamental because they are early—remains the most important group educationally.

The students of culture emphasize one semicircle of the cycle in which needs are made and met; we emphasize the other. They describe the pattern of needs and the standard procedures for satisfying them that a society has developed, and the way the pattern is taught to children. To this extent, they describe the norms of so-

ciety—what behavior ought to be, not necessarily what it is—and
the process of education in norms. Then they go deeper and show
how the application to babies of the society's norms of child rearing has consequences for the ripening personality of individuals.
The society breeds its own character-type, its basic personality.
But the culturalists are always thinking in terms of a social mold
theory; they are thinking of society putting its stamp on the individual, and they neglect to consider how the stamp, the culture,
gets to be what it is. They seem to feel no need for a principle of
social development and change; at least they do not talk much
about one. As far as they are concerned, a culture could go on being taught, lived, and retaught unchanged forever. In their accounts
of field work, they are apt to be bored with the physical environment, the technology (except toilet-training techniques), the organization of a society, and the relations of these to one another.[18]
We here, on the other hand, emphasize the process of organization,
in a changing environment and technology, to meet needs, and
how this process creates the culture that may then be taught to
the new generation. For full understanding, both halves of the
cycle—and we repeat, *both* halves—must be studied.

THE PROBLEM OF LIBERTY

These ideas can also be applied to the problem of individual
freedom. One might think that so dear a thing would by this time
have been well analyzed, but it never has. The moralists recognize
that liberty means neither isolation nor absence of restraint. Men
do not live in isolation from one another; in fact they will do any
mad thing, even submit to a tyrant, in order to escape from freedom of this kind.[19] They get their satisfactions, including liberty,
from collaboration with others,[20] and we know that all collaboration
implies norms and that departures from norms are punished. The

---

[18] This is not altogether fair. The problem of social organization, and changes
in social organization, is not sufficiently recognized in the general theories of
the culturalists. But when, in studies of particular groups, they have to deal
with social change, they do take into consideration the environment, technology, and organization. See, for instance, the study of Comanche history in
A. Kardiner, *The Individual and His Society.*

[19] See E. Fromm, *Escape from Freedom.*

[20] See B. Malinowski, *Freedom and Civilization,* 25.

individual is constrained to obey, and, some would ask, if there is constraint, where has liberty gone? Nor is liberty in collaborative groups always a matter of particular "freedoms": of speech, or religion, *habeas corpus,* and the rest. They are dear to us, being what we are. The savage has none of them; indeed he is said to be tyrannized by custom, and yet when we see him in the bush he does not *look* oppressed. Apparently what custom requires him to do he also deeply wants to do. A man, then, is free if he feels free. Admitting this, can we do nothing to describe a free society? We certainly talk about one all the time. If the last passage we quoted from Durkheim is correct, a society is free so far as the behavior it makes appropriate and natural for its citizens—the behavior they feel is good—is also the behavior its controls demand of them. Liberty is a beloved discipline. This is the old definition in the prayer, where we say of God, "His service is perfect freedom." We, lovers of liberty in a republic, must always be asking ourselves how far the machinery of a "free society" breeds liberty in this deeper sense.

CHAPTER 13

Social Disintegration: Hilltown

SO FAR we have had little to do with time as a
dimension of the social system. The investigations we have followed were based on only a few months' observation in the field;
further, they were written up from the point of view of the immediate *now*, without thought given to past, present, or future
change. In each study the group was treated statically, as though
stained for the microscope. This method has advantages. We cannot
lay hold on a puzzle as slippery as ours unless at the beginning
we simplify as far as we dare, and the easiest simplification is to
omit the time dimension. But in the end the method does violence
to the facts. In Chapter 11, with our analysis of social control, we
began to look at small changes in time, and their effect on other
aspects of the social system. We found that stability itself can only
be described in terms of change. Statics is, in fact, a special case of
dynamics, and the study of equilibrium is the bridge between the
two. In the present chapter and those following, we shall frankly
go over to the dynamic side, studying longer and more persistent
changes than any we have considered hitherto. But perhaps it is
better not to draw any line. We have argued for the unity of sociol-

ogy, for a sociology that is not labeled family or community, industrial or agricultural, rural or urban. Nor, if our position is sound, is there reason for drawing a line between social statics and social dynamics so long as the same scheme of analysis serves for the study of both.

THE STUDY OF DYNAMICS

The study of dynamics opens a whole new range of problems; it also puts in our power a more convincing method of exposition than any we have had up to now, though we may not be able to use the method for all it is worth. Over and over again we have said that the elements of social behavior are mutually dependent, that, for example, the more frequently persons interact with one another, the stronger, in general, are their favorable sentiments toward one another. In a group described as if it existed at only one moment of time, all we can do to establish this hypothesis is point to one subgroup and the strength of friendly sentiments within it, and then to another subgroup and the less friendly sentiments of the members of the first for the members of the second. This is, indeed, the method we used in studying the Bank Wiring Observation Room. Logically it may be valid, but psychologically it is less convincing to a student of society than watching the interactions between members of a subgroup decrease in frequency and studying the changes in sentiment that follow. When we have said that two elements are mutually dependent, we have said that if one changes the other will too. The proof of the link is in the pull.

Something of the same sort may be said about the comparative and historical methods: we may compare groups or we may follow at least one group through time. Here is one group, a primitive family let us say. In this group a series of items of social behavior—agricultural techniques, division of labor, locus of authority, attitudes within the nuclear family, attitudes toward more distant kinsmen, etc.—take such and such forms. Here is another group, where the comparable items take somewhat different forms. We may be able to make some sense out of the differences by appealing to the internal coherence of each set of items. Thus we may point out that certain attitudes within one group are compatible with the locus of authority in this group, and that different attitudes within the other group are compatible with the different locus of authority in that group. This is what we did when we compared the attitudes of father and son toward one another in the Tikopia and Trobriand families. But the fact remains that the groups differ in a number of ways, and we may have no example of forms of behavior intermediate between those of the two groups. The variations are discontinuous; there is a jump. A historical study of a single group has no such disadvantage. The changes in the various items of behavior can be traced continuously while the group, preserving its identity, changes from one state into another. We are no longer limited to two separate sets of items, but can follow the change in each of the items in relation to the others over a period of time. We have used the comparative method, at least by implication, in studying our first three groups. In the remaining chapters we shall be following changes of single groups in time. Eventually someone will go further and back up a comparative statics with a comparative dynamics.

TYPES OF SOCIAL CHANGE

No classification of types of social change is going to last forever. The further our analysis is pursued, the clearer it is that all types flow into one another. But just for convenience and to fix our ideas at the outset, let us block out at least two main types and give them names. In this chapter, we shall study a case of *social disintegration,* and in the next, one of *social conflict.*

Within sociology as a whole there used to be a recognized subfield called social pathology that dealt with such things as crime, alcoholism, divorce, suicide, and psychoneurosis. In one sense these are all troubles of the individual, since we can always point to an individual criminal, alcoholic, divorcee, suicide, or neurotic. But the individual and his society are never independent of one another, and in the study of social pathology it soon became clear that a particularly large number of persons suffering from behavior disorders are apt to appear in a society showing certain other symptoms besides the behavior disorders themselves. This state of society was called by Durkheim *anomie,* and he said it was marked by the small number of activities in which individuals collaborate, by the low degree of contact between individuals, and by a lack of control by the group over its members.[1] The last characteristic gave this state of society its name: *anomie* comes from a Greek word meaning "lack of law." The rooming-house areas of some of our big cities are examples of anomic society, as are some of our country districts. Society in this state was said to be *disorganized*, and social pathology was sometimes called social disorganization.

Further study showed that many places—for example, many slums marked by high rates of crime—which looked, because something was obviously wrong, as if they must be disorganized were not in fact disorganized, if that word means a lack of social control and of intimate contact between men. Indeed these areas were over-organized rather than under-organized. The criminals—that is, the persons so called by the state—were far from being neurotics and outcasts. They were healthy, hearty, happy, and much admired; it was not too much to say that in these areas only a person who was *not* a criminal showed any sign of personality disorder. A diagnosis of *anomie* could not be made, and yet all was not well with the community. It was in some sense organized in opposition to the larger society of which it was a part. Criminality—that is, violation of the norms of the state—was an expression of this opposition: the persons standing lowest by the norms of the state were the ones standing highest by the norms of the community. Cornerville, with its rackets, is an example of such a community.

The process that produces a society of the first kind will be called *social disintegration*, and the one that produces a society of the second kind, *social conflict*. In this way we avoid the ambiguity that lurks in the phrase *social disorganization*. In social conflict, there may be no decrease in the number of activities the group carries out, no decreasing frequency of interaction, and no loss of control in the sense of social restraints on individual behavior. But there is loss of control in another sense; through a process of change a subgroup is coming into conflict with another subgroup or with the larger society of which it is a part. It is true that if we point to social disintegration and social conflict, we should also point to

[1] E. Durkheim, *Le suicide* (new ed., Paris, 1930), 272-82.

processes running in the other direction: social integration and the resolution of conflict. And in fact, in our earlier chapters, the idea of social integration was implicit in our study of the build-up or elaboration of social systems. Social integration may, moreover, be linked with social conflict. Thus the internal integration of the Bank Wiring group was determined in part by the external conflict between the group and the Western Electric Company. But in the next few chapters we shall be entirely concerned with the processes that some people look upon as unpleasant: with social disintegration in this one, and with social conflict in the next two.

HILLTOWN

Our method requires that we study social disintegration by taking up a particular instance of it, and here at once we are in difficulties. In the study of social change we have, to be sure, the facts of history, and history will yield sooner or later to our kind of attack. The "newer" history, not the "new" history, which is already decades old, will treat any single set of events, economic, technological, religious, or political, as one aspect, which can only be understood as reflecting all other aspects, of a society changing as a whole. History and sociology—for that matter, political science and sociology—will merge, to the advantage of both parties. But this is prophecy. History does not often deal with small groups, and we students of social change should not begin with societies as wholes, but with something much smaller. Yet we are scarcely better off at this simpler level. It is a bitter reproach to sociologists and social psychologists that they have made few studies of small groups that give us all the facts we need for close analysis, fewer still of small groups under the impact of change, and almost none at all of groups in which the change was "natural" rather than "forced," that is, made experimentally. The deficiency is being made up, but in the meantime our choice of studies is restricted.

In the case we have chosen as an illustration of social disintegration, the social unit is a New England "town" with a population in 1945 of about one thousand persons. By our own definition this is hardly a group at all. It may once have been barely possible, though practically very difficult, for each one of the townspeople to have had some contact with each of the others, but such wide acquaintanceship is certainly not a fact of the present day. We shall, nevertheless, present the case without apology, since apology is superfluous when the choice of alternatives is so narrow. We shall study this community as if it were a small group, leaving out much of the detail that a more profound study could not afford to neglect. We shall, for instance, treat the families in the town as if each were a single person and not several persons. And we have no doubt that, with simplifications like these, a method of analyzing small groups may be extended to the study of larger units.

Hilltown[2] looks the way New England towns are expected to look. It is set on the shoulder of a hill in green and rolling uplands. The spires of two white churches rise from either end of Main Street and serve as landmarks many miles across the country. Between them, elms and maples shade big white houses in the Federalist and neoclassic styles of the early nineteenth century, plain but refined, relying for their beauty on proportion rather than ornament. This is the "center"; farmhouses scatter out across the hills.

Foreigners—foreign, that is, to New England—may not know what a "town," in the technical sense, is. A town is a geographical area with definite boundaries, and in this sense it is often called a township. It is also a geographical area whose inhabitants are governed in a particular way. The voters of the town, gathered together in annual town meeting, adopt legislation governing the conduct of town affairs, make appropriations, levy taxes, and finally, elect their town officials, chief among whom are three selectmen. In the past, as we shall see, the town had other functions besides these. The word *town* is the old English word for the rural community, and town institutions are historically continuous with English village institutions.

The first colonists of New England settled close to the coast or in a few specially favored places inland, particularly the Connecti-

---

[2] The present account is based on D. L. Hatch, "Changes in the Structure and Function of a Rural New England Community since 1900," Ph.D. thesis, Harvard University, 1948. The author is grateful to Dr. Hatch for permission to use and quote his data. A description of this community as it was in mid-depression appears in C. C. Zimmerman, *The Changing Community* (1938), 248-70, where it is called "Indecisive Hamlet." This name is cumbersome and misleading. The present author is responsible for choosing "Hilltown."

cut Valley. The hill country of the interior was not covered with continuous settlements until surprisingly late, more than a century after the founding of Plymouth and Boston. Most of the chosen town sites were in high places, on the backs of ridges, on the sides and shoulders of hills, rather than in the valleys. Hilltown "center," for instance, is at an altitude of about 1,000 feet above sea level. No doubt the valleyland was low and swampy, the high ground much more easily cleared and tilled. Whatever the reason for it, the first settlements were seldom on the lowest land, though they tended to move down later, when the streams and their water power became important for industry. The settlements were on hilltops in a hilly country. From a time to which the memory of man runneth not to the contrary, they have been called the "hill towns." And since it is one of them, we shall call the community we are going to study "Hilltown," though that is not its real name nor anything like it.

HILLTOWN: THE FIRST PHASE

Hilltown was incorporated as a town by the colonial legislature in 1767, and its first town meeting met on July 3 of that year. At that time about one hundred and fifty persons lived within its borders.

Let us look first at the political organization of Hilltown in the first years of its existence. In those days a town had many more responsibilities than it has now and was much less circumscribed in its action by state and national laws. It built the schools and chose the schoolmasters, built the highways and provided relief for the needy. The town meeting acted as court of justice of first resort: most of our representative institutions begin as courts. It raised and provided for the periodic drill of a company of militia, the men who were soon to march to Concord and Bunker Hill. It elected and sent its representatives to the colonial and later to the state legislature. Most important of all was the duty of the town, in town meeting assembled, to choose the minister of the gospel, provide for his livelihood, judge complaints about his ministry, punish undisciplined church members, and maintain the meetinghouse. State and church were one; the town as a political unit was indistinguishable from the town as a religious unit—a single congregation, Calvinist in doctrine, "Independent," that is, Congregational, in its form of church government. For all these purposes, the town voted, assessed, and levied its own taxes. No wonder that membership in town meeting was a privilege. Not all inhabitants, not all adult males even, were members—one had to meet certain property qualifications—but a large majority of the men were eligibile to go to meeting. All of the items on the "warrant" that served as notice and agenda for the meeting were shrewdly debated. In these debates each townsman became familiar with the character and habits of his fellows, and built up skill in self-expression and political management. In all these respects, Hilltown cannot have been much different from other New England towns of its time.

The settlement of Hilltown was late, compared with that of most towns in the neighborhood. It lay on no main road; it stood at a higher elevation than most, so that its weather was more severe. Its soil, though rich enough in the beginning, was shallow. The town contained few patches of level land and was heavily forested. This was marginal farmland in the eighteenth century and it has remained so up to now. Yet Hilltown was from the outset a settlement of farmers, and until about 1900 each Hilltown farm produced the food needed for a family. Besides growing such basic crops as corn, grain, and hay, each farm had a garden and an apple orchard, and kept pigs, cows, and chickens. With the continued growth of the surrounding communities, more and more of Hilltown's produce was sent to market and brought in a little cash, which was used to buy commodities like salt that could not be produced at home. But not until after 1900 were the farms predominantly commercial.

Farm work was carried on by the family, which had as its nucleus then the same unit that it has today: a married couple and their children. But the household, the group of people living under the same roof, was a good deal larger than most modern households, as the big farmhouses of the early days will testify. Each couple had on the average more children than they do today; children were essential if all the farm work was to be done, especially in the years when the land was still being cleared. Parents, as they grew old, kept on living with their children. And every farm had at least one hired man, who was treated as a member of the family. In farm work, a rather strict division of labor was the rule; for instance, the women were not expected to work in the fields, in contrast to the practice of some peasant peoples of Europe.

The Yankee tradition was one of self-reliance and independence. (Its critics have used the words "suspicion" and "distrust.") In theory a man should be able to take care of himself. In practice, especially in the early days of the settlement, an individual household would hardly have survived if it had not been able to rely, in certain tight spots, on the help of neighbors. Suppose a man wanted the frame of a barn raised, or had lost his plow oxen through no fault of his own. (Moral blamelessness was a great point.) Then the man's kinsmen and neighbors would get together to put up the frame or plow a field. Though there was no money payment for the work, the farmer was bound to provide food and drink in plenty for everybody that helped. Such were the New England "bees."

ECONOMIC CHANGES IN THE NINETEENTH CENTURY

From this brief view of the original constitution of Hiltown, we turn to its social history. The following table gives Hilltown's population in roughly ten-year intervals from its founding to the present.

Year	Population	Year	Population
1767	150	1870	1,654
1776	488	1880	1,385
1790	933	1890	1,346
1800	1,113	1900	1,227
1810	1,127	1910	1,073
1820	1,367	1920	1,045
1830	1,674	1930	1,010
1840	1,784	1940	1,022
1850	1,825	1945	1,019
1860	1,621		

Many of the hill towns could show a population curve like this one. There was a fairly rapid increase up to 1800. This was the period of settlement, of getting the stones out of the fields and into the walls, of building the first big farmhouses. Thereafter the increase was slower, and the population reached a peak sometime between 1840 and 1850. We must note, for what significance it may have, that the decades in which towns like this were most prosperous and populous were also the ones in which New England literature and philosophy reached their full flower in Emerson, Thoreau, and Hawthorne. In the years following, Hilltown lost so many people that in 1910 the population was no larger than it had been a century earlier. About 1910 population stabilized and has remained fairly constant to this day.

The conditions leading to this decline in population are not hard to find. In 1835 the first major railroads from Boston to its immediate hinterland were opened, and only six years later, in 1841, an all-rail connection was completed between Boston and the Middle West by way of Albany. Yankees had long been emigrating to New York, Ohio, and the tier of states beyond. Even today much of eastern Ohio, the old Western Reserve of Connecticut, looks like a gentler New England, and New England has left its stamp all over the Middle West. With the completion of the railroad, the stream of emigrants became a flood, and in the next decade the population of Hilltown and most of its neighbors began to decline. The emigrants, moreover, may have come from the most fertile part of the population, so that the long decline may have been a result not only of sheer emigration but also of the lower natural birth rate characteristic of the people who stayed at home.[3] New England's greatest export has always been men, and its most striking monument the abandoned farm. The rail connection to the Middle West made emigration easier; it also made emigration more necessary, for soon the produce of the fertile prairies came into competition in eastern markets with that of the hill towns. The practicability of marketing grain and cattle grown on rocky New England farms came to an end. Only specialties like dairying and chicken farming could long survive and provide the farmers with a cash crop to eke out their bare subsistence. Hilltown's shallow soil, already impoverished, had clearly become marginal.

If agricultural New England declined after the 1840's, industrial New England was still on the rise. It has been said that the Yankee —the word is used in New England in the special sense of a New

[3] See W. H. Bash, "Factors Influencing Family and Community Organization in a New England Town, 1730 to 1940," Ph.D. thesis, Harvard University, 1941, pp. 125-82.

Englander of colonial, usually English, descent—was never really a
farmer in the sense that a French-Canadian is one: he was not attached to the soil. The Yankee originally came from industrial areas
of England, industrial, that is, by the standards of the seventeenth
and not the twentieth century.[4] He was a tradesman squatting on
the land and working it, but always ready to leave if opportunity
offered. At any rate, household industry was active in old-time
New England. Every farm was in some measure a shop, where, in
the slack time of winter, furniture, shoes, and small articles of hard-
ware were turned out. One of the former selectmen of Hilltown
described the arrangements in force toward the end of the nineteenth century:

Every farm had a workshop. It might have been a whole ell or just a
room, or even a separate shed. Whenever anyone would go to town, he
would bring back a load of boot tops and soles to be pegged. The head
of the house, his wife, the sons and daughters, and even the hired man,
all of them were expert in pegging shoes. The farm provided most of
the necessities of life. From these workshops would come the extra cash
which bought luxuries and built up savings accounts. It provided a margin between bare subsistence and fairly comfortable living—mind you,
we had to work for a living all right. Just as sure as God made apples,
everybody had to work. But Hilltown was prosperous. Transportation
was slow everywhere, and the fact that Hilltown was not close to the
big cities did not seem to make much difference. Then came a change.
They began to manufacture footwear by machine, and the machinery
was set up in Lynn and Brockton and other cities like that, not out
here in the country. There was nothing we could do about it.[5]

Thus Hilltown went through at least one of the main stages of
industrial organization, the "putting-out" system. Under this system
the industrial worker got raw or partly finished materials from
some central distributing point, worked them up further, or partly
assembled them, in his home, and then took them back to the
central point, from which they would be once more "put out" for
the completion of another operation. The worker was paid by the
piece. During the course of the nineteenth century, this system
was replaced by the factory. Power-driven machinery was first in-

[4] G. C. Homans, "The Puritans and the Clothing Industry in England," *New
England Quarterly*, XIII (1940), 519-29.
[5] Hatch, thesis, 148.

troduced into the cotton textile industry of New England. It was soon applied to other trades; mills sprang up at likely places along the brooks and rivers and employed a population already accustomed to domestic industry. The Milltowns began to supplant the Hilltowns. In particular, three large factory communities grew up within twenty miles of Hilltown itself, a fact which in part explains Hilltown's decline in population.

Hilltown was not left altogether behind in the new development. Water power was available, and in time small tinware and blanket factories were built. But the chief inducement for industry to enter the town was the forests. Throughout the nineteenth century sawmills were active, and just before the Civil War six small plants turned out various wooden products such as furniture and carriages. A few French-Canadians and Nova Scotians came to work in the woods. Hilltown's industrial prosperity reached its climax in the middle of the century, but even at that time only about one-third of the population was supported by manufacturing. Afterwards the importance of manufacturing steadily diminished, and even the arrival of a minor railroad line in 1874 did not stimulate a revival.

SCHISM IN THE CHURCH

These were the main events of Hilltown's social history in the nineteenth century, except for two crises of a different kind, the Unitarian controversy and the Civil War. The oneness of church and state, characteristic of the town at its founding, was dissolved in the first quarter of the century. The Unitarian movement, whose manifesto was William Ellery Channing's Baltimore sermon of 1819, challenged doctrines that had been central not only in Calvinism but in all Christian belief: the doctrines of original sin and the divinity of Christ. The Unitarians, making God less because they made man more, asserted the mere humanity of Christ and denied the original depravity of man. The dethronement of Jesus broke up the Trinity; hence the members of the new sect were called Unitarians—believers in the unity of the Godhead—in distinction from the adherents of the old faith, who were Trinitarians.

From an original focus in Boston, the new faith spread quickly across New England. Since church affairs in every town were under the control of the town meeting, the Unitarians, as soon as they commanded a majority, were able to control the meetinghouse and its equipment, eject the minister if he did not conform to their views, and leave the faithful of the old religion, now called Congregationalism, without any place to worship unless they chose to listen to heresy. This is just what happened in Hilltown. The Unitarians were a majority in town meeting and took over control of the meetinghouse and its affairs. The Congregational minority formed, in 1827, a new society, The First Calvinistic Society of Hilltown, and after a time built a new church. Finally, in 1838, a third denomination, the Methodist, entered the town, and the schism of Puritanism was complete. In the end, by act of the state legislature, the town meetings were deprived of all power to regulate church affairs.

Antagonism between the sects is said to have been strong. "The Unitarians are the devil's own people," the Congregational minister declared from the pulpit in 1880. One faithful churchgoer may have been too dramatic in saying, "It was almost a crime to speak to another church member on the street. When I was a kid they were just as stiff-necked as they could be. If you were not in their church you were out." "Each society thought the other wrong," said another.[6] We are apt to think that the choice of a church, among people brought up in the Protestant tradition, is a matter of individual conscience. No doubt it is. But it is certainly also true that the membership of churches, in Hilltown as in Boston, tended to correlate roughly with that of certain social groups. A large part of the upper class was Unitarian; the persons who remained faithful to the old creed were apt to stand somewhat lower in the social scale, and the Methodists lower still.

The religious convictions of Hilltowners were strong, and so were their political convictions, if we can judge by their readiness to back up belief with action. One hundred and twenty Hilltown men served in the Union Army in the Civil War and, of these, forty-one were killed in action or died in the service. No American town of recent times has had to stand a drain like this.[7]

6 Hatch, thesis, 209-10.
7 C. C. Zimmerman, *The Changing Community*, 250.

SOCIAL LIFE IN THE NINETEENTH CENTURY

Let us turn now to less formally organized activities. We have already mentioned the bees, at which a group of neighbors would collaborate in particularly difficult tasks, and which were, in Hilltown as in most old-time rural communities, occasions for a party as well as for necessary work. But there were many activities still more purely "social." "Years ago," one old townsman said, "there was more interest in each other on the farm. Neighbors would run in." As another put it, "There were great arguments over politics, but there didn't seem to be any real grievances of one neighbor against another." Or again, "We always had good times. There was something doing most of the time. We had skating and sleigh-ride parties, and inside we had charades." To the kitchen, the only room in the farmhouse that was warm in winter, company came for "kitchen junkets." Spelling bees, organized, except for the activity itself, just like the farm bees, brought crowds to the district schools: "The school was the only building big enough to hold them." [8] In evaluating these comments we must allow for some idealization of the past, but we must also note the large number of different social events that were held.

In those days a Hilltowner visited one of the industrial cities of the county as seldom as three times a year, and the social life within the town was intense in inverse measure. The three general stores were favorite meeting places for the men. One of the old-timers said, "On a Saturday night there were ten men at least. Twenty or thirty would be in or out. We didn't play no cards because we didn't want it to be a hang-out. . . . They used to say everything for town meeting was decided at Litchfield's, but it wasn't really, no more than at Willard's." [9] Besides the general stores, several of the fraternal orders had vigorous chapters in town which provided further occasions for meetings of fellow townspeople.

Each of the three churches, moreover, supported a women's organization, a young people's club, and a Sunday school. The Unitarians went further and formed a society, the Social Union, that included both men and women and held biweekly socials. These

[8] Hatch, thesis, 265-6.
[9] *Ibid.*, 261. Personal names have been changed.

groups carried out works of charity and raised money for the church at church suppers and other meetings that were at once social and practical in purpose. In fact each congregation was a united social group, and every family in town was identified with one of them.

As late as 1900, people in Hilltown knew each other well, if not in person then at least by reputation. Families had been in town for as much as four generations, and their standing in relation to one another was pretty well established. Although in Hilltown as elsewhere in America the lines between classes were so vague that a student of society would have difficulty, with a few persons, in assigning them definitely to one class rather than another, yet three main social classes were recognized: a smallish upper class, a large middle class, and a lower class made up partly of hired men and partly of the French-Canadians and Nova Scotians who had come to work in the forests. The factors that determined social rank can best be seen in the upper class, which was made up of the families whose heads were the substantial farmers or merchants in town and owned the big white houses along Main Street. These were also the men who took the lead in town enterprises and held the chief town offices, such as selectman, treasurer, chairman of the school board, and representative in the state legislature. One leading family was the chief influence in the Unitarian church; another supplied deacons for the Congregationalists. Townspeople had in mind a clear picture of the qualities that made a good citizen; in the upper class, possessions, a high level of morality, and actual leadership all reinforced one another in agreement with the norm.

ECONOMIC CHANGES IN THE TWENTIETH CENTURY

Although the town had reached the end of a long period of declining population, during which it had lost almost half the number of its inhabitants at its most prosperous era, the old order of things in Hilltown was still, in the year 1900, substantially intact. By the year 1945, when the study we have been reporting was completed, great changes had taken place.

As we have seen, Hilltown had never been a rich farming community. The shallow soil had been misused for one hundred years. Yet even in 1900 a large part of the food needed to support a family was still grown on the farm. From that time on, Yankee farmers became increasingly unwilling to accept the standard of living associated with subsistence farming. And if they could not maintain what they believed to be a reasonable standard by concentrating on a cash crop, they would not farm at all. Today most Hilltown farms specialize in milk or poultry. There are more fowl than in 1900, and more cows (though not as many as in 1850), but the ownership of fowl and cows is in fewer hands. No longer does anyone keep pigs and maintain an orchard as a matter of ordinary good farm management. As the older Yankee families have died out, the farms have become larger; there are fewer of them, and they are acquired more often by purchase than by inheritance. Although good roads, trucks, and the growth of population in the factory cities around Hilltown have increased the chances of success in specialized farming, they have also made the farms much more dependent than those of the last century on factors of supply and demand that are beyond local control. The cost of feed, the price of milk and chickens are determined outside Hilltown.

The history of farming in Hilltown has been complicated by the Finns. From the middle of the nineteenth century, when a few Irish arrived, there had always been ethnic minorities in town, but they had never been large. The Irish soon moved away or intermarried with the Yankees. The French-Canadians and Nova Scotians, who came to work in the woods, left town again with the decline of the lumbering industries. But the Finns were different. They first came to Hilltown in 1898, not straight from the old country but from New England industrial cities, where they worked in the mills until they had saved enough money to buy at cheap prices the farms that Yankees were ready to abandon. In the old country they had been used to tilling a hard, cold, forested earth. They were fanatically ambitious to get ahead in the world and, to do so, were willing to work hard and at a low standard of living. This did not mean that they were any more ready than the Yankees to maintain a peasant economy. Simply as a means of saving money they subsisted as far as possible on food raised on the farm, but their methods were those of commercial farming. They restored to good heart the wasted soil, and many of them went on to make good profits from dairying and poultry raising. The original Finnish settlers were followed by others until, in 1945, about one quarter of Hilltown's population was of Finnish descent.

In order to cut down the size of the group with which we must deal, and which is already too large, we shall for the most part leave the Finns out of our description of Hilltown. In doing so, we have the justification that the Finns for many years lived as a community apart from the rest of the town. The Yankees had always been reluctant to take in outsiders and were particularly unwilling to accept "foreigners" like the Finns, who had a different language, socialist sympathies, and a lower standard of living. The attitude of the Yankees was one of mingled suspicion and jealousy of the Finns' success in farming. The Finns have had hardly any part in the political control of town affairs, and do not seem interested in having any. In the younger generation, whose members were brought up together in the public schools, the association between Finns and Yankees is much closer, and the attitudes of the ethnic group have come to be scarcely distinguishable from those of other Americans. As we have said, the Finns never intended to remain peasant farmers, and today the ambitious young Finns are just as ready as any of the Yankees to leave town and pursue better opportunities elsewhere.

If the Finns have kept farming alive in Hilltown, no one has been able to do the same for industry. After failing for many years to show a profit, the blanket mill finally burned down; the furniture factories have consolidated with larger establishments elsewhere; the shoe shops have gone. Only two sawmills remain, and only at times of unusually heavy demand can they compete with western lumbering. This does not mean that Hilltown has run out of trees. A visitor would think it particularly heavily wooded. But the second growth is scrub oak and pine, the kind of timber, suitable only for cordwood, that grows when trees are cut without thought of their replacement.

The old hotel has gone; the railroad no longer keeps the express office open. The automobile and truck have put an end to Hilltown as a retail center. People drive to the nearby cities to do most of their shopping. Besides the Finnish Co-operative and a small chain grocery store, where people buy in limited amounts the supplies needed from day to day, only one of the general stores remains, and no effort has been made to keep its salesroom and stock up to date, which has had the unintended but favorable result that summer visitors patronize the store because they find it quaint. But if the automobile has almost destroyed retail trade, it has also brought people into the town. Hilltown has become a lower-middle-class suburb of the neighboring industrial cities because it is within easy commuting distance and because, in its state of decay, rents are quite low. Without this immigration, the population of the town would have declined even more than it has. The commuters have little connection with, or interest in, town activities, but we shall consider them a part of the town.

POLITICAL AND RELIGIOUS AFFAIRS

What has been the fate of town activities? Except on extraordinary occasions, town meeting is sparsely attended. The selectmen, the lesser town officers, and thirty or forty others come. "Town meeting don't amount to that," says a town officer with a snap of his fingers. "Town meeting is an awful dull affair," another complains. "One out of ten knows what he's voting for." [10] The fact is that activities once controlled by the town have become too big and expensive for it to handle now. In the automobile age, roads are no longer the responsibility of the town alone: in 1945 it paid less than half of the cost of road repair, the balance being made up by the state. The same is true of the schools, and Hilltown, too small to support a high school of its own, sends its high-school students by bus to a neighboring city. Nor, by modern standards, is a town poor farm a respectable way of dealing with relief, especially when most of the relief funds are supplied by state and federal government. The sums of money that Hilltown must appropriate every year for these purposes are practically dictated by the outside agencies that can withhold their share of the costs if the town does not do as it is told. The items on the warrant cannot be understood without reference to the state and federal statute books. Under these circumstances, the prestige of holding town office has declined. Few elections are contested, and once in office a man stays there as long as he wishes.

[10] Hatch, thesis, 192.

More serious still is the indifference of townspeople to dishonesty in their officers. Since 1885, for instance, no less than six town tax collectors have run off with town money, but as the years have gone by the reactions of people to the theft of public funds have changed. In the two cases that occurred before 1900, the lost money was repaid to the town, in the first case by the widow of the thief and in the second by three leading members of the community, who had signed his bond. The men themselves never came back to town, and no one would have spoken to them if they had. In the most recent case, the tax collector took $8,000, spent a year in the reformatory, and then returned to Hilltown, where he was cordially received. A bonding company made good the loss.

The Methodist church has disappeared, both building and congregation; the buildings of the Congregational and Unitarian churches still stand, but the faithful are few. The Unitarians can no longer support a full-time minister, and a small endowment fund yields just enough interest to keep the church fabric in repair. In 1945 the Congregational church, with the aid of the state missions fund, was able to pay its minister $23.50 a week. The minister was obviously one of the poorest men in town.

His parishioners regard him as a poorly paid servant, and the deacons take pleasure in exercising their authority over him. The church pays the minister partly in cordwood, and admonishes him not to keep the kitchen stove going except for meals. In six of the coldest winter weeks he burned a cord of wood. (Most householders burned three or four.) The deacon was indignant: "Something is wrong somewhere. I guess I'll call on them this evening to see if they keep the damper open. It should be fixed so there's only enough space to let the smoke out." [11]

Only very young ministers or those who have been failures elsewhere will stand for treatment like this. None of the Protestant churches is attended by more than thirty persons on Sunday. As for lay leaders, in 1900 every one of the half-dozen outstanding men in town was a church trustee. Today no leading man is prominent in a church or even a regular churchgoer. The affairs of the churches are in the hands of a few elderly women, descendants of families that once were highly respected but are now disappearing.

[11] Hatch, thesis, 212.

SOCIAL LIFE

Since the turn of the century, the old Yankee families have been dying out. Let us look at some of the facts. In 1900 twenty Yankee families had sons who might have carried on the family farm or business; only five did so, and of the five only one was followed in turn by his son. Out of fifty houses identified with particular families fifty years ago, only three are now occupied by members of the same families. Finally, only seventeen families whose ancestors lived in town in 1800 now remain there. Fewer of the old lineages are represented, and those that remain have decreased in size. But when we say "dying out," we mean dying out so far as Hilltown is concerned. To be sure, Yankee families today may produce fewer children, on the average, than they did in the past, but the greater part of the loss in Hilltown has come from youngsters leaving town to get jobs elsewhere. One man said of an old Yankee whose farm had been taken over by a Finn: "John Adams died on the farm; there were no children to take over. All the boys went to shops in the big cities. They were mechanically inclined, and factory work seemed to appeal to them more than farming." A former selectman said: "As the mills moved out of Hilltown a lot of the old families moved too; the young folk went to the cities to get jobs. With the shift in population, a new group of people came into town, though the number that moved out was greater than the number that came in." [12] In 1900 no Hilltown girl was employed out of town; since that time the women have left town in even greater numbers than the men. The fact is that, as we have seen, the population of Hilltown has remained practically constant for the last fifty years. The loss in the old families has been made up by the influx of Finns and of city workers looking for cheap housing and easy commuting.

There is evidence that social activity is impoverished compared with that of fifty years ago. The fraternal orders have left town; young people's clubs continue, not because the young feel any spontaneous enthusiasm for them but because they are backed by adults; a few clubs for older women are active. On winter evenings, only one or two men sit in the general store, and they are present only

[12] *Ibid.,* 45.

for the sake of the wood fire. "It isn't a place to visit now. Folks just wait here for a car to go to work in, that's all," the proprietor says.[13] The only local event that attracts large numbers of persons is the weekly dance at the Finnish Co-operative. But even on these occasions, a couple spends only a short time at the dance and then goes off to another dance or gets a drink in the car or a tavern. Several bars and movie houses in neighboring cities see more Hilltowners on an average evening than any meeting place in Hilltown itself. Said one informant, a sociable person herself, "In twenty years in Hilltown, I have never been invited out for a meal. I have been invited into a resident's house once. People never exchange meals. It's too much work. They never have people in for tea because three meals a day is enough to get ready." [14]

The social impoverishment seems particularly great in the upper class. Many of these families have no children, or the children have left home for good. They rarely entertain guests, partly, perhaps, because they have no tradition of entertaining, partly because there are, every year, fewer persons in town that are their social equals. We might expect that the Hilltown upper class, cut off from companions at home, would associate with upper-class people of neighboring towns and cities, but the fact is that, in his general level of living, a man who is upper-class in Hilltown is middle-class elsewhere. When he leaves town, he goes, literally and socially, downhill.

The standards of morality in relations between the sexes have changed from what they were fifty years ago. Then the boys and girls had, in theory, free choice in the matter of a marriage partner. In practice choice was limited. Social contacts, restricted to rather few persons but intense within this group, and the clear recognition of the social standing of every family in relation to the others, brought it about that a person's range of choice was narrow, although his chances of finding a compatible partner—compatible in social rank and background—were high within this range. Whatever the reason, the results seem to have been good, if one takes the stability of marriage to be good. In 1900 divorce was unequiv-

[13] Hatch, thesis, 261.
[14] *Ibid.*, 266.

ocally condemned, and only one divorced person lived in Hilltown, an outcast from the church and from everyday society. In 1945 there were twenty-three such persons, in all social classes, and no stigma was attached to them.

About 1900 three cases of forced marriage occurred in the town. The women concerned suffered from the ill will of the community; two of them are still in town and lead exemplary lives, but they still keep themselves apart from other people. In the younger generation, however, seven young women in the upper and middle groups are known to have been pregnant before marriage. They try to hide nothing; their families have nothing to say against them, and general knowledge of their difficulties has not hurt their social standing.

When a boy takes a girl out to the movies or a dance hall, pleasant conversation and good companionship are not considered a sufficient return for her to make, nor is the date a part of courtship leading to marriage. "The girl is expected to 'come across' or 'put it out,'" and the girl who, by these standards, cheats her escort gets few dates. "There is a common pooling of information among boys. No conventions of Victorian gallantry restrain young men from a frank discussion of their dating experiences. The expression is heard: 'I paid for her dinner and I didn't get a *damn* thing out of her.'" [15] The investigator who wrote the report on Hilltown says—and the attitudes of townspeople may have more variation than he indicates —that no one disapproves very strongly of sex relations before marriage. The tone of discussion is one of amused tolerance. "There's not a single girl in town who hasn't had a taste of it before she's married," is one remark often heard. Others are: "It makes them cranky if they don't get it"; and "If a girl goes out with a fellow and wants to, that's OK, but she shouldn't go with one fellow one night and three the next." [16] The nearest thing to an old-fashioned moral standard is a holier-than-thou attitude on the part of a few old defenders of the Calvinist dogma. But these people do not shun the sinners nor avoid the thought of evil. Instead they discuss exhaustively the details of their neighbors' trespasses. We are not

[15] *Ibid.*, 100-1.
[16] *Ibid.*, 86.

passing judgment on present standards but only noting that there has been a change.

Fifty years ago, the social standing of every family in town was pretty well established. By 1945, no such consensus remained. The persons with whom the investigator worked in trying to elucidate the social organization had been in town for more than twenty-five years and were scions of families that had lived there much longer, yet none was able with any confidence to place people in an order of relative social standing. They were not often ready to answer the question: "Is the Jones family better thought of than the Smith family?" It was not that no language for talking about social classes was available. People did not think in terms of "class," "society," "rank," and "prestige," but they had their own words for the same things. The real reason for their failure was that accepted standards no longer existed on which an estimate of a family's standing could be based. This, again, did not mean that people had no definite opinions about their neighbors. It did mean that these opinions implied no general standard by which an individual or a family might be evaluated. Opinions, in fact, were apt to be contradictory. Only three families—not all old families—were accorded high prestige, and only a very few more, which made no pretense of living up to any community standard, were generally admitted to stand at the bottom of society. The bulk of the townspeople—about nine-tenths of them—fell into a middle group where distinctions could be drawn much less easily. We must remember that the town had become a lower-middle-class suburb of larger urban centers.

Hilltown still looks as a New England town ought to look: white churches, green elms, classic houses, and all. But the activities that created the setting are dead. The churches are deserted; many of the farms are abandoned; the families that once kept up the houses on Main Street are represented now by the spinsters and the child-less; the other town institutions carry out only a small part of what was once their duty and their pride.

ANALYSIS

In the last few pages of this chapter, we make, as usual, an analysis of our case in the language of our conceptual scheme. For two reasons the analysis will not be lengthy. First, the material itself is familiar. The decay of New England has been an object of delighted study for many outsiders and even, since they are a perverse breed, for New Englanders themselves, the delight being in proportion to New England's conviction that it is superior to other parts of the country. Perhaps these analysts have been more ready to count the Yankees out than the facts warrant, and no claim is made here that Hilltown is typical of New England, but no one can deny the interest that the question of Yankee degeneracy has aroused. Second, we have described Hilltown briefly, although the town is rather large for a "small group." We have not been able to go into great detail, and our analysis must accordingly make only the most simple and obvious points. Our chief purpose is to show that the problem of social disintegration can be studied with the same analytical tools as those we used, in earlier chapters, to study the problem of social integration or "build-up." The one process is the negative of the other.

THE ENVIRONMENT

Following our regular procedure—and its effectiveness lies in its regularity, like a net that makes sure that if any fish are lost they will be small—we shall look first at changes in the environment in which Hilltown as a group has survived. All these changes have been mentioned; we need only cite them briefly. In the first place, the Hilltowners themselves brought about important changes in their physical environment. The land was cleared; the barns and houses built. The soil, once quite rich but always shallow, became depleted beyond the possibility of recovery by ordinary Yankee methods of farming. The forests were cut off, only timber for cordwood remaining.

Many other important changes, outside the control of Hilltowners, took place in the physical and technical environment. In particular, transportation was improved in scope, speed, and carrying capacity far beyond anything known at the beginning of the nineteenth century. Perhaps the most important event in the social history of Hilltown, and even in that of New England, was the opening of through railroads to the Great Lakes and the Ohio Valley.

This meant that the products of Hilltown farms and shops had to compete in a national market with the products of richer areas. Later the appearance of the hard-surfaced road, the automobile, and the truck hastened the same process, but at the same time enabled Hilltowners to sell perishable produce, such as milk and chickens, more widely than they had before, and, with the rise of factory towns in the neighborhood, allowed them to sleep in town but work and play outside.

The physical and technical changes in the nation at large stimulated change in another field, the national standard of living. By a national standard of living we do not mean actual expenditures for different kinds of goods, but the scale of expenditure that many people feel to be appropriate: the standard of living is one of the norms of a society. Suppose the people of one part of the country—Hollywood is a good example at the present day—are able to buy certain kinds of houses, clothes, gadgets, and entertainment that other people have not yet enjoyed. The knowledge of this fact is then, in one way and another, transmitted to, and acts as an influence on, the people of hundreds of other communities. They develop a new level of aspiration for the enjoyment of material goods. Certainly the rising standard of living of the nineteenth and twentieth centuries taught the Hilltowners to aspire to something better than subsistence farming. And national standards in such matters as road maintenance, poor relief, and children's schooling became so high that Hilltown could not meet those standards without help from outside. A concomitant of a rising standard of living is an increase in the scope and power of state and national government.

Finally, the Hilltowners were communicants in what the anthropologists would call New England culture. Its norms, far from checking the influence of rising living standards, encouraged Yankees to attain them. This effect of the cultural environment may be hard to describe but it cannot be ignored. We have said that the Yankees were, in effect, mere squatters on the land, content to till the soil only so long as no better opportunity presented itself. Unlike the French-Canadians, they were not indoctrinated in devotion to family, land, church, and tradition. Instead, their spiritual leaders, from John Wycliffe through Calvin to Emerson, had taught them for centuries the value of self-reliance and individual decision in the conduct of life. Translated from the spiritual plane to the half-conscious assumptions of everyday life, conveyed from parent to child, from teacher to pupil, from minister to churchgoer and even, for the Yankees were readers and their literature was flourishing, from writer to reader, this doctrine encouraged a conviction that every person should "make something of himself," "get ahead in the world," and submit to no group controls that might prevent his attaining these ends. At times Yankees seemed to believe, not that wealth came next to godliness, but that the two were identical. We are not arguing that even the kind of norms taught to French-Canadians will keep men subsistence farmers in the face of a rising standard of living. After all, a norm alone is not enough to preserve behavior unchanged; controls must back up the norm. We are arguing that the norms instilled in Yankees positively encouraged them to pursue the characteristic goals of American civilization in the nineteenth and twentieth centuries.

In short, the changes in the technical and physical environment made Hilltowners poorer, in comparison with other people, than they had once been, while the changes in the cultural environment made them anxious to get richer.

THE EXTERNAL SYSTEM

We turn now from the environment to the external system of social relationships in Hilltown, that is, the relationships determined by the survival of the group in its environment. We will remember that the sentiments entering the external system are those that men bring to a group rather than those that result from their membership in the group. These sentiments are often called individual self-interest. It is clear that in the course of Hilltown's history, *the number and strength of the sentiments that led members of the group to collaborate with other members had declined.* When the land had been cleared, and the barns and houses raised, the need for neighbors to work together became much less than it had been. As transportation improved, local industry declined, and mill towns grew up round about, the interests of Hilltowners led them to take part in organizations, such as markets and factories, outside the town rather than inside it.

At the same time, *the number of activities that members of the group carried on together decreased.* It is revealing just to count the number of activities in which Hilltowners collaborated with their fellow townsmen in the early part of the nineteenth century and then to count the ones that were still carried on in 1945. The farm bees had gone; farming itself was in decline; the local industries, first the small shops and then the factories, had been unable to survive; the general stores, once their customers began to trade in larger centers, lost money until finally only one of them was left. Though town government and town meeting remained, their activities were greatly curtailed. Militia training and the management of church affairs had vanished altogether; control of highways, schools, and relief was greatly reduced. Hilltown no longer sent its own representative to the state legislature—it was merely part of a larger electoral district. Finally, the church itself had been broken by schism.

This does not mean, of course, that individual Hilltowners had nothing to do. It does mean that they had much less to do with other Hilltowners. As the number of activities that members of the group carried on together declined, so *the frequency of interaction between members of the group decreased.* The sentiments, activities, and interactions of Hilltowners had become centrifugal rather than centripetal.

THE INTERNAL SYSTEM

The decline in the external system was accompanied by a decline in the internal. In studying the Bank Wiring Observation Room, we saw that when the wiremen were "thrown together" in the room, they soon developed "social" sentiments, activities, and interactions, over and above those necessary for the accomplishment of the wiring job itself. But if the process can run in one direction, it can also run in the other. *As the frequency of interaction between the members of a group decreases in the external system, so the frequency of interaction decreases in the internal system.* If we had known this rule and had been watching Hilltown at the turn of the century and afterwards, we should have been able to predict what happened. In a comparison of the Hilltown of 1850 or even 1900 with the Hilltown of 1945, even the crudest observations reveal an enormous impoverishment of social life. At the later date, there was much less informal visiting, and there were fewer parties. The decline was so great that some persons, particularly in the upper group, saw almost nobody outside of business. The fraternal orders disappeared, and the men stopped spending the time of day in the general store. The social occasions, such as church suppers, connected with the formal organs of Hilltown life, were much less frequent than they had once been. Even town meeting and church services were sparsely attended. Once again, it is important to state, in order to avoid misunderstanding, that this does not necessarily imply any lack of social life on the part of individual Hilltowners. It does imply that a citizen of the town today has fewer contacts with other Hilltowners than his ancestor had in the past. And it may imply something more, namely that, inside Hilltown or outside, the social life of an individual is made up of fewer occasions at every one of which substantially the same persons appear. There are fewer groups that come near being exclusive.

Just as an increase in the frequency of interaction between the members of a group will bring about an increase in the intensity of the sentiments they feel toward one another, so *a decrease in the frequency of interaction will bring about a decrease in the strength of interpersonal sentiments.* In Hilltown this rule seems to have held good for sentiments of antagonism as well as for sentiments of friendliness. Both retreated toward some neutral value. The words of informants suggest that, if there was less mutual good feeling in 1945 than in 1845, there was also, in certain fields, less mutual bad feeling. Certainly the attitudes of a townsman toward a member of a church different from his own were much more moderate. People were more nearly indifferent to one another. Again, this does not mean that people did not talk about one another. There is no evidence that gossip was in abeyance, but the gossip did not carry the same emotional tone.

This we should have been able to predict from what we know already. We have seen in the Bank Wiring group, and it is a commonplace of small-town life, that a sharp division into subgroups is quite compatible with a definite unity of the group as a whole.

We should expect then that, if the unity of the group as a whole disintegrates, the division into subgroups disintegrates too. Something like this we find in Hilltown. If, in 1945, there was less positive antagonism dividing one subgroup from another than there had been in 1845, this did not bring positive good feeling within the group as a whole but rather emotional indifference, that is, the absence of social organization.

NORMS AND SOCIAL CLASS

The emotional indifference of persons toward one another may increase through two processes, one direct and the other indirect. Sheer decline in the frequency of interaction may be one: a man may have a hard time feeling strongly about someone he does not see. But the decline may also affect sentiments through the medium of norms. No more than other aspects of the social system do norms exist in a vacuum. Norms—notions of proper forms of behavior—are not left untouched by real behavior. The degree to which norms are held in common by the members of a group must bear a relation to the frequency of interaction of the members, and the definiteness of norms, to the frequency with which the activities, whose standard form they describe, are repeated. Thus in Hilltown, as elsewhere, *a decrease in the frequency of interaction between the members of a group and in the number of activities they participate in together entails a decline in the extent to which norms are common and clear.* In Hilltown this process is best illustrated in the decay of the Protestant churches, the guardians of the most important norms. The disintegration of the community led to a weakening of the norms and this in turn to a weakening of the churches. But the circle is vicious, and the weakening of the churches led to a further weakening of the norms. Through ritual and preaching, churches drill people in norms, so that any decline in the churches contributes to social disintegration, since fewer people get the old thorough training in social standards. We can recognize this process at work in Hilltown, while still admitting that a general decline in the attitudes supporting the Protestant churches in America contributed to the decline in this single community. At least one point is clear: in the Hilltown of 1945 one important factor in the indifference of persons toward one another was their lack of an accepted standard for judging one another's behavior. A person is ready to look down on someone who has acted wrongly, but what if there is no definition of wrong?

The decline in the extent to which norms of behavior were clear and held in common by all members of the community had an effect on the class structure. Since we have been dealing with the small group rather than with society at large, we have not yet had to face the phenomenon of social class. But our ideas can be easily extended to deal with it. The relation between the social classes of a community and the community as a whole has much in common with the relation between subgroups and the group as a whole in any of the situations we have studied. First, a member of a given class interacts with members of that class more often than he does with members of other classes. In fact, class membership, like membership in any group, is defined by interaction. The interaction is particularly frequent in the internal system, so that, in trying to decide if two persons are members of the same class, we must pay more attention to whether they dine together than to whether they do business together. Second, a member of a given class resembles other members of that class in his activities more than he does members of other classes. He will buy the same kind of house, wear the same kind of clothes, and read the same kind of book as others in his class. In a hundred subtle ways his style of behavior will resemble theirs. Third, a member of a given class will share many of the sentiments of other members of the class. In particular, he will be apt to resent the assumed superiority of the classes above his own, while yielding them at the same time a grudging admiration; and he will look down a little upon the classes beneath him. Fourth, there is often some agreement in the community as to the ranking of the classes from top to bottom: one class is felt to be somewhat better than another. Fifth, this ranking is made according to the norms of the community, these norms ranging all the way from moral values and notions of what the "best" occupations are, down to standards of personal cleanliness. The more nearly a class realizes these norms, the higher, in general, it ranks, although in a large community the picture is complicated by the fact that the norms are many and no upper class lives up to all

of them equally well. Sixth, in any activity where members of different classes participate, a member of a higher class is apt to originate interaction for members of a lower one. This is an element in
the belief that upper-class people generally have better jobs than
lower-class ones. Moreover, all the elements of social class are
mutually dependent. To take a simple example, a dirty child in a
public school is apt for good reasons to be a lower-class child. But
the relationship between class membership and personal characteristics also works in the other direction. In an American community, a child who is known to come from a lower-class family
is apt to be called dirty whether he is dirty or not.[17] It is this mutual
dependence of elements that makes class lines so hard to break. We
will also note that these characteristics, used to define social class
in a community, are the characteristics that we have already used
to define subgroups within a larger unit.

Of these characteristics of social class, the most obvious in Hilltown was the relation between social norms and social rank. In the
middle of the nineteenth century, people had a clear idea of the
qualities that made a "good, respectable citizen," and the ranking
of the different families in town, according to the degree in which
they realized these norms, was well established. There were three
main classes; the members of the upper class not only owned the
best businesses, farms, and houses in town, but also maintained
the highest moral standards and took the lead in the chief town
activities: government and the church. In 1945 no such class alignment existed. One reason for the change was that Hilltown had become a lower-middle-class suburb of other communities, so that
more people stood at about the same socio-economic level, but this
was not the only reason. Townspeople were much less able than
they had been one hundred years ago to rank their fellows on some
such scale as respectability. Only a very few families were recognized to be superior. The upper class stood no higher in its morality
than any other, and, with the decline in church and government, no
longer exercised decisive leadership in town affairs. We can say
then that *as the number of activities carried out by the members of
a group declines, the social ranking based on leadership in these*

[17] W. L. Warner, M. Meeker, and K. Eells, *Social Class in America*, 83.

activities will become less definite. And we can also say that *as the norms of a group decline in the degree to which they are clear to, and held in common by, all members of the group, so the ranking of members of the group will become less definite.*

SOCIAL CONTROL

In Chapter 11 a simple but important point was made: that social control is not a separate department of group life; it is not a "function" that the group performs, or that someone performs for it. Instead, control, to a greater or lesser degree, is inherent in the everyday relationships between the members of the group. Now it is clear that social control was weaker in the Hilltown of 1945 than in the Hilltown of the nineteenth century. We do not have as much evidence as we should like, but we have enough. Reactions to the sexual irresponsibility of the young and to the misappropriation of town funds were very different in the two eras. When the tax collector, a few years ago, went off with town money, he was, to be sure, caught and put in jail, but so far as the town was concerned, nothing happened. The townspeople did nothing to catch him, and no one in town felt bound to make good the loss. When he got out of jail, he came back to town and was received as though everything was the same as before; no one was indignant and refused to associate with him; his social standing did not suffer. In short his action had none of the social consequences it would have had in an earlier generation. Yet it is a definition of stable equilibrium in a group that when a norm is violated something does happen. If a change takes place in a single element of behavior, there is a change in the other elements, and that of a certain kind: one tending to restore the previous state of the system. In the example we are using, the mere return of the funds would not have been enough to restore the previous state. If that had been enough, the equilibrium of Hilltown could have been preserved by a bonding company. Something more was needed: the supremacy of the violated norm should have been re-established, and this certainly did not take place.

The reaction of the town to the pregnancy of young women before marriage was of much the same kind. But let us be perfectly clear. Although we use, for convenience, such words as "decline" and "disintegration," we are not taking a moral stand here. The point we are making is not that sexual continency in the young is, by absolute standards, a particularly valuable norm, but rather that it had once been a Hilltown norm and in 1945 was one no longer. There are plenty of societies in which the young people enjoy sexual freedom before marriage and in which, at the same time, social control is strong. The norms of these societies are not those of old-time New England, and yet a breach of the norms, such as they are, is at once met by a strong reaction. Hilltown, on the contrary, had been losing its old norms, and the controls associated with them, without acquiring others to take their place. No doubt we exaggerate, but this seems to have been the general direction of change.

We observe the fact that social control had weakened; *if, moreover, social control is implicit in the relationships of the social system, any change in the strength of control must be determined by changes in the relationships.* And this is just what we can begin to see in Hilltown. Control ultimately is a matter of the punishment or reward of individuals. If social interaction is rewarding to a man, then loss of social interaction will hurt him. But if loss of social interaction—that is, avoidance—does not follow a breach of a norm, where is the punishment, especially when, as in Hilltown, the frequency of interaction is low to start with? If the good opinion of his neighbors is a reward to a man, then a loss of their good opinion will hurt him, but if this loss does not follow a breach of a norm, where is the punishment? And how can it follow, when the norms themselves are not well defined? If social ranking in the community is not established, how can a man suffer loss of social rank? In short, the social system of Hilltown has become such as to bring very little automatic punishment upon a man if he departs from his existing degree of obedience to a norm.

Moreover, a decline in control to such an extent that a man who commits a serious offense is not driven out of town probably implies also that a good citizen is less apt to be kept in. If reward is the other side of punishment, a group that cannot induce the bad to leave cannot induce the good to stay. If a man enjoys working with others in a common enterprise, and cannot find one; if he wants to gain, by achievement, the good opinion of his neighbors, and there is no foundation, in a common body of norms, for that good opinion, then, in effect, his social system will not reward him sufficiently, and he will be apt to leave it. Emigration from Hilltown, which was partly determined by changes in environmental conditions, must also have been determined in part by changes in the social system. What we can see is that interaction, activity, sentiment, and norms in Hilltown, unlike some other groups we have studied, were not working together to maintain the *status quo* or to achieve further integration of the group. Instead the relationships between the elements of behavior were such as to lead, in time, toward the condition Durkheim called *anomie,* a lack of contact between the members of a group, and a loss of control by the group over individual behavior. Let us hasten to add, lest we be accused of a conservative bias, that changes in the *status quo* are not, in our view, always and necessarily in the direction of *anomie.*

Many people would see the problem of Hilltown as a moral one: a weakening of the moral fiber of its inhabitants or, in some way, an increasing flabbiness in the community considered as a person. But surely we have learned that conscience itself is, in part at least, a function of the social circumstances in which conscience develops, and that for conscience to decide on action in accord with community norms, the community must make conscience more, rather than less, easily able to choose right. Because Hilltown still has a name, geographical boundaries, and people who live within the boundaries, we assume that it is still a community and therefore judge that it is rotten. It would be wiser to see that it is no longer, except in the most trivial sense, a community at all.

The decline of a community means decreasing control by that community over individual behavior. Since the group can support the individual and help him to maintain his personal equilibrium under the ordinary shocks of life, this decline in control may mean damage to individual personalities, provided the individuals are members of no other community that will take up the slack. Extrapolating from Hilltown to modern America, or indeed to the modern world, we recognize that what we have been studying is very common. Civilization has fed on the rot of the village. This in itself is not the problem. It becomes a problem only when the organizations to which the former Hilltowners go, such as the big new industries, fail to develop some of the characteristics that Hilltown once had. If they do fail, then the disorders of personal behavior increase. To this question, the leaders of these organizations have, on the whole, failed to address themselves.

CHAPTER **14**

The Electrical Equipment Company

*The Problem . . . Methods of Investigation . . . Norms
and Opinion in the Company . . . Attitudes of
Management and the Design Engineers . . . Attitudes
Toward the Design Committee . . . Changes in
Company Organization: First Phase . . . Changes in
Company Organization: Second Phase . . . Changes in
Company Organization: Third Phase . . . Preliminary
Analysis . . . The Authority of the President . . . The
New Line Organization . . . Staff-to-Line Relations . . .
Flow-of-Work Relations . . . Summary . . . Recommen-
dations of the Investigators*

IN THE last chapter we made a distinction be-
tween two kinds of social change in a group, calling one social disintegration and the other social conflict. Social disintegration is
marked by a decline in the number of activities in which the members of a group collaborate, by a decrease in the frequency of interaction between these members, and by a weakening of the control exercised by the group over the behavior of individuals. Social
conflict is not necessarily marked by a decrease in the activities
of the group and the interaction of its members, but it is marked
by a weakening of control, though not the same kind of weakening
as occurs in social disintegration. Instead, a subgroup comes into
conflict with another subgroup or with the group as a whole. We
made this distinction only for convenience, and not because we
thought that the differences between the two varieties of social
change were differences of kind rather than differences of degree.
In the last chapter we studied a case of social disintegration: the
community of Hilltown; in this chapter and the next we shall study

a case of social conflict: The Electrical Equipment Company. Following our usual procedure, we shall state the facts of the case in the present chapter and analyze the facts in the ·chapter following.[1]

THE PROBLEM

The Electrical Equipment Company was engaged in the design and manufacture of special measuring devices for the electrical industry. It developed new instruments tailored to the individual needs of customers in a highly technical field, instruments ordered in small numbers and built at high cost. In 1939, when the study that we shall describe was made, the firm employed about five hundred persons, and thus was small in size as American companies go; but what it lacked in size it made up for in the quality of its personnel. Most of the owners and officers of the company, as well as the salaried employees, were highly trained and professionally competent engineers, capable not only of designing new instruments but also of carrying out research and promotion.

Our concern is with this upper group of men connected with the company, about forty in number. At the head of the firm was the president, surrounded by a small body of officers who made the final operating decisions and whom we shall speak of as the management. The management was almost identical with the board of directors, and this latter body was responsible in the usual way to the stockholders, many of whom were also employees of the company. Below the management, the salaried employees were divided into two subgroups, each with its own duties. The so-called general engineers dealt with matters that were not engineering in the strict sense: finance, promotion, and sales; while the design engineers, about one dozen in all, did a job that was much closer to the accepted picture of engineering: they developed the designs for new instruments, tested the models, and made the drawings.

The company had been successful. Through the depression years, from 1932 to 1939, it had grown, though slowly. But the manage-

[1] The facts are drawn from C. M. Arensberg and D. Macgregor, "Determination of Morale in an Industrial Company," *Applied Anthropology*, I (1942), 12-34. Grateful acknowledgment is made to the authors and to the editors of *Applied Anthropology* for permission to quote from this article and to reproduce its charts in modified form. The name of the company and of all persons within it are fictitious.

ment was not altogether satisfied. It felt that one group in the firm, the design engineers, presented a problem. These men were well paid, and they freely admitted that they could not have done better for themselves financially in any other firm. Yet the management feared that they were not as contented as they might have been, and that any appreciable amount of discontent among them might hurt the enterprise as a whole, since their work was not just mechanical but demanded enthusiasm, spontaneity, and an easy ability to co-operate with the rest of the organization. With these ideas in mind, the management, in 1939, called in two social scientists, Conrad Arensberg and Douglas Macgregor, to study the problem. They were not asked to suggest a solution but only to make a diagnosis by answering two questions: Were the design engineers really discontented? And if they were discontented, why were they? The report of the investigators is the basis of our case.

METHODS OF INVESTIGATION

In making their study, the social scientists used two methods: the interview and the questionnaire. In their hands, the interview came close to following what is now called the "nondirective" approach.[2] That is, one of the investigators or the other had a talk with every member of the upper group in the company. The investigator made no effort to direct the conversation toward any particular topic, certainly no effort to find out something "wrong" that could be righted. He assumed that the man he was talking to would choose his subjects in something like the order of their importance to him; and what was important to him was just what the investigator wanted to discover. Broadly, each man was asked to describe "the happenings of his life in the company as he saw them." The stories he chose to tell and the language in which he told them were such as occurred to him and presumably had meaning for him, and not such as might have been put in his mouth by the investigator.

Questionnaires of two kinds were used to back up the interview data: first, a simple form of the familiar public opinion question-

[2] See F. J. Roethlisberger and W. J. Dickson, *Management and the Worker*, Chap. XIII, "The Interviewing Method," and C. Rogers, *Counselling and Psychotherapy*.

naire, designed to get quantitative data on attitudes in the company, and second, a questionnaire about personal contacts at work. In the latter, each member of the upper group was asked to estimate how often each week he talked to each other member and for how long a time on each occasion. In our language, the questionnaire was concerned with interaction. Note that the public opinion type of questionnaire was used in connection with other methods of investigation. In the future, the results of opinion polls will increase in interest as they are brought into closer relation with the results of other methods of social research. If the elements of behavior are interrelated, the methods of studying them must be interrelated also.

NORMS AND OPINION IN THE COMPANY

The problem, as management saw it, was the discontent of the design engineers. The investigators therefore began by studying the state of opinion in the company, their purpose being to learn whether management's ideas about attitudes in the upper group were correct. First they analyzed the diffuse information they got from the interviews and then they backed up their analysis with quantitative data obtained by the public opinion questionnaire.

In their interviews, many members of the upper group, and particularly the management, tried to describe the kind of interpersonal relations that they felt ought to exist in the company. They tried to express a norm of behavior. The company had begun as a very small concern, and it should, they felt, preserve the informal atmosphere natural in those early days. So the boast was made, as it is made in many small firms and, for that matter, in some big ones, that the company had no organization chart. Another formula often repeated was that "The competent man needs no supervision." A man's authority was not to be "personal" but "functional." That is, if he did a certain kind of work and was skilled in doing it, that fact should give him authority in questions concerning the work, but no one should boss or be bossed. The executives and research workers were all engineers, all members of a guild of experts, and in that guild, management felt, a man's command of a specialty determined his range of authority.

Management held, then, that organization should be informal and official lines of authority should not be stressed. These norms were echoed, to a degree, by all members of the upper group and formed an official body of doctrine. Yet in their interviews the general and design engineers made comments showing that difficulties arose in the relation between official doctrine and actual behavior in the company. Some men, who showed they believed the lines of authority to be as informal in fact as they were in theory, found in that informality a source of conflicting authority. They felt uncertain whether they should go ahead with the work they were doing: one member of the management might authorize it and another later countermand it. An engineer in the company, these men felt, should have some supervisor whose advice he could take without fear of later contradiction. They felt the insecurity inherent in the informal type of organization. Yet, on the whole, more men favored the flexibility of relationships than opposed it.

Some other men, while approving the company's norms, held that the norms were not maintained in practice. If, as was claimed, the competent man needed no supervision, then either no attention was paid to the rule or there were no competent men in the company. The investigators paraphrased a number of characteristic comments as follows:

Although it may be true that the competent man needs no supervision, it is obvious that no individual is completely competent in everything. It follows that that idea applied to that area where the individual is demonstrably competent. But, in practice, he is not given freedom to make decisions even within that area. There is little consistency with respect to the way his decisions are treated. A relatively major decision may be carried out without interference, and a minor one overruled. A decision with respect to the design of an instrument may pass today without notice, but a decision of a very similar sort tomorrow may be violently criticized. One will be told in private to carry out a given course of action, and that course of action will be criticized or even vetoed in public.

The inconsistency of discipline, it was often said, arose because management tried to avoid unpleasant situations rather than deal with them. In private conversation, an officer of the company would agree with a man's ideas and then, as soon as he was gone, take steps to see that the ideas were not carried out. The officer would not tell a man to his face that he was doing unsatisfactory work but would not hesitate to criticize him to others. Finally, the belief was often expressed that, contrary to doctrine, the least competent man received least supervision. Some engineers were ready to point out men who had proved their incompetence in more than one job, but, nevertheless, had been given with each job more responsibility and less supervision. In short, the men that made comments of this kind reached the same conclusions as the other group but from a different point of view. They approved the theory of informal organization, but held that, because the theory was not carried out in practice, the result was inconsistent and contradictory supervision.

One set of norms, widely held in the company, had to do with the nature of supervision; another with the method by which decisions should be reached. All members of the upper group, including the management, said that the firm should be run along "democratic" lines, a corollary being that "Committee management is superior to individual management," and, as we shall see, the company was in fact organized as a pyramid of committees. But many members of the upper group asked whether the management really meant to be democratic in its methods. These men assumed that, if the firm were a true democracy, the employees, particularly those who were also stockholders, would determine policy by majority vote, and the management would then carry out the policy. Some engineers thought that the directors were really following democratic procedure, others that, although the intention of the directors was sincere, autocracy prevailed in practice. Some went further and argued that the directors wanted to give an impression of democratic control but had no serious idea of abandoning autocratic power. These men felt that management would do well to state its philosophy frankly. And finally some held that management meant neither to be democratic nor to give that impression. The members of this group, small in number, came mostly from the board of directors itself.

Norms are not always unambiguous. Often the question is not whether norms conflict with realities but whether persons in different positions understand the norms in the same way. Such statements, current in the Electrical Equipment Company, as the following: "No formal lines of authority; the competent man needs no supervision; formal rules are unnecessary encumbrances; committee management is superior to individual management; the directors are gradually handing over the management of the company to those within it that have proved their competence; the company belongs to the shareholders"—such statements did not mean to management what they could easily mean to other members of the upper group. Although management, without question, expressed in these words its sincere feeling that company activities and policies should be discussed as widely as possible by all concerned, it certainly did not feel that the final decisions should be taken by popular vote. And yet persons not members of management might easily assume that the statements did mean something of just this sort. No criticism of the management is implied here. It meant what it said, but the words it used could bear more than one construction.

ATTITUDES OF MANAGEMENT AND THE DESIGN ENGINEERS

Up to now we have been considering some of the norms held by the upper group in the company and some of the attitudes stimulated by the contrast between the norms and the reality of company organization. Let us now separate the upper group into its contituent parts and study the opinions that management and the design engineers held toward one another. Management felt the design engineers were "prima donnas." The phrase seemed to imply that a design engineer was interested in the instrument he happened to be designing at the moment and in matters of administration threatening his freedom of action but not in the welfare of the company as a whole. Management also held the design engineers to be "temperamental"; that is, they allowed small annoyances to interfere with their work and spent their time looking for—and so of course finding—matters to complain about. Their indifference to the general welfare of the company was shown by their lack of concern with finance, sales, and the practical needs of the consumer and by their habit of spending months on an aspect of design that had only theoretical importance. Moreover, they disliked and shirked the necessary drudgery of making final working drawings.

Naturally, the engineers did not take quite the same view of themselves. They were ready enough to admit that they were individualists but not that they were heedless of broad company problems. On the contrary, they showed their awareness of these problems in the long discussions they held among themselves on matters of design. If they expressed some dissent from management's policy, the reason was that management, in the democratic tradition of the company, had encouraged criticism. They themselves resented criticism only when it was incompetent. They agreed, of course, that the customer must be encouraged to describe what he wanted in the way of an instrument, but only an engineer, they contended, was capable of designing one that would meet the customer's needs. Sales and financial considerations should have no controlling influence on design, and persons in these fields should pay more attention to the engineers' point of view.

Both management and the design engineers themselves had decided views about the morale of the latter. Both admitted that it was neither as bad nor as good as it might have been. No engineer made any complaint whatever about the pay he was getting. This issue was certainly not the one that made the co-operative spirit of the engineers something less than excellent. But many persons felt that the engineers had become disillusioned because the company had promised them, when they were engaged, more than it could ever give. The company had the reputation of being an engineer's paradise, and young engineers were, deliberately or by implication, made to feel that when they joined the company they would be given highly responsible assignments and much freedom in carrying them out. A new recruit did indeed acquire some such privileges rather early in his career, but he acquired few more until he showed that he could carry responsibilities greater than and different from those of an engineer, and in a small company opportunities for making this kind of a showing were few.

ATTITUDES TOWARD THE DESIGN COMMITTEE

Early in their interviewing program, the investigators encountered one subject on which every member of the upper group was eager to talk, and on this subject they decided to back up the evidence of the interviews with quantitative data to be gathered by a questionnaire. This subject was the design committee. When we describe in detail the organization of the company, we shall have much to say about this committee, and perhaps all we need say at this point is that some agency in the company had to decide what instruments should be designed, which engineers should design them, and how much time and money should be spent on each project. It then had to keep track of the progress of each design. In accordance with the doctrine that "committee management is superior to individual management," this agency in the Electrical Equipment Company was a committee—the design committee. Almost everyone had some question to raise about it. Was the committee really more efficient than administration by an individual, a chief engineer, for instance? Were the right men on the committee? Did it do the job properly? The committee seemed to be a focus of interest and uncertainty.

On the question of committee versus individual administration, the investigators found from their interviews that, in the opinion of some members of the upper group, no individual could hope to be competent in all the fields of engineering in which he might be called on to make a decision, that a committee could, without loss of face, change its mind more easily than an individual, and that a committee could be more impersonal and therefore more objective. Therefore they favored committee government. But others suggested that a committee could change its mind too easily and be too impersonal. They claimed that, in fact, individual members of the design committee expressed views very different from what the committee, as a body, had decided.

In the questionnaire administered to all members of the upper group—management, general engineers, and design engineers—one question was addressed to this problem: "Do you believe that some other form of direction of the engineer should be substituted for a design committee?" The results were as follows:

Definitely yes	6%
Yes	25
Undecided	13
No	31
Definitely no	25
	100%

While there was a good deal of spread in these opinions, the main weight was in favor of the committee form of government. This opinion was even more widely held by the design engineers than by the upper group as a whole.

As for the personnel of the design committee, the interviews had revealed the belief, held by the design engineers, that representatives of the sales organization of the company dominated the committee, and that at least one more design engineer ought to be a member of it. In the upper group as a whole, many admitted the control by the sales repreesntatives, but argued that sales ought to dominate because the needs of the customer necessarily determined what instruments were to be developed. Others felt that, although the sales department should have a strong voice, final control should lie with the engineers: a design committee ought to be concerned with design, that is, with technical matters in which engineers alone were competent.

In the questionnaire, the item: "Do you believe that the design committee should have a different personnel?" brought answers distributed as follows:

Definitely yes	25%
Yes	38
Undecided	18
No	18
Definitely no	0
	100%

The weight here was decidedly in favor of change, and the design engineers were more heavily of this opinion than the group as a whole.[3] Not all the men, to be sure, who felt the need for change would have agreed on what the change should be.

In the interviews, some men seemed convinced that government by committee was excellent and that the members of the design committee were well chosen, but they felt at the same time that the committee was not doing the right kind of job. Several of the design engineers said that the committee told them not only the

[3] In studying the questions and their answers, the student should remember that the way a question is phrased may have an effect on the way it is answered.

kind of work it wanted them to do, which was proper enough, but also just how it wanted them to do it, which was certainly not proper. Some members of the committee itself claimed that the committee never dictated to the engineers on technical matters; but the general consensus was that it did supervise the work of the engineers too closely. Another common opinion was that liaison between the committee and the design engineering staff was weak, that an engineer did not always understand what the committee wanted, and that the committee, for its part, did not understand what the technical problems were.

In the questionnaire, the item: "Do you believe that the design committee as it is functioning at present provides a satisfactory way of directing the work of the engineer?" brought forth answers distributed as follows:

Completely satisfactory	6%
Reasonably satisfactory	50
Barely satisfactory	18
Somewhat unsatisfactory	6
Highly unsatisfactory	18
	100%

Clearly the weight of opinion was that the committee was doing a satisfactory job, but again the attitudes of the design engineers differed somewhat from those of the group as a whole. None of them felt that the committee was "completely satisfactory."

On this same point, a second question was asked: "Aside from its personnel, do you believe that the design committee should alter its present methods of directing the engineers?" The answers were distributed as follows:

Definitely yes	13%
Yes	18
Undecided	36
No	31
Definitely no	0
	100%

In their answers to this question, the design engineers were somewhat more in favor of change than the group as a whole.

Let us sum up what we have learned so far. The social scientists, Arensberg and Macgregor, were called in by the management of the Electrical Equipment Company to study and make a diagnosis of what the management believed to be the company's chief problem: the design engineers were somewhat discontented and in danger of not co-operating easily with the other members of the upper group in the company. The investigators began their study by asking the members of the whole upper group, and not the design engineers alone, their opinions about life in the company. The investigators did not ask what was wrong, but were prepared to take note of anything people volunteered on the subject. And they made the assumption that, although opinion might not constitute in itself a good diagnosis of the problem—supposing there really was a problem—, it would at least point to the direction in which a diagnosis might be reached.

Members of every organization have their gripes and perhaps would not be happy without them, but neither the interviews nor the questionnaire in the Electrical Equipment Company revealed a body of men maddened by frustration. Most members of the upper group openly stated that they would rather work for the company than for any other they knew. At the same time, they were quite sure there were "bugs" in the company's organization that required the same kind of attention as bugs in the design of an instrument. If somewhat more feeling was aroused by the organizational bugs, the reason was simply that people instead of things were concerned. Some men questioned whether the expressed ideals of the company were, or could be, realized in practice, and whether the supervision of the design engineers, particularly by the design committee, was satisfactory. The design engineers were somewhat more emphatic than other members of the upper group in stating their misgivings. Their attitude might perhaps amount to discontent, and to this extent the fears of management were justified.

The next question for the investigators was: Why were the design engineers discontented? The opinions the members of the upper group themselves expressed might point the way to a diagnosis, but the investigators were unwilling to rely on opinion alone. They wanted to get independent evidence before accepting opinion as correct. They determined to study next the past and present organization of the company, not just the organization as formally set up, but the realities of everyday relations between members of the upper group, with the purpose of discovering whether the discontent of the design engineers could be linked with specific organizational changes. Unlike many students of public opinion, they proposed to correlate the attitudes they discovered with other features of social behavior as much subject to careful description as opinion itself.

CHANGES IN COMPANY ORGANIZATION: FIRST PHASE

In analyzing the past and present organization of the company, the investigators were aided by the interviews. In his interview, almost every man in the upper group told several stories of his past experience in the company, and in taking down the stories, the investigators were careful to identify the particular persons and activities mentioned. Thus, if the man being interviewed said that on the occasion in question he was dealing with the "office," the interviewer asked him to say what person or persons he meant. In the context of the stories, words like "office" and "shop" always did mean particular men and women. The sequence of events between individuals was also established. Thus if A made a suggestion that was followed by a question from B, the direction of interaction was taken to be from A to B. Finally, the investigators made sure that they knew the kind of activity carried on by every individual in every incident. Thus, in a particular incident, one man may have been urging the adoption of a certain design, the other man criticizing the design. No doubt the investigators would rather have observed the incidents directly than have accepted the evidence of stories. But they could not observe directly, and they felt that, whatever may have been the emotions aroused by the incidents, the members of the upper group could be objective in specifying the individuals and activities that came into their stories. Moreover, the questionnaire on personal contacts at work, in which, we will remember, each member of the upper group was asked to estimate how often each week he talked to every other member and for how long a time on each occasion, provided some check on the interview material as far as the present organization of the company was concerned. The collection of incidents, backed up by the questionnaire on personal contacts, provided the investi-

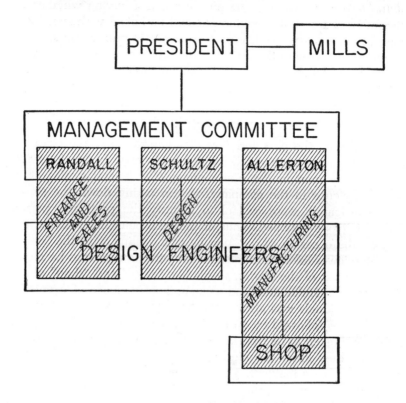

Fig. 16. Electrical Equipment Company:
Original organization plan

gators with a means of describing the relations between persons in the company at the time of the investigation and a means of reconstructing the changes in these relations that had taken place in the recent past.

The investigation was made in December, 1939. In telling the story of his life in the company, almost every person began with the year 1932, in the depths of the depression. (Refer to Fig. 16).

The company was small then and principally owned by Mr. Hubbard, the president, and Mr. Mills, his associate, both of whom were also directors. At the level below these two in the organization, Mr. Randall advised the president on matters of finance and sales; Mr. Allerton, as vice-president in charge of production, kept him in touch with the shop where the electrical equipment was manufactured, and Mr. Schultz, with the title of chief engineer, acted as leader of the design engineers. All three of these men were directors, and they were also members of a management committee, which, under the leadership of the president, decided all questions of co-ordination. Although they were said to be heads of "functional departments," we shall go wrong if we think of their having the same kind of responsibility as department heads in a large industrial concern. The design engineers formed the largest and most important group of salaried employees, yet they were not just employees and not just engineers. Schultz, the chief engineer, was only first among equals, and although Randall had some overall concern with sales, each design engineer in his own right kept in touch with old customers and made contact with new ones whose needs he thought the company might be able to meet. Nor did his activity end with the finished design. He might, by direct orders to men in the shop, change a design while the equipment was in process of manufacture, and he might suggest plans for the company's future development. In short, as the investigators pointed out, the firm at this time "looked more like a group of professional associates than an industrial company."

It was at this time that many of the norms of the upper group, and particularly those of the design engineers, became established. The committee form of administration was reflected in the belief in the "democratic" organization of the company. The large number of fields in which the design engineers could in fact give orders was reflected in the belief in "functional authority." The actual looseness of control was reflected in the belief that "the good man needs no supervision." It was a fact that all members of the upper group behaved as engineers and equals, and the company norms were very largely in agreement with the facts of company life.

CHANGES IN COMPANY ORGANIZATION: SECOND PHASE

In 1932 Schultz, the chief engineer, who was well liked by the
other design engineers, was fired. In their report the investigators
say that they are not competent to judge why this change took
place, but an alert reader will notice that it took place in the depths

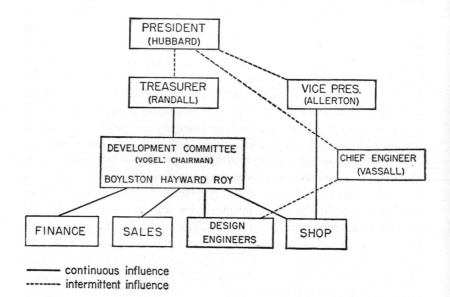

Fig. 17. Electrical Equipment Company:
Second organization plan

of the depression, and that afterwards the company's customers
increased steadily in number. Perhaps in a time of financial squeeze
the management decided that Schultz was putting too much
emphasis on design and too little on getting orders. Other changes
followed from this first one. (See Fig. 17.) A separate sales force
was brought into being. This force estimated and budgeted the
costs, in money and time, of developing the market for new instruments, and it began to replace the design engineers as the link
between customers and company. Randall, the treasurer, remained

in charge of both finance and sales, but Mr. Hayward, a man we have not mentioned so far, became, under him, head of sales and "general engineering." (We will remember that a man who, even though he held an engineering degree, did not work on design, was called a general engineer.) A separate sales force required a separate financial force as well. Financial practice was studied and made regular. Mr. Boylston took charge of this job, essentially an accounting job, as comptroller, also under Randall. These changes affected the position of the design engineers. Their contacts with the customers decreased as the sales organization rose in importance, and they found themselves, in some small ways, more closely supervised than they had been in the past. For instance, approval of travel expenses had once been handled informally; now the design engineers had to get approval from both a financial and a sales officer.

A new committee, the development committee, was set up to consider suggestions for the development of new instruments, choose the best suggestions in the light of possible sales and probable costs, and then supervise production. Suggestions came to the committee from the design engineers and, through salesmen, from customers. Thus the engineers submitted ideas to the committee and then, when it had decided what ideas should be carried out and in what manner, obeyed its orders. Mr. Vogel, a general engineer, was made chairman of this committee, so that decisions about designs were to be made by a body presided over by a man who was not himself a design engineer. Hayward, the head of sales and general engineering, was put on the committee with a controlling voice in matters of sales and finance.

The president, moreover, announced his intention of retiring. He did not, to be sure, retire at once, but his chief interest had always been engineering in the strict sense of the word, and he began slowly to limit his excise of authority to this field. From time to time, though less and less often, he still asserted his over-all administrative direction, so that it became difficult to separate his activity as an advisor on engineering matters from his activity as executive. With the gradual retirement of the president, Randall, the treasurer, began to emerge as chief administrative officer of the whole enterprise. As the last of the changes, Allerton, who had been in charge of production, a member of the management committee, and vice-president, decided that he too would soon retire. His place as head of the shop was taken by Mr. Roy. The new chief engineer was Mr. Vassall, who was not, however, placed on the development committee but acted as assistant to the president on engineering matters.

CHANGES IN COMPANY ORGANIZATION: THIRD PHASE

The organizational changes in the company took place in three main stages: that in which the company was, in effect, a group of engineering associates, that marked by the emergence of the development committee, and the final one. The second stage turned out to be unstable, and ended in what was called in the company the "October Revolution." Next to the dismissal of Schultz, no event in the history of the company was mentioned more often in the interviews. The most prominent incident of the Revolution was the decision of the management to split the development committee into two parts, a design committee and a planning committee. Vogel, the chairman of the old committee, became chairman of the new planning committee.

As for the design committee, we have seen how much discussion its personnel and policies aroused in the upper group in the company, and particularly among the design engineers. The president of the company sat with the committee but does not seem to have taken a leading part in discussion. Randall, the treasurer, was not a member, although he was by this time, in name if not in title, the chief executive of the company. Instead, one of his chief subordinates, Hayward, who was in charge of sales and had been a member of the old development committee, became chairman of the design committee. Boylston, the comptroller, and Roy, head of the shop, sat on this committee.[4] Vassall, the chief engineer, was a member and represented the design engineers, but we must note that the design engineers held neither the chairmanship nor more than one membership on the design committee.

A man who has not yet been mentioned, Mr. O'Malley, became

---

[4] The investigators' report does not make this clear, but it is consistent with their other statements.

the fifth member of the committee. His position needs a few words of explanation. Hayward had been head of sales under the treasurer. Now he was chairman of the design committee and, as such, had a big job to do. To give him time for his work he was relieved of the supervision of domestic sales and made nominal head of foreign sales, a small activity conducted in the past by the president and treasurer jointly. O'Malley, a former subordinate of Hayward's, became the new head of domestic sales, that is, head of the larger part of the salesmen called general engineers. Besides sitting on the design committee, he reported directly to the treasurer. (These changes should be carefully followed in Figs. 18 and 19.)

As head of the design committee, Hayward became in effect the chief co-ordinating officer at his level of the company's organization, like Randall, the treasurer, at the next higher level. The chief stages in the flow of work in the company from getting an order to shipping the completed equipment—sales, design, and manufacture—were represented on his committee. Hayward was given the responsibility of scheduling. That is, he had to decide, for all departments, what kinds of work were to be undertaken and at what times. Vogel and his planning committee, the second of the two committees into which the former development committee had been split, advised Hayward on technical problems of design, but did not give the controlling orders.

The growth of the company and the concomitant development of distinct departments within it made necessary a co-ordination that could only be achieved by an officer in a position like Hayward's. But if he was to do his job well, he himself had to be backed by his superiors, especially the members of the management committee, in theory the highest operating authority in the company. The members of the committee at this time were the president, the treasurer, and Allerton, vice-president in charge of production. But the gradual retirement of the president and vice-president meant that the treasurer was the only member of the committee who was steadily active. As a matter of course Hayward went to the treasurer with his problems and from him got the support he needed. Unlike that of the president, the influence of the treasurer was continuous. For all practical purpose he became president; the nominal president behaved much more like a chairman

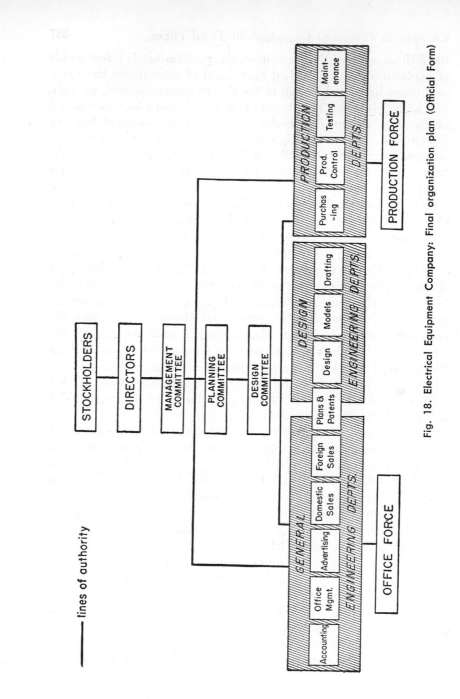

— lines of authority

Fig. 18. Electrical Equipment Company: Final organization plan (Official Form)

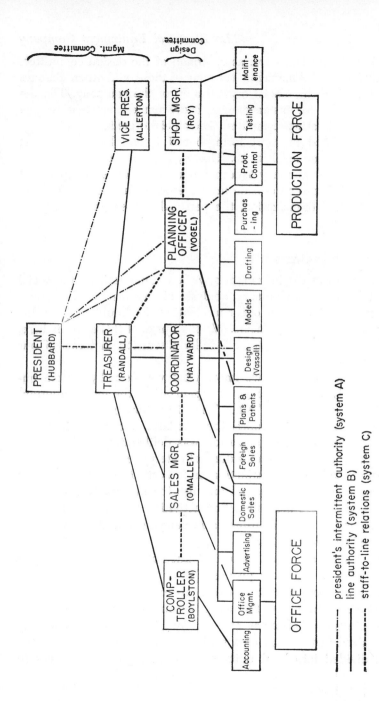

Fig. 19. Electrical Equipment Company: The structure of interpersonal relations

— · · — president's intermittent authority (system A)

——— line authority (system B)

— — — staff-to-line relations (system C)

of the board, and Hayward, as chairman of the design committee, was really a general manager. Yet none of these, and other, changes was reflected in the official organization of the company. The design committee, for instance, was badly named, since it was in reality a co-ordinating committee. The official organization plan was never represented in chart form, but if it had been, the chart would have resembled Fig. 18. That is, Fig. 18 represents the organization of the company as a member of the upper group would have described it to an outside investigator, whereas Fig. 19 represents the actual organization, the personal influences of everyday life.

PRELIMINARY ANALYSIS

On the basis of the information we have summarized, the social scientists made a preliminary analysis of organizational changes in the company and their effect in creating the "problem"—the discontent of the design engineers. We shall present this analysis here, reserving for the next chapter a fuller discussion in terms of our conceptual scheme.

Let us first make sure we know what we mean by certain important words in the language of organization, the most important of which are "line" and "staff." The distinction between the two was originally made in armies, the first large enterprises in Western civilization whose organization was deliberately planned. But we are dealing here with an industrial enterprise, and therefore we had better explain the distinction as it is made in industry. The main purposes of an industrial firm are the manufacture and sale of goods, and these are called line activities. Communications between superiors and subordinates in carrying out these activities will be called *line relations*.

Various other activities, important but not central, may support or contribute to the main purposes of an organization. In an industrial firm, these activities, which are called staff activities, include one or more of the following: accounting, finance, engineering, maintenance, personnel, and planning, and each of them may be organized in the form of a staff department. If, moreover, the firm is divided into local units—for instance, plants or offices in different cities—each unit may include, besides its operating or line personnel, representatives of the accounting, engineering, personnel, and other staff departments. Each of these representatives then has a dual responsibility: to the operating boss of his local unit and to the head of his staff department in the central offices of the company. In this way the organization becomes a pyramid rather than a triangle; it has depth as well as height and breadth. Communications between members of a staff department and persons concerned with line activities will be called *staff-to-line relations*. These are often advisory. For instance, the engineering staff officer will inform the line officer on technical matters of engineering that the latter needs to know in order to reach a wise decision, but the latter will make the decision by which this information is translated into manufacturing operations. The distinction between line and staff is never as sharp as the metaphysicians of organization like to say it is, but it is quite sharp enough for our present purpose.

We go on now to something else. In some kinds of enterprise, the required results can be obtained only if a number of processes are performed in a sequence. Thus the job of making woolen cloth begins, let us say, with the purchase of the wool, then goes through the stages of carding the wool, spinning the yarn, dyeing the yarn (if the cloth is to be "dyed in the wool"), and weaving the cloth, ending with the finishing processes such as shearing and fulling. There is a necessary flow of work, and the activities of the men who carry out the different processes are related to one another by reason of the flow. In the simplest case, a man who has performed one operation on an object hands it on to the man who will perform the next one. Or two foremen may have to work together because the workers each one supervises carry out successive steps in a sequence of operations. The necessary relations on the job between men whose activities fall into a determined sequence will be called *flow-of-work relations*.

With these definitions, we can begin to analyze the organizational changes in the Electrical Equipment Company. The investigators distinguished four systems of relations, which were of different degrees of importance at different times in the company's history. These they labeled as follows: System A, habitual, personal, but intermittent line authority surviving from early days in the company and becoming steadily less important, though still exercised from time to time; System B, habitual, personal line authority in process of emergence; System C, newly emergent staff-to-line relations; and System D, habitual flow-of-work relations. Let us take them up in order.

THE AUTHORITY OF THE PRESIDENT

System A was made up of the activity of the president in immediate contact with other members of the upper group. At one time it extended to all of them, but perhaps most often to the design engineers. The president himself had been a design engineer; in the early days, when the company was small, his problems had been theirs. As he gradually retired from the direction of the company, he dealt with the design engineers less and less frequently, though always more frequently than with most other members of the upper group. He associated with his fellow members of the management committee, with Vogel, chairman of the planning committee, and with the design engineers more often than he did with the sales and financial executives.

The president saw less and less of the design engineers. What was more important, this association was less and less apt to bring results. The interviews showed that it was quite easy for a design engineer with a problem on his mind to get the ear of the president, but much less easy to induce the president to take action. With the passage of time he became less inclined to intervene himself, as he would have done in the early days of the company; he preferred to turn the problem that had been described to him over to another officer, usually the treasurer. And the treasurer, if he took action at all, could not be counted on to take the kind of action desired by the man who originally brought up the problem. Yet it was difficult for some persons, still thinking of the original state of affairs in the company, to realize what had happened.

THE NEW LINE ORGANIZATION

On the other hand, the interviews revealed many occasions on which design engineers had not communicated with the president directly but had taken problems up through Vassall, the chief engineer, and Hayward, the chairman of the design committee, to the treasurer. And by this route, System B, successful results were achieved—successful from the point of view of the person who originally made the communication. We often forget that the process called communication is, for most men, concerned with action and not with abstract understanding. One man has successfully communicated with another if the latter puts the former's suggestion into effect. In a large organization, communication gravitates to the channels through which this kind of result is achieved. Though they may not be recognized on a company chart, they nevertheless determine the effective organization of the company.

In System B, communication was effective in the sense that it got results, but in this system a design engineer was separated from the highest authority by at least two steps—the chief engineer and the chairman of the design committee—and was not able to go directly to the top as he had before. As the company had grown, it had changed from a partnership of engineers to something much more like a conventional manufacturing enterprise with the usual hierarchy of authority. The accepted description of the organization did not accurately represent the change that had taken place, as a comparison of Figs. 18 and 19 will show, but the change had taken place nonetheless, and probably must necessarily have done so. No man could have avoided what happened, if the company was to survive and increase its sales. In terms of everyday methods of doing business, and not any official plan, the top level of the hierarchy was filled by the management committee, on which the treasurer was by this time the sole abiding influence. At the next level, the chief line authority was exercised by the chairman of the design committee. The third level was filled by the leaders of what had become in effect the various departments of the firm. For example, the head of the designing department was Vassall, the chief engineer, and the head of manufacturing was Roy, the shop manager, from whom the lines of communication ran to the foremen and workingmen in the shop.

STAFF-TO-LINE RELATIONS

We have traced out System A, the old line organization stemming from the president, and System B, the newly emergent line organization stemming from the treasurer. These were line organizations because they dealt with the basic activity of the company: manufacturing electrical equipment, and because in them the controlling decisions were made. But the investigators also discovered a third system of interpersonal relations in the company, which they called System C, newly emergent staff-to-line relations. In a sense there had always been staff officers in the firm, since the design engineers, besides doing their main job, had given advice on matters of sales and production. But in the process of change, the staff activities became more and more specialized, and more and more of them were taken away from the design engineers. The fact that the new activities were staff activities and encroached steadily on the sphere of competence of the design engineers was no more recognized in the official plan of organization than were most of the other changes. The newly emergent staff activities that made up System C were the following:

1. *Long-term engineering plans and development.* In the final phase of company organization, the development of ideas for new kinds of equipment was the responsibility of the planning committee under the chairmanship of Vogel. This work was one of the special interests of the president, who sometimes took the lead in person. According to the official plan of organization (Fig. 18), the planning committee was superior to the design committee, but in practice the former certainly did not order the latter to put into production the designs it had developed. Instead, Vogel transmitted suggested ideas either to the treasurer or to Hayward, chairman of the design committee. These men held the key positions in the line organization; they finally decided what should be done. Vogel and the planning committee only provided them with the material on which they could reach a decision. For this reason we must recognize the planning committee as a staff organ and, in the actual but unacknowledged organization of the company (Fig. 19), place Vogel not superior to Hayward but on a level with him and

linked with him by a staff-to-line relation. We must also note that the planning committee was doing a job that had once been done by individual design engineers.

2. *Financial development and control.* The development of accounting systems, whereby the contribution of every activity to the organization as a whole is evaluated in terms of cost and return, is an important function of any manufacturing enterprise. An accounting department had been growing steadily in the Electrical Equipment Company. Boylston, who was comptroller, assistant to the treasurer, and a member of the design committee, had been leading the department and transmitting the necessary technical advice on financial matters to the two principal line officers: the treasurer and the chairman of the design committee. But any clear recognition of his position was delayed by two circumstances. In the first place, Boylston and the lesser officers under him were still called "general engineers," though their functions were hardly engineering functions, and in the second place, the treasurer, by his very title, was taken to be in direct charge of financial matters. It is true that he was finally responsible for finance, but he was much more: he was in effect chief line officer of the company. These tricks of language, which had become hallowed by time, made it difficult for members of the firm to see that a new staff department had emerged, and Boylston was its head.

3. *Sales information and plans.* Something of the same sort had been taking place in the sales activity, especially if we consider sales planning, rather than the mechanics of getting orders, as a staff function. Hayward had first emerged as head of this activity, and he was still in charge of foreign sales, but he had gone on to become, as chairman of the design committee, the principal line officer at the second level. His place as head of sales had been taken by O'Malley, technically head of domestic sales only. Customers were now approached by O'Malley's subordinates and no longer by the design engineers. O'Malley transmitted information on orders received and on future sales plans to the treasurer as his immediate superior and to Hayward as chairman of the design committee, of which O'Malley was a member. In the actual rather than the theoretical organization of the company, O'Malley, like Boylston and Vogel, was on the same level as Hayward and in a

staff-to-line relation with him. The design committee co-ordinated the staff and line activities of the company at this level.

4. *Production plans, costs, and problems.* The production activity was in a position somewhat different from the others. In the language of organization, it was a line activity of the company, and orders as to the numbers and kinds of equipments to be manufactured were given to the shop by Hayward upon decision by his design committee. At the same time Hayward had to be informed about the costs and problems of production if he was to decide what the manufacturing orders were to be, and the transmission of this information may be considered a staff activity. Allerton, the vice-president, had been in charge of production and had conveyed this kind of advice to line authority through his membership on the management committee and the board of directors. But Allerton, like the president, was slowly withdrawing from the company, and Roy had emerged as shop manager and superintendent of production. As such, he was directly responsible to Hayward in the line organization, yet he still retained some of the independent advisory duties that Allerton had held, and, for that matter, he still reported from time to time to Allerton himself. Both as shop manager and as staff adviser on production problems, Roy's activity limited the former powers of the design engineers. At one time these men had given advice on production and had intervened directly in the production process. If the work was to go forward smoothly, and on a much larger scale than in the past, they could no longer be allowed to do so.

FLOW-OF-WORK RELATIONS

Besides line relations and staff-to-line relations, we can discern in this, as in most manufacturing firms, interpersonal relations based on the flow of work (System D). The making of an electrical measuring device began with the contact between customer and salesman. When the customer had given his order for a certain kind of equipment in certain quantities, the next steps in the flow of work were the planning and design of the equipment, then the testing of a model in the experimental shop, then the drafting of working plans, the purchase of materials for quantity production, production

itself, inspection and final testing, and, last, the shipping of the completed product. As the operations were linked, so the men that carried the operations out were linked in a certain order, and when the
company grew large and the different stages in the flow of work
separated out as technical specialties, the position of certain groups
in the sequence of operations tended to change. Thus the design engineers, who had originally taken the first step in the sequence by
getting in touch with the customers, were slowly replaced in this
position by the general engineers of the sales force, and whereas
the design engineers had once had a considerable amount of control over the whole flow of work, their activity was eventually limited to just one step, design and experiment, which was co-ordinated with the other steps by Hayward and the design committee.

SUMMARY

In summary, what had emerged was in fact, though not in theory,
much like a conventional industrial organization with line and staff
activities and several levels of authority. The president was still at
the top level, though his influence was becoming more and more
intermittent. At the same level, for all practical purposes, was the
treasurer, who was, his title to the contrary, the chief line officer
of the company. Co-ordinate with him was Allerton, the vice-president, who had once taken charge of production and still, from time
to time, gave advice on production problems. These men were
linked together by common membership on the management committee. At the next, or second, level, five officers were found: one
line officer, Hayward, co-ordinator and chairman of the design committee, and four staff officers: Boylston, comptroller and assistant to
the treasurer; O'Malley, in charge of domestic sales; Vogel, chairman of the planning committee; and Roy, the shop manager. The
four staff officers gave advice to Hayward on matters of finance,
sales, engineering, and production, respectively, and this relationship was reflected in the fact that most of them were members of
the design committee, which filled, at this level, the same function
as the management committee at the next higher one. Besides
belonging to the design committee, Boylston and O'Malley reported
to the treasurer as his immediate subordinates; Vogel advised both

the treasurer and the president; and Roy reported to the vice-president. Below the level of the design committee, the company was in effect divided into ordinary departments, one of which was design engineering. Some of these relations, though by no means all, were represented in the official plan of organization of the company (Fig. 18). They are much more fully represented in a chart of actual relations in the company (Fig. 19).

Let us now return to the problem with which the investigators started. The design engineers were said by management to be somewhat discontented. A study of their opinions showed that they, along with other members of the upper group, found some confusion in their supervision and some discrepancy between the current practices and the traditional norms of the company. In particular, they were not convinced that the design committee, at least as organized at the moment, provided the best possible supervision of their work. Study of organizational changes in the company from 1932 to 1939 showed that a new line organization had been emerging and in this organization the members of the design committee interposed at least one level of authority, which had not existed earlier, between the design engineers and the chief executive of the company. The design engineers had become the organizational equals of the accountants, the sales force, the shop force, and the draftsmen. The situation was confused by the fact that the old line organization, in which the design engineers had been in immediate touch with the president, was still intermittently active, so that the design engineers felt their supervision was contradictory and uncertain. The design engineers, moreover, had been at one time the only staff officers of the company. Since then a number of staff departments had grown up, and their leaders sat on the design committee. Every single new department had narrowed the sphere of activity of the design engineers. Once they had had much to say about sales and production and much power to regulate the flow of work. Now their authority was limited to the special function of design. Finally, the expressed norms of the company, and, to a great extent, the official organization plan as well, including the titles of many officers, reflected the conditions of 1932 better than those of 1939. It is not difficult to see a connection between these facts, on the one hand, and, on the other, the sentiments and opinions of the design engineers. But we shall postpone full analysis to the next chapter.

RECOMMENDATIONS OF THE INVESTIGATORS

In presenting their report on the situation in the Electrical Equipment Company, the social scientists made the diagnosis that we have just described. They had not been officially asked to give advice on the solution of the problem, but they did so nevertheless, and their advice followed directly from their diagnosis. They recommended that their report be circulated among the members of the upper group, and that the emergent but unacknowledged organization be recognized as the official organization of the company. In this way, any confusion in the lines of authority would be removed. The investigators believed that nothing could be done to restore the old position of the engineers, but that the engineers should at least know what their present position was. They recommended further that the various committees should be transformed into representative and advisory bodies, checking executive decision but not attempting to initiate it except in correction of grievances. For instance, the design committee should no longer, as a group, make the co-ordinating decisions at the second level of company organization. Hayward, chairman of the committee, should be solely responsible for these decisions, and the others should only advise him and, when necessary, ask him to change his action. In short, the relationship between line and staff officers should be recognized.

For the most part, the company took the action the investigators suggested. The report was circulated. The president completed his withdrawal from active participation in management, and the treasurer took his place as president. The members of the design committee were recognized as forming the second echelon in the company organization. All along the line, the theory of company organization was brought into agreement with practice. But the investigators do not to this day know how these changes were effected or how they were received when they took place,[5] and therefore this chapter cannot include a study of planned social change.

[5] Private communication from C. M. Arensberg.

CHAPTER **15**

Social Conflict

The Company and Its Environment . . . The External System . . . The Internal System: Social Rank . . . Sentiment and Norms . . . Reaction on the External System

BEFORE we analyze the case of the Electrical Equipment Company in terms of our conceptual scheme, let us be sure we know what manner of case we are dealing with. First, we are not, in this case, studying the internal organization of a small group. The investigators' report has, for instance, nothing to say about social differentiation within the body of design engineers. Instead we are studying the relation between the group of design engineers and the larger group, the company, of which they were a part. Second, we have presented the case as a problem of social conflict, but it is clear that the conflict was not severe. The design engineers were somewhat dissatisfied with their position in the company, but there is no evidence that dissatisfaction had reached the stage of open warfare or that the engineers were ready to resign. Yet conflict there was, even if it remained mild, and we hold that the processes leading to mild or to severe conflict differ in degree but not in kind. Third, the investigators studied the problem in a particular way. They studied the relation between public opinion in the company, on the one hand, and, on the other, changes in the way the company was organized to do its work. Thus they tell us only about the business contacts of the members of the upper group, and nothing about their "social" contacts.[1]

[1] These questions were not answered in the report. In a private communication C. M. Arensberg says that the design engineers had few off-the-job relations with the other executives, although they were of the same age as the younger executives in sales and other office positions, but formed a few small

Did the design engineers have dinner in each other's homes? Did the chairman of the design committee ever have lunch with the design engineers? What was the social rank of the design engineers in the company? Questions like these the investigators did not answer. We are not criticizing them for their failure to do so. Too often we sociologists damn research for what it does not do, and never intended to do, instead of welcoming what it does do. We can fairly complain that material has been left out of a piece of research only if we can show that the omitted material would have changed the results obtained, and in the case of the Electrical Equipment Company we may feel that, limited as it was, the investigators' report reached an adequate explanation of what happened. We are only saying that some kinds of information given us in earlier cases are not given us in this one. Therefore we shall not be able to make as full an analysis of this case as we made of earlier cases, and we may have to span gaps in knowledge with the bridge of conjecture.

THE COMPANY AND ITS ENVIRONMENT

The Electrical Equipment Company was trying to survive in an environment, and therefore it had to show a profit. In one way at least businessmen and radicals are alike. Both say that the "profit motive" is the incentive of American business, and neither takes time to examine what this means. Let us try briefly to make the examination for them, and let us agree, at the outset, that all the members of a firm, from president to common laborer, want to get some money for the work they do. In this they are no different from educators, soldiers, and clergymen, who are not supposed to be concerned with profits. Man does not live by bread alone, but he lives by bread at least. If this is the profit motive, let us admit it is powerful. But not all-powerful. To give the sheer hunger for money as an explanation for the observed behavior of American businessmen is grotesque in its simplicity. Yet some serious students of culture carry the idea far beyond business and say that Americans in general, compared with other people, are par-

cliques among themselves. The junior executives were not entertained by the directors of the company except at big office parties.

ticularly money-mad. Why, in this matter a French peasant puts
us to shame every hour of his life! A good case could be made for
the exact opposite: that of all the civilized societies, the American
is the one least concerned about money—perhaps because it has
so much of it. To get back to our point, if the money incentive
were as powerful as it is said to be, the best efforts of men could
be brought out far more easily than experience shows they can
now be. We should simply buy their efforts, and far higher salaries
and wages than we pay at present would be a cheap price for what
we should get. The fact is that, at every level of an organization,
money is only one of the incentives that must be offered to the
members. Pleasant companionship, prestige, connection with an
important business, and, not least, the sheer interest of the job
must also be provided, in different amounts for different persons,
if the full efforts of all members of the organization are to be enlisted.

But what are we talking about? Are we talking about the motives of individuals, or the considerations that determine what organizations do? We have not thought deeply if we think that these
two are always, or usually, the same or even comparable. If it is
proper to speak at all of the motives of an organization, we can
point to a motive more inclusive and fundamental than the desire
for profit, and that is the desire for survival. An organization, like
any group, is surviving in an environment. If the organization is
an American business firm, in an environment partly made up of
other firms and individuals governed by a particular code of laws,
the firm must, in order to survive, show at least an equality of income and expenditure. It does not have to show a profit in any
one year; indeed as we know from the history of several American
railroads, it can in some circumstances survive for many years
without showing any profit at all. But the Catholic Church must
also show an equality of money income and expenditures, and we
do not think of the church as driven by the profit motive. Most
organizations try to survive; for some of them, profit is the outward and visible sign of survival.

A firm, moreover, gets its profits by providing goods and services.
If a motive is a desire to achieve particular results, the desire to
provide goods and services is as truly a motive of businessmen as

the desire for profits. By emphasizing the need for profit as an in- centive, American business plays into the hands of the communists, who say that their industrial system produces goods for use, while ours produces them for profit. Analyze the meaning of the little word "for" in these phrases. As if the automobiles made by Gen- eral Motors were not produced for use! And as if an industrial trust in the Soviet Union was not expected to make a profit! Our ideological differences prevent us from seeing similarities in be- havior. But we have gone far enough to show that our everyday language, while useful for propaganda, is hopelessly unrealistic in the discussion of these matters. At one moment we talk about the motives of individuals, and at the next, all unconscious of the shift, we talk about the motives of organizations. And we speak of profits alone, when we ought to speak of profits, production, maintenance, credit, and good will, together with wages, salaries, and many other incentives, as elements, all interrelated with one another, that a business must keep in some kind of balance if it is going to survive. The problem of survival in an environment is the theme that links the elements together.

Finally, the problem, as we said in an earlier chapter, is not merely one of survival but also one of the level at which the or- ganization is going to survive. Many organizations try both to sur- vive and to achieve the conditions that will make them better able to survive in the future. Thus many enterprises try to increase in size, and even in American business firms the motive is not solely profit. Increased size may bring economies in the purchase of ma- terials and the scale of manufacturing: it may give the firm a greater diversity of products and a larger share of the market; it may en- able the firm to offer, in the way of prestige and influence, greater inducements for individuals to contribute their services. Whether or not profit is increased, these changes may help the firm to sur- vive, and increased size may have the same kind of effect on or- ganizations that do not have to show a profit. If we are looking at the characteristics that all organizations have in common, we shall do well to speak of the survival motive rather than the profit motive.

From this introduction let us return to the case before us. We cannot say that the environment determined the organization of the Electrical Equipment Company in the same way that the management of the Hawthorne Plant determined the setup of work in the Bank Wiring Observation Room. An independent enterprise must adapt itself to the environment or go under, but the environment does not often dictate an adaptation of any single kind; it only sets limits to the range of adaptations that can take place. We first encounter the Electrical Equipment Company in 1932, that is, in one of the worst years of the depression. At that time and under those circumstances, the leaders of the company evidently decided that the company was unlikely to survive if it did not put more effort into selling its products and less, relatively, into the niceties of design. If the company did not change its emphasis, it would be unable to sell to other companies enough instruments at a low enough price to bring in the money needed to buy materials and pay wages. The decision to put more emphasis on sales was marked by the discharge of Schultz, the original chief engineer. Our guess is that he opposed the new policy.

In one way the decision turned out well. The company's business increased somewhat more rapidly than the number of its employees, and to this extent the company was better able to survive. But the organizational changes that began by raising the company's capacity to survive ended in the dissatisfaction of the design engineers, and this put survival in jeopardy again. The problem put to the investigators was that if the engineers were not contented, their activities would not intermesh smoothly with those of others in the firm. The danger may not have been great, but difficulties of the same kind have been the death of other organizations. A superior adaptation in one field brings about, through the interconnectedness of the elements of organization, an inferior adaptation in another. We are killed by our best impulses.

THE EXTERNAL SYSTEM

We have looked briefly at the company's problem of adaptation to its environment. Let us now look at the changes in company organization that followed from the decision to seek a new adaptation based on expansion and increased sales. We will remember that, by our definition, the sentiments that enter the external system are those a man brings to a group from the other groups in society of which he is a member. The design engineers brought to the Electrical Equipment Company a desire for a good salary, some chance for advancement, and an opportunity to exercise the skills in which they had been trained. In the period of the company's expansion from 1932 to 1939, there is not much evidence that the degree to which these sentiments were satisfied had changed. As for pay, the engineers always admitted that they could not have done better in another company. As for the exercise of technical skills, the company was supposed to be an engineer's paradise. But there was some complaint that the company promised a newcomer more in the way of advancement and freedom at work than it was quite able to produce. It was not so much that the chances for advancement had decreased from 1932 to 1939, as that a man's advancement had come to depend on his developing capacities, such as administrative skill, somewhat different from those of a trained engineer.

The main weight of the investigators' report did not fall on the element of sentiment in the external system, but rather on the relationship of activity to interaction and the effect of this relationship on sentiment in the internal system. In the original organization of the company, the design engineers had carried on a number of activities besides those of engineering in the strict sense. On their own initiative they got in touch with customers, canvassed their needs, and drew up designs for the instruments that might be wanted. They had a great deal to do with seeing the instruments through the manufacturing shop. Naturally their range of interaction matched their range of work; they dealt with all kinds of people connected with the business, from customers through to shop-workers, and in these associations they made a good many decisions. That is, they initiated interaction to which others responded. Furthermore, they were often in touch with the president of the company and had much influence over him.

As the company increased in size, and certain functions were emphasized more than they had been in the past, activity became increasingly specialized. That is, the variety of activities carried out by a member of the upper group became smaller. A financial department emerged, charged with the job of estimating the costs and proceeds of company operations. A special sales department appeared, concerned with finding out what the customers needed and getting their orders. Something of the same sort occurred in the shop. Financial, sales, and production planning also became concentrated in fewer hands. Our assumption must be that here, as elsewhere, specialization brought economy of effort. A specialized department could, by putting a single-minded energy into it, do its particular job better than the design engineers could do the same job as a side line to their many other activities. But *an increasing specialization of activities will bring about a decrease in the range of interaction of a person concerned with any one of these activities and will limit the field in which he can originate interaction.* As time went on, the design engineers had less and less frequent contact with customers and shopworkers, and they took the initiative less often in matters of sales, finance, and production.

The activities in organization that are set apart must be brought together again. If the economies of specialization are not to be lost, these activities must be co-ordinated—a fact that is often forgotten in discussions of the division of labor. The co-ordination is achieved, more or less well, by the rise of new levels of organization, that is, by the rise of leaders who hear the reports of the individual specialists, or of the specialized departments, and on the basis of this information give the orders through which the specialists are brought into harmony with one another in their operations on the environment. Thus *an increase in the size of a group and in the specialization of activity will tend to increase the number of positions in the chain of interaction between the top leader and the ordinary member.* We exaggerate only a little when we say that the original organization of the Electrical Equipment Company took the form of a body of engineers, each of whom interacted directly with the president. As the company increased in size and specialization, at least two new levels of supervision emerged to carry out the necessary co-ordination. The treasurer came to the front as chief executive officer of the company, with the chairman of the design committee as chief co-ordinator at the level below him. In the new organization the design engineers were separated from the head of the company by a longer chain of interaction than in the past. We have already seen how they were hemmed in; they were also dropped down. The situation was confused by the fact that the old scheme of interaction, in which the design engineers had been in direct contact with the president, was still intermittently active, though the decisive communications no longer passed through this channel.

THE INTERNAL SYSTEM: SOCIAL RANK

We now take up a subject about which the investigators tell us nothing, but on which it may be profitable to speculate. A body of men such as the design engineers, doing the same kind of work, probably in the same surroundings, must have interacted frequently with one another and held a number of sentiments in common. They must have looked on themselves, and they were certainly looked on by others, as a separate group in the company. The nature of their work must also have made them feel superior. Engineers stand high in the American scale of social values. The design engineers were real engineers, doing engineers' work, while the other members of the upper group in the company, whatever their training and title, were not. It may have been some such feeling as this that earned for the design engineers the name of prima donnas.

And yet their social rank in the company, relative to that of other groups, may have been falling. Their job may not have been considered as good a job as it had once been. We know from the Norton Street Gang and other groups we have studied that high social rank is associated with a wide range of interaction. The leaders of the Nortons interacted more frequently with persons outside the group than did any of their followers. We know also that high rank is associated with the exercise of authority, and that the higher a man's rank, the more often he interacts with the leaders of his group. We can assume then that *as the range of a man's interaction declines, as he interacts less often with the leaders of his group, and as the field in which he exercises authority becomes more limited, his social rank will decline.* Now the changes in the external system of the Electrical Equipment Company had affected the design engineers in all these ways. They no longer contacted customers and shop workmen; they were separated from the effective head of the company by at least one more level of supervision than in the past; they no longer had authority over the whole flow of work or acted as staff advisors on financial, sales, and production problems. Their loss of all these privileges had, moreover, been matched by the rise of other groups in the company. Cannot we guess that the design engineers had suffered a loss in relative social rank?

And cannot we see a relation between their loss of rank and the sentiments they expressed? The design engineers expressed clear, if mild, dissatisfaction with the membership of the design committee and with the way the committee was doing its job; it also was a fact that the committee had thrust itself between them and final authority. The design engineers said that supervision was inconsistent and contradictory; and it was a fact that direct, if intermittent, contacts between the engineers and the president still persisted, although the longer chain of interaction that led to the treasurer was the one by which communication got results. The design engineers claimed that men who had proved their incompetence in more than one job had nevertheless been given more and more responsibility; and it was a fact that persons who were not design engineers in the technical sense held many of the new management positions that limited and controlled the engineers' own activities. Were not the design engineers expressing, in fact if not in form, some degree of antagonism for groups that had risen as they had fallen?

SENTIMENT AND NORMS

But can we dismiss the sentiments of the design engineers as mere resentment of their loss of social rank? This kind of question is one of the most important we ask in trying to understand our modern world. The little world of the group is a microcosm. Here is a man who says that public ownership of manufacturing enterprises may not work out for the advantage of the nation. We discover that he is a large stockholder in manufacturing enterprises, and we dismiss his argument with the words, "Oh, he would say that!" That is, we hold that his argument is a mere rationalization of his interests. But we may be taking too simple a view. Several influences may be determining his judgment and not, as we assume, just one. He may have some views about the general welfare and the way it is apt to be affected by public ownership that are not solely, though they may be in part, determined by his economic interests. They may be worth examining in their own right, apart from the source from which they come. In fact our simple-minded assumption has the effect of stopping public debate, for we can always find something in a man's interests or his social position and upbringing that would lead him to hold the views he does hold. If the views themselves are never of any importance, we may as well stop talking—all of us—about all opinions. Are there "good" opinions held for "bad" motives? And what do we mean by "bad" motives here? The fact is that, in the Electrical Equipment Company, the design engineers did not merely express discontent with the design committee and their supervision in general but gave reasons why they should be discontented. Were these reasons mere rationalizations?

Perhaps we need to consider more carefully what we mean by opinion. Suppose, to continue with our case, that one asks a design engineer to give his opinion on a certain subject. Suppose, for instance, one asks him some such question as this: "Do you believe that some other form of direction of the engineers should be substituted for a design committee?" His answer depends upon at least three factors that mutually influence one another. First, there is an existing state of affairs: the organization and personnel of the design committee, and the relation of the committee to the design engineers in the setting of the company at large—as this situation is seen by the person of whom the question is asked. Second, there is the expression of a sentiment (the word we prefer) or an attitude (the word often used) toward the existing situation, and this sentiment has as its focus a particular aspect of the situation, the aspect about which the question was asked. Is the design committee good, bad, or indifferent? No matter how the question is phrased, the answer inevitably expresses some degree of liking or disliking, favor or disfavor, approval or disapproval. If a design engineer wants to get rid of the design committee, the reason must be that he does not like it. But the answer to the question implies something more, for, third, there is some standard or norm on the basis of which the engineer decides whether he likes something or not. He measures what *is* against what *ought to be*. Sometimes we say that we dislike a person "instinctively," as we dislike physical pain. The reaction is so automatic that it seems silly to say we have acted on the basis of a standard of judgment, and perhaps the dislike that the members of a closely knit group feel toward outsiders is this kind of reaction. But at any higher level of judgment, the sentiment a man expresses about a situation facing him seems to have as a prerequisite some intellectual picture of the situation as it ought to be, a picture built up in the course of the man's past experience and social training. When we are asked not only how we feel about something, but why we feel as we do, we refer to the norm.

To understand any expression of opinion we must look at the three factors we have called situation, sentiment, and norm. Knowledge of the second of the three, the sentiment alone, is often useful. We know, for instance, that when a man, in answer to a questionnaire, expresses a preference for a certain candidate for public office, his answer will often, not always, predict how he is going to vote, although we may know very little about the situation in which the man is placed and to which his vote is presumably a reaction. But an expression of sentiment by itself is often ambiguous except as it foreshadows action. It does not tell us why a man feels as he does, and this may be the important question, for unless we know why, we shall be unable to do much to change his opinion. The famous refrain of the psychologist Titchener, "Meaning is always context," does not enlighten us much until we analyze the context. One of the great advantages of the investigators' report on the Electrical Equipment Company is that it tells us something about each of the three factors in opinion. It tells us something about the actual social situation in the company, past and present. It tells us, largely through the results of questionnaires, something about the sentiments the engineers held toward various aspects of the social situation. And it tells us something about the norms that helped determine sentiment. Future studies of opinion might well conform to this model.

What do we mean when we say that the factors determining opinion are mutually dependent? Let us take up this problem by asking what we mean by rationalization. A man behaves in a certain way. If what he does is not obviously appropriate, he will feel a need to justify his behavior, and the justification must be of a kind that others will accept, or it is not emotionally satisfactory even to the man himself. Under these circumstances he will explain his behavior by saying he is acting in accordance with norms commonly accepted in the group of which he is a member. If an outside observer then finds that the real reasons for the man's behavior have little to do with the explanation he has given, the observer will say that the man is rationalizing. Suppose, for instance, that a woman factory worker hates her foreman and says she does so because he is not giving her a fair deal. In effect she is justifying her hate by saying that the foreman is not living up to the norms of the group and that therefore, again according to the norms of the group, she ought to hate him. If an outside observer then finds that the foreman is not behaving unfairly but does bear a physical resemblance to the woman's hated stepfather, although she has not been conscious of the fact, the observer will say that her explanation for her behavior is a rationalization and not the real reason. His assumption is that the hate gives rise to the rationalization but that the factors cited in the rationalization have nothing to do with the hate. The relationship between the sentiment and the rationalization is one of cause-and-effect and not of mutual dependence.

But not all situations are as simple as this. Suppose we say that the reasons the design engineers gave for their discontent with supervision were "mere" rationalizations of the sentiments aroused by their declining social rank. In making this statement, we are accepting, by implication, two hypotheses: first, that the sentiments of the design engineers were determined entirely by their changing position in the company, and second, that the reasons they gave for their discontent were determined by their sentiments, and not their sentiments by their reasons. The engineers felt unhappy; they looked around for reasons for their unhappiness, reasons that could be made public and that everyone might accept, and, sure enough, they found some. But these two hypotheses may be an inadequate, though not wholly incorrect, explanation of the engineers' behavior. In particular, two other hypotheses are neglected. First, if sentiment determines norms, norms also determine sentiment. A man may feel disturbed because the reality of the situation does not match his view of what the situation ought to be. And second, the norms themselves may be determined by the situation, both past

and present, and are not always picked up haphazard as a justification for conduct. The mutual dependence of the factors in opinion makes the actual problem more complex than the usual theory
of rationalization will allow.

Both the two latter hypotheses may have held good for the design engineers in the Electrical Equipment Company. The real
situation in the company contrasted at every point with the norms
of behavior that the design engineers and other members of the
company had been taught to accept. In fact the whole language—
titles of officers, names of committees—in which the organization
of the company was described was unrealistic. "The competent
man needs no supervision"; "A man's authority is not to be personal but functional"; "Committee management is superior to individual management"; "Control should be democratic"—these
were the official slogans of the company and commanded the
wholehearted assent of many of its members. Yet what were the
facts? The engineers were more narrowly supervised than they
had been in the past. Authority was certainly not functional, in
the sense in which that word was used in the company. That is,
a man's authority did not depend on his competence to do a particular job of engineering but on his position in an organization
structure. The company was still organized in the form of committees, and yet the line authority in a committee like the design
committee was vested in one man, the chairman. Control, moreover, was certainly not democratic in the sense that it was achieved
by mutual agreement among a body of equals. The engineers were
confused by, and discontented with, their method of supervision
partly because the reality contrasted with their expectations as
expressed in the norms of the company.

The company norms had not materialized out of air. We emphasized earlier that *the norms of social behavior arise out of actual
social behavior.* Certainly the norms of the Electrical Equipment
Company described, after a fashion, the actual behavior of men in
the company at a time when it was, in effect, a group of engineering
associates. But we have also pointed out that *norms, once established, tend to change more slowly than actual social behavior.*
Thus the norms of family life in American society survive from a
time when the realities of family life were somewhat different from

what they are today, and, in the same way, the old norms of the Electrical Equipment Company persisted long after the realities of company organization had changed. When, moreover, the design engineers pointed to the contrast between the norms and the realities, they were not merely rationalizing a discontent that had quite other sources—the decline in their social rank. A man is rationalizing when his alleged reasons for his attitudes are different from his real reasons, but a man has a real reason for discontent when his leaders tell him to expect one situation but make him face another, and this was just what had happened to the design engineers.

The design engineers judged the state of affairs existing in 1939 by a set of norms appropriate to 1932; management gave its loud approval of the norms, yet it criticized the design engineers when they acted in accordance with the norms, when they showed that they were not altogether ready to accept their reduced sphere of activity and its necessary intermeshing with other spheres. The result was that the engineers at last turned their resentment on the norms themselves and said they were meaningless. It is true that men never do behave the way they say they ought to behave; in fact they never behave in quite the way they say they behave. At the same time, no set of norms can be wholly out of line with the possibilities of the real world. If it is, it loses its value both as an incentive and as a standard of judgment. For centuries moralists have tried to decide where the point of diminishing returns comes. For the norms of the Electrical Equipment Company, perhaps it had come. Certainly the tenor of the investigators' recommendations was that the norms of the company and the language in which its organization was described should be brought into agreement with reality.

After this long analysis, we can say that the discontent of the design engineers with their supervision was probably the result *both* of their lowered social rank in the company *and* of the contrast between the norms of company organization and the reality.

REACTION ON THE EXTERNAL SYSTEM

According to our method, we make a virtue of necessity and end where we began. As a result of changes in the external system of the company, partly a matter of natural growth and partly carried out by management in a deliberate effort to adjust the enterprise more effectively to its environment, certain other changes took place in the internal system. We have paid special attention to a decline in the social rank of the design engineers. Together with the survival from an earlier period in the company's history of a picture of company organization that could not easily be reconciled with existing facts, this decline in rank led to the dissatisfaction of the design engineers, and their dissatisfaction put in jeopardy their enthusiasm for work and their capacity for collaborating with others. The conflict was not violent, but it was serious enough to worry the management, who felt that much of the success of the enterprise depended on the contentment of the design engineers. In short, a better adjustment of the enterprise to its environment in one area led, through the connections of the external and internal systems with one another and of both with social norms, to a worse adjustment in another. In the Electrical Equipment Company the worse adjustment did not go so far as a breakdown; in other organizations it has. The evidence suggests that, in passing from one state of affairs to another, there may be some one path for a social system, some one set of concomitant changes in the elements of the system, that makes conflict minimal. The leader of an organization often attempts, rightly or wrongly, consciously or unconsciously, successfully or unsuccessfully, to find this path. To this question we shall return in the next chapter.

CHAPTER 16

The Job of the Leader

Orders and Norms . . . Authority and Control . . . A
Moving Equilibrium . . . The Behavior of the Leader

IN EARLIER chapters we have studied the posi-
tion of the leader in static groups, or groups that were described as
if they were static; that is, we have studied the leader as he pre-
sides over group activities that change little with the passage of
time. And we have studied social change, but, except to some extent in the Electrical Equipment Company, only such change as
takes place without planning and conscious direction. In this chapter we shall try to link the problem of the leader with the problem
of social change by examining the leader as he tries deliberately to
bring his group from one social state to another. For many persons,
this is the most interesting side of the study of group life; certainly
most has been written about it, and we shall have least to add.[1]

ORDERS AND NORMS

The leader brings his group from one social state to another
through giving orders that govern, in greater or less degree, the behavior of the members; at least giving orders is a part of what he
does. "Orders" may seem too strong a word for the directions given,
often very informally, by the leader of a small group, but there is,
perhaps, no single word that has just the right shade of meaning,
and if we remember that an order, in a group as in a formal organization, is a communication from the leader which governs the
behavior of the members, we shall not get into trouble. Surely much
that Doc said to the Nortons was orders in this sense.

[1] Particularly in this chapter, but in many of the earlier ones as well, our
ideas are in debt to C. I. Barnard, *The Functions of the Executive.*

Our first point is that orders are not different in kind from norms. Both norms and orders are verbal statements, and both specify what the behavior of the members of a certain group ought to be rather than what it really is. The only difference between the two is that norms apply to the maintenance of established behavior, orders to future changes in behavior. And between the norms of a group—the ideals of behavior that are deemed perennial—and the orders it obeys—the directions issued by a leader in order to adjust behavior to changing circumstances—there is every gradation of difference. Constitutions, laws, customs, standing orders, plans, directives, instructions, advice, suggestions—these are some of the words we apply to the gradations. When the head of a farm family gives the signal, every year, for starting activities that are the same every year, is he giving orders or putting old norms into effect? From fundamental law, to recurrences like the yearly cycle on a farm, to orders permanently changing the purposes of a group, to orders governing the behavior of an individual for a short time, there are only steps. And the impermanent is always becoming permanent: orders are always changing into law and custom.

Just as established behavior seldom coincides altogether with norms, so, as we all know and as social scientists must remember, orders are seldom obeyed to the letter and are often flagrantly disregarded. There is always a question of the degree to which behavior conforms to norms or orders; and it is not easy to say at what point the gap between the real and the ideal becomes so large that the norm or order, since it is so obviously unattainable, defeats its own purpose by turning men into cynics. Wise leaders know that nothing is so destructive of co-operation as the giving of orders that cannot or will not be obeyed.

Since orders envisage a future state of affairs for a group, the giving of orders may be looked on as the inculcation of group purposes. As usual in social science, two or more language systems are available for use in discussing the same problem: we may say that the leader gives orders or that he assigns purposes, but we must not think there are two problems just because there are two languages. A general order gives a broad or distant objective to the group; a specific order names a subsidiary objective that must be reached on the way to the major one—subsidiary for the group as a whole or subsidiary as applying to one subgroup or department within the group. When orders are transmitted downward from the leader, through his lieutenants, to the rank and file, the general purposes are often made progressively more specific.

Both norms and orders emerge from interaction between the members of a group, and again the differences seem to be matters of degree and not of kind. Norms often arise from the diffuse interaction of the members, who associate together for a while, and then, as if overnight, the group norms crystallize and take shape. One day they were followed, though not consciously held; the next day the group is aware of them. The origin of the norms, if it was ever known, is apt to be forgotten. The group has no memory of a time when the norms were *not* held, be that memory short or long. Thus no one knew the origin of the output standard in the Bank Wiring Observation Room. Orders, on the other hand, tend to arise from patterned rather than diffuse interaction. In the Norton Street Gang, we saw that, although a suggestion for group action might originate with anyone in the group, the suggestion had to get to the leader, who had to adopt it and transmit it to his lieutenants, before it could govern group behavior. Orders arise from interaction in established channels, but even in this respect the differences between orders and norms may not be great. Norms, like orders, may be established by the leader. It is hard to believe that bowling would have been adopted as a customary activity of the Nortons if Doc had not sanctioned it—and if he had not been skilled at bowling.

AUTHORITY AND CONTROL

The leader cannot bring his group from one social state to another unless his orders are, to some extent, obeyed. We have just seen that orders differ from norms not in kind but in degree: in the degree to which they apply to future change and in the degree to which they arise from patterned interaction. This suggests that a theory of authority—obedience to orders—will be of the same general kind as a theory of social control—obedience to norms, and if we recognize the similarity we may spare ourselves some repetition. We turn now to the theory of authority.

In studying the leaders who have appeared in our cases—Taylor (W3), Doc, the father of a Tikopia family—we have pointed out that one factor determining the social rank of the leader and the sentiments that the other members of the group adopt toward him is his origination of interaction to which the members respond. We spoke in this way only as a temporary expedient, because we wished to postpone the study of social control and authority, but now we must tuck in the loose ends of our argument. It is possible to pick out the leader of a group by following the chains of interaction in the group. The leader is at the center of the web of interaction: much interaction flows toward him and away from him. But it is impossible to define the leader merely by saying that he is the person who most often originates interaction for the other members of the group. We must also know the content of his orders and the degree to which they are obeyed. A member of a group may make a suggestion to the rest, and they will greet it with scornful laughter. He has originated interaction to which the others have responded, but the response is not the one he wished, and he is obviously not a leader. The high social rank of the leader and the respect that is accorded him are determined by the fact that he originates interaction for the group by giving orders that are in fact obeyed. In discussing the position of the leader we have simply, up to now, noted the fact that his orders are obeyed. Now we need to explain why his orders are obeyed; we need a theory of authority.

But what is authority? We need a definition, and here it is. *If an order given by a leader to a member of his group is accepted by the member and controls his activity in the group, then the order is said to carry authority.*[2] This definition implies that the authority of an order always rests on the willingness of the persons to whom it is addressed to obey it. Authority, like control, is always a matter of individual decision. This idea runs counter to ordinary forms of

[2] This definition is adapted from C. I. Barnard, *The Functions of the Executive*, 163. Barnard was writing about large formal organizations, but he feels that the nature of authority is the same in the group as in the formal organization. See *ibid.*, 161: "We may reasonably postulate that, whatever the nature of authority, it is inherent in the simple organization unit; and that a correct theory of authority must be consistent with what is essentially true of these unit organizations."

speech and legalistic definitions. We speak of leaders as "the authorities" or as "persons in authority," and we say that they can "delegate authority" to others. That is, we talk as if authority were something inherent in leaders and flowing from them. Our definition reminds us that the power of the leader always depends on his being able, by whatever methods, to carry his group with him; it reminds us of the great commonplace that government rests on the consent of the governed.

Following Chester Barnard, we must put out a warning here. Nothing in our definition implies that authority is gained only by democratic methods.[3] Indeed this word "democratic" may not be easily applicable to many small groups. Was control in the Nortons, for example, democratic or not? "Democracy" and "democratic" are best used to describe the actual machinery of government in countries like Great Britain and the United States. Freedom of speech, the habeas corpus, the secret ballot, the party system, the election of officers and representatives, and so forth, can be fairly well defined, and we can reason about democracy when it means these things. Sometimes democratic methods create and maintain authority; sometimes they are destructive of it. No democratic nation uses democratic methods in every sphere of its life, or can do so. But to talk about the democratic "atmosphere" or "way of life" of a group often leads away from careful reasoning, so ill defined are these terms, and it makes dictators happy by further muddying the meaning of "democracy," a result that they themselves have done their best to accomplish. The fact is that leadership in a group may be at one time abrupt, forceful, centralized, with all communications originating with the leader, and at another time slow, relaxed, dispersed, with much communication back and forth between leader and followers. Each mode is acceptable, appropriate, and authoritative, but each in different circumstances.

When we define authority as the decision of individual members of a group to obey orders, we raise the question why authority in many groups is the strong and stable thing we see it is. How can so firm a structure rest on such an apparently weak foundation as individual choice? The answer to this question is the same for au-

[3] *Ibid.*, 167n. See also C. I. Barnard, "Dilemmas of Leadership in the Democratic Process," in his *Organization and Management*, 24-50.

thority as for control. Although it is true that obedience is always
a matter of individual choice, yet the group, both leader and followers, does a great deal to see that the individual chooses right.
But let us make sure, by taking an example, that we know what
this very loose statement means.

Suppose that Doc, as leader of the Nortons, had decided to stage
a bowling match and had chosen the members of the team. What
incentives would lead a team member to obey Doc's orders and
appear for the match? He might enjoy the game for its own sake;
he would have the pleasure of associating with other members of
the group, and he would have a chance to improve his bowling
record, a matter of some importance, as social rank among the
Nortons was determined in part by bowling scores. If a member
failed to appear, he would forego all these advantages. He would
also spoil the sport for the others, who would have to find someone
to take his place, and therefore he would have to expect retaliation,
whether recognizable as such or not. On another occasion he might
not be asked to be a team member. Some of the other members
might become less friendly toward him, and he might suffer a fall in
his standing in the group. He might even get a bawling out from Doc,
which again would hurt his standing. Finally, he might be dropped
from the group altogether, and the strength of this threat would
depend on the relationship between the individual, the group, and
its social environment. Could he, for instance, find another group to
join? We need not pursue the example further, as the ideas are
already familiar to us. The points we need to make are these:
1. Authority, like control, depends on the fact that disobedience
brings about a number of punishments and not just one. The punishment does not fit the crime, but it is out of proportion to it.
2. The punishments are implicit in the relationships of the social
system. The elements of the system are interconnected in such a
way that if a man disobeys an order, his action automatically does
damage to his interactions, his friendships, his social rank, and the
attitude of the leader toward him. 3. The action of the leader to
punish the offender is only one of the controls that come into effect. The interests of the followers as well as those of the leader
are hurt, and this, we assert, will be found to hold good whenever
authority is effective in the small group.

A MOVING EQUILIBRIUM

Since we have been following out the parallel between control and authority, let us carry our comparison one step further. We have seen that control is not always effective. The reactions of a group to a man's departure from his existing degree of obedience to a norm may have the effect not of bringing his behavior back to that degree of obedience but of driving his behavior even further away from it. Therefore we have said that a social system is in equilibrium and control is effective only when the state of the elements that enter the system and of the mutual relations between them is such that any small change in one of the elements will be followed by changes in the other elements tending to reduce the amount of that change. By this definition, a social system is in equilibrium when any change is followed by a tendency of the system to return to its previous state. But what if the system is already in process of change? Shall we abandon the idea of equilibrium in these circumstances?

In this chapter we are studying the job of the leader as he tries, with conscious intent, to bring his group from one social state to another. Let us suppose, to take a hypothetical case, that a leader wants to change his industrial firm from a small one, carrying out a few, small-scale activities but also paying few workers and buying few supplies, into a somewhat larger one, carrying out large-scale activities but also paying many workers and buying many supplies. And let us suppose that he will wish, as of course he will, to maintain at a high level, throughout the period of change, the willingness of his workers to co-operate. We may think of the leader as causing the group, by the orders he gives, to follow a path leading from the initial state of the group to the final one. One path, moreover, may be better than another. Just as a man walking across rough country may reach his goal more quickly or with less fatigue by following a roundabout path along the contours of the land than by following a compass course uphill and downhill, so the leader in the group we are considering may attain his goal more easily by some other method than merely trying to increase the physical size of his firm. As we have seen, the expansion of the

Electrical Equipment Company and the increasing complexity of
its organization had results that ended in the discontent of the design engineers. If the leaders of the company, while trying to increase the size of the firm, had carried out compensatory changes
in other aspects of its social organization, changes tending, for instance, to maintain the rank of the design engineers and to keep
the norms of the firm in line with realities, they might have brought
about the expansion of the firm and kept the morale of its members
unimpaired as well. For any group moving toward a goal, there
may be some one path, some changing balance of conditions, in
which the willingness of its members to co-operate with one another and obey orders is most fully maintained.[4]

But let us suppose that the leader has chosen the path he will
try to get his group to follow, whether or not that path is the "best"
by some standard or other. He is not trying, by his orders, to maintain an existing state of affairs but to create a steadily changing
state. And we shall say that *a social system is in moving equilibrium
and authority exists when the state of the elements that enter the
system and of the relations between them, including the behavior of
the leader, is such that disobedience to the orders of the leader will
be followed by changes in the other elements tending to bring the
system back to the state the leader would have wished it to reach
if the disobedience had not taken place.* By this definition a social
system is in moving equilibrium when a departure from the path
the leader has laid out for it is followed by a tendency of the sys-

[4] Just as the path of a man walking across rough country is defined by the
space co-ordinates of every point on the path, so the path of the group would,
in theory, be defined by the simultaneously changing values of the very much
larger number of variables entering the social system. Some long-established
groups may have found paths of least disturbance for some often repeated
social changes. In describing the rules governing the choice of a wife in primitive societies, Coon writes, "The ideal or preferred mating is one which under
normal circumstances will produce the minimum of disturbance to all persons
in any way concerned."—C. S. Coon, *A Reader in General Anthropology,*
602-3. A. R. Radcliffe-Brown, whose ideas have become so much a part of
anthropological thinking that their author is often forgotten, was probably the
first to state this rule, but the reference has not been found. To a student
of mechanics the rule is particularly interesting, because in that science the
equation of equilibrium is the logical equivalent of the equation of least
action. See E. Mach, *The Science of Mechanics,* 470. See also G. K. Zipf,
Human Behavior and the Principle of Least Effort.

tem to return to the path. We shall make no effort here to define moving equilibrium for a group that is changing spontaneously, so to speak, and without much central direction, for in this case we have nothing like the intentions of a leader to indicate the path the group is following.

Just as not every state of a social system is one in which control is effective, so not every state is one in which authority, as we have defined it, exists. If, for instance, the officers of the Electrical Equipment Company had decided to punish the design engineers for their failure to collaborate with others in the firm, they might easily have created a condition in which any future orders they gave would not have brought the group closer to the goal they had in mind but driven the group farther away from it. The design engineers would have been rebellious and might even have resigned, putting the whole future of the company in jeopardy. Everyday exercise of leadership is full of results like this.

What we have been saying can be put in simpler, if less precise, language. Authority—the acceptance of orders—and control—obedience to the norms of a group—are not different in kind from one another but are two forms of the same process. And the job of a leader is twofold: (a) to attain the purposes of the group, and (b) in so doing to maintain a balance of incentives, both reward and punishment, sufficient to induce his followers to obey him.[5]

THE BEHAVIOR OF THE LEADER

Let us now turn to the question: How should the leader behave in order to maintain a moving equilibrium in his group? In trying to answer it, we shall state a few rules or maxims for the behavior of the leader. We shall not try to include all the rules that might be given, but only those that follow from what we have learned about the group, the position of the leader, and the nature of authority. All of the rules we give will be familiar, for humanity has had long experience of leadership and has thought long and hard about its problems. But the conclusions reached have been stated and learned as rules of thumb. We are less interested in the rules

[5] This is Barnard's distinction between *effectiveness* and *efficiency*. See C. I. Barnard, *The Functions of the Executive*, 55-9.

themselves than in their justification by a body of theory, less interested in what the rules are than in why they are good rules.

But one truth must first be made clear beyond possibility of misunderstanding. There are no rules for human behavior that apply in every situation without limit or change. Humanity yearns for certainty; it has looked for such rules for thousands of years but has not found them. For every principle it has discovered, it has also discovered a conflict of principles. In recent years men of practical affairs—industrial executives, for instance—have often come to psychologists and sociologists begging for a plan or set of rules that the executives can apply "across the board"—that is, in all circumstances—in dealing with their employees. There are no such rules, and if there were, they would be dangerous. They might work well for a time; then changing circumstances would make them inappropriate, and the leader would have to deal with a new situation while his mind was clogged with old rules. The maxims of leadership we shall state are, therefore, not to be taken as absolutes but only as convenient guides for the behavior of a leader. They apply only within limits determined by the situation that faces him, and there are situations in which the maxims will conflict with one another. What a leader needs to have is not a set of rules but a good method of analyzing the social situation in which he must act. If the analysis is adequate, a way of dealing with the situation will suggest itself. And if, as a working guide, the leader does have some simple rules in mind, analysis will show him where their limits lie. We do not mean that a leader need have no principles in the sense of moral standards. In fact, as we shall see, the leader must be more fully controlled by the morality of his group than any of his followers. We do mean that moral or other principles alone, unsupported by understanding, will not help him lead. It is a method of analysis rather than a set of rules that we learn in this book.

Let us also put on the record, lest we be accused of naïvety, that many men have been successful leaders without any conscious intellectual understanding whatever of the problem of leadership. We are merely stating explicitly what they do intuitively. This does not mean that conscious understanding is of no use. The number of "natural" leaders is probably inadequate to meet the needs of the complex modern world. The deficit can only be made up by leaders who are trained, and training implies conscious understanding—plus responsible practice under supervision.

And finally let us point out that we are making an important assumption, which may in many circumstances be contrary to fact. We are assuming that the leader is able to carry out the rules we propose. If he is the leader of an independent or semi-independent group he may be able to do so, but most small groups in our society are not of this sort. They are, instead, parts of larger formal organizations. The leader of a small group of this kind may not be in a position, by reason of the behavior of his own superior or of the organization and policies of the larger organization, to follow the rules that would make him, by our standards, an ideal leader. This may, indeed, be one of the most serious problems created by large formal organizations, and we cannot blame the leader if, in these circumstances, he adapts himself to realities and does the best he can.

With these points clear, let us go on to our rules of leadership.

1. *The leader will maintain his own position.*[6] A leader will be able to do nothing to lead his group unless he is established as a person from whom authoritative orders will come. The results of an order may or may not turn out to be acceptable to the members of a group, but if the members will not give the leader for a time the benefit of the doubt, if they are not willing to obey the order and wait and see whether the results are acceptable, the leader will not even begin to maintain moving equilibrium. He will have, so to speak, no working capital. The field within which orders are accepted by the members of a group without conscious questioning of their acceptability is called by Barnard the "zone of indifference."[7] The extent of the zone is determined by many factors, but one certainly is pre-eminent. The members of a group will obey many orders without consciously questioning their acceptability if they come from a person in constituted authority. In formal organizations the initial presumption that a man's orders are to be obeyed

---

[6] In setting up these rules we have been much helped by the best body of practical advice to supervisors we know: W. F. Whyte, *Human Relations in the Restaurant Industry*, Part IV.

[7] *The Functions of the Executive*, 168-9.

is established by giving him a title and an office, and by hedging the office about with the symbols of authority. In small, informal groups, the equivalent of office and title is high social rank. We have seen that, in the small group, the person who originates inter-action for other members of the group is in fact of higher rank than they. If, therefore, a leader is to originate interaction for a group, he must establish and maintain his rank. Many leaders, especially if they are new to a group, will, before they try to reach their ob-jectives, wait until they have established their own position. This may mean delay, but here as in so many other aspects of leadership, delay in the beginning means speed in the end.

2. *The leader will live up to the norms of his group.* But what must a leader do to maintain his social rank? We have seen that in the small group the person of the highest social rank is the person who comes closest to realizing in his behavior the norms of the group. Thus any failure on the part of the leader to live up to the group norms undermines his social rank and hence the presumption that his orders are to be obeyed. He must also be as zealous as any-one else in obeying his own orders. This is the truth we usually ex-press by saying *noblesse oblige* or "The leader must set an exam-ple." The old command, "Do as I say, not as I do," is fatal to leader-ship.

It is important to point out that the norms in question are the actual norms of the group and not what the leader believes the norms ought to be. In fact it is only when he has shown by his actions that he accepts the group norms that he can induce the group to adopt his own norms. We have been focusing on the small group, but much that we say can also be applied to larger social units. Thus one of the main problems in American industry today is that management often holds, perfectly sincerely, an idea of what constitutes right and proper behavior in industry that is rather unlike the idea held by the workingmen themselves. A politician like President Roosevelt had a much stronger hold on workingmen than any industrial leader because he showed in his behavior that he understood, and was working in accordance with, the working-man's actual norms.

What is important to the followers is always important to the leader. People often say that a leader should look after his men. Less often they add that he should look after them in the matters they consider important and not simply in the ones he considers important. If he only takes care of the latter, his men will feel that his behavior is paternalistic and will resent it, no matter how much good he may do. But if he looks after the interests they themselves have at heart, he cannot go wrong. People often believe that favors should not be done in an organization: that, for instance, a man should not be allowed to go home early from work on an occasion that is important for him, if the other men are not allowed to go too. This is supposed to lay the leader open to the charge of favoritism. Doing a favor will in fact hurt the leader only if the favor is one that the group feels should not be asked, if it is one that the leader will do for one man and not, on occasion, for another, and if the leader shows that he expects a return. A favor that the members of a group feel it is proper to ask is, as far as they are concerned, a right, and no return should be expected for a simple act of justice. Yet if he shows that he is not bargaining for favors, a leader who helps his men will be helped by them in turn.

The leader must live up to the norms of the group—all the norms —better than any follower. At the same time, he is the member of the group who is most in danger of violating the norms. In disputes between two followers, he is expected to do justice, as the group understands justice, but what man can always be just? And it is the leader who may sometimes act for the good of the group and still not act wholly acceptably. His action is appropriate to the group norms in one way, but does violence to them in another. For instance, he may have to drive a man out of the group, and yet the group may feel strongly that no one should be driven out. From this conflict of norms arises the condition of moral complexity in which all leaders, at every level, live.[8]

Some writers on leadership have been accused of teaching men how to "manipulate" others, but it is not always clear what this charge means. Sometimes it seems to mean that the writers in question have been teaching men to lead others in achieving ends that

[8] See *The Functions of the Executive,* Chap. 17.

the critics themselves will not accept. Some of the critics, for instance, will not accept a greater measure of co-operation between
management and workers in American industry as an end that
ought to be achieved. They would rather have conflict in industry
in the hope that out of the defeat of one of the parties—we all know
which one—a better society would emerge. Though we may well ask
if they expect the new society by its very nature to put an end to
the need for trained leadership, we can do no more. Their accusation implies a disagreement, which we cannot resolve, about ultimate ends. Sometimes the charge of "manipulation" seems to mean
that the leader is taught to be an all-wise outsider to the group,
influencing it without being influenced by it, and directing it toward
ends neither known to, nor accepted by, the members. If this is
the charge, the critics need not worry. The danger does not exist.
Men are not such fools that they cannot read their leader's intentions. Whether he likes it or not, the leader is always a part of the
group, and he can never, except by coercion—and this, we take it,
is not manipulation—, get the group to accept his ends until he has
shown, by his actions, that he has accepted its own. All the big-
time operators in the world cannot change this fact. If, finally, those
who condemn the teaching of leadership are questioning neither the
ends for which leadership is used nor the assumption that the leader
is an outsider directing the group to ends that it would not accept
if it knew them, we can only assume that they are questioning the
use of intelligence itself in human affairs. In this book we are assuming that any future society we can envisage—capitalistic, so-
cialistic, or communistic—will need more, rather than less, trained
leadership. So far as we can teach, we are teaching all the parties
and not any one. Is it impossible to be a man of good will?

   3. *The leader will lead.* If the leader is the person who originates
interaction for the other members of the group, any failure on his
part to originate interaction, to take the initiative, as we usually say,
will make him that much less a leader. This is obvious but worth
stating clearly. When a choice about the next move to make lies
before a group, the members will expect the leader to consult them,
but they certainly expect him to take action. At every level of
social rank, both advantages and disadvantages accrue to persons
at that level, and one of the advantages of holding low rank is

precisely the chance to avoid decision. An oversupply of men anxious to have responsibility is seldom a problem of organization. There is little evidence that people object to clear, firm orders, specifying just who is to do what, at what time, and in what way, just because they are orders. Rather they welcome orders in any situation in which they deem orders appropriate, and they would be confused without orders. We are not implying that the top leader of a group must take charge on all occasions; the decision in question may only concern a subgroup and can be left to a lieutenant. We are simply saying that the leader, whatever his rank, with whom the decision rests must in fact decide. Especially in an emergency that concerns the whole group, the members will expect the top leader to take charge and give the necessary orders with all the force at his command.

4. *The leader will not give orders that will not be obeyed.* This rule is the converse of the last. If he must give orders when they are expected and will be obeyed, he must not give orders when they will not and cannot be obeyed. The leader must maintain his own position. His social rank is in mutual dependence with the authority of his orders. When he gives orders that are not obeyed, he has by that fact undermined his rank and hence the presumption on the part of the members of his group that his future orders are to be obeyed. Nothing, moreover, will create more confusion in the minds of his followers, and nothing so quickly lead them to doubt his competence.

5. *In giving orders, the leader will use established channels.* We have seen what the leader must do to establish and maintain his own position. What must he do to maintain the position of others in the group? Even in quite small groups—the Norton Street Gang, for instance—we have seen that, although the leader may interact with every member of the group, he interacts most often with the persons nearest him in social rank, and his orders tend to be transmitted to the group through these men, his lieutenants. If an initial presumption is to exist in the minds of the members that the lieutenants' orders are to be obeyed, just as the leader's own orders are obeyed, the leader must do for his lieutenants what he has already done for himself, that is, maintain their social rank. And we have seen that one of the factors determining a lieutenant's social rank is

precisely interaction with the leader. Whenever the leader originates interaction by giving an order, and he does not transmit that
order to the lieutenant, he is, by that very fact, doing injury to
the latter's rank. He is hurting the lieutenant personally; he is also
throwing doubt on the presumption that the lieutenant's orders
are to be obeyed. If the leader will need in the future to transmit
orders through the lieutenant, he has, by undermining the latter's
authority, undermined his own. Therefore, to use the everyday language of organizations, the leader must not "jump the line."

As we have said, none of these rules is an absolute. Just as the
leader himself may decide he is not the man to lead the group and
may abandon his position, so he may decide that one of his lieutenants is incompetent and try to change the organization of the
group by by-passing the lieutenant. If he does so, he will have to
accept the risks of his action, and sooner or later, when he has every
man in the right position and he has to work with an established
organization, the rule will come into effect. Generally speaking, a
leader will have enough to do in adjusting his group to its environment without disturbing, at the same time, its internal or social
organization. In fact, the more severe a group's external environment,
as with ships and armies, the more stable its internal organization
tends to be.

The rule has several corollaries. The position of the lieutenants
is maintained not only by the leader's originating interaction through
them but also by their interacting with him. If it is vital to maintain
established channels for interaction in one direction, it is vital to do
so for interaction in the other. Therefore the leader must always
allow his lieutenants to have access to him. In fact he must encourage their access. There is a theory that a leader is showing himself incompetent if he asks help from his followers. On the contrary he will, by asking for advice, help establish the position of
his lieutenants; he will confirm their view, which will be a correct
one, that he is an intelligent man;—and he will have the advice to
boot. Note that he is not asking his lieutenants to decide for him;
in some circumstances that would destroy his position. Instead he is
asking for advice on which he can base his own decision. And for
the same reason that he will originate interaction through his lieutenants, the leader will discourage interaction from his followers

to himself that does not pass through his lieutenants, especially on occasions when that interaction might lead to an authoritative decision.

If, moreover, the leader is new to the group, his first effort will be to determine what the established channels of communication are, that is, which men hold high social rank. This will not always be easy. If the group is small and informal, there may be no way of recognizing these men except by watching the actual behavior of the group, which takes time. And if the group is more formal and has some official plan of organization, the plan may be misleading. The real leaders—the men through whom communications actually pass and through whom action is secured—may be different from the official leaders.

6. *The leader will not thrust himself upon his followers on social occasions.* This rule has something in common with the old army rule that an officer should not be familiar with his soldiers, and our claim that the army is not wholly incorrect may lead critics to charge that we support the military "caste system." We do not. To say that a leader should not thrust himself upon his followers on social occasions is not to say that any one particular line should be drawn between classes in an organization. The fact is that the traditional line between officers and enlisted men was appropriate in European armies and navies in the eighteenth and nineteenth centuries, when there was a real, if deplorable, distinction in society at large between gentlemen and nongentlemen. This line does not correspond to the social realities of the United States today. But even if all members of the armed forces attended the same clubs and used the same recreational facilities—and we believe they should—, certain persons would tend to eat together, drink together, and play games together, and these persons would tend to be social and organizational equals. The groups might be much more fluid than the present classes of officers and men, but there would be groups, and nothing whatever that anyone could do would prevent it. The fact is that, as we have seen, persons who are equal in social rank tend to interact frequently with one another in a "social" context, that is, in the internal system, and our present contention is simply that there are good reasons why this condition should exist. When a leader interacts often with an ordinary follower, rather

than with one of his lieutenants, he is, by so doing, lowering his social rank, and if his orders are to be obeyed, that is just what he must not do. Or, if he does not lower his social rank, his action will have another effect just as bad. He will originate interaction, and be expected to originate interaction, in the internal system as in the external. Everyone will wait for him to take the lead socially, and if he does so, he will destroy the easy give-and-take that is the charm of association among equals. By thrusting himself socially upon his followers, the leader will lower his own rank or embarrass his followers, or both. If, moreover, he associates frequently with the followers, he is putting himself in a position in which they can bring organizational demands to bear upon him without first going to his lieutenants, and, as we have seen, he needs to protect himself from such demands. The leader, like every other member of a group, must be able at times to "get away from it all."

To say that the leader will not thrust himself upon his followers does not mean that he will not interact with them at all. As we shall see, it does not mean that he will make no effort to "know his men." And on social occasions, such as the familiar office party, when all the members of the group are present, he will make it his business to be present too and for the time being to avoid behaving like a person in authority. More than any other member of the group, the leader must be flexible in his pattern of interaction. Perhaps it is best to say that, in maintaining his own position and that of his lieutenants, the leader will interact more frequently with his lieutenants than with any of his other followers. The larger the group concerned, and the more dangerous the environment it faces, the more appropriate this rule becomes. At least it is observed most strictly in army units and on ships, that is, in groups organized for emergency action in a dangerous environment. When orders must, at some time in the life of the group, be peremptory and accepted without question, the zone of indifference must be large, and it follows directly from our argument that, the larger the zone of indifference is to be, the more firmly the leader's social rank must be established. Although it may seem to run counter to the democratic creed, our contention is that the age-old experience of humanity with social units like armies and ships is not to be lightly dismissed as hidebound conservatism. Authority is a weighty thing and has inescapable consequences. But the rule can be, and obviously is, relaxed as the group becomes smaller and more nearly "autonomous."

7. *The leader will neither blame nor, in general, praise a member of his group before other members.* The leader has much to do with establishing the social rank of his followers. When he blames a man in public, he is lowering, or attempting to lower, the man's social rank, that is, the degree of esteem in which he is held by the members of the group. But the leader is not the only man who determines social rank; the opinions of the other members count for something too. They may not be ready to accept the leader's evaluation. When he blames a follower in public, he is not only humiliating the man; he may also be putting in doubt his own reputation for justice—his capacity for living up to the norms of the group. If, moreover, the person he blames is one of his lieutenants, he is impugning the source through which his own orders will pass, and therefore helping to destroy authority. Though it is not generally recognized, the same argument that applies to blame applies also to praise. Occasional public praise of a man is admirable, but frequent praise may embarrass him, because it may show that the leader is giving him an evaluation that the rest of the group is not ready to accept. So praise by all means. Nothing is more important. But praise in private.

8. *The leader will take into consideration the total situation.* We have studied what the leader must do to maintain his own position and that of others in the group. If he has done these things effectively, he will have created a zone of indifference, that is, an initial presumption that his orders and those of his lieutenants will be obeyed by members of the group without questioning whether these orders are acceptable or not. This is the leader's working capital. We now turn to the problem of what he does with it. What must the leader do to insure that he will give acceptable orders? If the results of his orders have satisfied individual motives for co-operation while the group has moved toward its objectives, this fact alone will do more to maintain the zone of indifference than any other action he can take. The leader's future orders will be obeyed because the members of the group have not regretted their obedience to his past orders. Or, as we say, nothing succeeds like success.

We cannot answer in detail the question what positive action the leader must take to maintain moving equilibrium, because the answer depends on the situation facing the group concerned, but we can say that he will be well advised to consider the total situation. Note that we say he must *consider* the total situation. He may not be able to act, and he may not need to act, on every element of it, but he certainly will not be able to act, because it will not have occurred to him to act, on an element he has not thought of. In achieving its purposes, the group will effect change, and will itself be affected by changes, in the following fields: (1) the environment, both physical and social, the latter including the larger groups of which the group itself is a part and the groups of which it is not a part but with which it is in contact; (2) the materials, tools, and techniques with which the group operates on the environment; (3) the external system, that is, the relations between the members of the group necessary for group action on the environment; (4) the internal system, that is, the further social relations that elaborate upon the external system and react upon it; and (5) the norms of the group. In the effort to maintain a moving equilibrium, the leader will have to remember that, since they are mutually dependent, a change in any one of these elements will, in general, bring about changes in *all* the others, changes for which he may have to allow and compensate.

The story of mankind is full of the unforeseen and unintended consequences of social action, and more often than not they were unforeseen because the mutual relations of the elements were not understood, particularly the mutual relations of the external and internal systems. The management of the Hawthorne Plant tried to set up the work in the Bank Wiring Room in such a way that output would steadily increase. Instead, the very setup of the work tended to put in motion a social development that partly defeated management's plan. The officers of the Electrical Equipment Company, trying to sell more of its products, put in motion further changes that ended in the discontent of the design engineers, thus placing the firm's survival in jeopardy again. In both cases, some of the results of social change were unintended and were determined by the mutual relations of the external and internal systems. The internal system is, in fact, the aspect of organization of which

Americans, in their conscious thinking, are least aware. They will design admirable technical processes and organizations for putting the processes into effect, but they do not understand, or do not understand in such a way that their understanding leads to effective action, the relations between technology, organization, and the other aspects of a social system. Perhaps they cannot see the relations. As we have said over and over again, for something to be seen it is not enough that it should be in plain sight. People have to be taught to see it. And they can think about nothing complex until they have a way of thinking about it. Americans are taught adequate ways of thinking about technology and organization; they are not taught adequate ways of thinking about social systems. A leader cannot examine the whole situation inside and outside his group unless he has a method for taking up each element of the situation in order and in its relation to the other elements. It is not enough to have a mystic sense of the whole; nor is it enough to have intuitive "social skills" that, all too easily, lead up a dead-end street to the "big-time operator." What is needed is explicit, conscious, intellectual understanding, and this is what a book like ours aims to produce. Even this is not enough, but, by all that is holy in the human spirit, without this the rest is dust and ashes.

9. *In maintaining discipline, the leader will be less concerned with inflicting punishment than with creating the conditions in which the group will discipline itself.* As leaders of small groups, many of us discovered that the more punishment we inflicted the more we had to inflict. We were led astray by the fallacy that a man disobeys orders out of sheer perversity. Usually there are more compelling reasons why he disobeys, though he may not be aware of them. If you punish him without considering or changing the reasons, they will persist and lead him to disobey you again, while his resentment of the punishment you have inflicted will give him still further reason for disobedience. He will want to get back at you, and he now knows how he can make you angry. In the Electrical Equipment Company, it would probably have been idle for the officers to bawl out the design engineers for their failure to cooperate fully with other members of the firm. The conditions that created their discontent would have remained; the engineers would have resented criticism and fought back.

When something has gone wrong in the group, the leader had better take aside the man who is apparently responsible and, instead of bawling him out, ask him to explain how the mistake was made and how it can be avoided another time. The leader will then accomplish several useful results: (1) He will escape the danger of punishing an innocent person. (2) If the man who seems to be responsible is in fact responsible, the leader will avoid humiliating him and hurting his standing in the group. (3) The leader may begin to learn what the underlying difficulty is. (4) By asking the man to explain what happened, the leader may be taking the most effective step toward preventing the mistake from happening again. In the course of his explanation, the man may begin to see the underlying difficulty for himself, and seeing is the first step toward correcting.

As we have observed in our study of authority, obedience to orders depends on the self-correcting relationships of the social system, and in these relationships the action of the leader in punishing a wrongdoer is only a part and often a small one. What the leader needs to do is not just punish the wrongdoer but examine the social system and correct the conditions that led to a breakdown of authority. Faced with the discontent of the design engineers, the leaders of the Electrical Equipment Company did something of just this sort. We will recognize that it is not always easy to do, but the leader should be thinking along these lines, rather than simply trying to determine responsibility and inflict punishment. We are not, be it clearly stated, saying that the leader should never inflict punishment. If the offense is important, if it is clearly a violation of group norms, and if the responsibility has been determined beyond a shadow of doubt, then the group and even the offender himself may expect the leader to punish, and he may weaken his position if he does not. But punishment without search for the underlying difficulty treats the symptoms and not the disease.

The rule we have stated is perhaps implied in a more inclusive one: the leader will treat the group as a group and not as a set of individuals. His actions will conform to the material in which he works. We have seen what an admirable discipline a group will spontaneously develop in support of a norm it has accepted for itself. The Bank Wiremen accepted, in support of restriction of output, a discipline more severe than any the company could impose on them to attain its aims. The leader will work with this characteristic of group behavior and not against it. He will not try to get individuals as such to adopt the purposes he has in mind but get the group as a whole to adopt them. In the Bank Wiring Observation Room, no individual could have increased output very far, without bringing down the overwhelming wrath of the others upon him, but the group as a whole could have decided to increase output. Let the leader first earn his leadership. Let him first establish with the group the kind of relationship summed up in our earlier rules. When he has established the relationship, then, if ever, the group will be ready to make his purposes theirs. And if they do accept his decision, they can be counted on to oversee its execution much more effectively than he can himself. All that we know of the group teaches us that an appropriate discipline will be forthcoming. The leader will not breathe down the necks of his men. Leave the group alone!

10. *The leader will listen.* If the leader is to give the orders that maintain a moving equilibrium, he must be informed about the whole situation inside and outside his group. But even in the small group, he is never adequately informed by his own direct observation; he must, in part at least, be informed by others. Although he is placed at the center of a web of communication in his group and therefore in a good position to get information, he will not get it just because the communication channels exist. The real question is how they are to be used. Everybody talks about the importance of two-way communication in an organization, the importance of communication from follower to leader as well as from leader to follower, but few people tell us what shall be communicated and how communication upward shall be encouraged. In the relationship between leader and follower we have found two opposing forces at work. On the one hand, a follower naturally seeks interaction with a leader he admires; on the other hand, authority is a weighty thing, and we have seen how it tends to cut down interaction between leader and follower and make the follower's attitude one of distance and respect rather than close friendliness. Between equals in an

organization, an easy give-and-take will tend to build itself up without deliberate contrivance. There is little to prevent it. But the leader cannot assume that free communication from his followers to him will come naturally. In his ambivalent position, he must *do* something to encourage it. There is a resistance, which he must work to overcome. Moreover, the leader must be informed about the whole situation, and many facts and feelings in the whole situation, particularly personal problems and social relationships, are inherently hard to communicate. A man does not want to talk about them, or he has no clear language in which to talk about them, as he would, for instance, have a precise terminology for talking about a piece of machinery. Here then is the twofold problem of the leader: (*a*) how to encourage his followers to talk about *anything* that is on their minds in (*b*) a situation that makes communication inherently difficult.

He cannot solve the problem merely by saying that he is always ready to see his followers, and that "his door is always open." This will be a joke in very bad taste if it remains merely a slogan. The leader must do something, not say something, and, first, he must seek interaction with his followers. This may seem to conflict with the rule that the leader should not thrust himself upon his followers on social occasions, but that rule applies most clearly to situations in which several of the followers are gathered together, and the leader will not violate it if he seeks interaction with each of his followers alone. When, moreover, he seeks an opportunity for interaction, his purpose must not be to pump the follower, for that will lead to less communication rather than more, but to do something very different—just pass the time of day with the follower and show that he, the leader, is friendly and interested. In short the leader must, if he is to receive communications, show by his actions that the channels are open. Or, as the rule is usually stated, "the leader must know his men."

But it is when a follower comes to him that the leader's real work begins, and it *is* work, though it may not sound so. For the hardest thing in the world for a man to do is keep his mouth shut, and that is just what the leader must do: he must listen. We shall not here go into the various means by which one man can encourage full communication from another. They are well stated elsewhere.[9] But the first and golden rule is: listen. Let the leader show he is interested, but let him not interrupt so long as his follower has anything he wants to say. It would seem obvious that if the leader is to be kept fully informed by the members of his group, he must allow them to inform him, which means that he must keep quiet himself, but no rule of leadership is more often violated, partly because leaders are apt to be active and energetic men and like to talk. The fact is that a leader should have a high capacity to vary his rate of activity: he must be active at one moment and passive at the next.

The second rule is: accept. The leader must not take a moral stand and show approval or disapproval of what is being said. He must accept—utterly, or, as some say, he must create a permissive atmosphere. No doubt there are occasions when it is appropriate for a man to take a moral stand, but he should never do so while he is listening to someone else trying to say what is on his mind. A leader is told only what he wants to hear; therefore he must show that he wants to hear *everything*. Moreover, he must not take action on what he is told unless the follower clearly shows that he wants action. Many questions that a follower will wish to discuss with his leader he will not discuss if he knows the leader is going to take immediate action on them. The greatest barrier to free communication between follower and leader is the leader's authority; a person in authority is a person who gives orders and upholds a moral norm. If, therefore, the leader, while he is listening to the follower, takes a moral stand or threatens to take action, he is bringing back the weight of authority, which is just what he wants to lift for the time being. The leader must not only be available—his door must be open—but also keep quiet when he is available.

If the leader listens and accepts, what will he accomplish? First, he will become better and better informed, and informed about more and more aspects of the whole situation, technical and social, facing his group. Let him remember that the problems important for his followers are always important for him. Second, the follower's thinking will change while he talks. As he talks about his own

[9] See especially, F. J. Roethlisberger and W. J. Dickson, *Management and the Worker*, Chap. XIII, "The Interviewing Method," and C. Rogers, *Counselling and Psychotherapy*.

problems and those of his group, he will see the problems more clearly, and his seeing them clearly is the first step toward his effective action on them. The leader will have to give fewer orders himself if the other members of the group have seen for themselves what the orders ought to be. Control will be decentralized. Third, the evidence is that nothing increases the respect and gratitude of one man for another more than the other's listening to him fully and with interest. This is part of the phenomenon the Freudians call *transference.* And finally, the encouragement of free communication on one occasion will lead to still freer communication on another. Communication feeds on communication.

11. *The leader will know himself.* This rule does not follow from our analysis of the group, but it badly needs stating. All of us who are, or have been, leaders of groups know most of these rules, intuitively or with conscious awareness. And yet how often we violate them! As Ovid said long ago, we see the better path and we approve of it, but we take the worse. From all that has gone before, it should be obvious that the leader himself is the greatest threat to the moving equilibrium of the group. He can do most to put it in jeopardy.[10] He may be the most active member of the group, and yet he must often keep silent. He must live up most fully to the group norms, and yet he, more than anyone else, must resolve conflicts of norms. More than anyone else, he has the ends of the group at heart. If something goes wrong, he will feel an overwhelming urge to bawl someone out, and yet a bawling out may outrage the group and humiliate the offender without changing his behavior. How often has the leader acted and later wished fervently he had not! He must be under great self-control in a situation where control is difficult. If, therefore, he must know his men well, he must know himself still better. He must know the passions in him that, unchecked, will destroy him as a leader, and he must know their sources in his personality. For how can we control a force, the source of whose energy we do not know? Self-knowledge is the first step in self-control.

[10] See G. C. Homans, "The Small Warship," *American Sociological Review,* XI (1946), 294-300.

Summary

A BOOK of exposition should state in the first chap-
ter what it intends to do; in the middle chapters it should carry out
its intention, and in the last chapter it should point out what it has
done. But the present book will depart somewhat from this whole-
some rule. The last chapter will foreshadow a broad problem suggested by the study just ending—the problem of the relation between small groups and the civilization of which they are a part—
and summary will be the job of this, the next to last, chapter. Yet
"summary" is not quite the right word. We shall not attempt to review in detail the results of our study; instead we shall try to show
what kind of study we have made. If, as we admit, ours is not the
only way of going to work in sociology, we are all the more bound
to point out the special features of the method we have used. We
shall be forgiven if we move rapidly, taking for granted an understanding of many points made earlier.

THE OFFICE OF THEORY

We began by saying that this book was to be a book on sociological theory, and we quoted Willard Gibbs' statement: "It is the office
of theoretical investigation to give the form in which the results of
experiment may be expressed." Since we were sociologists and not
physicists, we were more interested in observation than in experiment, but with this change we were ready to accept Gibbs' statement

of the job of the theorist. Our way of tackling this job was to ask ourselves what kinds of observations a few able students of social behavior had actually made. If we found that these students had made the same kinds of observations, we proposed to give names to these kinds, to call them the elements of behavior, and to make them the concepts with which we should work. Then we proposed to state, in terms of these concepts, the relationships that the students of small groups had found to exist between their different kinds of observations. In this way the physicists make observations they call pressures and temperatures and then state the relation between pressure and temperature. The physicists have a common language in which they can express the results of many different investigations, and we were trying to develop for sociology a common language of the same sort. We felt that only if we developed a common language could the results of one investigation be compared with those of another, and only in this way could a growing science of sociology construct and find applicable to many different groups a single body of hypotheses about social behavior. We were trying to move toward a general theory of the small group.

THE NATURE OF THE HYPOTHESES

With these ideas in mind, we first studied three groups, the Bank Wiring Observation Room, the Norton Street Gang, and the Tikopia family, that were described as if they were static and unchanging. In our study of these groups, we formulated a few hypotheses, some of which seemed to hold good for all three groups. We limited ourselves to the very simplest hypotheses, but we tried to state them in such a way that they could conceivably be tested by observation and experiment in other groups. Even among the simplest hypotheses in sociology, only a few have yet been stated in this way, and until they are so stated, the foundations of our science will not have been laid. We shall not now attempt to repeat these hypotheses but only show what kind of hypotheses they are. For instance, we saw, both in the Bank Wiring Observation Room and the Norton Street Gang, that the more closely a man, in the activities he performs, realizes the norms of his group, the higher is his social rank in the group. Note that this rule holds good no matter

what the activities and the norms may be. The norms of the Bank
Wiremen and the activities they carried out were somewhat different from the norms and activities of the Nortons, and yet, given
the particular norms and activities of each group, the same general hypothesis held in both cases. Our elements of behavior—interaction, sentiment, activity, and norms—were in fact chosen so that
these underlying relationships, which we have called analytical
hypotheses, could be brought out. At first sight, human groups are
very different from one another. One group dwells in tents, makes
its living by herding camels, and sets a high value on the courage
men display in raiding other groups. Another group lives in houses,
works in a factory, and sets a high value on "doing a fair day's
work for a fair day's wage." At this level of investigation, the anthropologists are right in emphasizing cultural relativity and in
heaping scorn on the old saw, "Human nature is the same the
world over." Human behavior in fact varies greatly the world over.
But though behavior may vary, our belief is that the relationships
between the elements of behavior may remain the same.

We have offered our analytical hypotheses only as hypotheses. A
statistician would require much more validation before he would
accept them as proven theorems. He would have to be shown that
they hold good for many more groups than our small sample of
five: the three static groups and the two groups, Hilltown and the
Electrical Equipment Company, in process of social change. Further study may well show that our hypotheses are incorrect; it will
certainly show that they can be more precisely formulated, and
that many additional hypotheses are necessary for an adequate
analysis of even the simplest human group. We have not pretended
to tell the whole story. Yet it is an article of our faith that, correct
or incorrect, sufficient or insufficient in number though they be, our
hypotheses are of the kind that a developed social science will formulate, in that they are statements of uniformities underlying the
superficial differences in the behavior of human groups.

THE SYSTEM OF HYPOTHESES

For each group we have studied we have not presented a single
hypothesis but rather a series, or system, of hypotheses that hold

good simultaneously for the group in question. The hypotheses are many, and they are related to one another in the sense that any element that enters one hypothesis also enters some of the others. Thus an increase in the frequency of interaction between persons may increase the strength of their favorable sentiments toward one another, and it may also increase the number of activities they carry out together. It was this effort to formulate a series of related hypotheses that limited the size of our sample to five groups. If we had been interested in only one hypothesis, we could have backed it up with evidence from many more groups than five. But the presentation of enough material to support a system of hypotheses has necessarily limited the number of groups we have been able to consider.[1]

In the system of hypotheses, each one sets limits to the applicability of the others. Let us again take an example. We have seen that the more frequent the interaction between people, the stronger in general their sentiments of liking or affection for one another. But in the interaction between people we have also seen that, as one person gives orders that another must obey, the interaction between them tends to decrease toward the amount required by the external system—interaction is largely "on business"—and the emotional attitude of the subordinate toward the superior tends to be one of respect rather than close friendship. The relationship between a given leader and his follower will be determined by both of these hypotheses. To the extent that the two merely interact with one another, sentiments of affection will grow up between them, and their interaction will increase "socially" beyond the amount required by the external system. To the extent that one gives orders that the other must obey, social interaction will be held down, and sentiment will move in the direction of respect or, at worst, antagonism.

THE VALUES OF THE ELEMENTS

This discussion has thrown into high relief the greatest of the many weaknesses of our theory. How, for instance, shall we ac-

---

[1] For further discussion of some of the problems involved here, see G. C. Homans, "The Strategy of Industrial Sociology," *American Journal of Sociology,* LIV (1949), 330-7.

count for the actual relationship between a given superior and his subordinate? How shall we be able to specify the degree to which one hypothesis limits the applicability of another in a particular instance? A mathematician would say that it is one thing to set up a system of simultaneous equations and quite another to solve them. If a system of hypotheses is to account for, and ultimately to predict, the actual behavior of a group, the hypotheses themselves are not enough. We must also be able to assign values to the elements entering the hypotheses. The more often, we say, one man gives orders that another must obey, the less frequent their interaction outside the external system. This hypothesis may be true and still not tell us enough to account for the behavior of the two men. It assumes that the frequency of authoritative orders and the frequency of social interaction are mutually dependent; that is, if the first frequency is determined, the second is determined also. But if we cannot assign a value to one frequency, we cannot assign a value to the other. If we cannot say *just how often* one man gives authoritative orders to another, we cannot say *just how often* the two will interact socially. And this holds true, of course, for the other and related hypotheses in the system. In this book we have hardly begun to solve this problem. We have not been able to assign absolute values to the elements, but have only, for instance, been able to say, in comparing the Tikopia family with the Norton Street Gang, that the authority of the leader was greater and there was less social interaction between leader and followers in the former group than in the latter. That is, we have solved the problem only comparatively, in terms of less or more, not how much less or more. Progress in this direction will have to wait for the development of measurements through which we shall be able to assign values to the elements of behavior and get comparable results from group to group. We are not saying that the formulation of hypotheses is unnecessary; it is necessary and important in the highest degree. We are saying that it is insufficient. The complexities of social behavior may arise less from the hypotheses, which, though no doubt large in number, may be simple enough in form, than from their interrelationships in the circumstances of particular situations.

THE "GIVEN" FACTORS

Thus, from a new point of view, we come back to the differences between groups. Groups are alike in that many of the analytical hypotheses apply to all of them; they differ in the values of the elements entering the hypotheses. This is what we meant when we said, in earlier chapters, that groups differ in the degree to which they possess elements present in all. Moreover, the values of the elements are initially determined by what we call the "given" factors in the circumstances in which the group is placed, one of the most prominent of these factors, or sets of factors, being the group's social and physical environment. Let us go back to the relationship between superior and subordinate which we have used to illustrate the difficulties our theory gets into. In a group like the Tikopia family, which made its own living through a wide variety of operations on the physical environment, the relationship between superior and subordinate—for instance, between father and son—involved much less social interaction and much more emotional distance than did the relationship between superior and subordinate in the Norton Street Gang, a group that was largely "autonomous"; that is, its survival did not depend on the successful completion of a large number of operations on the physical environment. The hypotheses accounting for the superior-subordinate relationship are the same for both groups, but the values of the elements entering the hypotheses vary from one group to the other as the relationship between group and environment varies.

Though we have emphasized the environment at the expense of the others, it is not the only set of "given" factors. Other important factors are the size of the group and its composition in age and sex. The Tikopia family differed sharply from the other groups we studied in that it might include persons of any age and both sexes. Still another important factor is the past history of the group in question, which determines the norms handed down from one generation to another. Here again the Tikopia family differed from the other groups: it had a long cultural history behind it. Just as the characteristics of the magnetic field in and surrounding a piece of iron cannot be completely understood unless we know the past history of the iron—has it, for instance, been pounded with hammers or by the sea?—, so the behavior of a group cannot be understood without reference to its past history. Thus, the Navaho and Hopi peoples of the American Southwest now live in the same physical environment and use many of the same techniques. But these factors only set limits to the range of variation possible for the two groups, which are somewhat differently organized. The differences are determined, in part at least, by the different past histories of the two groups. In the distant past, the Hopis were, as they are now, settled farmers, whereas the Navahos were nomadic hunters.

EMERGENT EVOLUTION

We have been careful to say that the values of the variables entering the hypotheses are determined only initially by factors given by the circumstances in which the group is placed. No group adheres entirely to the relationships between its members established by the "given" factors. On the basis of these relationships new ones may emerge and react so as to change the "given" factors, for instance, the adaptation of the group to its environment or the cultural traditions handed down to the younger generation. We have tried to take account of the process of emergent evolution through our analysis of the mutual dependence of the external and internal systems.

Yet though the internal system always elaborates on the external, the "given" factors may still set limits on the distance this development can go. Thus leadership emerged in the Bank Wiring Observation Room just as it did in the Norton Street Gang and by the same processes, the processes described by our analytical hypotheses. But leadership, measured, for instance, in the frequency of the leader's origination of interaction, did not develop as far among the wiremen as it did among the Nortons. The reason for this difference seems to have been that the Western Electric Company had imposed its supervision on the group in the shape of the group chief and the section chief, and their control over the processes of work limited the field within which the informal leader could take charge. We can say, then, that groups are alike because many of the analytical hypotheses apply to all of them; that groups differ in the values of the elements entering the hypotheses; and that these values are determined by the "given" factors in the circumstances in which the group is placed and the degree to which these factors permit the internal development of the group.

SOCIAL CONTROL

We began by analyzing three groups that, because they were described as if they existed at one moment of time, could be treated as static. This allowed us to work out some of the analytical hypotheses without being encumbered by the complications of social change. In order to formulate the relationships of the social system, we assumed the stability of the system. But when the relationships had once been formulated, we turned the argument inside out and showed that stability itself depended on the relationships. We did so by looking at the relationships differentially, that is, by asking what would happen if a man's behavior departed in any way from what the investigator described it as being. Here is a man who adheres, in a certain degree, to the norms of his group. Suppose he departs a little further from the norms. Suppose, for instance, a selector wireman allows his output to fall a little below its already low level. What, if anything, then leads him to bring his output back toward the original level? We have assumed that he brings it back because the net satisfaction of his sentiments is less at the new level than it was at the old. And even if we make no assumption whatever about the satisfaction of his sentiments, we can see what the consequences of his lowered output will be. It will tend to bring him and other members of the group less pay; it will also tend to increase the strength of any sentiments of hostility his fellows hold toward him, to decrease the frequency of their interaction with him, and to lower his social rank. The consequences of his action are all determined by the relationships, which we have already discovered, between sentiment, activity, interaction, and norms. This is why we said that, at least at the level of the small group, there was nothing essentially new in the study of social control, and that control, or a method of reward and punishment, is implicit in the analytical hypotheses of the social system.

Control, moreover, is inherent in the whole system of relationships and not in one alone. Control is effective in so far as a man's departure from his existing degree of obedience to a norm has many consequences and not one only. The effects are, so to speak, out of proportion to the cause. A departure from his existing level of activity may have consequences for a man's material gains—his pay, or the favors that others do for him—for his interaction with others, and for his social rank, because his activity is related to all of these things and not one only. But again we have learned nothing we did not know already. We have merely looked differentially at the system of analytical hypotheses.

Finally, we saw that small changes do not always have results tending to bring the behavior of a member of a group back toward an earlier level. But when they do, we may give the state of the social system the same name that is given to analogous states of physical systems. Thus *equilibrium* is that special state of a social system in which the values of the elements entering the system and the relations between the elements are such that any small change in one of the elements sets in motion other changes that tend to restore the system to the condition that existed before the first change took place. Note that we have not claimed equilibrium or a tendency toward equilibrium as an inherent property of a social system. Equilibrium exists in some groups some of the time, not in all groups all of the time.

SOCIAL CHANGE

The study of equilibrium was our bridge to the study of social change. We began by assuming stability in a group; then we turned to the analysis of stability itself and studied the small changes in a social system that result in a restoration of the previous state of the system; and finally we studied the changes that do not result in a restoration of the previous state. In particular we studied two roughly distinguishable kinds of social change: social disintegration and social conflict. Hilltown was our example of social disintegration. A decrease in the number of activities in which members of the group collaborated resulted in the end in a weakening of the control exercised by the group over the behavior of its members. In fact the group hardly remained a group at all. The Electrical Equipment Company was our example of social conflict. An increase in the size of the firm and the complexity of its organization led to the lowered social rank of a group—the design engineers—within the firm and to a confusion between the norms and the realities of company life, and thus, in the end, to the discontent of the design engineers and a lowering of their capacity to work with others in the firm.

In studying social change, as in studying social control, we discovered nothing new in the relationships between the elements of behavior. We simply asked the old questions in a new way. Instead of asking how interaction and activity are related, we asked, for instance, what happens to the frequency of interaction between the members of a group when the activities performed by the group decrease in number. Thus, in studying Hilltown, we saw that as the activities the members of the group perform in the external system decrease in number, their interaction in the external system necessarily decreases. And as their interaction in the external system decreases, their interaction in the internal system—what we call, for want of a better word, their social interaction—decreases also. As the frequency of social interaction decreases, the norms of the group become less well defined and less strongly held, and, since social rank is determined by the degree to which a man lives up to the norms, social rank also becomes less firmly established. All of these changes mean that the group has fewer incentives to offer individuals for compliance with its norms and fewer punishments to impose for disobedience. The result is *anomie* or disintegration.

We must go back again to the obvious but important distinction between our system of analytical hypotheses and the values of the elements entering the hypotheses. In studying social change, we discovered no new hypotheses. What we did was watch how a change in the value of one of the elements effected changes in the values of the others. When we say that a decrease in the number of activities a group performs brings about a decrease in the frequency of interaction between the members of the group, we are stating no new hypothesis; we are studying changes in the values of elements entering a hypothesis we already know. We are studying dynamics.

But what starts these changes going in the first place? In analyzing our static groups, we pointed out that the values of the elements entering the social system were initially determined by certain "given" factors, particularly in the relation between the group and the environment in which it survives. In studying social change we did not treat these factors as given once and for all; we did not treat them as constant but as variable. Thus changes in Hilltown's environment—some of them, such as the clearing of land and the building of barns and houses, brought about by Hilltown itself, some of them, such as improved transportation, wider markets, and the rise of industry, beyond its control—made less necessary the collaboration of Hilltowners in the activities of the external system. But these external developments will not wholly account for what happened to Hilltown. The internal effects of the external changes fed back to accelerate still further the process of change. For instance, the decreasing control exercised by Hilltown society over its members may have led energetic Hilltowners to leave town still more rapidly than they would have done if the environmental change alone had been significant.

Finally, we turned to a particular form of social change: change consciously directed by the leader or leaders of a group in the effort to attain a group goal. We saw that the problem of the leader was the maintenance of moving equilibrium, the maintenance of the social system in a condition such that any departure from the path leading to the goal will set up further changes in the system tending to bring it back to the path. And we saw that the rules that must govern the leader's behavior if he is to solve his problem are contained by implication in all we have learned about the group, the relation between the leader and his followers, and the nature of social control. The best advice we could give the leader was to adapt his action to the medium in which he works.

But when we say that in studying social control and social change we have learned nothing new, we are not trying to turn our science into dust and ashes. What we have said is that the phenomena of social statics, social control, and social change, which are sometimes treated as separate fields of sociology, can be stated with more simplicity, elegance, and insight when they are considered to be contained by implication in a single series of hypotheses. But the disillusion of simplicity is not the disillusion of finality. We have stated only a few of the most elementary hypotheses in what will become a long series. The student of human affairs must always remember that his search is at its beginning, not its end.

CHAPTER 18

Groups and Civilization

The Group and Social Cohesion . . . The Birth of Civilization . . . Decline and Fall . . . The Dissolution of the Group . . . The New Groups . . . Group Conflict . . . Circulation, Communication, and Control . . . Democracy . . . The Solutions of the Problem

IN THE last chapter we need withdraw nothing we said in the first. There is still only one sufficient reason for studying the group: the sheer beauty of the subject and the delight in bringing out the formal relationships that lie within the apparent confusion of everyday behavior. No one studies, in the way that makes study count, a subject he is not passionately interested in. But if there is only one sufficient reason for studying the group, there are several other good reasons. A method of analyzing a social system might make a better leader of a man who did not ask for principles he could apply "across the board" and who knew the limitations, in practice, of all abstract studies such as ours has been. An even better reason is this: men and women who are thinking about the present state of the world may find an understanding of small group behavior illuminating. Why this is so, we shall, at the end here, try to explain, insisting that by this time we have earned the right to skip the details, to suggest rather than demonstrate. We shall in fact raise questions rather than answer them. For we are in no position to answer them. This chapter does not release us from work; it shows us the next job. We never make an end, but a new start.

THE GROUP AND SOCIAL COHESION

At the level of the tribe, the village, the small group, at the level, that is, of a social unit (no matter what name we call it by) each of whose members can have some firsthand knowledge of each of the others, human society, for many millenia longer than written history, has been able to cohere. To be sure, the cohesion has been achieved at a price. Intelligent men have always found small-town life dull, and the internal solidarity of the group has implied a distrust and hatred of outsiders. But society has at least been able to cohere. This is not to deny that groups have succumbed to the severity of the environment and the violence of enemies, but they have had at the same time few problems of internal social organization. They have even tended, as we have seen, to produce a surplus of the goods that make organization successful: morale, leadership, and co-operation between increasingly large numbers of people.

THE BIRTH OF CIVILIZATION

Throughout human history, groups have used this surplus in the attempt to grow. For most of them, the environment, physical and social, has put an end to the process before it went very far. A few have been more successful. Given an environment neither too severe nor too luxurious, groups have grown and multiplied, and social units larger than the group have begun to appear. The challenge of the environment, to use Toynbee's phrase, posed an internal challenge: If large-scale co-operation could be achieved, it would pay for itself in an increased control over a bountiful nature. In the beginning, the challenge was met most successfully in broad river valleys. There the surplus of co-operativeness, applied to clearing, draining, damming, and irrigating, brought enormous returns and encouraged further co-operation. Finally, one of the groups, much like the others but possessing some of their qualities in a higher degree, consolidated the gains, and a civilization was born. Again and again this has happened. Now a little Chinese principality at the Great Bend of the Yellow River acts as the catalyst, now a city-state in central Italy, and now a tribe, called the Franks, settled on the south shore of the English Channel. The tribes have multiplied; one, more tribal than the rest, has brought the others together.

In our view, and here we are following Toynbee again,[1] ancient Egypt and Mesopotamia were civilizations. So were classical India and China; so was the Greco-Roman civilization, and so is our own Western civilization that grew out of medieval Christendom. These societies on the grand scale have had many characteristics in common. At its height, each has been inventive: it has devised and used a more powerful technology than any at the command of the tribes coming before and after it. Each has been coterminous geographically with a communications network. In fact the existence of such a network has been the necessary precondition allowing one tribe to unite the others. Thus the Mediterranean Sea, with its satellite roads, made possible the Roman Empire. Since the organization of a tribe is incapable of controlling an empire, each civilization has also developed new formal organizations, in law, government, warfare, and religion, linking the tribes to the new center. And almost every one of the civilizations has worked out and adopted a single body of values and beliefs, shared in some degree by all the citizens. Such until recently was Christianity for the Western world.

DECLINE AND FALL

The appalling fact is that, after flourishing for a span of time, every civilization but one has collapsed. The ruling class, if there was one, has lost its capacity to lead; the formal organizations that articulated the whole have fallen to pieces; the faith has no longer commanded the allegiance of the citizens; much of the technology has even been forgotten for lack of the large-scale co-operation that could put it in effect; and after a last and inevitably futile effort to hold society together by force, the civilization has slowly sunk back to a Dark Age, a situation, much like the one from which it started out on its upward path, in which the mutual hostility of small groups is the condition of the internal cohesion of each one. At the end of the cycle the names of the tribes are different from what they were in the beginning—the Saxons are not the Sabines—but

[1] A. J. Toynbee, *A Study of History.*

tribal behavior is much the same. Society can fall this far, but apparently no farther, and having fallen this far, it may start all over again. In some parts of the world, the cycle of civilization and decay has been repeated at least twice. One can read the dismal story, eloquently told, in the historians of civilization from Gibbon to Toynbee. The one civilization that has not entirely gone to pieces is our own Western civilization, and we are desperately anxious about it. Can it get out of the rut into which the others have fallen?

To account for the decay, the historians have developed many explanations, each more adequate than the last, but the sociologists may still be able to contribute something. Our own theory, in its main lines, would run as follows. At the level of the tribe or group, society has always found itself able to cohere. We infer, therefore, that a civilization, if it is in turn to maintain itself, must preserve at least a few of the characteristics of the group, though necessarily on a much expanded scale. Civilizations have failed in failing to solve this problem. In fact the very process by which civilization emerges has, up to now, made failure inevitable. But let us look more closely.

THE DISSOLUTION OF THE GROUP

The development of civilization has meant technical change, economic expansion, and warfare, usually all three. All have the effect of breaking up old social units without putting anything in their place. One characteristic result was the great cities of the Roman Empire, especially those of the Near East, filled with traders, artisans, and slaves, uprooted from their former homes, whether in Egypt, Canaan, Greece, Gaul, or Spain, and huddled into slums with other people of many different traditions. Another such result is our own great cities, like Detroit and Los Angeles, where, save for some difference in physical surroundings, the same conditions hold. Our study of Hilltown is typical of the reverse of the coin: the decaying society from which the uprooted come. In the old society, man was linked to man; in the new agglomeration—it cannot be called a society—he is alone. He has not had time to be anything else.

Now all the evidence of psychiatry, and it has not been our purpose to include it here, shows that membership in a group sustains a man, enables him to maintain his equilibrium under the ordinary shocks of life, and helps him to bring up children who will in turn be happy and resilient. If his group is shattered around him, if he leaves a group in which he was a valued member, and if, above all, he finds no new group to which he can relate himself, he will, under stress, develop disorders of thought, feeling, and behavior. His thinking will be obsessive, elaborated without sufficient reference to reality; he will be anxious or angry, destructive to himself or to others; his behavior will be compulsive, not controlled; and, if the process of education that makes a man easily able to relate himself to others is itself social, he will, as a lonely man, bring up children who have a lowered social capacity. The cycle is vicious; loss of group membership in one generation may make men less capable of group membership in the next. The civilization that, by its very process of growth, shatters small group life will leave men and women lonely and unhappy.

No harm would be done if new groups appeared to take the place of the old ones, new groups with some of the characteristics of the old. And we know that in fact such groups are always forming. The seed of society is always fertile. Yet it may be that at times the new growth does not keep pace with the rot, and that there is a net increase in the number of isolated individuals, superficially attached to the bare skeleton of formal organization but lacking the old feeling of belongingness. Each of the sociologists—Durkheim, LeBon, Figgis, Brooks Adams—who began, just before World War I, to point out the signs of decay in our society, used the same metaphor. They said that society was becoming a dust heap of individuals without links to one another.[2]

THE NEW GROUPS

The process cannot go on unchecked indefinitely. Society does not dissolve without a struggle, but produces antibodies to check the rot. The reaction often takes a religious form. Among the up-

---

[2] E. Durkheim, *De la division du travail social* (1902), xxxii; G. LeBon, *Psychologie des foules* (1910), 190; B. Adams, *The Theory of Social Revolutions* (1913), 228; R. N. Figgis, *Churches and the Modern State* (1914), 47, 87.

rooted of the big cities—Antioch, Alexandria, Ephesus, Rome, Detroit, Los Angeles—all sorts of religions spring up. They are seldom the religions of the tribes from which the uprooted come, and never the religion of the civilization itself. If men have not found a society satisfying, they will not find its beliefs satisfying either. Whatever spiritual unity the civilization may once have had is broken. The new religions are highly emotional: they cater to the exaggerated emotionality of the isolate. Their elaborate theology is a tribute to his obsessions. But they have something more important to offer than a release for the emotions and a subject for metaphysics. Each new religion is also a new society. Each is made up of cells or congregations, which offer to the isolate some of the feeling of full belongingness that he has lost. This was true of early Christianity, as the Acts of the Apostles and the Epistles of St. Paul bear witness. It was probably true of the mystery cults of the Roman Empire. Who shall say it is not true of the sects that fester in the social wilderness of our own cities, from Jehovah's Witnesses to Communism? Not all the cults survive. In the Roman Empire, Christianity was the only one that survived in strength, and some hope for mankind lies in the fact that Christianity set high ethical standards and addressed itself to man's spiritual, not just his physical, needs. If our civilization goes the way of the others, it may, like the Europe of the Dark Ages, be stimulated to recovery by some new synthesis of moral norms. But whatever the influence of its doctrines may have been, Christianity at least spread its network of new and tough groups, which finally set a term to the decay of the Empire, and, together with the Germanic tribes, formed the matrix out of which a new society could be carved.

In the end, the new groups provided a basis for the reconstruction of civilization, but we must notice that in the beginning they were irreconcilably hostile to the reigning order. Rome was the whore of Babylon, whose destruction St. John confidently predicted. A frustrated person, we are often told, turns to aggression. One is not loyal to a society in which one has been lonely and anxious. The decay of civilization would be much less rapid than history shows it to be if the new groups that absorb the isolated individuals did not have opposition to existing society as their very principle of organization and did not therefore, in the beginning, accelerate the decay.

In the history of Western civilization, the successor of the classical, the problem can be stated in much the same way. Erich Fromm, in his *Escape from Freedom,* says that in the last four hundred years men have been gradually set free from the restraints of traditional society. But in losing these restraints, they have also lost the sense of belonging to a group whose members co-operate in securing the deepest interests of each. If freedom is to mean no more than emotional isolation, it will not survive. Men will do any mad thing, even merge in a mass under the sword of a tyrant, to escape from a freedom of this kind. Every religion, every revolutionary movement claims it will restore the brotherhood of man, and sometimes has really done so in the form of the congregation or cell. Brotherhood, of the kind they get in a small and successful group, men must have. But at the level of civilization, the search for the lost brotherhood of man, by creating antagonisms that can only be resolved by force, may end in the worst of tyrannies. Our best instincts hurt us most. Although society, like the human body, has immense restorative powers, they are blind. Left to itself, a broken leg may knit again, but it will certainly knit crooked, and in the same way the forces of equilibrium in society will restore some kind of integration, though the new level may well be lower than the last. To achieve an advancing adaptation, the maintenance of a civilization rather than a relapse before a new start, intelligence must direct the restorative powers.

GROUP CONFLICT

The problem of emotional isolation, or psychosocial isolation as the social scientists call it, is not the only one that civilization raises, and it may not be the most important. We have already seen that this problem is inextricably intermixed with the problem of group conflict. As civilization advances, a process often takes place on a large scale that much resembles what took place on a small scale in the Electrical Equipment Company. An advancing civilization means, among other things, that the technical and economic adaptation of society to its environment changes. Since the internal system is continuous with the external, this change disturbs the relations between groups within society and exacerbates their mutual antagonisms. The antagonisms find expression in ideological differences, and civil war may break out. Something very much like this occurred in the sixteenth century, in the last great crisis of Western civilization before the present one. With economic expansion and organizational changes in industry and agriculture, the middle class rose rapidly in importance. The members of this class were apt to be isolates; they also came, as a group, into conflict with the other classes in society. The former balance between the classes was destroyed, and antagonisms one kept under control awoke. In the ideological controversies, which were then religious and political as they are now economic and political, the middle class took one side; the upper and lower classes together took the other. The issues were not considered on their merits; they became the mere flags of parties whose real energy was drawn from class antagonisms. The result was the civil wars in France and England, and the Thirty Years' War in Germany. Civilization escaped wreck, but only just escaped. England suffered least and even gained by the conflict, which was less severe there than elsewhere; France survived at the price of adopting absolute monarchy, and the development of Germany was so retarded that she has suffered from a national feeling of inferiority ever since. Perhaps we are going through a similar conflict today, but our capacities for wrecking are much greater.

CIRCULATION, COMMUNICATION, AND CONTROL

Other problems raised by an advancing civilization, and closely related both to emotional isolation and to group conflict, are the problems of circulation, communication, and control. Let us take them up in this order. By *circulation* we shall mean the process by which able persons are brought to positions of responsibility in a society. In the small group, the choice of a leader is an obvious and natural thing. The leader is the man who most fully lives up to the ideals of the group. He expresses the aspirations of the group, and it is this, more than anything else, that allows him to carry the group with him. In a civilization at its best, the leaders are of the same kind. Scipio Africanus, William of Orange, Elizabeth, and

Washington not only possessed great intellectual capacity but were also felt by their followers to represent the best in society. Their strength lay in this double fact. Yet as civilization advances, as the channels of advancement become more complex, and as conflict widens, the choice of leaders who have the twofold qualification for their job becomes more difficult. Able men may be available, but their skill lies in making money, in intrigue, in using force, or in exploiting the increasing antagonisms between groups. A split grows up between leaders and led, until the latter are no longer led but driven or bribed.

The problem of *communication* is close to that of circulation. We have seen that, in the small group, communication flows naturally toward the leader, and that he cannot do his job unless he is well informed in this way. Now civilization, which is, in one of its aspects, centralization, implies a lengthening of the channels of communication between followers and top leaders in the great formal organizations that articulate the whole. Even in the small group, the seeds of breakdown are latent in the emotional relation between leader and follower, and with every lengthening of the channels of communication, the difficulties increase. The subordinate, dependent on his superior for advancement, may tell the latter only what he wants to hear and only so much as will protect the subordinate's position. It is not enough that good communication should exist between most neighboring positions in the communication lines. If only one link is weak, the flow of information from bottom to top will be impaired. The separate channels of communication from bottom to top may multiply, as the rise of staff departments in every large organization shows, and yet this very multiplication may impede communication. Each channel transmits only part of the story; no one is responsible for paying attention to the whole. And every new channel may increase the insecurity of men located on the other channel, for it by-passes these men and transmits information that, in the hands of a leader inadequately skilled, may bring criticism back down upon them.[3] Finally, adequate communication depends to a great degree on the leader's awareness of the items that ought to be communicated. He hears

[3] For an example, see F. J. Roethlisberger, "The Foreman: Master and Victim of Double-talk," *Harvard Business Review,* XXIII (1945), 283-98.

what he wants to hear, and he wants to hear only what he has been trained to hear. In American industry, for instance, communication is excellent on questions of sales and engineering, but tends to be poor on questions of internal social organization. This kind of information may be inherently hard to communicate, but it is also true that the American administrator is not taught to think it important.

For the ordinary follower in an organization, communication is not a matter of transmitting abstract understanding of a situation. It is a matter of transmitting to the leader an awareness of those problems on which, in the follower's view, action needs to be taken, and of the fact that the follower feels as he does. If action is not then taken by the leader, communication, for the follower, has failed. In the big organizations of modern society, communication in this sense is all too liable to failure. Trade and industrial unions may arise in an unconscious attempt to repair some of the damage, but they are big organizations too, and may fall into the old difficulties.[4] We are in danger of producing a body of men wholly lacking confidence in leadership and organization of any kind whatever. Such a group would much resemble the "internal proletariat," demoralized, without opportunity for spontaneous group action of its own, and sullenly resistant toward its leaders, so characteristic of the later Roman Empire. For the problem is not just that of communication from follower to leader. The leader must also explain, in such a way that the followers will accept it, the plan of action that the society needs to adopt. If communication fails in one direction, it will fail in the other.

We have seen that in the small group, control over persons that threaten to depart from the norms of the group is often exceedingly effective but is not imposed from without. Instead it is implicit in the system of relations in the group. We have also seen that the leader, in close communication with his followers, does not ask them to take action that will not receive their spontaneous obedience. As civilization develops, as groups dissolve, as society divides into warring groups, and as the difficulties of communication be-

---

[4] See J. F. Scott and G. C. Homans, "Reflections on the Wildcat Strikes," *American Sociological Review*, XII (1947), 378-87.

tween leader and follower increase, this spontaneous control tends to dissolve in favor of a control imposed by force and by the central power. Of course it is true that a certain amount of force must always be used in controlling society. What we are talking about now is a civilization that has reached the stage at which, in the view of its leaders, it can be held together only by force. Their diagnosis may be correct, if the dissolution of groups and the increase of conflict have gone far enough. But as for force as a long-run remedy, the evidence of history is that this stage marks the beginning of the downward path of civilization. Forced co-operation only hastens the decay that would have taken place in any event. In the words of Durkheim, "A society made up of a boundless dust-heap of unrelated individuals, whom an overdeveloped state tries to hem and hold in, is a true sociological monstrosity."[5] And yet all dictators, from Napoleon onward, have tried to create something like this monstrosity. Just as Napoleon broke up the ancient provinces of France and divided them into departments, fearing that the provinces with their local loyalties and traditions of self-government would provide centers of resistance to his regime, so all dictators since his time have tried to break up or bring under central domination all social units independent of the state. Rousseau provided them with a rationale for their actions. He argued that the individual should be set free from the trammels of society, but when he faced the question how this should be done, he went on to say that "every citizen should be wholly independent of all the others and excessively dependent on the state . . ., for only the force of the state makes the liberty of its members."[6] In short, man must be compelled to be free.

Let us repeat: all of these problems—psychosocial isolation, conflict, circulation, communication, and control—are handled more or less well at the level of the group. Therefore human society never dissolves beyond this level. What is true of the group must also be

---

[5] E. Durkheim, *De la division du travail social* (2nd ed.), xxxii.

[6] J. J. Rousseau, *Contrat Social*, Bk. II, Chap. 12. See also R. A. Nisbet, "The French Revolution and the Rise of Sociology in France," *American Journal of Sociology*, XLIX (1943), 156-64. "De Bonald and the Concept of the Social Group," *Journal of the History of Ideas*, V (1944), 315-31; "The Politics of Social Pluralism: Some Reflections on Lammenais," *The Journal of Politics*, X (1948), 764-86.

true of the civilization if the latter is to maintain itself. Civilization fails when it cannot solve these problems on its own vast scale, and when it even prevents its constituent groups from solving them.

DEMOCRACY

Our own civilization has not wholly failed. It has made some institutional inventions that have turned out, in certain times and circumstances, to be valuable in solving the problems of the group at the level of the civilization. One complex of such inventions is democracy. We do not use the word here in its literal sense of "rule of the people." That gets us into the question of the location of sovereignty in a nation. Sovereignty, which is another word for authority, does not lie in any one element or organ of a nation but in the social system as a whole. Nor do we use it in the sense of "democratic way of life." That, as we have said, gives aid and comfort to the dictators by letting them say that they are as "democratic" as anyone else. So loose is the meaning of democracy in this sense that no one can prove they are not. We use the word here to mean the complex of governmental and legal institutions common to such nations as the United Kingdom and the United States: representative and parliamentary government, universal suffrage, the secret ballot, the habeas corpus, trial by jury, and the various freedoms named in the Bill of Rights.

Note how all these devices are addressed to the problem of maintaining, at the level of a nation if not of a civilization, the values of the small group. The election of executive officers and representatives aims at maintaining for the nation the method of choosing leaders that is characteristic of the small group. Together with the freedoms of speech and press, it also aims at effective communication between the led and the leaders. Trial by jury and the various freedoms are so many admissions that the spontaneous self-control of a society may be much more effective than any imposed control. Finally, representative government is an effort to establish that kind of relationship between leaders and followers on which a spontaneous obedience, rather than a forced one, can be based. A further pursuit of this main idea might lead to many important insights.

But democratic institutions do not exist in a vacuum; they exist in a society, and they cannot live long unless the society is of a certain kind. This is a field in which political science, in co-operation with sociology, must do much more work than it has so far. Democracy cannot be successful unless the nation is well educated and enjoys a standard of living so high that men do not have to worry about sheer survival. Just how high the standard of education and the standard of living need to be we cannot say, but we recognize that at least some minimum level must be achieved. How few countries in which we Americans blithely ask that democratic government be established meet these conditions! How unrealistic we are, and what frustration our unrealism leads us to!

These are only the minimum conditions. There are others. If democratic institutions do something to create the conditions in which they can survive, they do not do everything. Democracy cannot solve the problem of psychosocial isolation, and it cannot help greatly to solve the problem of conflict. No one believes that, even in the most flourishing circumstances, conflict disappears in a society. Conflict is built deeply into any social order, which would be uninteresting without it. As usual, the question is: How much conflict and in what areas? If social conflict does not go too deep, representative government provides a method for deciding the issues, with much salutary release of emotion. We are all ready to accept a large amount of verbal violence in our politics. Our tolerance for it is high, and we admire a man that gives and takes hard knocks. But if conflict goes deep enough, as the United States once learned, and as the communist propagandists know well, democratic methods do not lead to the peaceful resolution of conflict but to civil war. For democracy to survive, the members of society must enjoy some area of consensus, supported by the informal contacts of daily life, by formal communication networks, and by common ideals. We know little of the nature of this consensus, but we are aware that in some countries of Europe, which were formerly, or now are, democracies in the technical sense, this consensus never existed. Moreover, as we have seen, some characteristics of a developing civilization tend to put the consensus in danger.

Democracy does something to solve the problems of circulation, communication, and control, but its machinery is not applied, and probably cannot be applied, in vast areas of our national life. No one has seriously suggested that production schedules in a factory should be determined by popular vote or even that the factory manager should be elected. And yet in these vast areas the tensions of modern civilization are being generated. We can resolve them not by blindly applying existing democratic methods but by addressing ourselves to the problem to which democracy itself was addressed: How can the values of the small group be maintained on the scale of the civilization?

THE SOLUTIONS OF THE PROBLEM

We have seen some of the problems that an advancing civilization makes for itself. Apparently its rise creates the conditions that lead to its fall. How shall we escape from this dreary cycle? The usual conservative has nothing more to offer than the advice: "Stop change. Any change will be for the worse." But from beginning to end civilization means change. Stop change and, we infer, civilization also stops. And while the conservative is giving his advice, the business firms he admires are making his words idle by stimulating enormous social change. The real problem is this: How can a social order change without either dissolution into a dust heap or cleavage into hostile camps? How can we, to use Elton Mayo's phrase, create an "adaptive society"? [7] Another kind of conservative—he is usually called an "old-fashioned liberal"—growls about "the curse of bigness" and argues that social groups of all kinds should be more independent of state control. He has some idea of the nature of the problem, but his solution is mistaken. Civilization means centralization. It means that men and women will be related to one another in increasingly large organizations, and that these organizations will be brought more and more under the influence of the central directing body of the society, the government. Whether or not modern society requires large-scale organization if it is to maintain its complex adaptation to the natural environment, the

[7] E. Mayo, *The Social Problems of an Industrial Civilization*, 31. The reader should also study Brooks Adams, *The Theory of Social Revolutions*, Chap. VI, a chapter that, as Elton Mayo used to say, should be printed in letters of gold.

fact certainly is that the process of centralization is still going on both in business and in government. If government did not centralize, business would; neither one is in a position to blame the other. The real problem is not how to keep social groups wholly independent and autonomous but how to organize their relation to central control in such a way that they can maintain their own life while contributing to the life of organized society. In the social organism, how can we keep the center strong without destroying the life of the periphery? How can we centralize without stagnating?

As for the modern liberal, not the old-fashioned one, all he has to offer to solve the problems of large-scale organization is more of the same. For big private business he would substitute bigger government business. He rushes into the leviathan state without having the faintest notion how to deal with some of its important human problems. He assumes our present methods are adequate. Take, for instance, the problem of restriction of output, which is a typical problem of the relation between the central direction of an organization and the small working groups of which the organization is made up. The liberal may not know about restriction in American industry, but if he does, he will say that it is specifically a result of business organization and not of modern big organization in general, including the kind he advocates, and that restriction will wither away when the government becomes socialist and the labor leaders are in power. But the difficulties are stubborn and their roots run deeper than we thought. Society is made up, among other elements, of countless small groups of the kind we have described in this book. If advancing civilization, which means an increasingly centralized control, does not destroy them altogether, which hardly seems likely, it will have to deal with them, and yet, as we have seen, advancing civilization tends to weaken the kind of relation between leader and follower in which the leader can carry the group wholeheartedly with him and the follower can accept leadership without fear that his views will be disregarded. Suppose we organize the welfare state and still find thousands of small groups sullenly resisting the advice of their official leaders? That the problem is not academic, the industrial experience of Socialist government shows. If social control is increasingly centralized, the reason must be that such control is necessary, but a central control that cannot be exercised would seem to mean stagnation and not progress. Shall we then use force to bring the recalcitrant into line? History seems to show that this does not solve the problem but rather starts civilization on its downward path. The decline of the Roman Empire began with its birth—the dictatorship of Augustus. This is not an argument against the welfare state; it is a plea that we study more carefully than we have so far the conditions that must be realized if the centralized state is not to stagnate. Let us put our case for the last time: At the level of the small group, society has always been able to cohere. We infer, therefore, that if civilization is to stand, it must maintain, in the relation between the groups that make up society and the central direction of society, some of the features of the small group itself. If we do not solve this problem, the effort to achieve our most high-minded purposes may lead us not to Utopia but to Byzantium. The problem will not be easily solved, but one step we can take in the beginning is to learn the characteristics of the human group.

Index

T 2
U 3
V 4
W 5
X 6
Y 7
Z 8